U·X·L
Sustainable Living

U·X·L
Sustainable Living

VOLUME 1: A–E

Jason M. Everett, Project Editor

U·X·L
A part of Gale, Cengage Learning

Matawan Aberdeen Public Library
165 Main Street
Matawan, NJ 07747
(732) 583-9100

GALE
CENGAGE Learning

Farmington Hills, Mich • San Francisco • New York • Waterville, Maine
Meriden, Conn • Mason, Ohio • Chicago

GALE CENGAGE Learning

U•X•L Sustainable Living

Project Editor: Jason M. Everett

Product Manager: Christine Slovey

Rights Acquisition and Management: Moriam Aigoro and Ashley Maynard

Imaging and Multimedia: John L. Watkins

Composition: Evi Abou-El-Seoud

Manufacturing: Wendy Blurton

Product Design: Kristine A. Julien

Indexing: Laurie Andriot

© 2016 Gale, Cengage Learning

WCN: 01-100-101

ALL RIGHTS RESERVED. No part of this work covered by the copyright herein may be reproduced, transmitted, stored, or used in any form or by any means graphic, electronic, or mechanical, including but not limited to photocopying, recording, scanning, digitizing, taping, Web distribution, information networks, or information storage and retrieval systems, except as permitted under Section 107 or 108 of the 1976 United States Copyright Act, without the prior written permission of the publisher.

For product information and technology assistance, contact us at
Gale Customer Support, 1-800-877-4253.
For permission to use material from this text or product, submit all requests online at **www.cengage.com/permissions.**
Further permissions questions can be emailed to
permissionrequest@cengage.com

Cover photographs: © Lynnya/Shutterstock.com (Monarch butterflies); © Betty LaRue/Shutterstock.com (river); © Denis and Yulia Pogostins/Shutterstock.com (carrots); © gornjak/Shutterstock.com (sunflowers); © spwidoff/Shutterstock.com (recycling); © Sopotnicki/Shutterstock.com (car recharging station); © majeczka/Shutterstock.com (wind turbines).

While every effort has been made to ensure the reliability of the information presented in this publication, Gale, a part of Cengage Learning, does not guarantee the accuracy of the data contained herein. Gale accepts no payment for listing; and inclusion in the publication of any organization, agency, institution, publication, service, or individual does not imply endorsement of the editors or publisher. Errors brought to the attention of the publisher and verified to the satisfaction of the publisher will be corrected in future editions.

LIBRARY OF CONGRESS CATALOGING-IN-PUBLICATION DATA

U-X-L sustainable living / Jason M. Everett, Project Editor.
    pages cm
  Includes bibliographical references and index.
  ISBN 978-1-4103-1783-4 (set : alk. paper) — ISBN 978-1-4103-1784-1 (volume 1 : alk. paper) — ISBN 978-1-4103-1785-8 (volume 2 : alk. paper) — ISBN 978-1-4103-1786-5 (volume 3 : alk. paper)
  1. Sustainable living—Juvenile literature. 2. Environmentalism—Juvenile literature. I. Everett, Jason M. II. Title: UXL sustainable living.
  GE196.U95 2015
  304.2—dc23   2015026530

Gale
27500 Drake Rd.
Farmington Hills, MI 48331-3535

978-1-4103-1783-4 (set)   978-1-4103-1785-8 (vol. 2)
978-1-4103-1784-1 (vol. 1)   978-1-4103-1786-5 (vol. 3)

This title is also available as an e-book.
ISBN-13: 978-1-4103-1787-2
Contact your Gale, a part of Cengage Learning, sales representative for ordering information.

Printed in China
1 2 3 4 5 6 7 19 18 17 16 15

Table of Contents

Entries by Component of Sustainability **xi**

Reader's Guide **xix**

Advisory Board **xxi**

Chronology of Important Events **xxiii**

Words to Know **xxxvii**

VOLUME 1: A–E

Abundance **1**

Acid Rain **3**

Activism **7**

Agriculture **11**

Air Pollution **17**

Alter-Globalization Movement **24**

Alternative Energy **29**

Aquaculture **32**

Aquifers **38**

Automobiles **40**

Batteries **47**

Biodiversity **50**

Biofuel Energy **60**

Table of Contents

Biomimicry **66**

Bioregionalism **70**

Biosecurity **74**

Biotechnology **78**

Brundtland Report **83**

Building Design **88**

Carbon Cycle **95**

Carrying Capacity **100**

Citizen Science **104**

Citizenship **107**

Climate Change **111**

Coal **123**

Community-Supported Agriculture (CSA) **129**

Composting **137**

Comprehensive Environmental Response, Compensation, and Liability Act (CERCLA) **140**

Conservation **143**

Consumption **149**

Cradle-to-Cradle Design **155**

Deep Ecology **159**

Desalination **161**

Desertification **164**

Drought **170**

Ecological Footprint **177**

Ecological Restoration **184**

Ecology **188**

Economics **196**

Ecosystems **203**

Ecotourism **212**

Ecovillages **217**

Endangered and Threatened Species **221**

Energy Conservation **227**

Environmental Justice **236**

Environmental Law **241**

Environmental Policy **247**

VOLUME 2: F–N

Fair Trade **253**

Farm Bill, U.S. **257**

Farming, Industrial **260**

Farming, Sustainable **266**

Food Security **271**

Food Systems **278**

Food Waste **284**

Food Web **287**

Fossil Fuels **290**

Free Trade **298**

Genetically Modified Organisms (GMOs) **303**

Geothermal Power **306**

Globalization **310**

Green Economy **312**

Greenhouse Gas Emissions **319**

Hazardous Waste **327**

Human Rights **333**

Hydraulic Fracturing **338**

Hydropower **346**

Industrial Ecology **351**

Intergenerational Responsibility **355**

Invasive Species **359**

Jobs **367**

Land **375**

Light Pollution **383**

Local Economy **385**

Locavores and the Local Food Movement **389**

Table of Contents

Mass Transit **397**

Millennium Development Goals **402**

Mining **407**

Monoculture **414**

Natural Gas **419**

Natural Law Theory **424**

Natural Resources **426**

Nitrogen Cycle **433**

Noise Pollution **437**

Nongovernmental Organizations (NGOs) **440**

Nuclear Power **447**

Nutrition **454**

VOLUME 3: O–Z

Oil **461**

Ozone Depletion **468**

Permaculture **475**

Pesticides **478**

Plastics **486**

Polar Melting **489**

Pollution **494**

Population, Human **501**

Precautionary Principle **507**

Preservation **511**

Public Health **516**

Quality of Life Indicators **523**

Recycling **529**

Risk Assessment **535**

Seed Banks **545**

Social Justice **548**

Soil **552**

Soil Pollution **557**

Table of Contents

Solar Power **561**

Sustainability **568**

Systems and Systems Thinking **576**

Thermal Pollution **581**

Tidal Power **584**

Tragedy of the Commons **586**

Transition Towns Movement **590**

Transportation **593**

United Nations Conference on Environment and Development (UNCED) **599**

Upcycling **603**

Urban Farming **605**

Urbanization **608**

War **615**

Waste Management **620**

Water Access and Sanitation **627**

Water Cycle **633**

Water Pollution **637**

Wildlife Management **644**

Wind Power **648**

Zero Waste **653**

Where to Learn More **liii**

List of Organizations **lix**

Index **lxiii**

Entries by Component of Sustainability

The entries below are organized by the three pillars of sustainability: environment, economy, and society. Entries are broken down further under broad categories. As the pillars of sustainability overlap, entries may appear under more than one heading. Boldface indicates volume numbers.

Environment
  Air/Atmosphere

Acid Rain	**1**: 3
Air Pollution	**1**: 17
Alternative Energy	**1**: 29
Automobiles	**1**: 40
Biofuel Energy	**1**: 60
Biotechnology	**1**: 78
Brundtland Report	**1**: 83
Carbon Cycle	**1**: 95
Climate Change	**1**: 111
Coal	**1**: 123
Ecological Footprint	**1**: 177
Ecological Restoration	**1**: 184
Ecology	**1**: 188
Ecosystems	**1**: 203
Environmental Justice	**1**: 236
Environmental Law	**1**: 241
Environmental Policy	**1**: 247
Food Web	**2**: 287
Fossil Fuels	**2**: 290
Green Economy	**2**: 312
Greenhouse Gas Emissions	**2**: 319
Hazardous Waste	**2**: 327
Industrial Ecology	**2**: 351
Light Pollution	**2**: 383
Mass Transit	**2**: 397
Natural Gas	**2**: 419
Natural Resources	**2**: 426
Nitrogen Cycle	**2**: 433
Oil	**3**: 461
Ozone Depletion	**3**: 468
Polar Melting	**3**: 489
Pollution	**3**: 494
Recycling	**3**: 529
Sustainability	**3**: 568
Thermal Pollution	**3**: 581
Transportation	**3**: 593
United Nations Conference on Environment and Development (UNCED)	**3**: 599
Waste Management	**3**: 620
Water Cycle	**3**: 633
Wind Power	**3**: 648

  Energy

Agriculture	**1**: 11
Alternative Energy	**1**: 29
Automobiles	**1**: 40
Batteries	**1**: 47
Biofuel Energy	**1**: 60
Biotechnology	**1**: 78
Brundtland Report	**1**: 83
Carbon Cycle	**1**: 95
Climate Change	**1**: 111
Coal	**1**: 123
Ecology	**1**: 188

xi

Entries by Component of Sustainability

Ecosystems	**1**: 203	Coal	**1**: 123
Ecotourism	**1**: 212	Community-Supported Agriculture	
Energy Conservation	**1**: 227	(CSA)	**1**: 129
Environmental Justice	**1**: 236	Composting	**1**: 137
Environmental Law	**1**: 241	Comprehensive Environmental	
Environmental Policy	**1**: 247	Response, Compensation, and	
Fossil Fuels	**2**: 290	Liability Act (CERCLA)	**1**: 140
Geothermal Power	**2**: 306	Conservation	**1**: 143
Green Economy	**2**: 312	Desertification	**1**: 164
Greenhouse Gas Emissions	**2**: 319	Drought	**1**: 170
Hazardous Waste	**2**: 327	Ecological Footprint	**1**: 177
Hydraulic Fracturing	**2**: 338	Ecological Restoration	**1**: 184
Hydropower	**2**: 346	Ecology	**1**: 188
Industrial Ecology	**2**: 351	Ecosystems	**1**: 203
Light Pollution	**2**: 383	Ecovillages	**1**: 217
Mass Transit	**2**: 397	Environmental Justice	**1**: 236
Mining	**2**: 407	Environmental Law	**1**: 241
Natural Gas	**2**: 419	Environmental Policy	**1**: 247
Natural Resources	**2**: 426	Farm Bill, U.S.	**2**: 257
Nuclear Power	**2**: 447	Farming, Industrial	**2**: 260
Oil	**3**: 461	Farming, Sustainable	**2**: 266
Plastics	**3**: 486	Food Security	**2**: 271
Solar Power	**3**: 561	Food Systems	**2**: 278
Sustainability	**3**: 568	Food Web	**2**: 287
Systems and Systems Thinking	**3**: 576	Green Economy	**2**: 312
Tidal Power	**3**: 584	Greenhouse Gas Emissions	**2**: 319
Transition Towns Movement	**3**: 590	Hazardous Waste	**2**: 327
Transportation	**3**: 593	Hydraulic Fracturing	**2**: 338
Wind Power	**3**: 648	Industrial Ecology	**2**: 351
Land/Soil		Land	**2**: 375
Acid Rain	**1**: 3	Mass Transit	**2**: 397
Agriculture	**1**: 11	Mining	**2**: 407
Alternative Energy	**1**: 29	Monoculture	**2**: 414
Aquifers	**1**: 38	Natural Gas	**2**: 419
Biodiversity	**1**: 50	Natural Resources	**2**: 426
Biofuel Energy	**1**: 60	Nitrogen Cycle	**2**: 433
Biosecurity	**1**: 74	Oil	**3**: 461
Biotechnology	**1**: 78	Permaculture	**3**: 475
Carbon Cycle	**1**: 95	Polar Melting	**3**: 489
Carrying Capacity	**1**: 100	Pollution	**3**: 494
Climate Change	**1**: 111	Preservation	**3**: 511

Entries by Component of Sustainability

Recycling	**3**: 529	Green Economy	**2**: 312
Soil	**3**: 552	Invasive Species	**2**: 359
Soil Pollution	**3**: 557	Land	**2**: 375
Sustainability	**3**: 568	Locavores and the Local Food	
Transition Towns Movement	**3**: 590	Movement	**2**: 389
Transportation	**3**: 593	Monoculture	**2**: 414
United Nations Conference on		Natural Resources	**2**: 426
Environment and Development		Nitrogen Cycle	**2**: 433
(UNCED)	**3**: 599	Noise Pollution	**2**: 437
Urbanization	**3**: 608	Nutrition	**2**: 454
Waste Management	**3**: 620	Pesticides	**3**: 478
Water Cycle	**3**: 633	Precautionary Principle	**3**: 507
Wildlife Management	**3**: 644	Preservation	**3**: 511
Wind Power	**3**: 648	Seed Banks	**3**: 545

Plants/Animals

Agriculture	**1**: 11	Sustainability	**3**: 568
Aquaculture	**1**: 32	United Nations Conference on	
Biodiversity	**1**: 50	Environment and Development	
Biofuel Energy	**1**: 60	(UNCED)	**3**: 599
Biomimicry	**1**: 66	Urban Farming	**3**: 605
Biosecurity	**1**: 74	Water Cycle	**3**: 633
Biotechnology	**1**: 78	Wildlife Management	**3**: 644

Waste

Carrying Capacity	**1**: 100	Climate Change	**1**: 111
Climate Change	**1**: 111	Composting	**1**: 137
Composting	**1**: 137	Cradle-to-Cradle Design	**1**: 155
Conservation	**1**: 143	Environmental Justice	**1**: 236
Deep Ecology	**1**: 159	Environmental Law	**1**: 241
Ecology	**1**: 188	Environmental Policy	**1**: 247
Ecosystems	**1**: 203	Food Waste	**2**: 284
Endangered and Threatened		Food Web	**2**: 287
Species	**1**: 221	Green Economy	**2**: 312
Environmental Justice	**1**: 236	Greenhouse Gas Emissions	**2**: 319
Environmental Law	**1**: 241	Hazardous Waste	**2**: 327
Environmental Policy	**1**: 247	Industrial Ecology	**2**: 351
Farm Bill, U.S.	**2**: 257	Light Pollution	**2**: 383
Farming, Industrial	**2**: 260	Pollution	**3**: 494
Farming, Sustainable	**2**: 266	Recycling	**3**: 529
Food Security	**2**: 271	Soil Pollution	**3**: 557
Food Systems	**2**: 278	Sustainability	**3**: 568
Food Web	**2**: 287	Thermal Pollution	**3**: 581
Genetically Modified Organisms		Upcycling	**3**: 603
(GMOs)	**2**: 303		

U•X•L Sustainable Living   xiii

Entries by Component of Sustainability

Waste Management	**3**: 620	United Nations Conference on	
Water Access and Sanitation	**3**: 627	Environment and Development	
Water Pollution	**3**: 637	(UNCED)	**3**: 599
Zero Waste	**3**: 653	Water Access and Sanitation	**3**: 627
Water		Water Cycle	**3**: 633
Acid Rain	**1**: 3	Water Pollution	**3**: 637
Agriculture	**1**: 11	**Economy**	
Alternative Energy	**1**: 29	Business	
Aquaculture	**1**: 32	Alter-Globalization Movement	**1**: 24
Aquifers	**1**: 38	Alternative Energy	**1**: 29
Biofuel Energy	**1**: 60	Automobiles	**1**: 40
Biosecurity	**1**: 74	Community-Supported Agriculture	
Carbon Cycle	**1**: 95	(CSA)	**1**: 129
Climate Change	**1**: 111	Economics	**1**: 196
Conservation	**1**: 143	Ecotourism	**1**: 212
Desalination	**1**: 161	Fair Trade	**2**: 253
Desertification	**1**: 164	Farming, Industrial	**2**: 260
Drought	**1**: 170	Farming, Sustainable	**2**: 266
Ecological Footprint	**1**: 177	Food Systems	**2**: 278
Ecological Restoration	**1**: 184	Fossil Fuels	**2**: 290
Ecology	**1**: 188	Free Trade	**2**: 298
Ecosystems	**1**: 203	Globalization	**2**: 306
Environmental Justice	**1**: 236	Green Economy	**2**: 312
Environmental Law	**1**: 241	Jobs	**2**: 367
Environmental Policy	**1**: 247	Local Economy	**2**: 385
Farm Bill, U.S.	**2**: 257	Locavores and the Local Food	
Farming, Industrial	**2**: 260	Movement	**2**: 389
Farming, Sustainable	**2**: 266	Mass Transit	**2**: 397
Food Web	**2**: 287	Oil	**3**: 461
Geothermal Power	**2**: 306	Public Health	**3**: 516
Green Economy	**2**: 312	Quality of Life Indicators	**3**: 523
Hazardous Waste	**2**: 327	Solar Power	**3**: 561
Hydropower	**2**: 346	Sustainability	**3**: 568
Millennium Development Goals	**2**: 402	Systems and Systems Thinking	**3**: 576
Natural Resources	**2**: 426	Transition Towns Movement	**3**: 590
Polar Melting	**3**: 489	Transportation	**3**: 593
Pollution	**3**: 494	Employment	
Preservation	**3**: 511	Alternative Energy	**1**: 29
Sustainability	**3**: 568	Community-Supported Agriculture	
Thermal Pollution	**3**: 581	(CSA)	**1**: 129
Tidal Power	**3**: 584	Economics	**1**: 196

Entries by Component of Sustainability

Ecotourism	**1**: 212
Fair Trade	**2**: 253
Food Systems	**2**: 278
Free Trade	**2**: 298
Globalization	**2**: 306
Green Economy	**2**: 312
Jobs	**2**: 367
Local Economy	**2**: 385
Locavores and the Local Food Movement	**2**: 389
Millennium Development Goals	**2**: 402
Population, Human	**3**: 501
Quality of Life Indicators	**3**: 523
Sustainability	**3**: 568
Transition Towns Movement	**3**: 590

Income

Brundtland Report	**1**: 83
Consumption	**1**: 149
Economics	**1**: 196
Fair Trade	**2**: 253
Food Security	**2**: 271
Free Trade	**2**: 298
Globalization	**2**: 306
Green Economy	**2**: 312
Jobs	**2**: 367
Local Economy	**2**: 385
Millennium Development Goals	**2**: 402
Public Health	**3**: 516
Sustainability	**3**: 568
United Nations Conference on Environment and Development (UNCED)	**3**: 599

Production/Consumption

Abundance	**1**: 1
Alter-Globalization Movement	**1**: 24
Alternative Energy	**1**: 29
Automobiles	**1**: 40
Batteries	**1**: 47
Bioregionalism	**1**: 70
Brundtland Report	**1**: 83
Carbon Cycle	**1**: 95
Climate Change	**1**: 111
Coal	**1**: 123
Community-Supported Agriculture (CSA)	**1**: 129
Consumption	**1**: 149
Cradle-to-Cradle Design	**1**: 155
Ecological Footprint	**1**: 177
Economics	**1**: 196
Ecovillages	**1**: 217
Energy Conservation	**1**: 227
Fair Trade	**2**: 253
Farm Bill, U.S.	**2**: 257
Farming, Industrial	**2**: 260
Farming, Sustainable	**2**: 266
Food Security	**2**: 271
Food Systems	**2**: 278
Food Waste	**2**: 284
Fossil Fuels	**2**: 290
Free Trade	**2**: 298
Globalization	**2**: 306
Green Economy	**2**: 312
Greenhouse Gas Emissions	**2**: 319
Hazardous Waste	**2**: 327
Hydraulic Fracturing	**2**: 338
Hydropower	**2**: 346
Industrial Ecology	**2**: 351
Jobs	**2**: 367
Local Economy	**2**: 385
Locavores and the Local Food Movement	**2**: 389
Mass Transit	**2**: 397
Mining	**2**: 407
Monoculture	**2**: 414
Natural Gas	**2**: 419
Natural Resources	**2**: 426
Nuclear Power	**2**: 447
Oil	**3**: 461
Plastics	**3**: 486
Pollution	**3**: 494

U•X•L *Sustainable Living*

Entries by Component of Sustainability

Population, Human	**3**: 501
Precautionary Principle	**3**: 507
Recycling	**3**: 529
Risk Assessment	**3**: 535
Solar Power	**3**: 561
Sustainability	**3**: 568
Systems and Systems Thinking	**3**: 576
Tragedy of the Commons	**3**: 586
Transition Towns Movement	**3**: 590
Transportation	**3**: 593
United Nations Conference on Environment and Development (UNCED)	**3**: 599
Upcycing	**3**: 603
Urbanization	**3**: 608
War	**3**: 615
Waste Management	**3**: 620
Water Access and Sanitation	**3**: 627
Wind Power	**3**: 648
Zero Waste	**3**: 653

Trade
Alter-Globalization Movement	**1**: 24
Automobiles	**1**: 40
Bioregionalism	**1**: 70
Climate Change	**1**: 111
Economics	**1**: 196
Fair Trade	**2**: 253
Food Security	**2**: 271
Free Trade	**2**: 298
Globalization	**2**: 306
Green Economy	**2**: 312
Hazardous Waste	**2**: 327
Jobs	**2**: 367
Local Economy	**2**: 385
Millennium Development Goals	**2**: 402
Natural Resources	**2**: 426
Seed Banks	**3**: 545
Sustainability	**3**: 568
Transition Towns Movement	**3**: 590
Transportation	**3**: 593
Waste Management	**3**: 620

Society

Culture
Abundance	**1**: 1
Automobiles	**1**: 40
Bioregionalism	**1**: 70
Citizenship	**1**: 107
Deep Ecology	**1**: 159
Ecotourism	**1**: 212
Ecovillages	**1**: 217
Human Rights	**2**: 333
Intergenerational Responsibility	**2**: 355
Jobs	**2**: 367
Locavores and the Local Food Movement	**2**: 389
Natural Law Theory	**2**: 424
Nongovernmental Organizations (NGOs)	**2**: 440
Permaculture	**3**: 475
Sustainability	**3**: 568
Tragedy of the Commons	**3**: 586
Urbanization	**3**: 608

Education
Activism	**1**: 7
Citizen Science	**1**: 104
Citizenship	**1**: 107
Conservation	**1**: 143
Ecotourism	**1**: 212
Intergenerational Responsibility	**2**: 355
Preservation	**3**: 511
Sustainability	**3**: 568
Systems and Systems Thinking	**3**: 576

Governance
Abundance	**1**: 1
Activism	**1**: 7
Automobiles	**1**: 40
Bioregionalism	**1**: 70
Brundtland Report	**1**: 83
Carrying Capacity	**1**: 100
Citizenship	**1**: 107
Climate Change	**1**: 111

Entries by Component of Sustainability

Comprehensive Environmental Response, Compensation, and Liability Act (CERCLA)	**1**: 140
Conservation	**1**: 143
Economics	**1**: 196
Ecovillages	**1**: 217
Endangered and Threatened Species	**1**: 221
Environmental Law	**1**: 241
Environmental Policy	**1**: 247
Farm Bill, U.S.	**2**: 257
Globalization	**2**: 306
Land	**2**: 375
Mass Transit	**2**: 397
Millennium Development Goals	**2**: 402
Natural Resources	**2**: 426
Ozone Depletion	**3**: 468
Pollution	**3**: 494
Population, Human	**3**: 501
Precautionary Principle	**3**: 507
Preservation	**3**: 511
Risk Assessment	**3**: 535
Sustainability	**3**: 568
Transition Towns Movement	**3**: 590
Transportation	**3**: 593
United Nations Conference on Environment and Development (UNCED)	**3**: 599
Urbanization	**3**: 608
War	**3**: 615
Water Access and Sanitation	**3**: 627
Wildlife Management	**3**: 644
Health	
Air Pollution	**1**: 17
Brundtland Report	**1**: 83
Climate Change	**1**: 111
Comprehensive Environmental Response, Compensation, and Liability Act (CERCLA)	**1**: 140
Ecology	**1**: 188
Environmental Justice	**1**: 236
Food Security	**2**: 271
Fossil Fuels	**2**: 290
Genetically Modified Organisms (GMOs)	**2**: 303
Greenhouse Gas Emissions	**2**: 319
Hazardous Waste	**2**: 327
Human Rights	**2**: 333
Intergenerational Responsibility	**2**: 355
Millennium Development Goals	**2**: 402
Noise Pollution	**2**: 437
Nongovernmental Organizations (NGOs)	**2**: 440
Nutrition	**2**: 454
Ozone Depletion	**3**: 468
Pesticides	**3**: 478
Pollution	**3**: 494
Precautionary Principle	**3**: 507
Public Health	**3**: 516
Quality of Life Indicators	**3**: 523
Risk Assessment	**3**: 535
Sustainability	**3**: 568
United Nations Conference on Environment and Development (UNCED)	**3**: 599
Water Access and Sanitation	**3**: 627
Water Pollution	**3**: 637
Justice	
Abundance	**1**: 1
Activism	**1**: 7
Carrying Capacity	**1**: 100
Citizenship	**1**: 107
Climate Change	**1**: 111
Deep Ecology	**1**: 159
Economics	**1**: 196
Environmental Justice	**1**: 236
Environmental Law	**1**: 241
Environmental Policy	**1**: 247
Food Security	**2**: 271
Fossil Fuels	**2**: 290
Globalization	**2**: 306
Human Rights	**2**: 333

U•X•L Sustainable Living

Entries by Component of Sustainability

Intergenerational Responsibility	**2**: 355	Environmental Policy	**1**: 247
Land	**2**: 375	Food Security	**2**: 271
Millennium Development Goals	**2**: 402	Globalization	**2**: 306
Natural Law Theory	**2**: 424	Human Rights	**2**: 333
Nongovernmental Organizations (NGOs)	**2**: 440	Intergenerational Responsibility	**2**: 355
		Jobs	**2**: 367
Oil	**3**: 461	Land	**2**: 375
Pollution	**3**: 494	Millennium Development Goals	**2**: 402
Public Health	**3**: 516		
Quality of Life Indicators	**3**: 523	Nongovernmental Organizations (NGOs)	**2**: 440
Social Justice	**3**: 548		
Sustainability	**3**: 568	Nuclear Power	**2**: 447
Transportation	**3**: 593	Public Health	**3**: 516
United Nations Conference on Environment and Development (UNCED)	**3**: 599	Quality of Life Indicators	**3**: 523
		Risk Assessment	**3**: 535
		Seed Banks	**3**: 545
War	**3**: 615	Sustainability	**3**: 568
Water Access and Sanitation	**3**: 627	Transition Towns Movement	**3**: 590
Security		United Nations Conference on Environment and Development (UNCED)	**3**: 599
Biosecurity	**1**: 74		
Brundtland Report	**1**: 83		
Carrying Capacity	**1**: 100	War	**3**: 615
Climate Change	**1**: 111	Water Access and Sanitation	**3**: 627
Environmental Law	**1**: 241		

Reader's Guide

Living sustainably means that people take no more resources from the earth than can be replenished naturally. It also means that people not overload the environment's capacity to renew itself. Human lives and the global economy depend on the earth's natural resources and ecosystems, but many aspects of modern life have made essential resources scarce and are destroying vital ecosystems. From the fossil fuels we burn to the waste we create, the challenge for humans is to learn how to live more sustainably to preserve the earth for future generations.

U•X•L Sustainable Living is devoted to helping students and general readers understand the economic, social, and environmental issues humans face today. As such, this full-color, three-volume set addresses sustainability challenges and opportunities, from air pollution to natural resources, to zero waste. All 124 entries start with an overview of the topic, followed by more in-depth information which discusses its scientific, societal, and sustainable context. Entries are arranged alphabetically throughout the volumes.

One hundred fifteen photos and illustrations provide engaging visual content that enlivens and adds context to the text. *U•X•L Sustainable Living* entries also contain sidebars on related topics and a "For More Information" section that lists sources to guide readers to reliable additional information. Twenty of the entries contain important primary source documents that will help students meet Common Core literacy standards by offering the opportunity to read and understand scientific and historical sources that support and provide context to the material in the entries. *See Also* references at the end of entries alert readers to related

Reader's Guide

articles across the three-volume set that may provide additional information or insights on each topic.

Additional Features

The front matter of each volume of *U•X•L Sustainable Living* contains a thematic table of contents that organizes the entries under the three pillars of sustainability: environment, economy, and society; an overall chronology of important events related to sustainability; and a general glossary. The back matter of each volume includes a "Where to Learn More" section that lists books and websites to help with further research, a list of organizations, and a subject index.

Advisory Board

Susan Jane Gentile

Executive Director, Living Routes: Study Abroad in Sustainable Communities

Affiliate Faculty, Urban Sustainability Master of Arts Program, Antioch University Los Angeles

Adjunct Faculty, Department of Environmental Studies and Department of Education, Antioch University New England

Managing Editor, Whole Terrain

Board Member, US Partnership for Education for Sustainable Development

Pamela Rogers Harmon

Middle school science teacher, St. Andrew's Episcopal School, Austin, Texas

Emily Hoyler

Curriculum Specialist, Shelburne Farms, Shelburne, Vermont

Upper elementary teacher, Cornwall School, Cornwall, Vermont

Molly McKay

Middle school dean of students and seventh and eighth grade teacher, Berwick Academy, South Berwick, Maine

Glen Denys

Science teacher, Oak Street School, Bernards Township, New Jersey

Chronology of Important Events

1962 Rachel Carson's *Silent Spring,* a book outlining the dangerous effects of pesticides on the environment, is published. Her claim that the pesticide DDT results in thinning eggshells that cause birds to die prematurely is initially met with derision among many scientists, but over time she is proven correct. The book is widely credited as the beginning of the modern environmental movement.

1963 The U.S. Clean Air Act is enacted by Congress on December 17. The law is the federal government's first attempt to improve air quality nationally. The law is amended significantly to include tighter pollution restrictions in 1970, 1977, and 1990.

1966 The Rance Tidal Power Station in Brittany, France, becomes the world's first tidal power station, generating electricity by harnessing the energy from water rushing out of the estuary during low tide. Twenty-four turbines are capable of producing up to 240 megawatts.

1967 The Environmental Defense Fund is founded in New York to promote a variety of issues after winning a lawsuit that prevents the spraying of DDT in New York State. Major efforts over the years include working to ban whale hunting, phasing out chloroflurocarbons (CFCs) that destroy the ozone layer, and promoting economic policies to combat climate change.

1968 Stanford University professor Paul R. Ehrlich publishes *The Population Bomb,* a book that declares that "the battle to feed all of humanity is over." Ehrlich predicts that growing world population will result in an era of mass starvation because of an inadequate food supply. While many of Ehrlich's predictions do not come to pass, throughout the years he continues to stand by his hypothesis.

1968 Ecologist Garrett Hardin publishes his essay "The Tragedy of the Commons" in the journal *Science*. The essay describes how unregulated common ownership of natural resources results in unsustainable overuse.

1969 The Cuyahoga River in Cleveland catches fire on June 22, as it has several times in the past due to chemicals pumped into the river from nearby industries. The fire is mentioned in *Time* magazine and raises awareness of the river's high toxicity. Public outrage results in efforts to clean up the river, and by the late 1990s it once again supports fish and other aquatic life.

1970 U.S. senator Gaylord Nelson helps organize the first Earth Day celebration on April 22. Millions of people in New York, Philadelphia, and other cities gather to celebrate and mobilize around local and national environmental issues, including pollution, overpopulation, and nuclear disarmament.

1970 The U.S. Environmental Protection Agency is formed on December 2 as a result of an executive order signed by President Richard Nixon. The agency is responsible for enforcing legislation passed by Congress regarding human health and the environment. Over the years it is tasked with enforcing the Clean Air Act, the Clean Water Act, the Safe Drinking Water Act, the Endangered Species Act, and many others.

1970 The Natural Resources Defense Council is formed in New York City. The organization works on the local, state, and federal levels to strengthen existing environmental standards and implement new laws as needed. Wildlife conservation, limiting climate change, pollution prevention, and sustainable development remain its core issues.

1970 American agronomist Norman Borlaug receives the Nobel Peace Prize for his role in the Green Revolution. His advances in developing high-yield, drought-resistant varieties of grains and then introducing them to famine-prone countries is credited with saving millions of people from starvation throughout the middle decades of the twentieth century.

Chronology of Important Events

1971 After a series of protests against nuclear testing in Alaska, activists based in Vancouver, British Columbia, form Greenpeace to stop environmentally destructive practices worldwide. As a major international NGO, Greenpeace rallies for peace and promotes direct action to end climate change and to protect the planet's oceans over the coming decades.

1971 Frances Moore Lappe publishes *Diet for a Small Planet,* which promotes vegetarianism as an environmentally sustainable way to produce enough food for the planet's population. The book sells over three million copies and changes the way many people relate to food as a natural resource.

1971 Alice Waters, chef and cofounder of the Berkeley, California, restaurant Chez Panisse, pioneers the farm-to-table concept by establishing a local network of farmers, ranchers, and dairies to provide fresh and organic ingredients for the restaurant on a continuing basis. Over the next several decades, the farm-to-table and locavore movements raise awareness of sustainable food production around the country.

1972 The United Nations Conference on the Human Environment is held in Stockholm, Sweden, in June. The conference results in the Stockholm Declaration, twenty-six principles for safeguarding the environment. These principles become the foundation for the UN's later sustainability efforts and include a commitment to human rights, protecting natural resources, and limiting pollution.

1972 The Trans-Amazonian Highway opens in Brazil on September 27. The 2,485-mile (4,000-km) road through the world's largest rainforest provides access to loggers, who cause deforestation in order to create large cattle grazing lands. The destruction of the most biodiverse place on earth results in a rapid extinction of thousands of species of plants and animals before they can even be catalogued by scientists. Additionally, deforestation interferes with the rainforest's ability to act as a carbon sink for the entire planet.

1972 U.S. Congress passes the Clean Water Act on October 18. It is the first comprehensive U.S. law designed to improve the water quality of the nation's navigable waterways. It addresses point source pollution, primarily from industry. Major amendments to the law are passed in 1977 and 1987 that cover nonpoint source pollution, including storm water and agricultural runoff.

1972 The pesticide DDT, widely used during World War II to prevent malaria, is banned in the United States after it is proven to cause cancer and have negative effects on the environment. However, it is still used in small amounts in some parts of the world to combat malaria.

1973 An energy crisis caused by an oil embargo against the United States by OPEC member states begins in October. This "first oil shock" causes the price of oil to nearly quadruple within a few months, and Americans suffer long lines and rising prices at the gas pump. The event highlights the geopolitical consequences of U.S. dependency on foreign oil.

1973 The Endangered Species Act goes into effect on December 28. The effort to halt the extinction of animals focuses on protecting delicate ecosystems and habitats. By 2012, fifty-six previously endangered species are delisted due to the law's success.

1974 Pioneering environmentalist Lester Brown establishes the Washington, D.C.-based Worldwatch Institute, whose mission is "to accelerate the transition to a sustainable world that meets human needs." Beginning in 1984 the organization publishes the annual *State of the World* report, highlighting the most pressing environmental issues of the day.

1975 Environmental activist Edward Abbey publishes the novel *The Monkey Wrench Gang,* in which a small group of activists sabotage companies and individuals they believe are destroying the environment of the American West. The book inspires future generations of eco-activists who advocate direct action in order to stop development of the wilderness.

1977 Wangari Maathai establishes the Green Belt Movement in Nairobi, Kenya, which organizes women in rural areas to plant trees. This green belt provides jobs and economic independence for women, halts deforestation, prevents soil erosion, and provides fuel for cooking. Maathai becomes the first African woman to receive the Nobel Peace Prize in 2004.

Chronology of Important Events

1978 Decades-old toxic waste in the Love Canal neighborhood near Niagara Falls, New York, is revealed to have caused an unusual number of birth defects and health problems in the area. President Carter declares a federal health emergency and eight hundred families are relocated and the neighborhood is razed. The incident is instrumental in the passage of the 1980 Superfund law.

1978 In an attempt to halt the spread of the Gobi Desert into populated areas, China launches a reforestation program that later becomes known as the Green Wall of China. Billions of trees will be planted through 2050 in a 2,800-mile (4,500-kilometer) network in order to maintain topsoil and prevent further desertification of highly populated areas.

1979 A partial nuclear meltdown on March 28 at the Three Mile Island nuclear power plant in Pennsylvania becomes the worst nuclear accident on U.S. soil. The accident is caused by a mechanical malfunction intensified by human error. Although no one is injured or dies, concerns about radiation released into the atmosphere cause many people to question the safety of nuclear power in general. Clean-up takes more than a decade and costs over $1 billion.

1979 Swiss politician Daniel Brelaz becomes the first member of the Green Party to be elected to a national legislative body. The Green Party promotes policies of environmental sustainability, social justice, and nonviolence. Within thirty years, the Green Party evolves into the Global Greens, a network of political parties active in over ninety countries.

1980 Congress passes the Comprehensive Environmental Response, Compensation, and Liability Act (CERCLA), commonly known as the Superfund Law. The legislation provides funds for and requires clean-up of hazardous waste sites that are named to a National Priorities List. CERCLA is administered by the EPA.

1984 The world's worst industrial accident takes place in Bhopal, India, on December 2 and 3 when 30 metric tons of the pesticide methyl isocyanate leaks from a tank into the atmosphere at a Union Carbide plant and kills over 3,700 people. Survivors suffer for decades with various health problems.

Chronology of Important Events

1984 Farm labor activist Cesar Chavez launches his Wrath of Grapes boycott with a 36-day hunger strike to raise awareness of the dangers of pesticide spraying of grape crops in California.

1985 The French foreign intelligence service intentionally bombs and sinks Greenpeace's flagship, the *Rainbow Warrior*, while it is docked in Auckland, New Zealand, on July 10, before it sets sail to protest an upcoming French nuclear test. One person dies in the blast.

1986 The Chernobyl nuclear power plant in Pripyat, Ukraine, suffers a catastrophic meltdown on April 26 that releases radiation that drifts over much of Europe. Thirty-one people die directly from the accident, and the city of 50,000 people is evacuated as workers entomb the damaged reactor in concrete. A radius of 18.6 miles (30 kilometers) around the facility becomes the Chernobyl Exclusion Zone, which is off-limits to all individuals except military personnel for decades.

1987 General Motors' Sunraycer wins the first World Solar Challenge, a 1,867-mile (3,005 km) race across Australia in November, with an average speed of 42 mph (67 kmh). The ultra-lightweight Sunraycer features 8,800 solar cells and was driven by Australian race car driver John Harvey.

1987 *Our Common Future*, better known as the Brundtland Report, is published following the United Nations Conference on the Human Environment. The document defines the term *sustainable development* and explains how issues such as poverty, gender equity, and hunger have a negative impact on the natural environment. The report proves influential in future conferences designed to address environmental and sustainability issues worldwide.

1987 Yucca Mountain in Nevada is identified by Congress as a suitable site for permanent placement of the nation's high-level radioactive waste, which has been stored in unsecured, temporary locations around the nation's nuclear power plants for decades. Federal funding for the site is withdrawn in 2010, leaving many tons of radioactive waste in limbo.

1988 Brazilian environmental activist Chico Mendes is assassinated on December 22. Mendes's efforts to stop the destruction of the Amazon rainforest and promote human rights of indigenous people conflicts with ranchers' efforts to clear cut the rainforest. His murder by a local rancher brings international attention to the issue of deforestation.

1988 Entomologist Edward O. Wilson popularizes the term *biodiversity* in *Papers from the 1st National Forum on Biodiversity*. The collection highlights the proceedings from a conference sponsored by the National Academy of Sciences to address the rapid extinction of plant and animal species due to human intervention in nature.

1988 The Intergovernmental Panel on Climate Change is established by the United Nations to assess scientific research on climate change and promote options for adaptation and mitigation. Its fifth assessment report, published in 2014, states that with 95 to 100 percent probability, human influence is the dominant cause of current global warming.

1989 The Montreal Protocol on Substances that Deplete the Ozone Layer goes into effect on January 1. The international treaty is designed to phase out the use of chlorofluorocarbons (CFCs) that have damaged the ozone layer, thereby allowing dangerous levels of ultraviolet radiation to reach earth. Twenty-five years later, with the ozone layer steadily healing, the Montreal Protocol is hailed as one of the most successful international environmental treaties in history.

1989 The oil tanker *Exxon Valdez* runs aground in Prince William Sound, Alaska, on March 24, spilling between 11 and 38 million gallons of crude oil into the ocean, becoming the largest oil spill in U.S. history. Clean up is difficult because of the remote location. Hundreds of thousands of animals die in the disaster, and the spill continues to have a negative effect on the marine environment for decades.

1991 At the end of the Persian Gulf War in January, Iraqi troops retreating from U.S.-led military forces set fire to about seven hundred of Kuwait's oil wells, and many of the fires continue to burn until November. An estimated one billion barrels of oil are burned.

1992 The United Nations Conference on Environment and Development, better known as the Earth Summit, is held from June 3 to 14 in Rio de Janeiro, Brazil. Representatives from 172 countries and thousands of NGOs discuss how to achieve sustainable development. The results are published as Agenda 21.

Chronology of Important Events

1993 The first mission in Biosphere 2, built by Space Biosphere Ventures in Arizona, ends on September 26 after two years. A crew of eight scientists have been isolated in an artificial, supposedly self-sustaining biome with no outside input of air, water, food, or other resources to test the feasibility of creating artificial sustainable environments. Results are mixed; many food species die off and oxygen levels run too low for optimal health, among other factors.

1994 The U.S. Food and Drug Administration determines that Calgene's Flavr Savr tomato is safe for human consumption, and it becomes the first genetically modified (GM) food to reach the marketplace. The tomato has been altered with a gene that slows down the ripening process, thereby extending the time between harvest and consumption. However, consumers are not impressed with the new fruit and it is taken off the market within three years.

1994 The U.S. Green Building Council begins developing Leadership in Energy and Environmental Design (LEED) standards to promote environmentally responsible design, construction, operation, and maintenance of commercial and residential buildings. By 2012 more than one thousand buildings worldwide have attained LEED platinum status, meaning that they implement green practices and materials to a highly sustainable degree.

1997 The Toyota Prius goes on sale in Japan and quickly becomes the bestselling hybrid electric vehicle (HEV) in history, selling 4.8 million units by 2014. The Prius has a traditional internal combustion engine, an electric propulsion system, and regenerative brakes that help charge the battery. The vehicle has ultra-low emissions and gets up to 50 miles per gallon of gasoline, about twice that of the average car.

2000 All 189 United Nations member states adopt the Millennium Development Goals (MDGs). These eight goals are to be achieved by 2015. They are: eradicate extreme poverty and hunger; achieve universal primary education; promote gender equality; reduce child mortality; improve maternal health; combat HIV/AIDS, malaria, and other diseases; ensure environmental sustainability; and develop a global partnership for development. Worldwide there has been progress on achieving many of the goals. However, the achievements have been uneven.

Chronology of Important Events

2002 The World Summit on Sustainable Development takes place in Johannesburg, South Africa in August and September. The conference results in the Johannesburg Declaration, which builds on agreements outlined at the 1992 Earth Summit in Rio de Janeiro and recognizes that major impediments to sustainable development worldwide include poverty, hunger, armed conflict and other forms of violence, corruption, natural disasters, and disease.

2002 China's massive South-to-North Water Diversion project begins. Over the next fifty years, the country plans to build a series of canals to transfer water from the Yangtze River in the south to the more populated areas in the north. The project may displace hundreds of thousands of people and introduce new, unforeseen environmental problems.

2003 Tesla Motors is founded in San Carlos, California, by Martin Eberhard and Marc Tarpenning to create an affordable, high-performance all-electric vehicle. Within ten years the Tesla Model S earns the highest ranking ever given to a vehicle by *Consumer Reports*. Sales of Tesla cars are aided by the development of a worldwide network of Supercharger stations.

2004 On December 15, NASA announces that a "brown cloud" of smog has formed over the Indian subcontinent and South Asia. The cloud is largely the result of millions of cooking fires, which release unhealthy levels of soot that linger in the atmosphere and drift across the globe. The soot also traps particles of ozone near the earth's surface, where it can harm respiratory health and damage crops.

2004 The Stockholm Convention on Persistent Organic Pollutants goes into effect on May 17. This international treaty limits the production and use of persistent organic pollutants (POPs), which are chemicals that can remain in the environment for many years and bioaccumulate in the fatty tissue of animals and people, thereby causing major health problems. Substances that are banned or severely limited include DDT, PCBs, Aldrin, and Chlordane.

2004 Fairtrade International (FLO) is founded in Bonn, Germany, to certify products as fair trade, meaning farmers and workers in developing countries receive a fair price for their goods that are sold internationally. The fair trade movement is intended to empower impoverished farmers and peasants worldwide by preventing unfair labor practices in their industries.

2004 The Subaru plant in Lafayette, Indiana, becomes the first U.S. facility to reach zero-landfill status. This means all waste material is reused, recycled, or converted into electricity.

2005 The Kyoto Protocol to the United Nations Framework Convention on Climate Change becomes effective on February 16. Signed and ratified by nearly every nation in the world except the United States, the protocol is designed to combat climate change by reducing each state's greenhouse gas emissions gradually in accordance with several target dates. Over the next ten years, some countries do meet their reduced greenhouse gas targets, but their gains are offset by a steep increase in other countries' emissions.

2007 The bald eagle is removed from the list of endangered and threatened wildlife on June 28. Its population had been drastically curtailed by the 1970s due to hunting and its susceptibility to DDT, but protection of its habitat and a ban on DDT increase the number of nesting pairs in the lower 48 states from 412 in the 1950s to many thousands.

2007 On October 24, thirty-five nations join ITER, the International Thermonuclear Experimental Reactor, a massive research and engineering project aimed at building the world's first nuclear fusion reactor. Located in the south of France, the fusion reactor, if successful, will provide practically limitless energy with minimal environmental impact and have an unprecedented impact on sustainability.

2007 The Aral Sea in Central Asia, once the fourth largest lake in the world, shrinks to 10 percent its original size due to Soviet irrigation projects that divert its water. By 2014 the eastern basin dries up completely and becomes known as the Aralkum Desert.

2007 Former U.S. Vice President Al Gore wins the Academy Award for best documentary for *An Inconvenient Truth,* a film version of his slide show about global warming. Gore's presentation, first developed in the late 1980s, walks viewers through the science of climate change and some possible future scenarios based on current and projected levels of greenhouse gas emissions.

Chronology of Important Events

2007 According to the Global Footprint Network, the world is consuming natural resources 1.5 times as fast as they can be renewed. The organization measures each country's ecological footprint in hectares per person and determines that the United Arab Emirates uses more resources per person than any other country in the world, although the United States is not far behind. The purpose of the ecological footprint is to provide a visualization of unsustainable development.

2008 On February 26, the Svalbard Global Seed Vault opens on the Norwegian island of Spitsbergen just 800 miles from the North Pole. The repository of seeds and genetic diversity is insurance against global catastrophe. The highly secure facility is the largest of its kind in the world and has the capacity to store samples of 4.5 million varieties of plant seeds.

2008 The United Nations estimates that for the first time in history, more people live in urban areas than rural areas worldwide. This population shift has wide ramifications regarding the use of natural resources, food production, poverty, and other issues pertaining to sustainability.

2010 On April 20 the *Deepwater Horizon* oil rig in the Gulf of Mexico explodes and sinks. Eleven people die, and oil gushes from the ocean floor for 87 days, becoming the largest accidental oil spill in history. An estimated 4.9 million barrels of oil pollute the Gulf and the coast line of Mississippi, causing billions of dollars of damage to delicate wetlands and estuary ecosystems.

2010 The controversial practice of hydraulic fracturing, or fracking, is the subject of Josh Fox's Academy Award-nominated documentary *Gasland*. The film highlights the environmental problems with the fracking process to recover natural gas from shale formations. The process uses immense amounts of water and chemicals, which have been proven to contaminate local drinking water sources and soil.

2011 On March 11 the Fukushima Daichii nuclear power plant in Japan is struck by a massive tsunami caused by a magnitude 9.0 earthquake. The resulting nuclear meltdown is the second largest in history, following the Chernobyl disaster of 1986. No immediate deaths are reported as a result of the meltdown, and future elevated risks of cancer for those in the immediate area are determined two years later by the World Health Organization to be minimal.

Chronology of Important Events

2012 The Rio+20 Summit is held in Rio de Janeiro, Brazil, in June to follow up on sustainability progress outlined at the first Earth Summit in 1992. Conference participants focus on establishing a worldwide green economy and creating an institutional framework to support global sustainable development.

2012 The Three Gorges Dam on the Yangtze River in Hubei, China, becomes the world's largest power plant on July 4. The project brings electricity to millions of people, but it forces the relocation of 1.3 million people. The unprecedented scale of the dam floods over 1,500 villages, towns, and cities and alters the environment of the area beyond what some experts believe is sustainable.

2013 The London Array becomes the world's largest offshore wind farm when it opens on July 4, twelve miles off the coast of the Thames Estuary in Kent, England. The farm is comprised of 175 turbines and two substations that can produce 630 MW at peak production.

2013 The Sorek reverse osmosis desalination plant near Tel Aviv, Israel, becomes the world's largest facility for producing freshwater from sea water, providing residents in the arid nation up to 627,000 cubic meters of water each day. Within a few years, half of Israel's water is derived from desalination plants.

2014 According to the Organic Trade Association, U.S. sales of organic products reaches $39 billion, representing the commitment that many consumers have made to eating foods they believe are more healthful and environmentally sustainable than their factory-farmed counterparts.

2015 California governor Jerry Brown declares a state of emergency on January 17 as the state's worst drought in 1,200 years enters its third year. The drought has brought record high temperatures, lack of precipitation, and the evaporation of most of the mountain snowpack from which the state obtains a third of its water.

2015 On February 24, President Obama vetoes a bill that would have approved construction of the Keystone XL Pipeline through environmentally sensitive areas of Nebraska. Environmentalists oppose the bill because of the potential for oil spills along the route and because it carries crude oil derived from oil sands, which requires much more energy and causes more pollution than traditional oil-drilling processes.

2015 The Topaz Solar Farm and the Desert Sunlight Solar Farm, both constructed by First Solar in Southern California, become the world's largest solar farms, each capable of generating 550 MW, enough to power about 160,000 homes.

Words to Know

A

Abiotic Not involving living organisms. Nonliving components in an ecosystem include air, sunlight, minerals, and water.

Abundance An economic concept that describes universal accessibility of goods and services to all members of a society.

Acid mine drainage Outflow of acidic water from metal and coal mines; common in areas containing high levels of sulfide minerals. Also known as acid rock drainage.

Acid rain Precipitation, which can be rain, fog, or snow, that is acidic. It is caused by sulfur dioxide and nitrogen dioxide emissions and can kill plants and trees, corrode (eat away by chemical action) cars and buildings, and pollute water.

Active solar heating A method of heating in which mechanical means such as pumps are used to collect, store, and distribute solar energy.

Activism Taking public action to cause social change.

Agenda 21 Plan of action for sustainable development from the first Earth Summit in 1992.

Agribusiness Large-scale corporate farming.

Agriculture Growing plants and animals for food or as raw materials for goods.

Air pollution All substances in the earth's atmosphere that are dangerous to human health or the environment.

Alternative energy An energy source that is renewable and sustainable. Or, a traditional form of energy used in a more efficient way.

Words to Know

Anthropogenic Caused by human activity.

Aquaculture Growing and harvesting of fish and shellfish for human use.

Aquatic ecosystem A community of living organisms interacting with their nonliving environment in a body of water.

Aquifer An underground formation of rock, gravel, and sand that stores freshwater.

Atmosphere The layer of gases that surrounds the earth's surface and makes life possible.

B

Battery A portable device that stores chemical energy, which can be converted into electrical energy.

Bioaccumulation The process whereby a substance, such as a pesticide, persists in the environment by moving up the food chain as larger animals eat the smaller animals that have consumed it.

Biocapacity The amount of resources available in an area, or on all of earth, expressed in terms of the area of land needed to produce the resources.

Biodegradable Able to be broken down by natural processes.

Biodiversity The variety of species or organisms in a given environment or ecosystem. A large range of plant and animal life in a given region is symptomatic of its health; a narrow range or declining number of species in a region may indicate environmental damage or stress.

Biofuel A gas or liquid fuel made from plant material, which makes them a renewable resource, unlike fossil fuels.

Biomass Plant materials and animal wastes used as fuel.

Biome A habitat consisting of a community of naturally occurring plants and animals that may consist of many ecosystems.

Biomimicry Using processes found in nature to solve human problems.

Bioregionalism The belief that human activities should be based on bioregions, rather than political or economic boundaries.

Bioremediation Using living organisms to remove pollution from the environment.

Biosphere The part of the earth in which life can exist.

Biotechnology The use of any biological process for agricultural, medical, industrial, or environmental purposes.

Biotic Describing a living organism. Living components in an ecosystem include bacteria, animals, plants, and fungi.

Boycott A ban organized by a group of people against a company to protest what the group sees as unfair or unethical business practices.

Brundtland Report Authored in 1987 by the United Nations World Commission on Environment and Development (WCED), the report was the first international plan for sustainable development, which it defined as "development that meets the needs of the present without compromising the ability of future generations to meet their own needs."

C

Campaign A coordinated effort to achieve a goal, such as winning an election or promoting social, political, or environmental change.

Carbon An element that is found in all life on the earth.

Carbon footprint The total amount of greenhouse gases produced by human activity. A person's carbon footprint includes, for example, the fuel to power a car or heat a house or cook food and would extend to the power used to produce and transport the goods a person uses.

Carbon sequestration A pollution-control process in which carbon dioxide generated by power plants is pumped underground to be stored indefinitely so it does not contribute to climate change.

Carbon sink A reservoir that stores carbon over a long period of time. Carbon sinks can be natural or human made.

Carcinogen A chemical or other agent that can cause cancer.

Carpool The practice of commuters riding together in one car instead of separately in different cars.

Carrying capacity The maximum number of one species that can survive in one area at a time.

CERCLA (Comprehensive Environmental Response, Compensation, and Liability Act of 1980) Comprehensive Environmental Response, Compensation, and Liability Act, the U.S. federal law that requires and regulates the cleanup of hazardous waste sites. Also known as the Superfund law.

Words to Know

Chlorofluorocarbons (CFCs) An organic compound consisting of carbon, chlorine, and fluorine and used in the manufacture of aerosol sprays, foams, packing materials, and refrigerants.

Chronic disease A long-lasting condition that can be controlled with medicine or lifestyle changes but that cannot be cured. Chronic disease is more common in developed countries than in developing countries.

Circular economy An economy that uses resources effectively so that waste is drastically reduced and becomes reusable material for products or food for organisms in the soil.

Citizen science The involvement of the general public in science inquiry and research.

Citizenship The rights and duties, such as voting, working, and living within the country, held by a person that is recognized as a citizen by their government.

Civic engagement The involvement of the public in the political process and the issues that affect the public.

Climate change Gradual and enduring changes in weather patterns over the earth that impact numerous ecosystems in different and often dramatic ways.

Community-supported agriculture (CSA) A farming enterprise that sells shares to individuals and relies on these members to help run the operation. Shareholders receive an amount of produce and goods proportionate to their ownership stake in the farm.

Compost A decayed mixture of plants (such as leaves and grass) that is used to improve the soil in a garden.

Composting The practice of helping along the decay of organic matter (such as leaves and grass) so that it can be used in agriculture or gardening as a nutrient-rich soil amendment.

Condensation The process of turning a gas into a liquid.

Conservation The protection of natural resources, plants and animals, and their habitats to prevent unnecessary loss of resources or biodiversity.

Consumption The using of resources.

Cost-benefit analysis An economic tool that helps businesses determine if the benefits of a new product or service will outweigh its costs. In traditional economics, this process usually fails to accurately assess ecosystem services or natural capital.

Cover crop A crop planted to minimize soil erosion and improve its quality and to manage weeds, pests, and diseases.

Cradle-to-cradle design The manufacture of products in a closed-loop cycle to save natural resources and energy. All used goods are either broken down into components that are recycled and made into other goods or returned to the earth as food for organisms in the soil.

Crop rotation The practice of growing first one and then another crop on the same land especially to preserve the ability of the soil to produce crops.

Crude oil A thick, blackish liquid created over millions of years through the decay of the remains of plants and animals subjected to heat and pressure beneath the surface of the earth. Also called petroleum and oil.

Cultural heritage Refers to parts of culture you can see and touch (for example, artifacts, buildings, and monuments) as well as things that you can't see or touch (for example, traditions, languages, and rituals).

D

Deep Ecology An environmental philosophy in which the value of human life is no greater than the value of any other organism's life.

Deforestation Removing trees from a forest, especially to the point that the forested area is cleared.

Desalination The process of turning saltwater into freshwater for human consumption and agricultural uses.

Desertification Breakdown of the soil when it becomes increasingly dry and can no longer support the amount and variety of plant and animal life it once did.

Developed country A country that has developed industries, technology, and a mature economy, as compared to less developed countries. The United States, Canada, and Germany are examples.

Developing country A country that has a low standard of living, including low average annual income per person, high infant mortality rates, widespread poverty, and an underdeveloped economy. Most of these countries are located in Africa, Asia, and Latin America.

Drought An extended period with little or no rainfall.

Words to Know

E

Earth Summit Also known as the Rio Summit. A conference held in Rio de Janeiro, Brazil, in 1992. It resulted in numerous documents and international agreements regarding sustainable development, including the Rio Declaration and Agenda 21.

Ecological footprint The measure of human stress on the planet's ecosystems. The footprint considers how much land and water resources a population consumes and the ability of the environment to absorb the population's corresponding waste.

Ecology The study of the relations and interactions between organisms and their environment.

Economy The wealth and resources of a country or region, especially in terms of the production and consumption of goods and services.

Ecosystem A complete and interdependent system of biotic (living) and abiotic (nonliving) components that cycles matter and transfers energy within a given area. The three major types of ecosystems are freshwater, terrestrial, and marine.

Ecosystem restoration The process of returning a damaged ecosystem to its original condition.

Ecosystem services The benefits an ecosystem provides to humankind. The four main categories are provisioning, regulating, supporting, and cultural.

Ecotourism The practice of traveling to beautiful natural places for pleasure in a way that does not damage the environment there.

Emigration The movement of an individual out of a population.

Emissions The production and discharge of something, especially gas or radiation.

Endangered At high risk of extinction.

Energy conservation Using less energy by doing less of what uses the energy, for example driving less.

Energy efficiency Using less energy to accomplish the same task, for example using fluorescent instead of incandescent light bulbs to produce the same amount of light.

Energy footprint A measure of the land required to absorb carbon dioxide emissions.

Environmental degradation The change in or decline of an environment or ecosystem through the depletion (or lessening) of resources such as air, water, and soil.

Environmental justice Equality for all people regarding environmental laws, regulations, and policies.

Environmental policy The laws, regulations, and programs that are designed, funded, and enforced by government agencies to protect public health and natural resources.

Equity The condition of being fair and reasonable.

Erosion The movement of soil and rock from one area to another caused by the flow of water or wind.

Ethanol An alcohol fuel that is manufactured by fermenting and distilling crops with a high starch or sugar content, such as grains, sugarcane, or corn.

Evaporation The process of turning a liquid into a gas.

Evolution The change and adaptation of organisms to their environments.

Extinct No longer in existence.

F

Fair trade An economic partnership founded upon principles of sustainability and equity in trade so that producers and workers in poorer countries receive a fair price or wage to reduce poverty.

Food access One of the three pillars of food security, concerning whether everyone has sufficient ability to grow or buy food.

Food availability One of the three pillars of food security, concerning whether enough food is provided to feed a population.

Food desert An urban or rural, high-poverty area in which residents do not have easy access to grocery stores that stock a variety of reasonably priced and healthy produce.

Food insecurity Limited consistent and constant access to adequate food as the result of a lack of money and other resources.

Food security Access to safe, affordable, and nutritious food for everyone at all times.

Food shed The geographical area between where food is produced and where that food is consumed.

Words to Know

Food use One of the three pillars of food security, concerning whether food that is available is used properly.

Food waste Food that is discarded or cannot be used.

Fossil fuel Nonrenewable energy source formed over millions of years through geological processes. Includes coal, oil, and natural gas, which when burned to release energy also emit greenhouse gases that contribute to climate change and air pollution.

Freshwater Water that has a low level of salt and is suitable for drinking and irrigation of agriculture.

G

Gasoline Refined oil that is burned as transportation fuel in internal combustion engines—engines that are found mainly in cars but also in motorcycles, buses, trucks, and some other vehicles.

Genetically Modified Organism (GMO) An organism whose genetic makeup has been altered by genetic engineering.

Geothermal Referring to heat from inside the earth.

Geothermal power Electricity generated from the earth's internal heat.

Globalization The process of people and economies around the world becoming more linked to each other because of the spread of culture, ideas, and goods through modern technology and transportation systems.

Grassroots activism Organizing individuals at the local level to make changes that affect their community.

Grassroots organization A group of ordinary citizens who work toward specific goals driven by a community's politics.

Green economy A system in which the production and consumption of goods and services are profitable, environmentally sustainable, and socially just.

Green Revolution Scientific advances of the twentieth century that greatly increased food production.

Greenhouse effect The process whereby gases in the atmosphere allow sunlight to enter the atmosphere but do not allow its heat to escape.

Greenhouse gases Any of the gases in the earth's atmosphere that absorb or reflect back to earth infrared radiation from the sun, thereby trapping heat close to the earth's surface. An increase in greenhouse gases corresponds with climate change. The main greenhouse gases are carbon dioxide, methane, nitrous oxide, and ozone. Clouds and water vapor also function as greenhouse gases.

Groundwater Freshwater that accumulates underground, usually in aquifers.

H

Haber Process An industrial process to efficiently make ammonia from atmospheric nitrogen. Afterward, it can be utilized as a nitrogen fertilizer for plant growth.

Habitat The natural environment where a living organism lives.

Hazardous waste Waste that can be solid, liquid, or gas and that is harmful to living things and the environment. Hazardous waste can be discarded commercial products, like cleaning fluids or pesticides, or the by-products of manufacturing processes.

Human rights The fundamental rights, based on moral principles and society's norms, to which a person is entitled regardless of race, nationality, religion, gender, ability, or socioeconomic status.

Hydraulic fracturing A process for extracting natural gas from shale rock by injecting the rock with a stream of highly pressurized water mixed with chemicals and sand.

Hydrochorofluorocarbons (HCFCs) Chemicals used in manufacturing that contain chlorine and hydrogen, which can break down ozone.

Hydropower Electricity generated from flowing water.

I

Indigenous Living and having historical ties to a particular country or region, often with a distinctive culture.

Indoor air pollution Smoke, particulates, and poisons that contaminate interior spaces and that can cause disease leading to premature death.

Industrial Revolution The period of time between the mid-1700s and the mid-1800s when society transitioned to new manufacturing processes.

Infrastructure Basic physical and organizational structures, like buildings and roads, needed for the operation of a society.

Introduced species A species introduced deliberately or inadvertently to one part of the world from another that benefits or causes no harm in the new area.

Invasive species A species that is intentionally or unintentionally introduced to one part of the world from another that causes harm in the new area. Invasive species may become competitors, predators, or parasites of native species.

L

Landfill A site where solid waste (the garbage of a particular community) is buried.

Law of Conservation of Matter The natural law that states that in chemical reactions matter cannot be created or destroyed.

LEED standards A set of voluntary standards that show a building or factory exhibits Leadership in Energy and Environmental Design, awarded by the U.S. Green Building Council.

Life expectancy Age to which a person is expected to live.

Lobby To try to influence a company or government to change its practices or laws.

Lobbyist A representative for an interest group that meets with elected officials to persuade them to act in the interest group's favor.

Local currency Money issued in only a limited location and only usable in that location to promote the local economy.

Locavore A person who aims to eat only or mostly locally grown or produced food.

M

Mass transit A system of large-scale public transportation.

Maximum carrying capacity A carrying capacity in which the population uses as many resources as are necessary to support the largest possible population.

Mitigation Measures taken to control, reduce, or halt the impacts of environmental change.

Monoculture The cultivation or growth of a single crop or organism especially on agricultural or forest land.

Montreal Protocol A treaty developed by the United Nations to regulate or eliminate the emission of ozone-depleting substances.

Municipal solid waste (MSW) Household garbage and other items that a consumer throws out.

N

Native species The species of organisms normally found in a given habitat.

Natural capital Any natural resource that can be used to create a good or service. This includes obvious substances such as minerals and water, as well as less obvious things such as pollination or biodiversity hotspots.

Natural gas A fossil fuel made of organic material that is transformed over millions of years into methane, butane, propane, and other gases.

Natural resource A material that occurs in nature that can be used for economic gain.

Natural selection Evolution that occurs through an organism's interactions with the natural world.

Nongovernmental organization A nonprofit group that is associated with neither a for-profit business nor a government and that raises funds to address a specific issue.

Nonpoint source pollution Air, water, or soil pollution that has many sources.

Nonrenewable resource A resource that cannot be easily replenished or that is consumed much faster than nature can create it, like oil and gas.

Nuclear fission The splitting of atomic nuclei to produce energy.

Nuclear fusion Fusing, or joining, atomic nuclei together to produce energy.

Nuclear power The production of electricity by harnessing the energy stored in the nucleus (center) of atoms.

O

Oil A thick, blackish liquid created over millions of years through the decay of the remains of plants and animals subjected to heat and pressure beneath the surface of the earth. Also called petroleum and crude oil.

Words to Know

Optimum carrying capacity A carrying capacity in which the population only uses resources as quickly as the ecosystem can replace them.

Organic farming Raising food without the use of synthetic, or artificial, fertilizers and pesticides, and raising livestock without growth hormones and antibiotics.

Overfishing The situation in which humans deplete wild fish populations faster than the fish can reproduce, leading to their endangerment or extinction.

Ozone A form of oxygen that exists naturally in the upper atmosphere, but causes pollution in the lower atmosphere.

Ozone depletion Destruction of the protective layer of ozone molecules in the stratosphere that allows dangerous ultraviolet radiation from the sun to reach the earth's surface.

Ozone layer A layer of atmosphere 10–20 miles (16–32 kilometers) above the earth that contains a large amount of ozone, which absorbs ultraviolet radiation from the sun and prevents heat loss from the earth.

P

Peak oil The point in time at which worldwide oil production reaches its all-time high, which will be followed by a sharp and steady decrease due to dwindling supplies.

Permaculture Agriculture that is designed to work with the natural surroundings and to be sustainable and self-sufficient.

Pesticides Chemical or biological substances that kill organisms that harm plants, animals, and people.

Photosynthesis The process by which plants make food from sunlight.

Point source pollution Air, water, or soil pollution that comes from a specific source.

Pollutant Any substance, such as certain chemicals or waste products, that renders the air, soil, water, or other natural resource harmful or unsuitable for a specific purpose.

Polluter pays principle The notion that any individual or corporation who pollutes the environment must pay to clean it up.

Polyculture The practice of growing many different types of crops in a single area.

Population A group of individuals of the same species living in an area.

Power grid A system of electrical transmission lines and other facilities that distributes electricity from power plants to users over a wide area.

Precautionary principle When there is significant scientific uncertainty about potentially serious harm from chemicals or technologies, decision makers should act to prevent harm to humans and the environment.

Precipitation Liquid or solid water that falls to the earth's surface as a product of condensation.

Preservation The maintenance of wilderness areas in an undisturbed state.

Public health The science of preventing disease and promoting healthful habits so people in a given community live longer and healthier lives.

R

Rainforest A temperate or tropical forest with tall, broad-leaved trees which require a humid climate and a large amount of precipitation.

Recycling To turn waste materials into new products and in this way conserving natural resources and energy.

Remediation Stopping and correcting environmental damage.

Renewable resource A resource that can be replenished through natural processes at a rate that matches consumption, such as trees and plants.

Rio Declaration List of principles for sustainable development from the first Earth Summit in 1992.

Risk assessment The process by which people weigh the pros and cons in making a decision.

S

Seed bank A repository of different strains of plant seed to preserve genetic variation for future need.

Self-reliance Depending on one's own resources.

Social justice Equal distribution of wealth, opportunities, and privileges in a society, which allows all individuals to live up to their potential.

Socioeconomic Relating to both social and economic factors and how they interact with one another.

Words to Know

Solar power Energy obtained from sunlight.

Species The basic unit or category of classification for living things. A group of organisms that have unique common characteristics and can breed with each other.

Stratosphere The layer of atmosphere that lies just above the troposphere, starting six miles (9.6 kilometers) above the earth.

Strip mining Surface mining that continues horizontally after removing all vegetation, soil, and the top layer of rock. This is common practice for recovering coal that is often found in horizontal layers just below the surface of the earth.

Subsidy A sum of money granted by the government to assist a business.

Subsistence farming Farming focused on growing enough food to feed one's family rather than farming to produce food to sell.

Surface water Water that collects on the surface of the earth from rain and snow.

Sustainability The capacity of the earth's natural systems and human cultural systems to survive, flourish, and adapt to changing environmental conditions for many years into the future.

Sustainable development Development that meets the needs of the present without compromising the ability of future generations to meet their own needs.

Sustainable farming A set of agricultural practices that conserves resources, namely water and soil, and protects the well-being of an entire ecosystem.

T

Thermal pollution Worsening of water quality as the result of a rise in water temperature.

Thermodynamics, First Law of The natural law that states that in any physical or chemical change, matter is neither created nor destroyed but merely changed from one form to another.

Thermodynamics, Second Law of The natural law that states that energy always changes from a more useful, more highly organized form to a less useful, less organized form.

Threatened Species that are considered critically endangered, endangered, or vulnerable.

Three pillars of sustainability Achieving sustainability means balancing the three pillars: environment, economy, and society. The first pillar, the environment, involves making sure that humans consume the earth's natural resources at a sustainable rate and in a way that does not damage the earth's ecosystems. The second pillar, the economy, addresses the need for current and future jobs, economic growth, and for businesses to use resources efficiently and responsibly for the long term. The third pillar, society, focuses on the social well-being of people living in a community, country, and around the world.

Time bank Currency system that uses hours of labor instead of units of money.

Topsoil The top layer of soil, which contains the most organic matter and has the most biological activity.

Transition Town A local community that is seeking to build a less energy dependent and more local, resilient, and self-sufficient economy.

Treaty An agreement or arrangement made by negotiation, especially one between two or more states or rulers.

Trophic level The position an organism occupies in a food chain.

U

Upcycling Recycling that involves reusing an item by using it to create a new product of higher value or quality than the original item.

Urban In, or having to do with, a city or large town.

Urban farming Produce and meat grown or raised in an urban or suburban setting.

Urban heat island A portion of a city or metropolitan area that is hotter than surrounding suburban or rural areas.

Urban sprawl The poorly controlled spread of cities and suburbs onto rural lands.

V

Vulnerable Species that are considered critically endangered, endangered, or vulnerable.

W

Wastewater Water that has been used.

Water cycle The continuous movement of water between the oceans, atmosphere, and soil.

Watershed An area of land from which all of the rain and melted snow drain into a particular body of water, such as a river or lake.

Weather Short-term variations in the temperature, rainfall, and wind over a small area.

Wetland An area of land that is saturated with water and has its own distinct ecosystem.

Wind farm A large group of wind turbines located at a site that has dependable, strong winds.

Wind power Electricity generated from wind turbines.

Wind turbine A device that converts energy from the wind into electric power.

Z

Zero waste The process of creating goods that generate little waste; any waste generated is used as a raw material for other goods instead of being placed in a landfill or incinerated.

A

Abundance

Abundance is an economic term that describes universal accessibility of goods and services. A society of abundance is one in which everyone has access to what they need to thrive physically and mentally. Sustainability and abundance go hand in hand. When resources are used responsibly and distributed fairly, people will have enough to maintain a comfortable standard of living without compromising the ability of future generations to also have a similar standard of living.

Achieving sustainable abundance requires good governance. Societies must value resources enough to protect them. They must also value the rights of all people to live free from hunger and poverty. Thus, legal protection of human rights and economic justice are also aspects of abundance. Psychologically, people achieve abundance when they realize that their happiness is not tied to overconsumption of consumer goods (that is, having a large house, expensive cars, or designer clothes). Abundance is achieved only when there is little economic divide between individuals within a society.

The circular economy

One concept crucial to abundance is the circular economy. In a circular economy, natural resources are never wasted. They are turned into either technical or biological nutrients. Technical nutrients are materials like steel or glass that can be used repeatedly without losing value. Biological nutrients are materials such as cotton fabric, paper, or wood, which when they are no longer useful can be returned to the earth to build and regenerate soil as they become food for microorganisms.

> ## WORDS TO KNOW
>
> **Abundance:** An economic concept that describes universal accessibility of goods and services to all members of a society.
>
> **Circular economy:** An economy that uses resources effectively so that waste is drastically reduced and becomes reusable material for products or food for organisms in the soil.
>
> **Cradle-to-cradle design:** The manufacture of products in a closed-loop cycle to save natural resources and energy. All used goods are either broken down into components that are recycled and made into other goods or returned to the earth as food for organisms in the soil.

A circular economy produces no waste and is therefore much more sustainable than an economy based on goods that have a short life span and are disposed of in a landfill or burned in an incinerator. Cradle-to-cradle design, which is the manufacturing of products in a closed-loop cycle to save natural resources and energy, is key to establishing a circular economy. Switching over to nonpolluting forms of renewable energy is also vital for abundance. Unpolluted ecosystems help ensure that the planet retains the biodiversity (variety of life-forms) necessary for its own health and that of its current and future inhabitants.

Threats to abundance

A worldwide culture of sustainable abundance is threatened by many countries' reliance on environmentally destructive means of providing essential goods and services. For example, unsustainable agricultural practices that deplete the soil and reduce and pollute water supplies leave millions worldwide in poverty, promote deforestation and desertification, and limit biodiversity. Desertification happens when soil becomes dry as a desert and can no longer sustain the life it once did. The clearing of trees with deforestation can contribute to soil erosion that makes way for desertification. If these trends continue unchecked, it will be harder and harder for future generations to attain abundant food on their own.

Reliance on nonrenewable fossil fuels is another major threat to abundance. Mining coal, petroleum, and natural gas damages ecosystems; pollutes water, air, and soil; and threatens biodiversity. Burning fossil fuels also increases the level of carbon dioxide (CO_2)—a greenhouse gas—in the atmosphere. Increasing levels of CO_2 are believed to play a significant role in climate change. Climate change will limit millions of people's access to food, water, and clean air—all of which are considered human rights. In a society of abundance, the shortcomings of the wasteful use of natural resources are recognized and addressed.

SEE ALSO Citizenship; Consumption; Cradle-to-Cradle Design; Human Rights; Social Justice

For more information

BOOKS
McDonough, William, and Michael Braungart. *The Upcycle: Beyond Sustainability—Designing for Abundance.* New York: North Point Press, 2013.

PERIODICALS
Tantram, Joss. "Valuing Abundance: Breaking the Tyranny of Resource Scarcity." *The Guardian* (August 8, 2012). Available online at http://www.theguardian.com/sustainable-business/blog/valuing-abundance-breaking-resource-scarcity (accessed April 20, 2015).

WEBSITES
"Circular Economy Reports." Ellen MacArthur Foundation. http://www.ellenmacarthurfoundation.org/business/reports (accessed April 20, 2015).

Acid Rain

Precipitation, which consists of rain, snow, sleet, hail, and fog, normally contains water that is slightly acidic. This level of acidity does no harm to the environment. However, under certain circumstances the acidity of precipitation increases to a level that is harmful to living things, some buildings, bridges, statues, and even the coatings of cars. Precipitation with a higher-than-normal acid concentration is called "acid rain" or "acid precipitation." Moisture that is acidic, or wet deposition, and dry materials that are acidic, or dry deposition, together are referred to as "acid deposition." In both cases, acidic substances fall through the atmosphere and are "deposited" on the earth's surface.

How acid rain forms and where it is most concentrated

Acid rain results from industrial processes and transportation. Many industries, especially some electrical power plants, and most forms of transportation, such as cars and trucks, burn fossil fuels such as coal, oil, and natural gas to produce usable energy. When fossil fuels burn, they produce a

Acid Rain

WORDS TO KNOW

Acid rain: Precipitation, which can be rain, fog, or snow, that is acidic. It is caused by sulfur dioxide and nitrogen dioxide emissions and can kill plants and trees, corrode (eat away by chemical action) cars and buildings, and pollute water.

Dry deposition: Acidic particles that fall from the air to the earth's surface.

Fossil fuel: Nonrenewable energy source formed over millions of years through geological processes. Includes coal, oil, and natural gas, which when burned to release energy also emit greenhouse gases that contribute to climate change and air pollution.

Wet deposition: Acidic moisture that falls from the air to the earth's surface.

---

number of gases. One of these gases is sulfur dioxide (SO_2). Another group of gases are made up of nitrogen oxides (NOx). When these gases rise into the atmosphere, they react chemically with oxygen (O_2), water (H_2O), and other substances to form a variety of acids. The main products of these reactions are sulfuric acid (H_2SO_4) and nitric acid (HNO_3).

If winds blow these acids into wet areas of the atmosphere, the acids will mix with water. If winds blow the acids into dry areas of the atmosphere, the acids will mix with dry particles, such as dust and smoke. As they mix, the acids increase the acidity of the water and dry particles in the air. The acidic mixtures may then fall to the ground as wet or dry deposition. According to the U.S. Environmental Protection Agency (EPA), roughly equal amounts of wet and dry acid deposition fall on earth's surface.

Not all parts of the world, or the United States, receive equal amounts of acid rain. Areas with high concentrations of industries and automobiles produce more acid-forming gases than sparsely populated areas or areas with few industries. Therefore, more acid rain falls in the northeastern United States than on the plains in the central part of the country. Prevailing winds are another contributing factor to where acid rain becomes concentrated. In the United States, these winds blow from west to east, carrying additional acid-producing gases from the industrial Midwest to areas in the Northeast.

How acid rain affects the sustainability of living things

Acid rain affects both organisms and nonliving objects on earth. Plants and animals have adapted over time to environments with particular levels of acidity. With industrialization, and consequently acid rain, these environments have changed in many places on earth. If the plants and animals cannot adapt to their changing environment, they may be harmed and die.

Some organisms are directly affected by acid rain. For example, as acid rain flows through soil it picks up the element aluminum. Aluminum is poisonous to many forms of aquatic life, such as fish. Lakes and streams become highly acidic and overloaded with aluminum. The fish lose weight and do not grow to a normal size. As a consequence, they lose the ability to compete with other organisms for food and living space. In addition, if the acidity of the water increases too much, fish eggs will not hatch. This may threaten the survival of an entire population of fish.

Sometimes acid pollution indirectly affects the survival of organisms. Frogs can survive in fairly acidic water. However, mayflies, which are a main source of food for frogs, do not survive in such water. Mayflies are more sensitive to acidic water than frogs. If the mayfly population of a pond dies, frogs lose a source of food, which may threaten their population's survival.

Trees are also vulnerable to acid rain. When exposed to acid rain, the leaves of trees turn brown and fall off. Acid rain also dissolves and washes away nutrients in the soil. As a result, trees may not be able to produce or obtain the nutrients they need. This weakens trees and reduces their ability to survive when other threatening conditions occur.

Acid rain has caused the needles to drop from these spruce trees. Trees exposed to acid rain are also less able to withstand drought and disease. © MARY TERRIBERRY/SHUTTERSTOCK.COM

More on Acid Rain

The acidity of most lakes and ponds affected by acid rain is similar to that of bananas, but not as great as vinegar or lemon juice. One of the most acidic bodies of water in the United States is Little Echo Pond in Franklin, New York. It is as acidic as tomato juice. Aquatic animals possess different tolerances to acidic water. Here is a partial list from most tolerant to least tolerant: frogs; perch; salamanders and trout; bass, crayfish, and mayflies; snails and clams.

In the United States, about 67 percent of sulfur dioxide (SO_2) and 25 percent of nitrogen oxides (NOx) enter the atmosphere from the burning of fossil fuels, such as coal, by electric power plants.

Due to weather patterns, acid rain may fall hundreds or thousands of miles from where it originally forms. Acid rain produced in the U.S. Midwest can fall on eastern Canada as well as the U.S. Northeast, and acid rain produced in northern European countries such as England and Germany can fall on Scandanavian countries. Acid rain knows no boundaries. It crosses the borders of states and nations and can cause political conflicts between acid rain producers and victims of the pollution.

Although human beings cannot sense the difference between normal rain and acid rain, and can safely walk in it or swim in lakes acidified by it without harm, people can be affected by some of the products of acid rain. The gases that produce acid rain also produce chemicals called sulfates and nitrates. Scientific studies show that when small particles of sulfates and nitrates are inhaled, they can cause or aggravate respiratory illnesses such as asthma and bronchitis.

How acid rain affects the sustainability of nonliving things

Acids react chemically with a wide variety of substances and materials. Among these substances is the mineral calcite (calcium carbonate). The acids in acid rain dissolve calcite. Calcite is the main component of limestone and marble. Next to granite, limestone is the most used building material. Marble is also used as a building material and as a material for sculptures. When acid rain dissolves the calcite in these materials, they become pitted, crumble, and flake. In addition to acid rain's impact on modern buildings, some archaeological sites have been negatively affected by acid rain, including the buildings of the Acropolis in Greece and the Taj Mahal in India. Metals used to construct some statues, such as bronze, are also damaged by acid rain.

Controlling acid rain

Various laws, programs, and technologies are being used to limit the production of acid rain. Devices called scrubbers are attached to smokestacks to capture gases that produce acid rain before they can escape into the atmosphere. Similar devices are built into car exhaust systems. The Clean Air Act passed by the U.S. Congress in 1970 and revised in 1977 and 1990 spells out how states and the EPA should solve a variety of air pollution problems through programs based on the latest science and technology information. The EPA's Acid Rain Program focuses specifically on ways to reduce the production and effects of acid rain.

SEE ALSO Air Pollution; Coal; Fossil Fuels; Natural Gas; Oil; Pollution; Soil Pollution; Water Pollution

For more information

BOOKS

Haerens, Margaret, ed. *Air Pollution*. Detroit, MI: Greenhaven Press, 2011.

Raven, Peter H., David M. Hassenzahl, and Linda R. Berg. *Environment*. 8th ed. Hoboken, NJ: Wiley, 2012.

PERIODICALS

Weiss, Marissa. "Decades after Battle against Acid Rain Began, Soils Are Still Recovering." *Washington Post* (July 2, 2012). Available online at http://www.washingtonpost.com/national/health-science/decades-after-battle-against-acid-rain-began-soils-are-still-recovering/2012/07/02/gJQA28tfIW_story.html (accessed March 12, 2015).

WEBSITES

"Acid Rain: Do You Need to Start Wearing a Raincoat?" U.S. Geological Survey. http://water.usgs.gov/edu/acidrain.html (accessed March 12, 2015).

"Effects of Acid Rain." Environmental Protection Agency. http://www.epa.gov/acidrain/effects/index.html (accessed March 12, 2015).

"What is Acid Rain?" Environmental Protection Agency. http://www.epa.gov/acidrain/what/index.html (accessed March 12, 2015).

Activism

Activism is the use of individual or group action to cause social change. The desired change may take the form of a passage of a new law or a repeal of an existing law, a change to the practices of a business or other organization, or a change in public opinion. In the United States, activism has promoted changes related to a wide variety of issues, including voting rights, immigration laws, issues of war and peace, health matters, and environmental protection.

Citizens sometimes engage in activism individually, such as by writing a letter to a newspaper or to a public official. However, activism often involves many people acting together in a coordinated way. At rallies and marches, groups of people proclaim their opinion in a public setting.

Activism

WORDS TO KNOW

Activism: Taking public action to cause social change.

Boycott: A ban organized by a group of people against a company to protest what the group sees as unfair or unethical business practices.

Campaign: A coordinated effort to achieve a goal, such as winning an election or promoting social, political, or environmental change.

Zoning: A legal practice that specifies or limits the use of land.

A boycott is another form of activism. In a boycott against a business, people protest the actions of a company by refusing to buy its products or services. The purpose of the boycott is not only to voice the opinions of the group, but it is also an attempt to get that business to change its actions, usually by threatening the business's profits, as well as generating negative publicity. Campaigns for public office may also be a form of activism. A candidate for the office may take stands on a variety of issues. Citizens who agree with the candidate work together to help win the election.

Young activists bring awareness to the killing of elephants for their tusks. © SIMON MAINA/AFP/GETTY IMAGES

Activism for sustainability

Activism has proven to be an important tool for promoting sustainable living efforts. For example, in many communities, developers often want to buy small farms or wilderness areas so that they can construct new houses or other buildings on the land, thereby disrupting or destroying the existing habitat. Local residents may use the methods of activism to prevent these changes from happening. They can circulate petitions that gather signatures of registered community voters who are also against the proposed development and present these to the town officials. Activists may attend community-planning meetings, so that they can encourage local government officials to either pass new ordinances or strengthen the existing zoning laws, which are laws that communities may use to limit development, as a way to protect the existing environment.

Activism also promotes sustainability issues at national and global levels. In September 2014, over 400,000 people gathered in New York City for the People's Climate March. Their goal was to convince world leaders to take action to fight global climate change. Other marches and rallies against climate change have taken place in cities around the world.

Launching a business that promotes sustainable living is also a form of activism. An example of this type of business launched in 2013 by University of Illinois at Chicago student Harish Patel. On a trip to India, Patel observed that clothing was often produced by poorly treated workers and through methods that polluted the local environment. Patel had no special skills in business or fashion design. However, he wanted to make a difference in the lives of workers. He recognized that many people in the United States agreed with his goals and were interested in buying attractive, handmade clothing. For these reasons, Patel founded "ishi vest," a line of clothes that are developed in a sustainable way. The clothes are colored with natural dyes and use organically grown cotton for their lining. The goal of the company is to make a profit while protecting both its workers and the environment.

Organizations for activism

Many nonprofit organizations promote activism in support of sustainability. Generally, these organizations employ only a few full-time or part-time staff members. The organizations depend on volunteers who contribute money and/or effort.

A few examples are the Environmental Defense Fund (http://www.edf.org/), which works with government agencies and businesses in the United States on climate and energy, health, and ecosystems issues. The Kindling Trust (http://kindling.org.uk/) promotes local farms and sustainable agriculture in the United Kingdom. An international organization called 350.org (http://350.org/) is building a global climate movement. 350.org supports thousands of activists who organize actions in over 188 countries to hold "our leaders accountable to the realities of science and the principles of justice. [This] movement is rising from the bottom up all over the world, and is uniting to create the solutions that will ensure a better future for all." These three organizations accomplish their goals in very different ways, yet each practices activism in doing so.

Activism

> **PRIMARY SOURCE**
>
> ## Love Canal: My Story
>
> **Book (excerpt)**
>
> **By:** Lois Gibbs
>
> **Source:** Gibbs, Lois, and Murray Levine. *Love Canal: My Story.* Albany: State University of New York Press, 1982, 1.
>
> **About the document:** In 1978 the residents of Love Canal, a neighborhood in Niagara Falls, New York, discovered that their elementary school and many homes were built on top of 20,000 tons (18,000 metric tons) of toxic chemical waste. Lois Gibbs, a housewife and mother of two, organized her neighbors to fight to have the government relocate them to another area. In her book, *Love Canal,* Gibbs describes her frustration with government, as the threats to the health of people living in the community became more obvious and as it became clearer that no one would be able to move because no one could sell their homes. After a battle that lasted years, the government was forced to buy eight hundred houses in the area, allowing residents to move away. In the following excerpt, Gibbs talks about the importance of fighting for change at all costs.
>
> I want to tell you our story—my story—because I believe that ordinary citizens—using the tools of dignity, self-respect, common sense, and perseverance—can influence solutions to important problems in our society. To a great extent, we won our fight. It wasn't easy, that's for sure. In solving any difficult problem, you have to be prepared to fight long and hard, sometimes at great personal cost; but it can be done. It must be done if we are to survive as a democratic society—indeed, if we are to survive at all.

SEE ALSO Alter-Globalization Movement; Citizenship; Environmental Justice; Environmental Law; Nongovernmental Organizations (NGOs); Social Justice; Sustainability

For more information

BOOKS

Friedman, Lauri S., ed. *Environmentalism.* Detroit, MI: Greenhaven Press, 2012.

Gibbs, Lois, and Murray Levine. *Love Canal: My Story.* Albany: State University of New York Press, 1982.

PERIODICALS

Grid Business. "Can an Urban Planning Grad Student Change the Fashion Industry?" *Chicago Sun-Times* (August 22, 2013). Available online at http://voices.suntimes.com/business-2/grid/ishi-vest-kickstarter/ (accessed April 8, 2015).

Semuels, Alana. "New York March Seeks to be Largest Climate Change Event Ever." *Los Angeles Times* (September 18, 2014). Available online at http://www.latimes.com/nation/nationnow/la-na-nn-peoples-climate-march-20140918-story.html (accessed March 13, 2015).

WEBSITES

Boehrer, Katherine. "People's Climate March Preparation in Full Swing." *The Huffington Post,* September 19, 2014. http://www.huffingtonpost.com/2014/09/19/climate-march-preparation_n_5843584.html (accessed March 13, 2015).

"Introduction to Activism." Permanent Culture Now. http://www.permanentculturenow.com/what-is-activism (accessed March 13, 2015).

"Our History." Greenpeace USA. http://www.greenpeace.org/usa/en/campaigns/history/ (accessed March 13, 2015).

"What We Do." 350.org. http://350.org/about/what-we-do/ (accessed April 8, 2015).

Agenda 21

See **Brundtland Report; Economics; United Nations Conference on Environment and Development (UNCED).**

Agriculture

Agriculture is farming. The word *agriculture* comes from two Latin words that together mean "field cultivation." The three main forms of agriculture are cropland farming, livestock farming, and aquaculture. Cropland farming provides about 77 percent of the world's food. By the mid-twentieth century, just three plants—rice, wheat, and corn—accounted for 60 percent of all calories consumed worldwide. A significant amount of the corn and wheat crops is used to feed livestock. Cropland agriculture also grows plants that are processed into biofuels (fuels that come entirely from the organic material of plants) or goods such as cotton fabric. Plantation crops, such as bananas, pineapples, and sugarcane, are grown in developing countries for export. Livestock farming is done on rangelands, pastures, and feedlots, where cattle, pigs, and other animals are raised for slaughter and supply about 16 percent of the world's food. Aquaculture, which includes wild-caught fish and farmed fish and seafood, makes up about 7 percent of the world's food supply.

Agriculture

WORDS TO KNOW

Agriculture: Growing plants and animals for food or as raw materials for goods.

Agronomy: The science and technology involved in producing and using plants.

Aquaculture: Growing and harvesting of fish and shellfish for human use.

Compost: A decayed mixture of plants (such as leaves and grass) that is used to improve the soil in a garden.

Cover crop: A crop planted to minimize soil erosion and improve its quality and to manage weeds, pests, and diseases.

Genetically Modified Organism (GMO): An organism whose genetic makeup has been altered by genetic engineering.

Green Revolution: Scientific advances of the twentieth century that greatly increased food production.

Monoculture: The planting of a single crop over a large area of land.

Nitrogen fixation: A process that frees the nitrogen in the atmosphere, changing it into a form that can be used by plants to help them grow. Nitrogen compounds are then held in the roots of plants and are released into the soil when a plant dies, fertilizing the soil.

Polyculture: The usually simultaneous cultivation or growth of two or more compatible plants or organisms, and especially crops or fish, in a single area.

Slash-and-burn agriculture: The practice of clear-cutting and burning forest area to convert it to farmland.

Subsistence farming: Farming focused on growing enough food to feed one's family rather than farming to produce food to sell.

When humans began to develop agriculture around twelve thousand years ago, it marked a turning point in human history. Once people learned how to grow their own food, they no longer had to rely on hunting and gathering. This meant they could stop moving from one area to another to find food and they could settle down. People formed towns and cities, where a few people took over the task of agriculture, while others specialized in tasks like baking bread, making pottery, or building houses. This division of labor contributed to the flourishing of civilization. Consistent adequate food supplies allowed the world's human population to increase rapidly.

Agriculture is a key component of sustainability because it is crucial for human survival and has an enormous impact on the planet's natural resources. Agriculture that damages land or uses water inefficiently is considered unsustainable. The fact that the world's food supply hinges on just a handful of plant and animal species means that many people are vulnerable to starvation. When the production of these crops is disrupted by disease, environmental degradation, or climate change, food supplies are threatened.

Was Adopting Agriculture a Mistake?

According to renowned American anthropologist Jared Diamond (1937–), agriculture is the worst development in human history. In his influential article for *Discover* magazine published in 1987, "The Worst Mistake in the History of the Human Race," Diamond states that agriculture is "a catastrophe from which we have never recovered."

Diamond backs up his claim with evidence that the remaining hunter-gatherer tribes in the modern world spend very little time foraging for food—just a few hours a week. The rest of the time they relax, sleep, and socialize. The abundance of edible plants and animals in their environment means that if one plant fails, there will still be plenty of others to eat. Compare this with the great potato famine in Ireland in the 1840s, when a million people died of starvation because their only crop—the potato—was killed by a blight.

Diamond recounts how studies of ancient skeletons reveal stark differences between hunting-gathering and farming communities. Hunter-gatherers were taller on average, were better nourished, suffered less infectious disease, and had a longer life expectancy. They ate a larger variety of plants (an estimated sixty to seventy) rather than subsisting mainly on starchy grains that lack many essential nutrients. Agriculture left people vulnerable to crop failure. Living in close quarters with their farm animals provided a breeding ground for disease.

Diamond's view is controversial. Many anthropologists believe it is too simplistic. Many hunter-gather cultures made the move to agriculture when their populations became too large to keep moving around. This means that agriculture was, at least initially, sustainable by definition. Moreover, after an initial period of adjustment lasting several thousand years, nutrition in most agricultural societies began to improve as technology increased, itself a product of the time savings agriculture afforded.

The Green Revolution

Between 1950 and 2000 the world's population was expected to grow from 2.5 billion to 6 billion. Many experts believed this would cause large-scale famines, especially in developing countries. They worried that there was not enough farmland to grow enough food to feed everyone. While some countries did indeed suffer terrible famines, these were usually caused by political situations, not by lack of farmland. The forecasted famine due to lack of food never happened, thanks to the Green Revolution.

The Green Revolution was a series of technical advances in agronomy, the science of farming. These advances drastically increased the amount of food that could be grown on a plot of land. These advances were developed by American agronomist Norman Borlaug (1914–2009), who developed new varieties of corn, wheat, and rice that had higher yields, or

Agriculture

Employees wrap recently harvested oranges as they travel on a conveyor belt. Sustainably increasing food production to feed the growing human population is a huge challenge. © ANGEL NAVARRETE/BLOOMBERG VIA GETTY IMAGES

outputs, and required much less water to grow than traditional varieties. He worked with farmers in countries that were at risk of famine because of poverty and high population growth, such as Mexico, India, and Pakistan. With these new varieties of staple crops, farmers were able to grow more food on the same amount of land. Borlaug, who has been called the father of the Green Revolution, was awarded the Noble Peace Prize in 1970 for his contribution to feeding the world's hungry. Since about 1950, 89 percent of the increase in global food production has been due to increased crop yields. By mid-2015 the world population had reached 7.3 billion, and although access to food was often a problem, the world's farmers continued to produce enough calories to feed everyone in the world each year.

Agriculture and the rise of monoculture

The Green Revolution in the developing world took place about the same time that developed countries began shifting toward monoculture and industrial farming. In the practice of monoculture, just one crop is grown, or one type of livestock is raised. Many family farms were purchased by corporations. These corporations applied concepts of industrialization to farming to increase yields and efficiency. Industrial farming practices included growing only a few varieties of seed crops over large areas, using extensive mechanical equipment for all farming processes, and also using larger amounts of pesticides, fertilizers, and water.

While monoculture and industrial farming result in larger crop yields than traditional farming, they also require greater inputs. Inputs are the seeds, fertilizers, pesticides, herbicides, and fossil fuels required for intensive farming. Pesticides and herbicides can kill beneficial species of insects, animals, microscopic organisms, and plants that are part of a natural ecosystem, thereby reducing local biodiversity (the variety of life-forms) and ecosystem resilience, that is, its ability to recover from environmental disturbances.

Unsustainable agricultural practices

Monoculture production is an unsustainable agricultural practice. It relies on too few species of plants and animals. It threatens the biodiversity of world food crops. Seed banks, which are repositories for seeds from plants around the world, offer some protection against the loss of this biodiversity, but, in general, monoculture farming leaves much of the world's population at risk of food insecurity and is unsustainable.

In contrast to monoculture farming, individuals in the developing world who grow their own food for survival carry out what is called subsistence agriculture. This, too, is considered unsustainable. About 2.7 million people worldwide practice subsistence farming, using up to 75 percent of cultivated land, but they generate only 20 percent of the world's food. Subsistence farmers live on the margins of society. They suffer more than other farmers during drought or warfare, when they may be forced from their land without any other means of economic survival.

In slash-and-burn agriculture, people cut down and burn forest areas to create new farmland. The areas of the world most affected by slash-and-burn agriculture are the tropical rain forests near the Amazon River in South America. Sixty to seventy percent of the rain forest has been cleared in Brazil to provide grazing land for cattle. Much of this beef is sent to the United States to be processed into hamburger. Since widespread deforestation began in the Amazon in the early 1970s, almost 20 percent of the rain forest has disappeared—some 293,438 square miles (about

Land has been cleared for agriculture in the Amazon Rainforest in Brazil.
© GUENTERMANAUS/ SHUTTERSTOCK.COM

760,000 square kilometers), an area larger than all of Alaska—enough to change weather patterns in the rain forest, resulting in less rainfall and drier soil. This is highly unsustainable because the Amazon rain forest is the most biodiverse area on the earth. Clear-cutting this land not only threatens thousands of plants, animals, and microorganisms with extinction; it also destroys the world's most important carbon sink. Plants act as carbon sinks that absorb carbon dioxide from the atmosphere. Carbon dioxide is a greenhouse gas, which contributes to the warming of the earth. Acting as carbon sinks, the world's forests are essential to combating climate change.

Sustainable agriculture techniques

Sustainable agriculture is farming that respects the relationship between crops and their environment. Most experts agree that polyculture agriculture, rather than monoculture agriculture, is the best way to move toward sustainable agriculture. In polyculture agriculture, many varieties of plants and animals are grown on the same land, either simultaneously or over the course of several growing seasons. Each crop affects the soil differently, ensuring that it never becomes completely deprived of the nutrients it needs to remain healthy. Many polyculture farms try to retain as much of the natural ecosystem surrounding the farm as possible. Instead of using pesticides, for example, farmers use natural pest control techniques that seek to limit pests that damage crops rather than attempting to destroy all of them.

Organic farming incorporates many techniques of sustainable agriculture and does not allow the use of genetically modified organisms (GMOs). GMOs are organisms whose genetic makeup has been formed or changed in a laboratory, creating an organism that does not exist in nature. For livestock, no growth hormones or antibiotics are used, and the animals are required to consume organic feed. Rather than using synthetic, or artificial, inputs for fertilizers and herbicides, organic farmers rely on compost, nitrogen-fixing cover crops, and animal manure to provide soil nutrients. Instead of pesticides, organic farmers often practice companion planting techniques, use strict plant rotation schedules, and, when needed, introduce beneficial insects for pest control. The goal is to grow as much food with as little water as possible. Conserving natural resources means generating less air and water pollution as well. Organic food tends to cost more than industrially farmed food because it is more labor intense and crop yields tend not to be as high.

SEE ALSO Aquaculture; Community-Supported Agriculture (CSA); Fair Trade; Farm Bill, U.S.; Farming, Industrial; Farming, Sustainable; Food Security; Food Systems; Locavores and the Local Food Movement; Monoculture; Permaculture; Pesticides; Seed Banks

For more information

BOOKS
Owings, Lisa. *Sustainable Agriculture.* Innovative Technologies series. Minneapolis, MN: Abdo Publishing, 2013.

PERIODICALS
Bialik, Carl. "How Much Water Goes into a Burger?" *Wall Street Journal* (January 11, 2008). Available online at http://www.wsj.com/articles/SB120001666638282817 (accessed April 2, 2015).

Diamond, Jared. "The Worst Mistake in the History of the Human Race." *Discover* (May, 1999). Available online at http://discovermagazine.com/1987/may/02-the-worst-mistake-in-the-history-of-the-human-race (accessed March 23, 2015).

O'Connell, Sanjida. "Is Farming the Root of All Evil?" *The Telegraph* (June 23, 2009). Available online at http://www.telegraph.co.uk/news/science/science-news/5604296/Is-farming-the-root-of-all-evil.html (accessed March 23, 2015).

WEBSITES
Diersing, Nancy. "Phytoplankton Blooms: The Basics." Florida Keys National Marine Sanctuary. May, 2009. http://floridakeys.noaa.gov/scisummaries/wqpb.pdf (accessed March 23, 2015).

"Staple Foods: What Do People Eat?" Food and Agriculture Organization. http://www.fao.org/docrep/u8480e/u8480e07.htm (accessed March 30, 2015).

Air Pollution

Air pollution refers to the substances in the earth's atmosphere that are dangerous to human health or the environment. Air pollution is usually considered anthropogenic, meaning "caused by humans." However it can also be a result of natural processes, such as forest fires and volcanoes, which release harmful gases into the atmosphere. Much air pollution is caused by the burning of fossil fuels to power cars and generate electricity. This has led to health problems, acid rain, ozone depletion, and climate change, all of which are serious issues facing humanity in the twenty-first century.

The earth's atmosphere is a combination of several gases that make life possible. It is 78 percent nitrogen, 21 percent oxygen, less than 1 percent argon, 0.4 percent water vapor, and—prior to the widespread use of

WORDS TO KNOW

Acid rain: Precipitation, which can be rain, fog, or snow, that is acidic. It is caused by sulfur dioxide and nitrogen dioxide emissions and can kill plants and trees, corrode (eat away by chemical action) cars and buildings, and pollute water.

Air pollution: All substances in the earth's atmosphere that are dangerous to human health or the environment.

Atmosphere: The layer of gases that surrounds the earth's surface and makes life possible.

Climate change: Gradual and enduring changes in weather patterns over the earth that impact numerous ecosystems in different and often dramatic ways.

Greenhouse effect: The process whereby gases in the atmosphere allow sunlight to enter the atmosphere but do not allow its heat to escape.

Greenhouse gases: Any of the gases in the earth's atmosphere that absorb or reflect back to earth infrared radiation from the sun, thereby trapping heat close to the earth's surface. An increase in greenhouse gases corresponds with climate change. The main greenhouse gases are carbon dioxide, methane, nitrous oxide, and ozone. Clouds and water vapor also function as greenhouse gases.

Indoor air pollution: Smoke, particulates, and poisons that contaminate interior spaces and that can cause disease leading to premature death.

Ozone depletion: Destruction of the protective layer of ozone molecules in the stratosphere that allows dangerous ultraviolet radiation from the sun to reach the earth's surface.

Positive feedback loop: A cyclic process where a small disturbance reinforces itself, leading to greater disturbance in the same direction.

Smog: Ozone in the troposphere; that is, the portion of the atmosphere closest to the earth's surface.

Stratosphere: The layer of atmosphere that lies just above the troposphere, starting six miles (about 9.6 kilometers) above the earth.

Toposphere: The layer of atmosphere that is closest to the earth's surface, just below the stratosphere.

---

fossil fuels—about 0.027 carbon dioxide. In addition to the burning of fossil fuels, carbon dioxide is also released into the atmosphere from open cooking fires and slash-and-burn clearing of forests that are converted for agriculture and cattle grazing. This has caused the amount of carbon dioxide in the atmosphere to rise to 0.04 percent (400 parts per million) in 2015. The result is climate change.

The greenhouse effect

Understanding climate change requires understanding the greenhouse effect. The greenhouse effect is the natural process by which radiation from the sun enters the earth's atmosphere. A little less than half of this solar radiation is absorbed by the earth's surface, and the other half is converted into heat energy. This heat energy is in the form of infrared radiation. Some infrared radiation bounces off the earth's surface and passes through the atmosphere on its way back into space, but a good portion of it gets trapped in the atmosphere by greenhouse gases (GHGs). The main GHGs are carbon dioxide, methane, nitrous oxide, and ozone. The more GHGs there are in the atmosphere, the more heat is trapped.

Air pollution upsets the natural balance of nitrogen, oxygen, carbon dioxide, and other gases in the atmosphere. In addition to leading to climate change, it causes health problems. The World Health Organization (WHO) estimated that in 2012 air pollution caused seven million deaths worldwide from asthma, respiratory diseases, cancer, and other diseases, making it "the world's largest single environmental health risk." Urban residents in developing countries often suffer the most because of air pollution from unregulated nearby factories and the tradition of cooking over open fires indoors.

A study released in May 2014 by the World Health Organization stated that New Delhi, India had the world's dirtiest air. © KUNI TAKAHASHI/ BLOOMBERG VIA GETTY IMAGES

Ozone depletion

Ozone is a molecule made of three atoms of oxygen. The ozone layer is a thin coating of these molecules six miles (about 9.6 kilometers) above the earth (in the atmospheric level called the stratosphere) that prevents some of the sun's harmful radiation from reaching the surface of the earth. Air pollution from ozone-depleting chemicals has damaged this protective layer of ozone molecules. As a result, dangerous ultraviolet radiation reaches the earth's surface and causes serious health problems, including skin cancer and eye diseases.

The air pollution that harms the ozone layer comes from substances known as chlorofluorocarbons (CFCs), hydrofluorocarbons (HFCs), and halogens. These chemicals were once common in aerosol spray bottles, solvents (a substance that dissolves another substance), air conditioners, and refrigerators. When they are emitted into the atmosphere, they drift

Air Pollution

The Atmospheric Brown Cloud

The atmospheric brown cloud is an annual phenomenon in which a giant cloud of air pollution arises from South Asia, namely India and Pakistan, and drifts over China, the Pacific Ocean, and the western United States before dissipating, or disappearing. This cloud can be seen from space and is caused mostly by cooking fires and slash-and-burn techniques for turning forests into land for farming. People in this part of the world mostly cook over open fires, which sends smoke into the air. One study estimated that about two million people die each year just in India from health effects related to the brown cloud. There is also evidence suggesting that the cloud delays the Asian monsoon season by several weeks; this affects drought and flood cycles that impact agriculture. Furthermore, the cloud pushes the monsoons southward toward Australia, which now receives more rain than it used to.

The brown cloud traps heat in the atmosphere, which in turn is making the Himalayan glaciers melt faster. When these glaciers are gone, hundreds of millions of people will be without their major source of water. The brown cloud also traps harmful ozone close to the earth's surface, which lowers the yields of some crops and causes many breathing problems, especially for young children and the elderly. The brown cloud also affects wind patterns to the east, over the Arabian Sea, which scientists believe is making cyclones more intense in the Middle East. Ultimately, researchers have found that the brown cloud amplifies the effects of climate change because of its high content of black carbon, or soot. This soot is much more effective in melting polar ice and snow than increased carbon dioxide levels in the atmosphere.

up to the ozone layer and destroy ozone molecules. The result was two large seasonal holes in the ozone layer at the North and South Poles. Ozone depletion also interferes with the growth cycle of plants and phytoplankton (tiny plant particles found in bodies of water) in marine ecosystems. Most ozone-depleting substances have now largely been banned.

Ozone can also occur near the ground. This ozone is not naturally occurring but is formed when man-made pollutants react with sunlight. When this ozone becomes trapped in the troposphere (the level of atmosphere closest to the earth's surface), it becomes smog. Smog can lead to serious health problems, such as asthma attacks, shortness of breath, and lung damage.

Acid rain

Acid rain is rain, snow, or fog that is acidic, meaning it has more hydrogen ions than alkaline rain. Acid rain is caused by sulfur dioxide and nitrogen dioxide emissions from the burning of fossil fuels. These

Air Pollution

Heavy haze from an atmospheric brown cloud appears thickest in north-central India (left) and clings to the face of the Himalayan Mountains (center). China is to the north (top). NASA. IMAGE BY JEFF SCHMALTZ, MODIS RAPID RESPONSE, NASA GODDARD SPACE FLIGHT CENTER.

chemicals mix with water vapor in the atmosphere to form acid. Acid rain has many harmful effects on the natural and built environments. It limits biodiversity (the overall variety of life-forms) and causes buildings, cars, and structures to wear away or be eaten away, for example, through rusting.

When acid rain cause lakes and rivers to become too acidic, some species of fish eggs will not hatch, and some species may die. When acid rain falls on soil, it affects the balance of microorganisms in the soil, which in turn affects how well plants grow. Soils that are too acidic disrupt a plant's ability to absorb essential nutrients. Trees at high altitude are especially vulnerable to acid rain. The fog and clouds at these altitudes can have high levels of acid in them. The acid damages the outer protective layers of leaves and pine needles, leading to stunted growth and poor health.

Climate change

According to the U.S. Environmental Protection Agency (EPA), "There is compelling evidence that many fundamental measures of climate in the United States are changing, and many of these changes are linked to the accumulation of GHGs in the atmosphere." Ozone in the upper reaches of the atmosphere is predicted to make global warming worse. Particles in the atmosphere, especially black carbon (that is, particles from burned fossil fuels), absorb sunlight. This means that heat stays in the atmosphere longer instead of being reflected back into space. When black carbon falls on snow and ice, the snow and ice melt faster. Fewer ice-covered surfaces result in less heat being reflected back into space. This creates a positive feedback loop that increases average global temperatures and thus melts more snow and ice. This rise in temperatures is increasing the rate at which the planet's glaciers and polar ice caps are disappearing, resulting in rising sea levels worldwide.

Indoor air pollution

Most people think of air pollution as an outdoor problem, but indoor air pollution, or poor indoor air quality, can also be a problem. Unhealthy air inside buildings and homes may be caused by cigarette smoke, cooking fires, and even gases such as formaldehyde and other chemicals given off by carpeting, plywood, electronics, plastics, and other materials. Older buildings can be contaminated with poisonous lead paint particles and asbestos dust. Faulty gas appliances can lead to carbon monoxide poisoning. Radon, a naturally occurring radioactive gas, can lead to lung cancer and causes thousands of deaths per year. Mold, dust mites, pollen, and other allergens can be spread through air conditioners and heating vents.

While indoor air pollution can be damaging to people in developed countries, in developing countries it tends to be worse. Cooking indoors over open wood or biomass (organic material) fires is a common practice that generates smoke and particles of pollution called "particulates." According to WHO, 3.8 million people die each year worldwide from diseases and health conditions caused by household air pollution.

Stopping air pollution

Air pollution causes heart disease, stroke, lung cancer, acute lower respiratory system infections, and more. By the time this problem became clear in the 1970s, many countries were beginning to create laws to limit air pollution.

In the United States, the Clean Air Act of 1963 was the first legislation designed to monitor and limit air pollution. It was expanded in 1970 and again in 1990 to address acid rain and ozone depletion. The laws established air-quality standards, guidelines for the migration of air pollutants across state lines, and motor vehicle emissions and smokestack emissions limits. The substances regulated by the Clean Air Act include ozone, particulates (such as soot), carbon monoxide (from vehicle exhaust), nitrogen oxides, sulfur dioxide, and lead. The EPA estimates that between 2010 and 2020, the Clean Air Act will prevent 230,000 early deaths. The EPA's Acid Rain Program has been especially successful. Between 1995 and 2011, sulfur dioxide emissions fell 64 percent, and nitrogen oxide emissions fell 67 percent.

Internationally, the most successful treaty dealing with air pollution has been the United Nations' 1987 Montreal Protocol on Substances That Deplete the Ozone Layer. The Montreal Protocol was the first universally ratified treaty in UN history, meaning that every nation on earth signed it. Since then, CFCs and HFCs have been largely phased out worldwide, and the hole in the ozone layer at the South Pole has gotten much smaller.

SEE ALSO Acid Rain; Automobiles; Climate Change; Coal; Greenhouse Gas Emissions; Ozone Depletion; Pollution; Public Health

For more information

BOOKS

Desonie, Dana. *Atmosphere: Air Pollution and Its Effects.* Our Fragile Planet series. New York: Chelsea House, 2007.

Haerens, Margaret. *Air Pollution.* Global Viewpoints series. Farmington Hills, MI: Greenhaven Press, 2011.

PERIODICALS

Grabar, Henry. "50 Years After Its Discovery, Acid Rain Has Lessons for Climate Change." *Mother Jones* (September 12, 2013). Available online at http://www.motherjones.com/environment/2013/09/acid-rain-lessons-climate-change (accessed April 20, 2015).

Petit, C. W. "A Darkening Sky: A Smoky Shroud over Asia Blocks Both Sun and Rain." *U.S. News & World Report* (March 17, 2003), 46–48.

WEBSITES

"Climate Change & Air Quality." U.S. Environmental Protection Agency. http://www.epa.gov/airquality/airtrends/2011/report/climatechange.pdf (accessed April 20, 2015).

"Effects of Acid Rain." U.S. Environmental Protection Agency. http://www.epa.gov/acidrain/effects/index.html (accessed April 20, 2015).

"Household Air Pollution and Health." World Health Organization. http://www.who.int/mediacentre/factsheets/fs292/en/ (accessed April 20, 2015).

"7 Million Premature Deaths Annually Linked to Air Pollution." World Health Organization, March 25, 2014. http://www.who.int/mediacentre/news/releases/2014/air-pollution/en/ (accessed April 20, 2015).

"Stratospheric Ozone Layer Depletion and Recovery." Earth System Research Laboratory. http://www.esrl.noaa.gov/research/themes/o3/ (accessed April 20, 2015).

Alter-Globalization Movement

Alter-globalization (alternative globalization or alter-globalism) is a movement that supports globalization—the process through which nations invest and integrate as their cultures, economies, and governments interact to promote trade and investment—as a positive trend for the world economy but rejects the aspects of it that place corporate profit-making goals above justice and human rights, actively advocating for regulations and practices that elevate the well-being of workers and the environment.

The overarching goals of alter-globalization are to promote locally controlled, sustainable practices and to reduce inequality. It seeks to promote social changes that benefit the quality of life for people across socioeconomic strata and in developing as well as wealthy countries by agitating to reverse climate change and enact cleaner methods of production, ensure worker rights and safety, guarantee access to high-quality food and water, protect indigenous cultures, and foster world peace. The movement's goal is not to end globalization, but rather to promote the idea that it can influence globalization for the betterment of humanity.

In specific terms, alter-globalization positions itself against the economic philosophy known as neoliberalism, which has, since the 1980s, sought to loosen governmental regulations in order to allow international economic markets to police themselves. Critics of neoliberalism, including alter-globalization supporters, maintain that it gives primacy to profit at all costs and that its principles were responsible for the worldwide economic crash of 2008.

History of globalization

Globalization has its roots in trade of goods and services, which has existed across human cultures for thousands of years. With the advent of seafaring exploration in the 1400s, previously unknown trade routes

WORDS TO KNOW

Agribusiness: Large-scale corporate farming.

Globalization: The process of people and economies around the world becoming more linked to each other because of the spread of culture, ideas, and goods through modern technology and transportation systems.

Greenhouse gases: Any of the gases in the earth's atmosphere that absorb or reflect back to earth infrared radiation from the sun, thereby trapping heat close to the earth's surface. An increase in greenhouse gases corresponds with climate change. The main greenhouse gases are carbon dioxide, methane, nitrous oxide, and ozone. Clouds and water vapor also function as greenhouse gases.

Monoculture: The cultivation or growth of a single crop or organism especially on agricultural or forest land.

Transnational: Literally "across nations"; often used to describe corporations that have a presence and interests in multiple countries.

---

opened, and with them came overseas empire-building, colonization, and the transatlantic slave trade. Globalization in modern times is generally dated to the 1944 Bretton Woods Conference, a meeting of experts to discuss the financial arrangements that would be necessary to ease countries through the rebuilding process following the anticipated end of World War II (1939–1945). Representatives at Bretton Woods drew up plans for an International Bank for Reconstruction and Development (now known as the World Bank) and the International Monetary Fund (IMF). These bodies would eventually aid in loosening international barriers to trade.

The 1980s experienced a growing interest in opening global markets under the leadership of England's prime minister Margaret Thatcher (1925–2013) and U.S. president Ronald Reagan (1911–2004), both of whom championed eased restrictions and lower taxes on businesses as well as increased international trade. This is often considered the start of contemporary globalization through neoliberal policies, marked by industry deregulation, cuts to government-funded social services, and the outsourcing of jobs overseas. In the twenty-first century, with greater access to transportation and new technological advances in communications, companies can increase productivity and profits by entering new markets and offering services to new customers. Free-trade agreements, which are treaties between countries who agree to open trade between them, allow corporations to relocate operations in other countries and to export goods and services to each other. This can give consumers more choices and stimulate economic growth by creating jobs and encouraging improvements in infrastructure, but it also comes with increased economic inequality, human rights abuses, and environmental damage. Alter-globalization emerged in the mid-1990s as a response to what was considered the failure of the World Trade Organization (WTO) to act as an effective force in policing the terms of international trade agreements and unfair labor practices in the developing world.

Four phases of alter-globalization

In its earliest phase, alter-globalization concerned itself chiefly with the rights of the "common citizen" in regions with a high degree of human-rights abuses, such as Asia and Central America. In particular, the movement sought to protect workers' rights, the rights of small farmers, and indigenous cultures. In 1993 the movement took shape in the form of a network of organizations called La Via Campesina, which brought together the various strains of workers' rights, small farmers' interests, women's rights, native issues, and various other activists under the single umbrella of "peasants' rights," which as of 2013 had 164 member organizations in 73 countries. Later in the 1990s, alter-globalization also sought to protect developing nations from excessive debt caused by exploitation from corporations due to the models of international trade that were in place at the time. This last point drew widespread protests during the World Trade Organization (WTO) conference that was held in Seattle, Washington, in 1999.

Tunisian youths hold banners during a demonstration as a part of the World Social Forum in Tunis, Tunisia, on March 27, 2013. © YASSINE GAIDI/ANADOLU AGENCY/ GETTY IMAGES

With global media attention on the sometimes violent protests in Seattle, the alter-globalization movement gained increased public notice and support, particularly with the first World Social Forum (WSF) held in Brazil in 2001. Subsequent international forums highlighting the social problems that often emerge out of unrestrained market growth were equally successful at drawing attention to the needs of economically marginalized groups, with the 2005 meeting, again in Brazil, hosting 170,000 activists from around the world. The movement faltered between 2006 and 2010 as some of its key founding organizations were disbanded or experienced internal discord. The forums held during these years had disappointing turnouts, and media coverage of key issues slowed dramatically. During these years, alter-globalization did, however, make important inroads into Africa, the Middle East, and the United States, as the economic collapse of 2008 spread around the world and countries with vulnerable economies felt the effects of government-imposed austerity measures (the drastic cutting of social and other programs considered extraneous) and citizens vocally protested. World Social Forums since 2011 have been held with more frequency and more success in Middle Eastern countries, and the movement found renewed energy in the Occupy Movement, which sought to bring attention to income inequality following the 2008 economic meltdown.

Human rights and environmental concerns

With its early focus on the struggles of agricultural workers through La Via Campesina, alter-globalism quickly developed an interest in ties between human rights and environmental sustainability. Championing the land rights of small and subsistence farmers against the encroachment of government and corporate development has been one of the movement's key issues since its inception. Unjust land distribution of this kind displaces families from their ancestral land and deprives them of their ability to feed their families and earn a living. A natural outgrowth of this is the concern that large-scale corporate farming, or agribusiness, relies on a method of farming known as monoculture, in which a single crop is grown for profit—often on thousands of acres—causing soil erosion and degradation as well as using potentially toxic pesticides, thereby polluting adjacent land and waterways. Toxic runoff further impacts the lives of local people, depriving them of clean water sources and degrading the land.

Alter-Globalization Movement

Alter-Globalization Organizations

There are a number of different organizations around the world that have been involved with or been influential in the alter-globalization movement:

ATTAC (Association for the Taxation of financial Transactions and Aid to Citizens) is an international organization whose goals are to advance the social, environmental and democratic aspects of globalization. They advocate for the common good of humanity (access to health care, education, clean water, and protections against climate change) and propose these should be supported through the imposition of global taxes. See www.attac.org.

Global Trade Watch (GTW) is one of several policy groups of Public Citizen, a nonprofit organization who advocates on behalf of pubic interests. Started in 1995, GTW promotes the public interest perspectives on issues of globalization, including jobs, wages, food, health, environmental protection, and economic justice. See www.citizen.org.

La Via Campesina is an international grassroots movement of poor and women farmers, peasants, and rural youth that defends small-scale sustainable agricultural practices as a way to promote social justice and dignity. They are involved in a wide variety of issues, from agrarian reform to food sovereignty to protecting biodiversity in the food supply. See www.viacampesina.org.

Transnational Institute (TNI) is a worldwide group of scholar activists who provide informed analysis on issues of global importance, such as ownership of resources, environmental sustainability, and empowering the workforce. They are involved in worldwide movements to promote better social, economic, and environmental justice through research, information, and advocacy. See www.tni.org.

The overarching environmental concern of alter-globalization is climate change caused by human activity. With most land-rights issues centered in developing countries, forest land often is clear-cut by corporate developers, shrinking the area of carbon dioxide-absorbing plant life and adding greenhouse gases like methane to the environment through the development of cattle ranches to meet the high demand for beef in wealthier countries. As greenhouse gases have accumulated in the atmosphere, global temperatures have risen and continue to rise. Attempts to regulate and reduce emissions of these gases have not been successful. Changes to existing practices would not be in the interests of governments and corporations that stand to benefit most from the processes that cause the emissions.

There is hope for progress, though, and it comes from alliances among policy makers that seek to address causes such as climate change.

Particularly in Latin America, there is a movement to forsake short-term profit for *buen vivir* (literally "good life"). The complementary benefits from grassroots activism, international alliances, and the election of alter-globalist-sympathizers are increasing as leaders have accelerated reforms in this area of the world. Other signs of progress include the spread of political reforms to Middle Eastern countries and more widespread acceptance of alter-globalist points of view.

SEE ALSO Activism; Agriculture; Climate Change; Economics; Free Trade; Human Rights; Pesticides; Social Justice; Sustainability

For more information

PERIODICALS
Folbre, Nancy. "Is Another Economics Possible?" *New York Times* (July 19, 2010). Available online at http://economix.blogs.nytimes.com/2010/07/19/is-another-economics-possible/ (accessed March 18, 2015).

WEBSITES
"History of Globalization." Yale Global Online. Yale University. http://yaleglobal.yale.edu/about/history.jsp (accessed March 18, 2015).

Houtart, François. "From 'Common Goods' to the 'Common Good of Humanity.'" Brussels: Rosa Luxembourg Foundation, November 2011. http://rosalux-europa.info/publications/articles/common_good_of_humanity/ (accessed March 18, 2015).

Pleyers, Geoffrey. "A Brief History of the Alter-Globalization Movement." Books and Ideas.net (June 20, 2013). http://www.booksandideas.net/A-Brief-History-of-the-Alter.html (accessed March 18, 2015).

Alternative Energy

Alternative energy is usually defined as an energy source that is an alternative to fossil fuels. The main forms of alternative energy are solar, wind, geothermal, and hydroelectric power. Unlike the burning of fossil fuels, these alternative energy sources do not emit harmful greenhouse gases such as carbon dioxide that contribute to climate change. For this reason, alternative energy is sometimes called clean energy. Most types of alternative energy are also renewable, meaning we won't run out of them; the sun will shine for billions of years and the wind will continue to blow as long as the earth turns. Fossil fuels such as oil, natural gas, and coal are nonrenewable and unsustainable because we can't make more of them once they are used up.

WORDS TO KNOW

Alternative energy: An energy source that is renewable and sustainable. Or, a traditional form of energy used in a more efficient way.

Geothermal power: Electricity generated from the earth's internal heat.

Hydropower: Electricity generated from flowing water.

Renewable energy: An energy source that will never be exhausted.

Solar power: Energy obtained from sunlight.

Wind power: Electricity generated from wind turbines.

Alternative energy resources that have a low environmental impact are considered sustainable. For this reason, nuclear power is usually not considered an alternative energy because it can have a negative impact on the environment if nuclear waste is not disposed of properly or if a nuclear power plant malfunctions and releases radiation into the air or water. Biomass fuel, in which fast-growing organic material such as algae or grass is used as an energy source, is also often considered unsustainable because it causes air pollution when it is burned.

Wind power

Wind power has been used for millennia, since ships have used sails to move through the water and windmills have turned stones to grind grain. Modern wind turbines are usually grouped together in wind farms to generate a substantial amount of electricity. This is clean and sustainable energy because it produces no pollution. There are some drawbacks to wind power. The low-level noise emitted from the turbines may bother people. The turbines may also kill birds if they are not properly designed and located. In addition, electricity is not generated when there is no wind. Because of this, wind farms are built in places where the wind tends to be steady. According to the World Wind Energy Association, 4 percent of the world's electricity in 2014 was generated by wind.

Solar power

Solar power is the process of converting sunlight into electricity by means of a photovoltaic cell. Hundreds of photovoltaic cells, each embedded with electronic components, are grouped together in solar panels that can be placed on rooftops or on the ground to generate enough electricity to power houses and factories. Like wind power, solar power is clean, sustainable, and limited only by the fact that the sun does not always shine. The main problem with using solar power to produce electricity has been the high cost of manufacturing solar power systems. New breakthroughs in technology have increased the efficiency of photovoltaic cells substantially, which should lead to a worldwide increase in solar power.

Hydropower

Hydropower (also called hydroelectric power) is electricity that is generated from running water, usually by controlling the flow of water from a reservoir through a dam. Dams, like windmills, have been used for hundreds of years to generate power. While hydroelectric power is renewable as long as rivers and lakes don't dry up, it can have negative environmental impacts. Dams displace people from their homes, increase water evaporation, and crowd out native plants and animals in the ecosystem, leading to a loss of biodiversity. For this reason, hydroelectric power is considered unsustainable by some. Tidal power and wave power, in which the ocean's tides and waves are used to generate electricity, are two forms of hydroelectric power that are being used to a limited extent as large dam projects become less popular.

Alternative Energy in the United States

As of 2014 in the United States, about 6 percent of the country's electricity was generated by hydropower, and 7 percent came from other alternative sources, including wind (about 4 percent), biomass (about 2 percent), geothermal (less than 1 percent), and solar (less than 1 percent). While this totals only 13 percent of the energy generated in the country, this percentage is forecasted to grow in coming years. Many corporations as well as the federal government, especially the U.S. Department of Energy, have invested in alternative energy research and development since the 1990s in recognition of the environmental dangers of fossil fuels and their nonrenewable nature.

Geothermal Power

Geothermal power harnesses the earth's internal heat with a pump. Water is pumped underground where it is heated naturally. The hot water then drives a turbine that generates electricity. This is sustainable because the temperature inside the earth's crust will stay constant for millions of years. Geothermal power is generally limited to areas where heat from the planet's core reaches close to ground level. Geothermal power plants can generate greenhouse gases and toxins in the process of drawing up water and heat from inside the earth. However, many experts believe that this issue can be managed and that geothermal power can become an important form of sustainable, alternative energy.

SEE ALSO Biofuel Energy; Geothermal Power; Hydropower; Solar Power; Tidal Power; Wind Power

For more information

BOOKS
Becker, Peggy Daniels. *Alternative Energy.* Detroit, MI: Greenhaven Press, 2010.

PERIODICALS
Wolfson, Elijah. "Renewable Energy Farms Spread Through California Deserts." *Newsweek* (November 24, 2014). Available online at http://www.newsweek.com/renewable-energy-farms-populate-california-286644 (accessed March 4, 2015).

WEBSITES
2014 Half-year Report. World Wind Energy Association. http://www.wwindea.org/webimages/WWEA_half_year_report_2014.pdf (accessed March 4, 2015).

"What Is the Difference between Alternative and Renewable Energy?" Government of Alberta. http://www.energy.alberta.ca/BioEnergy/3796.asp (accessed March 3, 2015).

"What Is U.S. Electricity Generation by Energy Source?" U.S. Energy Information Administration, updated June 13, 2014. http://www.eia.gov/tools/faqs/faq.cfm?id=427&t=3 (accessed March 4, 2015).

Aquaculture

Populations of ocean and freshwater fishes, shellfish, crustaceans, and krill have fallen drastically since the middle of the twentieth century. Overfishing, habitat destruction, pollution, the accidental introduction of nonnative invasive species, and the damming of rivers are just some of the reasons for the decline. Environmental scientists estimate that overfishing to satisfy human demands for seafood has led to the extinction or endangerment of up to 90 percent of wild fish. Overfishing occurs when people catch fish faster than the fish are able to reproduce. Technologies such as the use of sonar and airplanes to spot fish, as well as the use of extra-long fishing lines and huge nets to harvest fish, have greatly accelerated unsustainable overfishing practices.

WORDS TO KNOW

Aquaculture: Growing and harvesting of fish and shellfish for human use.

Aquatic: Having to do with water.

Carnivorous: Meat-eating creatures.

Ecosystem: A complete and interdependent system of biotic (living) and abiotic (nonliving) components that cycles matter and transfers energy within a given area. The three major types of ecosystems are freshwater, terrestrial, and marine.

Endangered: At high risk of extinction.

Extinct: No longer in existence.

Habitat: The natural environment where a living organism lives.

Herbivorous: Plant-eating creatures.

Invasive species: A species that is intentionally or unintentionally introduced to one part of the world from another that causes harm in the new area. Invasive species may become competitors, predators, or parasites of native species.

Krill: A small crustacean that is a significant food source for many animals in the ocean.

Overfishing: The situation in which humans deplete wild fish populations faster than the fish can reproduce, leading to their endangerment or extinction.

Population: A group of organisms of one species (can interbreed) that live in a shared region at the same time.

The aquaculture solution

Despite international bans on overfishing and the designation of many species of fishes as protected, it is hard to enforce these restrictions in the vast oceans that surround the planet. Populations are not recovering quickly enough to sustain aquatic ecosystems. Aquaculture, or fish and shellfish farming, is a partial solution that is being used to attempt to sustainably meet the demand for food while reducing overfishing. The National Oceanic and Atmospheric Administration defines aquaculture as the "breeding, rearing, and harvesting of plants and animals in all types of water environments including ponds, rivers, lakes, and the ocean." Aquaculture is now the world's fastest-growing method of food production. It produces almost 50 percent of the fish and shellfish humans consume worldwide. It is also used to raise and replenish populations of endangered aquatic species back into the wild.

Nearly six hundred aquatic species are being farmed worldwide. The most commonly farmed species in the United States are oysters, clams, mussels, shrimp, and Atlantic salmon. Some organisms are farmed in

Aquaculture

Aquaculture is used to raise many important seafood animals, including salmon, shrimp, eels, and sea basses.
© VLADISLAV GAJIC/ SHUTTERSTOCK.COM

huge ocean cages, others are raised in ponds or tanks on land. Some species, such as tilapia, breed quickly and are easy to raise. Others, like bluefin tuna, are very difficult to raise in captivity. Aquaculture continues to be explored around the world as an efficient method of breeding fish, feeding people, and restoring fish populations.

The Challenges of Aquaculture

Despite successes, scientists warn that some aspects of aquaculture can harm the environment. In some cases, farmed fish escape from their cages and mate with wild fish. This can alter the genetics of wild fish populations.

Carnivorous farmed fish are often fed fishmeal made from wild caught fish. This has led to the overfishing of species used to make the fishmeal. Farming carnivorous fish is also inefficient. It takes about 6.6 pounds (3 kilograms) of wild fish to produce 2.2 pounds (1 kilogram) of farmed salmon. The ratio of wild fish needed to produce farmed tuna is even higher at 20:1 making its sustainability questionable. Farming plant-eating fish such as tilapia, carp, and catfish solves this problem. Sustainability experts emphasize that eating plant- and algae-eating farmed fish diminishes overfishing and is more likely to be a sustainable solution.

Aquaculture can have a negative effect on local water quality. Farmed fish are often kept in densely populated enclosures and can produce large amounts of waste. This can pollute oceans and rivers. Densely housed fish are more susceptible to disease than fish in the wild. Farmed fish are often given antibiotics to prevent and treat infections. These drugs enter the water, the local food webs, and the flesh of the animals. Scientists have not yet determined if eating animals that have consumed these drugs is safe for long-term human consumption.

Possible Solutions

Many solutions are being explored for these aquaculture challenges. Open-ocean aquaculture is a method of making aquaculture more sustainable. This involves raising large carnivorous fish in underwater pens as large as 6,000 square feet (557 square meters). These pens are located up to 190 miles (300 kilometers) offshore so that fast currents can sweep away and dilute fish wastes. The Scandinavian Silver Eel Farm in Sweden is using another method to limit offshore damage. They are capturing fish waste products and converting them into fertilizer.

Successful sustainable systems often mimic natural systems. Polyaquaculture is a sustainable aquaculture system that attempts to mimic natural aquatic ecosystems. Farmers raise fish and shellfish along with algae and seaweed in lagoons, ponds, or tanks on the coast. This creates mini-ecosystems that the designers hope will sustain themselves. The Maya Fish company, which operates an offshore fish farm in Campeche, Mexico, uses the algae produced in their system design to make flour. This flour is used to make an algae meal which is added to small amounts of fish meal to produce food for their farmed fish. Maya Fish plans to become one of the first farms to use no fishmeal at all in the near future. This will further enhance their sustainability through environmentally sound practices.

Raising public awareness of the critical worldwide depletion of wild fish populations and the promise of sustainable aquaculture practices will enhance aquaculture's sustainability. According to the United Nation's Food and Agriculture Organization, "It is likely that the future growth of the fisheries sector will come mainly from aquaculture."

Aquaculture

Bluefin Tuna and Aquaculture

One of the most overfished species is bluefin tuna. Soaring demand for this fish, particularly for making sushi in Japan, has led to bluefin being severely endangered and threatened with extinction. Fish farmers tried to breed bluefin for many years, but these fish are difficult to raise in captivity. Bluefin larvae are very fragile. The larvae die immediately if they hit the sides or bottom of a fish tank. The fish, which can grow to weigh 500 pounds (226 kilograms), have voracious appetites, and feeding them can be very expensive.

However, the demand for bluefin tuna has spurred aquaculture enterprises to keep trying. Companies in Japan have made the most progress, assisted by sustainable breeding and fish-raising technologies developed over nearly fifty years by scientists at Kinki University in Osaka, Japan. For many years, only one or two baby bluefin out of hundreds survived to adulthood in captivity. Now, using a combination of technologies including carefully regulating the water temperature and the amount of light to keep the fish from panicking and smashing into tank walls or nets, one or two baby bluefin out of one hundred survive to adulthood. Considering that only one in thirty million wild bluefish larvae survive after hatching from eggs, the fish farmers are pleased with this progress. One bluefin farming company owned by a subsidiary of the Toyota motor company produces about forty thousand fish per year. Depending on size and quality, these bluefin can sell to Japanese restaurants for anywhere from one thousand to more than one million dollars each.

The Japanese bluefin farming companies, along with other fish farms developing more sustainable bluefin breeding methods, believe increased fish production will help meet the vast demand for fish in the future. However, there are challenges that do not yet allow this method to be considered fully sustainable. It takes 15 pounds (6.75 kilograms) of food

SEE ALSO Agriculture; Ecosystems; Water Pollution

For more information

BOOKS

Bliss, John. *Catching and Raising Seafood* (Ethics of Food series). Mankato, MN: Heinemann, 2011.

Stickner, Robert R. *Aquaculture: An Introductory Text*. 2nd ed. Oxfordshire, UK: CABI, 2009.

PERIODICALS

Hayashi, Yuka. "Taming the Wild Tuna." *Aquaculture Magazine* (February–March 2015). Available online at www.aquaculturemag.com/magazine/february-march-2015/2015/03/01/taming-the-wild-tuna (accessed March 17, 2015).

Lutz, Greg. "Blue Ridge Aquaculture Story." *Aquaculture Magazine* (October-November 2014). Available online at www.aquaculturemagazine.com

fish (such as sardines or mackerel) to produce one pound (.45 kilograms) of farmed bluefin. Researchers are seeking to develop new types of artificial food products made with both fishmeal and vegetable protein, to feed the bluefin to reduce the number of wild fish that are caught to feed the farmed fish. Although farmed bluefin look like wild bluefin, they behave differently. Breeders describe farmed bluefin as being moody and less hardy. Farmed bluefin have an impaired ability to avoid dangerous situations, and often end up bumping into things and dying. They are inclined to change their food preferences from day to day. Scientists wonder if breeding large numbers of bluefin with identical genes will also lead to populations that are weaker than wild fish. Efforts have been made to mate wild and farmed fish to produce genetically diverse bluefin, but these efforts have not been successful. With continued research, many are optimistic that these challenges will be solved.

Bluefin tuna are large and difficult to raise in captivity. © HOLBOX/SHUTTERSTOCK.COM

/magazine/october-november-2014/2014/11/01/blue-ridge-aquaculture-story (accessed March 17, 2015).

WEBSITES

"Aquaculture." Food and Agriculture Organization of the United Nations. www.fao.org/aquaculture/en/ (accessed March 17, 2015).

"Aquaculture." United States Department of Agriculture. www.usda.gov/wps/portal/usda/usdahome?navid=AQUACULTURE (accessed March 17, 2015).

"Start Your Sustainable Seafood Search." Seafood Watch. http://www.seafoodwatch.org/ (accessed May 4, 2015).

"What is Aquaculture?" National Oceanic and Atmospheric Administration. www.nmfs.noaa.gov/aquaculture/what_is_aquaculture.html (accessed March 17, 2015).

"You Have One Body We Have One World." Maya Fish. www.mayafish.net/green.php (accessed March 26, 2015).

Aquifers

An aquifer is an underground layer of permeable, porous rock that contains groundwater. This groundwater can be pumped from the aquifer and used for drinking, watering lawns and golf courses, and irrigating farmland. While only 30 percent of the freshwater on the planet comes from aquifers, they hold 98 percent of the water that humans use for drinking and agriculture. Most other freshwater on earth is held in glaciers and the polar ice caps.

The fresh water in aquifers comes from rain and snow. This surface water seeps into the aquifers from above and recharges, or refills, the aquifer at different rates, depending on the characteristics of the land above the aquifer and the depth of the aquifer. It can take anywhere from a few hours to many years for rainwater or snowmelt to reach an aquifer. Surface water can also enter aquifers from rivers, streams, and lakes.

When more water is taken out of an aquifer than can be replenished naturally by the water cycle (the continuous movement of water between the oceans, atmosphere, and soil), the aquifer can become depleted, or empty. Removing water from an aquifer faster than it is replaced is unsustainable because it means that the communities that depend on the water from the aquifer may run out of water for drinking and growing food. Aquifer depletion is taking place throughout the world because steady population growth has led to a rising demand for water. Especially hard hit are aquifers in arid, or dry, areas that receive little rain or snow. Aquifers in these areas recharge slowly because water tends to evaporate before it can make its way underground. In other areas the soil above the aquifer may not absorb water well. This slows down the rate at which groundwater can be replenished.

Pumping too much water out of aquifers that are located near the ocean can cause the aquifers to fill with salt water instead of freshwater. This increase in salt content is a process called salinization. When an aquifer's water becomes salty it is no longer potable, or drinkable, and

---

Rainwater Harvesting

One way communities are trying to conserve their dwindling aquifers is by implementing sustainable capture and storage methods for surface water. This is sometimes called rainwater harvesting. It involves funneling water from gutters and downspouts to cisterns, or tanks, near houses and buildings. The water can easily be used to water gardens or crops. In addition to lowering the consumer's water bill, it also means that more water can remain in the aquifer.

Some parking lots also collect groundwater runoff through permeable pavement, which is a specialized pavement that allows water to filter through to the ground. When rain seeps back into the soil, it nourishes nearby plants, recharges groundwater supplies, and returns to the water cycle. This is preferable to having storm runoff end up in a sewer, where it can overwhelm the system.

> **WORDS TO KNOW**
>
> **Aquifer:** An underground formation of rock, gravel, and sand that stores freshwater.
>
> **Freshwater:** Water that has a low level of salt and is suitable for drinking and irrigation of agriculture.
>
> **Groundwater:** Freshwater that accumulates underground, usually in aquifers.
>
> **Salinization:** The process whereby water becomes contaminated with salt and is no longer fit for drinking or agriculture.
>
> **Surface water:** Water that collects on the surface of the earth from rain and snow.
>
> **Water cycle:** The continuous movement of water between the oceans, atmosphere, and soil.

cannot be used for agriculture because saltwater kills plants. Areas that have been damaged by salinization include farmland in central California and near the Aral Sea in Central Asia.

Many hydrologists, or scientists who study water, are concerned about the depletion of the world's aquifers and have encouraged farmers, who are the biggest users of groundwater, to practice water conservation methods. Methods of working the land that slow water down and allow it to seep into the soil can help to conserve water and recharge aquifers. Another strategy used to maintain aquifers since the early 2000s is aquifer storage and recovery (ASR). This involves injecting water back into aquifers when it is readily available, usually in the spring as the snow melts. An additional benefit of this process is that electricity can be generated when the water is injected. This offsets the environmental impact of the ASR process.

The sustainability of using the groundwater found in aquifers varies depending on the location of the aquifer, its ability to recharge, and the rate at which the water is withdrawn. For example, the Ogallala Aquifer in the United States is located in the Great Plains, with the bulk of its water beneath Nebraska. It is one of the world's largest aquifers and provides about 30 percent of the water needed for agriculture in the country and drinking water for millions of people from South Dakota to Texas. Although some areas of the aquifer are enjoying rising water levels, other areas are becoming seriously depleted, primarily because so much of its water is used to irrigate farmland in the region. According to the U.S. Geological Survey, the total amount of water stored in the aquifer decreased by 8 percent between the 1950s and 2013.

SEE ALSO Drought; Water Access and Sanitation; Water Cycle

For more information

BOOKS

Kallen, Stuart A. *Running Dry: The Global Water Crisis.* Minneapolis, MN: Twenty-first Century, 2015.

PERIODICALS

Associated Press. "Arsenic in Drinking Water Seen as Threat." USAToday.com (August 30, 2007). Available online at http://usatoday30.usatoday.com/news/world/2007-08-30-553404631_x.htm (accessed April 10, 2015).

Jehl, Douglas. "Saving Water, U.S. Farmers Are Worried They'll Parch." *New York Times,* August 28, 2002. Available online at http://www.nytimes.com/2002/08/28/international/worldspecial/28WATE.html (accessed April 10, 2015).

WEBSITES

"Aquifer Rechard (AR) and Aquifer Storage & Recovery (ASR)." U.S. Environmental Protection Agency. Updated May 4, 2012. http://water.epa.gov/type/groundwater/uic/aquiferrecharge.cfm (accessed March 4, 2015).

"Groundwater Facts." National Groundwater Association, updated October 18, 2010. http://www.ngwa.org/fundamentals/use/pages/groundwater-facts.aspx (accessed March 4, 2015).

McGuire, Virginia. L. "Water-Level Changes and Change in Storage in the High Plains Aquifer, Predevelopment to 2013 and 2011-13." U.S. Geological Survey Scientific Investigations Report 2014-5218. http://pubs.usgs.gov/sir/2014/5218/ (accessed May 21, 2015).

Architecture
See **Building Design.**

Automobiles

Automobiles are vehicles powered by an internal combustion engine. An internal combustion engine is one that runs on the heat and pressure produced when a mixture of fuel and air is burned in a cylinder. The term applies mainly to cars, but it is also relevant to trucks, buses, motorcycles, and tractors. The internal combustion engine requires nonrenewable fossil fuels in the form of gasoline or diesel fuel. The high demand for this limited resource is a primary reason why automobiles with internal combustion engines are unsustainable. Fossil fuels harm the environment both when they are recovered from the earth and when they are burned. Burning fossil fuels causes air pollution and is a major contributor to

> ## WORDS TO KNOW
>
> **Biofuel:** Liquid and gaseous fuels derived partially or completely from organic materials and are considered renewable.
>
> **CAFE:** Corporate Average Fuel Efficiency; the U.S. government standard of how many miles per gallon a specific vehicle must be able to travel.
>
> **Fossil fuel:** Nonrenewable energy source formed over millions of years through geological processes. Includes coal, oil, and natural gas, which when burned to release energy also emit greenhouse gases that contribute to climate change and air pollution.
>
> **Full-cost pricing:** The practice of making manufacturers and consumers pay for the harm they inflict on the environment.
>
> **Hybrid vehicle:** A vehicle that has two power systems, typically an electric motor and an internal combustion engine.
>
> **Internal combustion engine:** An engine that generates controlled explosions to convert chemical energy into mechanical energy.
>
> **Zero-emissions vehicle:** A vehicle that releases no tailpipe pollutants.

climate change. Furthermore, the natural resources and heavy industry required to build automobiles are intense and have also caused significant pollution and disruption of ecosystems.

The rise of the automobile throughout the twentieth century and into the twenty-first century has led to massive urban and suburban growth that, in turn, has made owning an automobile often a necessity rather than a convenience. Commerce reorganized around the mobility that the automobile allowed, and shopping malls, freeways, and sprawling neighborhoods have changed the landscape of the developed world. Half the urban land in the United States is dedicated to roads, parking lots, gas stations, and other infrastructure devoted to automobiles.

Companies that recover and refine petroleum, from which fuel is made, and those that manufacture automobiles have become the largest corporations in the world. Political, industrial, economic, and social roadblocks have prevented efforts to incorporate principles of sustainability within the industry and among automobile owners, even as the health and environmental dangers of the automobile have become widely acknowledged.

Oil

An automobile's internal combustion engine is propelled by a series of controlled explosions in which a fuel source is mixed with air. These explosions turn chemical energy into mechanical energy. For most of the automobile's history, the preferred fuel source has been gasoline or diesel fuel, which is derived from petroleum. Petroleum is a nonrenewable fossil fuel that, when burned, releases harmful greenhouse gases and particulates, or soot, into the atmosphere. Greenhouse gases trap heat in the atmosphere and have been linked to global climate change.

Petroleum is refined into gasoline, and each gallon (3.8 liters) of gasoline burned in a typical car releases over 19 pounds (8.6 kilograms) of carbon dioxide into the air. Cars and trucks in the United States alone consume over 19 million barrels of oil per day, which adds 589 million pounds (267.1 million kilograms) of carbon dioxide to the air. As of 2015 the United States used about 43 percent of the world's gasoline, far more than any other country. With over one billion vehicles on the world's roads, greenhouse gases from cars' tailpipe emissions have accumulated and warmed earth's atmosphere, resulting in climate change.

Automobiles and sustainability

Apart from the pollution caused by operating automobiles, the manufacturing of automobiles involves a number of industries, ranging from steel production to production of plastics, paint, and tires, that also contribute to air and water pollution and climate change owing to the chemicals and natural resources they use. Factories and roads have destroyed millions of acres of habitats and delicate ecosystems. Air pollution caused by emissions results in numerous health problems and deaths each year. The most common are lung diseases and respiratory illnesses that make breathing difficult. Additionally, the average American will spend about two years of his or her life stuck in traffic jams. While this is a sustainability issue as far as burning fuel while idling a car is concerned, it is also a quality-of-life issue that limits people's productivity and leisure time.

Automobiles have also negatively impacted human health through injuries and deaths due to accidents. In fact, more Americans have died in car accidents than in all the wars in the country's history. In 2013 over thirty-two thousand people died in automobile-related accidents in just the United States, although this represents a decline from a high of fifty-one thousand deaths in 1979. Much of this decline is due to more effective safety features, such as seat belts, airbags, and improved crumple zones. A crumple zone is a structural feature of a car that is designed to absorb the energy of an impact and in this way protect drivers. Worldwide, about 1.3 million people die in car accidents each year, and another fifty million are injured.

About fifty million animals die in collisions with cars each year, from family pets to endangered species in environmentally sensitive areas.

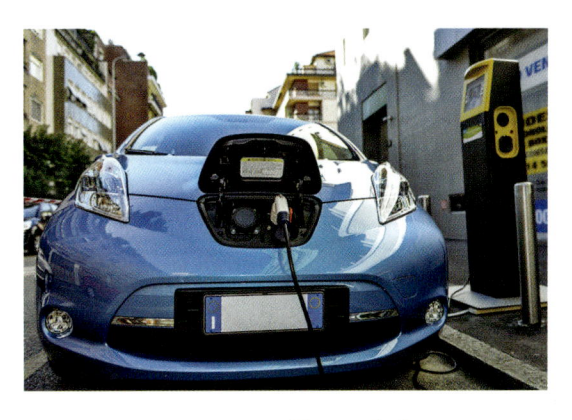

Efficiency

Beginning in the 1970s, changes in laws resulted in the first small steps toward creating a more sustainable automobile industry. Leaded gas was phased out in the 1970s, because lead was found to harm brain development in children. This greatly reduced pollution in automobile emissions. Congress also introduced the Corporate Average Fuel Economy (CAFE) standards in 1975 to make cars more fuel efficient. For example, in 1974 the average pickup truck got about 12 miles (19.3 kilometers) per gallon, and by 2014 that had doubled to 24 miles (38.6 kilometers) per gallon. Fuel-economy standards changed very little between 1985 and 2005 but rose again after that.

Electric vehicles are quiet, reliable, and use energy very efficiently. They do have drawbacks, however. © VIAPPY/SHUTTERSTOCK.COM

The Environmental Protection Agency and the National Highway Transportation and Safety Administration have ordered that by 2025 automobiles must achieve 54.5 miles (87.7 kilometers) per gallon (3.8 liters) on average. While this will represent considerable improvement from previous decades, it is also likely that any fuel savings will be offset by the fact that there will be more cars on the road and they will be driven more miles than in previous decades.

The future of the automobile

Automobile use continues to rise around the world as people in developing countries eagerly become car owners as their economic fortunes improve. Most experts agree that adopting renewable, clean fuels is important in the fight against climate change, because no one expects the demand for automobiles to decrease any time soon. Toward that end, many urban buses now run on natural gas, which burns cleaner than gasoline, although it is still a fossil fuel that contributes to climate change. Electric vehicles powered by batteries are rising in popularity; however, they are more expensive than internal combustion engine vehicles, and their range is limited. As of 2015 electric vehicles represented about 0.06 percent of vehicles on the road. Additionally, while electric vehicles may not produce tailpipe emissions that contribute directly to air pollution, their electricity may be generated at a power plant that generates electricity from fossil fuels. This means that electric vehicles may still contribute to climate change and other types of pollution, just not directly.

Hybrid vehicles combine traditional internal combustion engines with electric motors and have become popular since 2000. They conserve a fair amount of fuel, resulting in more miles per gallon and lower tailpipe emissions. Like electric vehicles, however, hybrids contain batteries that require rare earth materials. The mining of these materials often takes place in developing countries under conditions that raise serious concerns about human rights, social justice, and environmental impacts.

Using biofuels in traditional internal combustion engines is becoming more popular. Biofuels are made from renewable, easy-to-grow crops, such as corn, sugarcane, or soybeans. While burning biofuels does release carbon dioxide into the air, it is the same amount of carbon dioxide that the plants absorbed from the atmosphere as they were growing. Thus, biofuels are "carbon neutral," as opposed to fossil fuels that are made from plants that trapped carbon in the earth's crust millions of years ago. However, growing crops for biofuels requires lots of water for irrigation and contributes to monoculture. Monoculture is the growing of one crop over a wide area. This agricultural method limits biodiversity (the variety of life-forms) and can adversely affect the ecosystem of a region. Furthermore, fertilizers used in growing the crops can create runoff pollution into nearby waterways that harms aquatic life.

Full-cost pricing

Full-cost pricing is the practice of making manufacturers and consumers pay for the harm they inflict on the environment. This is one solution that sustainability advocates believe can help stop some of the pollution and environmental damage caused by automobiles. Full-cost pricing may mean that automobiles will cost more, to reflect the true value of the natural resources they use, and that gasoline will cost more, to reflect the pollution it causes. These extra costs may persuade people to cut down on the number of miles they drive or to reconsider driving altogether. At the very least, many people would choose to drive more efficient cars, take mass transportation, or ride a bike more often.

All these habits, if adopted widely enough, could have a real impact on the environment. However, much of this full-cost pricing would take place through tax increases on vehicles and gasoline, and higher taxes are politically unpopular. Two other tactics that have been used successfully in some urban areas are to charge drivers to enter a congested urban area and to establish car-sharing networks. In the United States, cities that have established a network of bike lanes and bike-sharing systems have been praised for taking a proactive stance in offering alternatives to single-occupant cars.

Automobiles are here to stay, but there are several ways they could become more sustainable. A continued transition to alternative fuel types, such as solar power and hydrogen fuel cells, may reduce the need for fossil fuels. Experimenting with lighter materials, such as aluminum, can make automobiles more fuel efficient. Urban areas can improve their mass transportation systems, which would tempt people to leave their cars at home more often. The increase in bike lanes, bike-share programs, and carpool lots in urban areas encourages behavior that is healthy and sustainable. People may choose to live closer to their workplace or to telecommute more often.

SEE ALSO Acid Rain; Air Pollution; Batteries; Biofuel Energy; Climate Change; Economics; Fossil Fuels; Green Economy; Greenhouse Gas Emissions; Human Rights; Mass Transit; Oil; Pollution; Quality of Life Indicators; Transportation

Fuel Cell Vehicles

A fuel cell vehicle (FCV) is an automobile with an electric motor that is powered by oxygen and hydrogen—two of the most common elements on the earth. When these elements are mixed inside the fuel cell, the only discharge from the tailpipe is harmless water vapor. Thus, they are also known as zero-emissions vehicles. Wide adoption of these vehicles would reduce greenhouse gases significantly as well as the United States' dependence on foreign oil. One of the greatest challenges to overcome is compressing hydrogen. This is a technically difficult and energy-intensive process that is still quite expensive.

Fuel cell technology is evolving. Fuel cells have been used in the Space Shuttle and various rockets over the years, but no fuel cell vehicle was commercially available as of 2015. Companies that have developed very limited numbers of FCVs in the past include Hyundai, Toyota, Honda, and Mercedes-Benz. These vehicles had an average range of 230 miles (370 kilometers). Forklifts, motorcycles, and bicycles are other types of FCVs on the market. One factor limiting the expansion of the FCV is the lack of hydrogen service stations, where drivers can go to recharge their vehicles when they start to run low. California has indicated its intention to build 100 hydrogen stations by 2023, but as of June 2015 only twelve hydrogen stations existed in the United States.

For more information

BOOKS

Newman, Peter, and Jeffrey Kenworthy. *The End of Automobile Dependence: How Cities Are Moving Beyond Car-Based Planning.* Washington, DC: Island Press, 2015.

Sperling, Daniel, and Deborah Gordon. *Two Billion Cars: Driving Toward Sustainability.* New York: Oxford University Press, 2008.

WEBSITES

"Driving to 54.5 MPG: The History of Fuel Economy." Pew Charitable Trusts, April 20, 2011. http://www.pewtrusts.org/en/research-and-analysis/fact-sheets/2011/04/20/driving-to-545-mpg-the-history-of-fuel-economy (accessed April 20, 2015).

"Greenhouse Gas Emissions from a Typical Passenger Vehicle." U.S. Environmental Protection Agency. http://www.epa.gov/otaq/climate/documents/420f14040a.pdf (accessed April 6, 2015).

"Progress and Accomplishments in Hydrogen and Fuel Cells." U.S. Department of Energy, March 2013. http://www1.eere.energy.gov/hydrogenandfuelcells/pdfs/accomplishments.pdf (accessed April 20, 2015).

"Road Traffic Deaths." World Health Organization. http://www.who.int/gho/road_safety/mortality/en/ (accessed April 20, 2015).

B

Batteries

A battery is a portable device that stores chemical energy that can be converted into electrical energy. When a wire is used to create a closed circuit between a battery and an external object, such as a flashlight bulb, the stored chemical energy is converted into electrical energy, and the bulb lights up. All batteries operate on the same principles. This is true of the tiny batteries that run watches and cell phones and the much larger batteries used to start and run cars, trucks, and buses and store energy in solar electric systems.

There are three types of widely used batteries: alkaline, lithium, and lithium-ion. Alkaline batteries depend on a reaction between zinc and manganese dioxide and can be either rechargeable or non-rechargeable. Lithium batteries may be used in items such as watches, digital cameras, toys, and other small devices. They depend on metallic lithium and manganese dioxide and, while more expensive than alkaline batteries, they have a significantly longer life. Lithium-ion batteries are rechargeable, have an extended life, and use a lithium compound in place of the metallic lithium used in regular lithium batteries. They are commonly used in electronic devices. Although they are rechargeable, they are also considered more hazardous than other batteries because the lithium compound they require is highly flammable.

Parts of a battery

A battery is made up of three parts: two electrodes separated by an electrolyte. Electrodes are also commonly called "poles." An electrolyte is a substance that conducts electricity. The two electrodes are made from

WORDS TO KNOW

Anode: The electrode that gives off electrons.

Battery: A portable device that stores chemical energy, which can be converted into electrical energy.

Cathode: The electrode that takes up electrons.

Electrode: A material that either gives off or takes up electrons.

Electrolyte: A substance that conducts electricity.

---

different materials that either give off or take up an electric charge. The electrode that gives off an electric charge is called the anode. The charge passes through the electrolyte and is taken up by the other electrode, called the cathode. The chemical energy of a battery is stored in the anode, cathode, and electrolyte. When a wire forms a closed circuit between the poles of a battery and an outside device, such as the starter of a car, an electric current flows from the anode through the car's starter and back to the cathode, and the car starts.

Rechargeable versus non-rechargeable

Batteries can either be rechargeable or non-rechargeable. The cylindrical dry cells used to operate devices such as flashlights, television remotes, and toys are non-rechargeable. When all of the chemical energy in this cell has been converted to electrical energy, the cell becomes permanently "dead." Rechargeable batteries such as those used in cars last much longer. Connecting them to an outside source of electricity or a generator can recharge them. This process supplies electrons to the anode and removes them from the cathode. This is the opposite of what happens when a battery is generating electricity. Instead of chemical energy being transformed into electrical energy, electrical energy is transformed back into chemical energy. Although rechargeable batteries have a longer lifespan than non-rechargeable batteries, they cannot be recharged forever and have to be replaced.

Batteries as alternative energy

Battery-operated vehicles and solar energy are two emerging technologies with great promise. In the case of solar energy, also known as photovoltaic systems, lead-acid batteries are used to power solar grids after dark. Battery-operated vehicles can be either electric vehicles with rechargeable battery packs and electric motors or fully battery-powered vehicles with no internal combustion engine, fuel cell, or fuel tank. Both reduce carbon emissions by not relying on refined crude oil in the form of gasoline. But even gasoline-powered automobiles need batteries, which are typically of the lead-acid variety, to power functions such as lights and ignition.

Recycling and disposal

The disposability of non-rechargeable batteries may seem appealing to consumers, but this type of battery contains toxic materials that may leak out over time due to exposure to heat or corrosion of the metal outer container. Until the passage of the Mercury-Containing and Rechargeable Battery Management Act of 1996, alkaline batteries were made with mercury; batteries produced since then are made without mercury. Most alkaline batteries do, however, contain some degree of heavy metals and should therefore be disposed of at hazardous waste sites, although these sites vary by state and local jurisdiction. Some components of batteries can be recycled, although the process is costly. Even rechargeable batteries have a lifespan, depending upon how often they are allowed to cycle through their full discharge.

Rechargeable batteries, such as those found in cell phones, have a longer life-span than regular batteries. © BRENT LEWIN/BLOOMBERG VIA GETTY IMAGES

The nonrenewable materials in all types of batteries can be recycled, sustaining their supply and making them available for the production of new batteries or for use in various industries. These materials include silver, cobalt, nickel, and lead. Recycling these substances reduces the need to mine them, a process that causes severe pollution of land, air, and water, although in the case of lithium-ion batteries, recycling is more costly than new manufacturing. Lithium-ion batteries are generally considered safe to dispose of in landfills. Manufacturers of batteries, even of the same type of battery, may use different materials in their making—for example, some lithium batteries are made with a toxic substance called perchlorate while others are not—so recommended disposal methods must be checked with state and local authorities. Different countries, states, and even local municipalities can have vastly different regulations regarding battery disposal.

SEE ALSO Air Pollution; Alternative Energy; Automobiles; Fossil Fuels; Pollution; Waste Management

For more information

BOOKS
Levine, Steven. *The Powerhouse: Inside the Invention of a Battery to Save the World.* New York: Viking, 2015.

PERIODICALS
Buckle, Kenneth. "How Do Batteries Store and Discharge Electricity?" *Scientific American* (May 29, 2006). Available online at http://www.scientificamerican.com/article/how-do-batteries-store-an/?print=true (accessed March 18, 2015).

Fleischer, Evan. "Those Revolutionary Technologies Promised to Help Save us from Climate Change. So What Happened?" *Washington Post* (August 29, 2014). Available online at http://www.washingtonpost.com/posteverything/wp/2014/08/27/these-revolutionary-technologies-promised-to-help-save-us-from-climate-change-so-what-happened/ (accessed March 18, 2015).

WEBSITES
"How Can Batteries Help Sustainable Development Worldwide?" Association of European Automotive and Industrial Battery Manufacturers. http://www.eurobat.org/sites/default/files/eurobat_poster_-_iarc_2011_budapest_0.pdf (accessed March 18, 2015).

Biodiversity

Biodiversity, or biological diversity, refers to the variety of life on the planet. Scientists think about biodiversity in three ways: the variety of plant and animal life in a given area, the genetic diversity within a given species, and the numbers of different ecosystems, or communities of life, in a region. An area with high biodiversity includes many different species of organisms, each with a high degree of genetic diversity among them. Genetic diversity describes the characteristic makeup of a species, the total number of genetic characteristics that it has. A biodiverse area will also include a number of healthy ecosystems. An ecosystem is a network of plants, animals, and microbes interacting with the nonliving

WORDS TO KNOW

Acid rain: Precipitation, which can be rain, fog, or snow, that is acidic. It is caused by sulfur dioxide and nitrogen dioxide emissions and can kill plants and trees, corrode (eat away by chemical action) cars and buildings, and pollute water.

Anthropogenic: Caused by human activity.

Biodiversity: The variety of species or organisms in a given environment or ecosystem. A large range of plant and animal life in a given region is symptomatic of its health; a narrow range or declining number of species in a region may indicate environmental damage or stress.

Carbon sequestration: A pollution-control process in which carbon dioxide generated by power plants is pumped underground to be stored indefinitely so it does not contribute to climate change.

Earth Summit: Also known as the Rio Summit. A conference held in Rio de Janeiro, Brazil, in 1992. It resulted in numerous documents and international agreements regarding sustainable development, including the Rio Declaration and Agenda 21.

Ecosystem: A complete and interdependent system of biotic (living) and abiotic (nonliving) components that cycles matter and transfers energy within a given area. The three major types of ecosystems are freshwater, terrestrial, and marine.

Ecosystem services: The benefits an ecosystem provides to humankind. The four main categories are provisioning, regulating, supporting, and cultural.

Invasive species: A species that is intentionally or unintentionally introduced to one part of the world from another that causes harm in the new area. Invasive species may become competitors, predators, or parasites of native species.

Overexploitation: Overuse of a natural resource to such an extent that it becomes unsustainable.

Payment for ecosystem services (PES): A system that assigns economic value to the act of conserving natural resources.

Seed bank: A repository of different strains of plant seed to preserve genetic variation for future need.

---

components of an environment (such as rocks, minerals, air, and water). Natural ecosystems engage in self-sustaining nutrient and chemical cycles. A high degree of biodiversity makes a system more resilient and is related to sustainability, while decreasing biodiversity is a warning that the area is under environmental stress.

Biodiversity is not evenly distributed across the planet. Some areas are more biodiverse than others. Tropical areas are more diverse than polar regions and arid deserts. They have more species of plants, animals, and microbes per square hectare (2.5 acres). Biodiversity extends to aquatic environments as well, with tropical coral reefs among the most species-rich areas of the oceans.

Biodiversity

Life ranges from the tiniest organisms, such as the **Paramecium** *as seen through a microscope on the left, to the blue whale, possibly the largest animal ever to live on earth on the right.* LEFT: © PAN XUNBIN/SHUTTERSTOCK.COM; RIGHT: © SCUBAZOO IMAGES

The rise of conservation biology

The concept of biodiversity evolved in the 1980s in conjunction with the establishment of conservation biology. Conservation biology is the scientific study of life on the earth for the purpose of protecting it and the habitats that support it. The field arose to halt the number of mass extinctions of plants and animals occurring in many of the world's ecosystems at that time as the result of human actions and influences, such as clear-cutting of old-growth forests and rain forests, air pollution leading to acid rain, and widespread contamination of waterways and oceans.

In 1986 conservation biologists sponsored the National Forum on BioDiversity in Washington, DC. The conference resulted in the landmark book *Biodiversity* (1988) by renowned American biologist Edward O. Wilson (1929–) This book highlighted the rate of species loss being seen around the globe. Wilson noted the importance of biodiversity for the well-being of humankind and how international cooperation could conserve the planet's biodiversity. Wilson likened biodiversity to an insurance policy for an ecosystem; the more species it has, the more likely it is to survive various threats. As the field matured, conservation biologists came to realize just how little they knew about the planet's biodiversity. In 2011 scientists estimated that 8.7 million species of living organisms inhabited the planet; of these, 86 percent of land species and 91 percent of ocean species had yet to be discovered.

Threats to biodiversity

Despite this apparent bounty of biological diversity, the planet is undergoing an event known as a die-off, that is, a mass extinction. The rate of loss of plant and animal species is as large as the extinction event sixty-five million years ago that killed the dinosaurs. While extinction is a natural process, scientists estimate it is now taking place at an unnaturally high rate—about one thousand to ten thousand times faster than normal. This loss of biodiversity, conservation biologists maintain, is anthropogenic, meaning that it is due to human activities. The five major processes responsible for the rapid and wide-scale die-off are habitat destruction, climate change, the spread of invasive species, overexploitation, and pollution.

Habitat destruction Habitat destruction reduces biodiversity by making an area uninhabitable for the plants and animals that used to call it home. Habitat destruction is the leading cause of biodiversity loss worldwide. Large tracts of wilderness have been and are being transformed to meet human needs. In the process, ecosystems are destroyed, and the plants and animals that rely on these ecosystems are threatened. Land is cleared for housing, commerce, and farmland to feed the world's surging population. Vast areas of farmland are obtained by clear-cutting areas of great biodiversity, such as the Amazon rain forest. This area is then used to graze cattle or to plant crops, such as corn or wheat. Large-scale agriculture further decreases genetic diversity because farmers tend to plant only one or two varieties of a crop that may regionally have had hundreds of genetic variations in the wild. These varieties are easily lost to extinction.

Climate change Climate change is the alteration of weather patterns due to a rise in average global temperatures. This may cause the extinction of up to 25 percent of all land species by 2050. Rapid changes in regional weather patterns disrupt ecosystems. Many species cannot survive outside a narrow temperature or precipitation range. When species fail to adapt to changing temperatures or changing rain amounts, they may die off and threaten the existence of other species that rely on them for food. It is predicted that rising ocean levels will submerge biodiverse coastal wetlands. This may cause many unforeseeable changes in marine ecosystems.

Invasive species Invasive species are plants and animals that have been imported to a region, either intentionally or unintentionally, by humans. Invasive organisms disrupt the ecosystems because they have no natural predators and their populations can explode. They can consume a large amount of resources, outcompeting native species. For example, settlers introduced many species of animals to Australia during colonization in the 1800s, such as cane toads, camels, goats, water buffalo, and pigs. These nonnative species have become more than a nuisance; they have upset many ecosystems through their drastic population surges and their destruction of vegetation, which has led to a decline of many of the native species of plants and animals found only in Australia.

Overexploitation Overexploitation is when a resource is used to such a degree that it becomes unsustainable. Examples of overexploited resources include groundwater, fish stocks, and old-growth forests. When these resources become scarce, they are no longer able to sustain the ecosystems that rely on them. For instance, when the Maori people of New Zealand hunted the moa, a large flightless bird, to extinction, the Haast's eagle also became extinct because it lost its main source of food. Today, overexploitation has placed many of the world's fisheries on the brink of collapse.

Pollution An ecosystem becomes polluted when it suffers negative effects from contaminants. Examples of contaminants, or pollutants, include exhaust from automobiles and other vehicles; chemicals that industrial plants dump into rivers; fertilizer, pesticide, and manures from industrial farming operations; and even trash that people toss on the side of the road. Air pollution can lead to acid rain, which changes the chemical makeup of soil, making it difficult for trees and plants to survive. It kills the oceans' coral reefs, which are home to thousands of aquatic plant and animal species. Air pollution also is linked to climate change. Soil that has been polluted by nitrogen and phosphorus, common chemical fertilizers that make large-scale agriculture possible, makes its way to rivers, streams, and oceans, where it leads to algae growth. The algae deplete oxygen and smother other organisms. This can lead to dead zones, areas with so little oxygen that they cannot support the aquatic ecosystem.

The Most Biodiverse Place on Earth

Yasuni National Park in the South American country of Ecuador is one of the most remote places on the earth and one of the most biodiverse. The park is home to 382 species of fish and 596 species of birds. The park contains many more species of trees, plants, amphibians, reptiles, and bats than any known area of its size in the world. It is primarily a rain forest ecosystem and is even home to a handful of people who want to remain isolated from modern society; these uncontacted tribes, as they are called, are extremely rare.

Yasuni National Park is also rich in oil, and oil is a valuable economic resource in a developing country such as Ecuador. In 2007 the government negotiated a plan using the concept of economic services to keep the area from being developed. They reasoned that its biodiversity was much more valuable to the planet in the long run than a few hundred million barrels of oil would be in the short run. It urged the international community to pay millions of dollars to keep the region pristine. When the hoped-for funds failed to materialize, the government abandoned the plan in 2013 and prepared to let oil companies drill in the region.

A snapshot of dense vegetation within Yasuni National Park, one of the most biodiverse areas in the world.
© KALYPSOWORLDPHOTOGRAPHY/SHUTTERSTOCK.COM

The Convention on Biological Diversity

The Convention on Biological Diversity is an international treaty designed to conserve biodiversity. It calls on countries to create and enforce strategies and action plans that halt the spread of invasive species and protect ecosystems and habitats through sustainable development. It also calls for the protection of genetic diversity by establishing seed banks.

The convention was opened for signature at the Earth Summit in Rio de Janeiro in 1992. Since then, every nation in the world except the United States has signed and ratified it. It took effect in 1993. To further its goals, the convention adopted the Cartagena Protocol on

Biosafety in 2000 and the Nagoya Protocol in 2010. The Cartagena Protocol addresses the issue of genetically modified organisms (GMOs.) It urges governments to adopt practices that require scientific evidence that genetically modified commodities like corn or cotton are generally safe before they are exported to other countries. The goal is to ensure that GMOs do not harm biological diversity in the manner seen with invasive species. The Nagoya Protocol includes a list of twenty biodiversity targets to be met by 2020. These targets are designed to create fair and evenhanded access among all parties to genetic resources (that is, all variants of all species) and to encourage the sharing of benefits arising from genetic resources.

Conserving biodiversity by giving it economic value

Many conservation biologists believe that the best way to preserve biodiversity is to highlight its economic benefits. The benefits that the natural world affords human beings are known as ecosystem services. Examples of ecosystem services include the food that we eat; the nitrogen cycle, which allows plants to grow; pollination of crops by bees, which allows plants to reproduce; the flowing water that powers hydroelectricity plants, carbon sequestration by plants, the filtering of pollutants by healthy soils, and even the recreational opportunities and psychological benefits that nature affords us.

According to a study known as "The Economics of Ecosystems and Biodiversity" (TEEB), the economic benefits of ecosystems amount to many trillions of dollars. Preserving biodiversity is far less expensive than having to adjust to a less biodiverse world. The problem is that most ecosystem services are not traded on the world market and thus have not become an integral part of the world economy. Payment for ecosystem services (PES) is a system that assigns economic value to the act of conserving natural resources and thus preserving biodiversity. This typically takes the form of payment by governments to landowners (usually farmers) to manage their land sustainably.

In the United States, the Conservation Reserve Program, which predates the concept of ecosystem services, serves as an example of the concept. The goal of the program is to prevent soil erosion by planting grasses and other ground-cover plants to help hold the soil in place. The program is designed to prevent another Dust Bowl scenario like the one that destroyed vital cropland during the Great Depression (1929–1941), a period of depressed world economies and high rates of unemployment. At that time, severe drought and farmers' use of methods that destroyed deep-rooted plant cover allowed soil to turn to dust, blowing away in high winds.

Individuals can help preserve biodiversity by supporting nonprofit conservation organizations such as the Sierra Club or the Nature Conservancy. The Sierra Club is the largest environmental organization in the United States. It has many local chapters that offer opportunities to take action and to enjoy nature responsibly. The Nature Conservancy works for sustainable growth and fosters economic partnerships that allow land to remain undeveloped. Individuals can protect biodiversity by educating themselves, by voting in favor of proposals that seek to maintain biodiversity, and by making informed decisions about the companies they support and the level of consumerism they engage in.

PRIMARY SOURCE

Convention on Biological Diversity

Article (excerpt)

By: United Nations Conference on Environment and Development

Source: United Nations Conference on Environment and Development, 1992. *Convention on Biological Diversity*. This document is available online at https://www.cbd.int/convention/text/default.shtml.

About the document: The Convention on Biological Diversity was opened for signature at the Earth Summit in Rio de Janeiro in 1992. It was the first international agreement recognizing the importance of biodiversity to humankind. All UN member states except for the United States have ratified, or consented to, its 42 articles. Here, the preamble and article one illustrate its far-reaching goals, which include conserving the planet's genetic diversity and using it sustainably and equitably between countries. In 2000 the Cartagena Protocol on Biosafety supplemented the treaty in recognition of advances in biotechnology and genetic engineering.

Preamble

The Contracting Parties,

Conscious of the intrinsic value of biological diversity and of the ecological, genetic, social, economic, scientific, educational, cultural, recreational and aesthetic values of biological diversity and its components,

Conscious also of the importance of biological diversity for evolution and for maintaining life sustaining systems of the biosphere,

Affirming that the conservation of biological diversity is a common concern of humankind,

Reaffirming that States have sovereign rights over their own biological resources,

Reaffirming also that States are responsible for conserving their biological diversity and for using their biological resources in a sustainable manner,

Concerned that biological diversity is being significantly reduced by certain human activities,

Aware of the general lack of information and knowledge regarding biological diversity and of the urgent need to develop scientific, technical and institutional capacities to provide the basic understanding upon which to plan and implement appropriate measures,

Noting that it is vital to anticipate, prevent and attack the causes of significant reduction or loss of biological diversity at source,

Noting also that where there is a threat of significant reduction or loss of biological diversity, lack of full scientific certainty should not be used as a reason for postponing measures to avoid or minimize such a threat,

Noting further that the fundamental requirement for the conservation of biological diversity is the in-situ conservation of ecosystems and natural habitats and the maintenance and recovery of viable populations of species in their natural surroundings,

Noting further that ex-situ measures, preferably in the country of origin, also have an important role to play,

Recognizing the close and traditional dependence of many indigenous and local communities embodying traditional lifestyles on biological resources, and the desirability of sharing equitably benefits arising from the use of traditional knowledge, innovations and practices relevant to the conservation of biological diversity and the sustainable use of its components,

Recognizing also the vital role that women play in the conservation and sustainable use of biological diversity and affirming the need for the full participation of women at all levels of policy-making and implementation for biological diversity conservation

Stressing the importance of, and the need to promote, international, regional and global cooperation among States and intergovernmental organizations and the non-governmental sector for the conservation of biological diversity and the sustainable use of its components,

Acknowledging that the provision of new and additional financial resources and appropriate access to relevant technologies can be expected to make a substantial difference in the world's ability to address the loss of biological diversity,

Acknowledging further that special provision is required to meet the needs of developing countries, including the provision of new and additional financial resources and appropriate access to relevant technologies,

Noting in this regard the special conditions of the least developed countries and small island States,

Acknowledging that substantial investments are required to conserve biological diversity and that there is the expectation of a broad range of environmental, economic and social benefits from those investments,

Recognizing that economic and social development and poverty eradication are the first and overriding priorities of developing countries,

Aware that conservation and sustainable use of biological diversity is of critical importance for meeting the food, health and other needs of the growing world population, for which purpose access to and sharing of both genetic resources and technologies are essential,

Noting that, ultimately, the conservation and sustainable use of biological diversity will strengthen friendly relations among States and contribute to peace for humankind,

Desiring to enhance and complement existing international arrangements for the conservation of biological diversity and sustainable use of its components, and

Determined to conserve and sustainably use biological diversity for the benefit of present and future generations,

Have agreed as follows:

Article 1. Objectives

The objectives of this Convention, to be pursued in accordance with its relevant provisions, are the conservation of biological diversity, the sustainable use of its components and the fair and equitable sharing of the benefits arising out of the utilization of genetic resources, including by appropriate access to genetic resources and by appropriate transfer of relevant technologies, taking into account all rights over those resources and to technologies, and by appropriate funding.

SEE ALSO Conservation; Ecological Restoration; Ecosystems; Genetically Modified Organisms (GMOs); Invasive Species; Seed Banks; Sustainability

For more information

BOOKS

DeCarlo, Jacqueline. *Fair Trade: A Beginner's Guide.* London: Oneworld Publications, 2007.

Miller, Debra A., ed. *Biodiversity.* Current Controversies series. Farmington Hills, MI: Greenhaven Press, 2012.

Strauss, Rochelle. *Tree of Life: The Incredible Biodiversity of Life on Earth.* Illustrated by Margot Thompson. Tonawanda, NY: CitizenKid, 2013.

PERIODICALS

Ingraham, Christopher. "We've Killed Off Half the World's Animals Since 1970." *Washington Post* (September 30, 2014). Available online at http://www.washingtonpost.com/blogs/wonkblog/wp/2014/09/30/weve-killed-off-half-the-worlds-animals-since-1970/ (accessed March 19, 2015).

WEBSITES

Bass, Margot S., et al. "Global Conservation Significance of Ecuador's Yasuni National Park." *PLOS One* January 19, 2010. DOI: 10.1371/journal.pone.0008767 (accessed March 9, 2015).

Center for Health and the Global Environment. "Climate Change and Biodiversity Loss." Harvard University School of Public Health. http://www.chgeharvard.org/topic/climate-change-and-biodiversity-loss (accessed March 10, 2015).

"The Extinction Crisis." Center for Biological Diversity. http://www.biologicaldiversity.org/programs/biodiversity/elements_of_biodiversity/extinction_crisis/ (accessed March 10, 2015).

"How Many Species on Earth?" California Academy of Sciences, August 24, 2011. http://www.calacademy.org/explore-science/how-many-species-on-earth (accessed March 10, 2015).

"Overview of the Millennium Ecosystem Assessment." United National Environmental Programme, updated 2005. http://www.unep.org/maweb/en/about (accessed March 10, 2015).

Biofuel Energy

The modern world runs on energy. Large amounts of energy are needed to provide electricity, transportation, food, water, medicines, and building materials around the world. The fossil fuels oil, coal, and natural gas provide most of the world's energy in the twenty-first century. The supply of fossil fuels, however, is limited and not renewable. Most experts agree that as fossil fuel supplies dwindle, the world will need alternative energy sources. In addition, burning fossil

WORDS TO KNOW

Acid rain: Precipitation with a higher-than-normal acid concentration. Also referred to as acid precipitation.

Biofuel: A gas or liquid fuel made from plant material, which makes them a renewable resource, unlike fossil fuels.

Biomass: Plant materials and animal wastes used as fuel.

Cellulose: The rigid substance that makes up a plant's cell walls.

Climate change: Gradual and enduring changes in weather patterns over the earth that impact numerous ecosystems in different and often dramatic ways.

Emissions: The production and discharge of something, especially gas or radiation.

Ethanol: An alcohol fuel that is manufactured by fermenting and distilling crops with a high starch or sugar content, such as grains, sugarcane, or corn.

Feedstock: A raw material to supply or fuel a machine or industrial process.

Fermented: A process that converts sugar to acids, gases, and/or alcohol.

Fossil fuel: Nonrenewable energy source formed over millions of years through geological processes. Includes coal, oil, and natural gas, which when burned to release energy also emit greenhouse gases that contribute to climate change and air pollution.

Greenhouse gases: Any of the gases in the earth's atmosphere that absorb or reflect back to earth infrared radiation from the sun, thereby trapping heat close to the earth's surface. An increase in greenhouse gases corresponds with climate change. The main greenhouse gases are carbon dioxide, methane, nitrous oxide, and ozone. Clouds and water vapor also function as greenhouse gases.

Pollutant: Any substance, such as certain chemicals or waste products, that renders the air, soil, water, or other natural resource harmful or unsuitable for a specific purpose.

Residue: A small amount of something that remains after the main part has gone or been taken or used.

---

fuels releases pollutants into the air, such as greenhouse gases (carbon dioxide, methane, nitrous oxide, and ozone), which have been linked to the warming of the earth's temperature, known as the greenhouse effect. Other pollutants cause acid rain when they react with water in the atmosphere, with associated harmful effects on plant, insect, and aquatic life. Concerns with fossil fuels have led to an increased focus on alternative and sustainable energy sources.

Biofuels are a potential replacement for fossil fuels and can be part of sustainable energy in the future. Biofuels are liquid and gaseous fuels produced from biomass, organic material from plants. Biomass energy comes from plant materials such as crop and forest residues, wood waste, corn kernels, energy crops (such as perennial grasses), food waste, and industrial waste materials. Biomass material can be burned in power plants to produce heat or electricity. It can be chemically fermented (broken down into a simple substance) to make liquid fuel such as ethanol or biodiesel. In addition, it can be digested by bacteria to create methane gas that powers turbines. It can also be heated under special conditions to produce a gas than can be burned for electricity or used in a variety of products. According to the Natural Resources Defense Council, in 2015 biomass was the source of about half of all the renewable energy produced in the United States.

Biofuels are not always sustainable, however. Their sustainability depends on how and where biofuel energy is produced. In some cases, biofuels can be less sustainable than fossil fuels. For example, biofuel production processes often use fossil fuels. If it takes more fossil fuel to produce a unit of biofuel than the biofuel replaces, the biofuel is less sustainable than the fossil fuel.

Types of biofuel

Ethanol Worldwide, ethanol is the most common biofuel. Ethanol is primarily used as a transportation fuel and blended with gasoline. According to the U.S. Department of Energy, the United States is the world's largest ethanol producer, generating over 13 billion gallons (49.2 billion liters) in 2013. Ethanol can be produced from different types of feedstock, including sugarcane in Brazil and corn in the United States.

Ethanol produced from sugarcane is considered to be more sustainable than corn-based ethanol. Sugarcane requires less fertilizer and creates less soil erosion. It also yields a waste product that can be used to generate steam that helps to power ethanol production. In comparison, corn-based ethanol uses larger amounts of fertilizer made from natural gas and also pesticides and herbicides made with petroleum. Corn crops used for ethanol production can cause significant soil erosion. In addition, high-nitrogen fertilizer runoff moves from corn cropland into the Mississippi River and travels into the Gulf of Mexico, where it has created a large dead zone—an area with low oxygen levels, which can be deadly to marine life.

Biofuel Energy

Workers harvest the sugarcane crop in Thailand. Ethanol, the most common biofuel, can be produced from sugarcane.
© SOPOSE/SHUTTERSTOCK.COM

Biodiesel Biodiesel, another type of biofuel, is derived from organic oils such as vegetable or microalgae (tiny plantlike organisms) oil. Biodiesel is a popular biofuel in Europe. It is often made from palm and soybean oil. It can also be made from recycled cooking grease. Most biodiesel is blended with petroleum-based diesel fuel. In some cases, it can be used alone to power a vehicle.

Cellulosic ethanol Instead of using food crops like corn and sugar to produce ethanol, researchers are developing biofuels from cellulose. Cellulose is found in many nonfood grasses and woody plants, such as switchgrass and willow. Switchgrass is a native, perennial prairie grass with several benefits that make it attractive as a biofuel source. Switchgrass is easier to grow than most food crops. When planted responsibly, it can also reduce erosion and nitrogen runoff and increase

U•X•L Sustainable Living

63

Biofuel Energy

> ### Unintended Consequences
>
> Sometimes the production of biofuels can have unintended consequences on economies and the environment. For example, using food crops such as corn or soybeans for biofuels diverts these crops from the food supply. If food supplies decrease, food prices may increase. In this way, using food crops for biofuels can lead to rising prices for livestock feed and food worldwide.
>
> Using whole trees instead of tree waste for biofuel energy also can have unintended environmental effects. Trees and forests absorb carbon from the air and play an important role in the defense against climate change. When a whole tree is cut down to produce biofuels, the tree loses its ability to absorb the atmosphere's carbon in the future. In this way, harvesting entire forests can increase carbon pollution and destroy forest habitats.

soil carbon levels. Increasing soil carbon can improve soil health and remove carbon dioxide from the air.

Cellulosic ethanol has the potential to be more efficient than food-crop biofuels because it uses more of the plant to produce fuel. Cellulosic sources of ethanol require less fossil fuel energy than food crops to grow. In addition, part of the biomass can be used to power the production process, further reducing the amount of fossil fuels needed in the production process. Another benefit of cellulose-based ethanol is that it results in lower levels of life-cycle greenhouse gas emissions.

Although it has promise, cellulosic ethanol has some drawbacks. Breaking down cellulose for biofuel is more difficult and expensive than creating biofuels from corn or sugarcane. As of 2015, there were no commercial-scale cellulosic biofuel plants operating in the United States, mainly because it was still too costly.

Landfill gas When solid waste in landfills decomposes, it releases landfill gas, another potential source of biofuel energy. Once converted into energy, landfill gas can be used to generate electricity, heat, or steam. Using landfill gas as an energy source also reduces the amount of methane released into the atmosphere. Methane is a powerful greenhouse gas that has been linked to climate change.

Biofuels and sustainability

Many people believe that biofuels are a promising energy source. Biofuels can be made from renewable resources that are found around the world and are not limited to specific geographic areas. Biofuels are also environmentally friendly. They contain no sulfur and have low carbon monoxide, particle, and toxic emissions. Exposure to high levels of environmental sulfur can affect people's breathing and be especially harmful to those with respiratory problems. In addition, using biofuels instead of fossil fuels can reduce greenhouse gas emissions.

At the same time, biofuel energy has drawbacks. While it can be produced in environmentally friendly ways, it can also be produced in less sustainable ways that harm lands, forests, water, and ecosystems and even increase pollution. Ethanol made from corn requires large amounts of land and water. Improper management of cropland can lead to increased soil erosion and pollution from fertilizer runoff. In addition, the production of corn ethanol can create more carbon pollution than the fossil fuel it is meant to replace.

Biofuel production also relies on fossil fuels in several ways. Corn and other crops grown for biofuel energy use fertilizers, pesticides, and herbicides made from fossil fuels. The biofuel production is often powered by fossil fuels. The production of biodiesel uses methanol, made from natural gas. Even transportation of biofuel to consumers uses fossil fuels to power the delivery vehicles. In these cases, biofuels are not truly renewable because they depend on fossil fuels.

In order for biofuel energy to be a truly sustainable energy source, it needs to provide energy in a better way than the fossil fuels it replaces. Scientists hope that better and more efficient technologies and changes to production processes will make biofuel a more sustainable energy source in the future.

SEE ALSO Agriculture; Alternative Energy; Automobiles; Carbon Cycle; Food Security; Fossil Fuels; Nitrogen Cycle; Soil; Transportation

For more information

BOOKS
Brown, Robert C., and Tristan R. Brown. *Why Are We Producing Biofuels?* Ames, IA: Brownia, 2012.

PERIODICALS
Cardwell, Diane. "Big Factories Go to Work on Biofuel." *New York Times* (September 19, 2014). Available online at http://www.nytimes.com/2014/09/20/business/energy-environment/big-factories-go-to-work-on-biofuel.html (accessed March 30, 2015).

WEBSITES
"Biomass Energy and Cellulosic Ethanol." Natural Resources Defense Council. http://www.nrdc.org/energy/renewables/biomass.asp (accessed March 28, 2015).
"Ethanol Fuel Basics." U.S. Department of Energy. http://www.afdc.energy.gov/fuels/ethanol_fuel_basics.html (accessed March 28, 2015).

"Landfill Gas to Energy." Energy Systems Group. http://www.energysystemsgroup.com/landfills.asp (accessed March 28, 2015).

Biomimicry

Biomimicry is when processes, structures, and systems found in nature are adapted to solve human or industrial problems. The term itself comes from the ancient Greek words *bios,* meaning *life,* and *mimesis,* meaning *imitation.* A simple example of biomimicry are airplane wings. The wings of an airplane are shaped like the wings of birds to generate lift. This allows airplanes to take advantage of the same principles of aerodynamics that birds use to fly. Biomimicry is studied in many scientific disciplines, including chemistry, robotics, and biology. By looking to nature for solutions to design and engineering issues, humans learn to value the complexity of nature, especially the relationships between plant and animal species and their environment. This is a crucial step in understanding sustainability.

The origin of biomimicry

The term *biomimicry* was coined by American physicist and inventor Otto Schmitt (1913–1998), who in the 1950s developed a type of electronic circuit based on the nervous system of the squid. The term was further popularized by science writer and president of the Biomimicry Institute Janine Benyus in her 1997 book *Biomimicry: Innovation Inspired by Nature.* At the heart of the matter, Benyus explains, "life creates conditions conducive to life." This is the foundation of sustainability. If humanity can learn how to harness these techniques we will move beyond environmental destruction toward conservation.

By studying how nature solves various problems, scientists are studying successful design. In other words, if an animal or plant is not designed to adapt to its habitat, it becomes extinct. Not only are natural designs successful, they are also energy efficient due to the scarcity of energy in the natural world. Predators must be able to catch their prey. This influences the shape of a bird's beak or a tiger's teeth. Plants must be able to transform water and sunlight into energy, this influences the shape of a plant's leaf. The natural world can also teach scientists how to create energy from waste, just as the natural world constantly recycles matter into new resources.

Biomimicry

WORDS TO KNOW

Biomimicry: Using processes found in nature to solve human problems.

Bioprocessing: Using living organisms to create new products.

Examples of biomimicry

Plants do an exceptional job of turning sunlight into energy so they can grow. Researchers investigating this process have learned to build solar cells that operate on the same principle, which makes them more efficient and powerful than previous generations of solar cells. Previous polymer (that is, plastic) solar cells had a smooth texture, but those that mimicked the wrinkles of a leaf were found to generate up to 47 percent more electricity. The wrinkles function like channels that guide the light where it needs to go and reduces the amount that bounces off the surface. Although these polymer solar cells are not as efficient as traditional silicon solar cells, they are flexible, durable, lightweight, and inexpensive to manufacture, which makes them suitable in a number of situations. They can act as portable sources of renewable energy, which will reduce the need for less sustainable, nonrenewable forms of energy in the future.

The front-end of the Shinkansen Bullet Train of the West Japan Railway Company (left) is modeled after the beak of the kingfisher (right) resulting in a quiter and faster ride while using less power to speed the train along its path. LEFT: © SEAN PAVONE/SHUTTERSTOCK.COM; RIGHT: © PANU RUANGJAN/SHUTTERSTOCK.COM

U•X•L Sustainable Living

Biomimicry

Using Biomimicry to Design a Sustainable City

Studying how nature solves problems is the big idea in sustainable design for the twenty-first century. A key concept in urban design is understanding how cities function like an ecosystem, in which everything has a purpose and little is wasted. Toward this end, Janine Benyus told journalist Margaret Badore that "a city [could] provide the same level of services as the forest next door." This, Badore explains, would mean "a city could build fertile soil, filter air, clean water, sequester carbon, cool the surrounding temperature, provide biodiversity and produce food." Rooftops can be designed to collect or evaporate rainwater like the tree canopy of the rain forest. Building materials can be designed to sequester, or hold, carbon in them so it stays out of the atmosphere. Systems to generate drinking water from fog or humid air can be devised based on the nanoscale bumps of the Namib desert beetle, which gathers water from the air. All these design ideas and more could create cleaner, healthier, and more sustainable cities in the future.

In medicine, researchers are studying how humans can achieve a state of hibernation similar to what bears undertake to survive in harsh climates. Bears survive the long, cold winter by reducing their body temperature and metabolism to a state of hyperthermia called torpor. This conserves crucial energy and eliminates their need to hunt and eat. If humans could mimic this process of torpor without tissue and cells dying, it would have a profound impact in treating conditions such as stroke, burns, insufficient blood or oxygen supply, and cancer by giving patients more time to heal.

Other researchers are investigating how spiders create their webs from a flexible protein fiber called spider silk, that is stronger than steel, without generating any waste or pollution. Genetically engineered silkworms could be programmed to produce spider silk that could be used as cables for suspension bridges or artificial ligaments for the human body. It could be turned into flexible fabric that is bullet-resistant.

One product already on the market is a swimsuit fabric that mimics shark skin. Shark skin is comprised of overlapping scales that funnel water in such a way that it does not create turbulent swirls as the shark glides through the water. These turbulent swirls create drag, which slows down swimmers. But a full-body swimsuit that mimics shark skin allows the wearer to avoid drag and swim faster than his or her competitors. In fact, this swimsuit has been banned in competition for giving swimmers an unfair advantage.

What biomimicry is not

It is important to note that biomimicry is not simply a matter of using natural processes to accomplish certain tasks. For example, most wastewater treatment plants use bacteria to filter wastewater so it can be used again. This is bioprocessing or biotechnology, which is using living organisms, such as bacteria, enzymes, or chloroplasts, to create new products (clean water, in this case). Biomimicry is learning how an organism goes about doing something and then recreating that process independently from the organism and applying it to solve a completely different problem.

Biomimicry and sustainability

Biomimicry embraces the idea that it is more efficient to use an already existing, and proven concept to solve an environmental problem than create a solution from scratch. As the Biomimicry Institute explains on its website, "a sustainable world already exists." This sustainable world is the natural world. The hope among scientists is that if humans can learn how plants and animals have adapted to their environment in order to survive, they can take advantage of the designs and patterns found in those adaptations to create sustainable solutions to current environmental problems.

For example, Zimbabwean ecologist and farmer Allan Savory (1935–) has studied how herds of wild animals graze over large areas for many generations. Their natural patterns of grazing, fertilizing, and trampling the soil before being chased off by predators has proven to be more sustainable for land than traditional forms of cattle raising. He believes that replicating this natural process can reverse desertification in many parts of the world. Desertification is the process whereby land is degraded by overuse and soil is robbed of its nutrients. This makes it unable to sustain life. Farmers, Savory believes, need to mimic the natural patterns of wild animal grazing on their own land in order to sustainably raise livestock.

SEE ALSO Biotechnology; Cradle-to-Cradle Design; Industrial Ecology

For more information

BOOKS

Benyus, Janine. *Biomimicry: Innovation Inspired by Nature.* New York: William Morrow, 1997.

Marshall, A. *Wild Design: The Ecomimicry Project.* Berkeley, CA: North Atlantic, 2009.

Pawlyn, Michael. *Biomimicry in Architecture.* London: RIBA Publishing, 2011.

PERIODICALS

Hutchins, Giles. "Biomimicry: Looking to Nature to Solve Human Problems." *The Guardian* (November 15, 2013). http://www.theguardian.com/sustainable-business/blog/biomimcry-nature-human-problems-sustainability (accessed April 21, 2015).

WEBSITES

Badore, Margaret. "Generous Cities: Biomimicry and Urban Design." Treehugger, June 22, 2013. http://www.treehugger.com/urban-design/generous-cities-biomimicry-and-urban-design.html (accessed April 12, 2015).

Benyus, Janine. "12 Sustainable Design Ideas from Nature." TED Talk, May 17, 2007. https://www.youtube.com/watch?v=n77BfxnVlyc (accessed April 12, 2015).

Benyus, Janine. "Biomimicry in Action." TED Talk, July 2009. http://www.ted.com/talks/janine_benyus_biomimicry_in_action (accessed April 12, 2015).

"Biomimicry Examples." Biomimicry Institute. http://biomimicry.org/biomimicry-examples/ (accessed April 12, 2015).

Merchant, Brian. "Fish-Inspired Wind Turbines to the Future of 3-D Printing." Treehugger, September 23, 2011. http://www.treehugger.com/clean-technology/how-biomimicry-drives-sustainability-from-fish-inspired-wind-turbines-to-the-future-of-3-d-printing-video.html (accessed April 12, 2015).

Pawlyn, Michael. "Using Nature's Genius in Architecture." TED Talk, November 2010. http://www.ted.com/talks/michael_pawlyn_using_nature_s_genius_in_architecture (accessed April 12, 2015).

Savory, Allen. "How to Green the Desert and Reverse Climate Change." TED Talk, February 2013. http://www.ted.com/talks/allan_savory_how_to_green_the_world_s_deserts_and_reverse_climate_change (accessed April 12, 2015).

"What Is Biomimicry?" Biomimicry Institute. http://biomimicry.org/what-is-biomimicry/ (accessed April 12, 2015).

Bioregionalism

Sustaining the future of natural resources begins with small regions and local communities. A bioregion is an area with similar natural characteristics, such as climate, soil, water, seasons, and native plants and animals. The idea of achieving sustainability by defining areas by their characteristics rather than by set geographic or political boundaries began in the mid-1970s, and provides a way for local activists and leaders to address ecological concerns within their cultural context.

> ## WORDS TO KNOW
>
> **Bioregion:** An area of land that is described by similar natural characteristics.
>
> **Bioregionalism:** The belief that human activities should be based on bioregions, rather than political or economic boundaries.
>
> **Deforestation:** The action or process of clearing an area of forests.
>
> **Watershed:** An area of land from which all of the rain and melted snow drain into a particular body of water, such as a river or lake.

The general objectives of those who act and think on the principle of bioregionalism are to protect and preserve ecosystems; practice sustainable ways to meet basic human needs, such as food and water; and integrate human communities into the natural environment.

A watershed is often used to identify a bioregion, and issues involving water are often part of bioregionalism. A watershed is an area of land from which all of the rain and melted snow drain into a particular body of water, such as a river or lake. People who live within the same watershed often share drinking water sources, and so have a good reason to cooperate with one another.

Examples of bioregions

Bioregional thinkers and activists believe that people in communities and regions can live happily by using their share of local resources, while saving resources and space for wildlife and natural wilderness. By developing bioregional programs or policies for sharing natural resources and open space, people can avoid duplication of efforts from one community to another. Even better, they can cooperate to improve their entire region. For example, if a river is home to salmon, and one community along the river has practices that harm salmon, the efforts of others to sustain the salmon population are affected.

Examples of bioregions include an area called Cascadia, which covers the northwest United States and British Columbia in Canada. Cascadia has forests, mild temperatures and frequent rain. The Sonoran Desert is a bioregion covering much of the southwestern United States and northern Mexico that is home to rapid population growth since the 1980s. Conserving water and using solar energy are important sustainability goals for the bioregion. The Po River Valley is a large bioregion of Italy where

Bioregionalism

A satellite photograph of the Western Hemisphere at night illustrates the clustering of human settlements. These clusters of lights are geographically defined by mountains, lakes, rivers, and other natural ecosystems. Bioregionalism emphasizes the connection between human civilization and the natural environment, especially at the local level. NASA/GODDARD SPACE FLIGHT CENTER SCIENTIFIC VISUALIZATION STUDIO nearly one-third of Italy's people live and farms provide much of the country's food. Deforestation has stressed the environment, and is being addressed by the Italian government.

Bioregionalism and sustainability

Many of the goals and principles of bioregionalism are similar or identical to those of other environmental movements. One difference, however, is that bioregionalism emphasizes the connection between human civilization and the natural environment, especially at the local level. According to bioregionalism, local culture should help people understand and respect their relationship with the place they live. Often, a bioregion's residents include descendants of the land's earliest inhabitants. For example, Native Americans live throughout the Sonoran Desert. Their historical and even spiritual links to some animals, land, and natural resources are important to their culture and may differ from the priorities of people who move to the area from other parts of the United States. Buildings and landscaping should also foster a connection between people and the environment.

In many ways, bioregionalism combines environmental concerns with philosophical and social ideals. Although sustaining the environment in a bioregion might require logical approaches such as conducting research, planning, and setting strategies, bioregionalists first approach sustainability with a holistic awareness of their surroundings and how people and resources fit together in those surroundings.

SEE ALSO Biodiversity; Building Design; Community-Supported Agriculture (CSA); Ecosystems; Farming, Sustainable; Food Systems; Local Economy; Permaculture; Sustainability; Transition Towns Movement

For more information

BOOKS
Thayer, Robert L. *Lifeplace: Bioregional Thought and Practice.* Berkeley: University of California Press, 2003.

WEBSITES
Berg, Peter. "The Bioregional Approach for Making Sustainable Cities." Planet Drum Foundation. http://www.planetdrum.org/biareg_approach_cities.htm (accessed March 13, 2015).
"Bioregionalism." Living Awareness Institute. http://lebendig.org/bioregion.htm#what (accessed March 13, 2015).
"Cascadian Bioregionalism." Cascadia Now. http://www.cascadianow.org/about-cascadia/cascadia-bioregionalism (accessed July 29, 2015).

Biosecurity

Biosecurity is the effort to protect an ecosystem or population from biological hazards, such as disease or invasive species, sometimes with the enactment of public policy measures. All living beings exist within ecosystems, or ecologies—communities of organisms that interact in specific ways with each other and their environment. Biosecurity seeks to maintain the biological integrity of ecosystems. Biological integrity is the ability of an ecosystem to support and maintain a balanced community of organisms. Biosecurity has slightly different meanings, depending on the field in which it is applied. In agriculture, for example, biosecurity refers to protecting crops and livestock from diseases and pests. In public health, the military, and law enforcement, biosecurity means protecting the human population from diseases, including biological warfare.

Biosecurity in ecosystems

Within an ecosystem, each organism has developed, through millions of years of evolution and adaptation, to fill a niche in a habitat and to protect itself from the threats it faces in that habitat. When a foreign organism, called an invasive species, is accidentally or deliberately released into a new area, it can harm the existing organisms because the native species have not evolved to defend themselves against it. The newly introduced organism may outcompete the native species for resources by eating all of a certain food resource, for example. By doing so, the invader wipes out not only the species that provided food but also the organisms that rely on that species for food. An invasive species can also be an agent of an infectious disease, or an efficient predator for which the native species have not evolved survival mechanisms. One example of an invasive species is the zebra mussel, which is a native mollusk of the freshwater lakes of the Baltic but has spread throughout the world by attaching to ships in huge clusters. Female zebra mussels can lay as many as half a million eggs per year, which quickly enter a larval stage and begin filtering plankton, causing overgrowth of aquatic plant life and starving native fish species. Biosecurity measures such as natural resources management policies may be put in place to combat the damage done to ecosystems by invasive species, or to prevent their introduction in the first place.

WORDS TO KNOW

Biodiversity: The variety of species or organisms in a given environment or ecosystem. A large range of plant and animal life in a given region is symptomatic of its health; a narrow range or declining number of species in a region may indicate environmental damage or stress.

Biological integrity: The ability of an ecosystem to support and maintain a balanced community of organisms.

Invasive species: A foreign organism accidentally or deliberately released into a new area.

Monoculture: The human cultivation of a single crop in agriculture.

Niche: The role of a species within an ecosystem.

Biosecurity in agriculture

Agriculture is the activity in which humans preferentially grow species beneficial to them in habitats that humans have altered for that particular species. One negative aspect of agriculture is reduced biodiversity due to monoculture—large areas of cropland with only one crop growing on them. Monocultures are vulnerable to pests and disease. Large concentrations of animals, such as a herd of cattle, are also vulnerable to diseases and parasites. The biosecurity of the ecosystems surrounding farmland can be threatened by agriculture when animals or plants escape from an agricultural setting and, in effect, become invasive species. There is also a danger that crops or livestock that are genetically modified will affect agriculture and other aspects of the environment in ways their creators did not envision.

According to the Food and Agriculture Organization of the United Nations (FAO), biosecurity is directly related to the sustainability of agriculture, food safety, and the protection of the environment, including biodiversity. The FAO has recommended that farmers strive to promote biosecurity in agriculture by implementing sustainable methods for animal and plant pest and disease control. Sustainable measures would ensure that the environment is not harmed by any measures that farmers take to control pests and diseases on their farms. For example, chemical pesticides used to kill insects on a farm may spread into areas surrounding the farm, killing insects that are part of and may be beneficial to the surrounding ecosystem. One method of avoiding chemical

Biosecurity

pesticides is to encourage or even to introduce natural predators, such as birds or other insects, among the crops, to naturally rid them of any pests as they appear.

Biosecurity in society

Humans often live in close proximity to each other, which can promote the spread of infectious diseases. Since ancient times, humans have used disease as a weapon of war. With current technology, the ability to produce and deliver very serious diseases or toxins as biological weapons has increased the threat. Most societies have made treaties to abolish these weapons, but others are not bound by such treaties and increase the danger that disease-causing organisms could be released deliberately.

All of the threats to biosecurity ultimately affect the sustainability of life on earth. Although disease and weaponized diseases pose a great threat to the lives of humans, other aspects of biosecurity threaten the biodiversity and food security of the planet. In North America, for example, bats have become endangered by the introduction from Europe of a highly contagious fungal infection called White Nose Syndrome, which is believed to have traveled to the continent on the shoe of a visitor to the caves where bats live and hibernate. According to *Wired* magazine's science writer Gwen Pearson, "Bats provide pest control services estimated

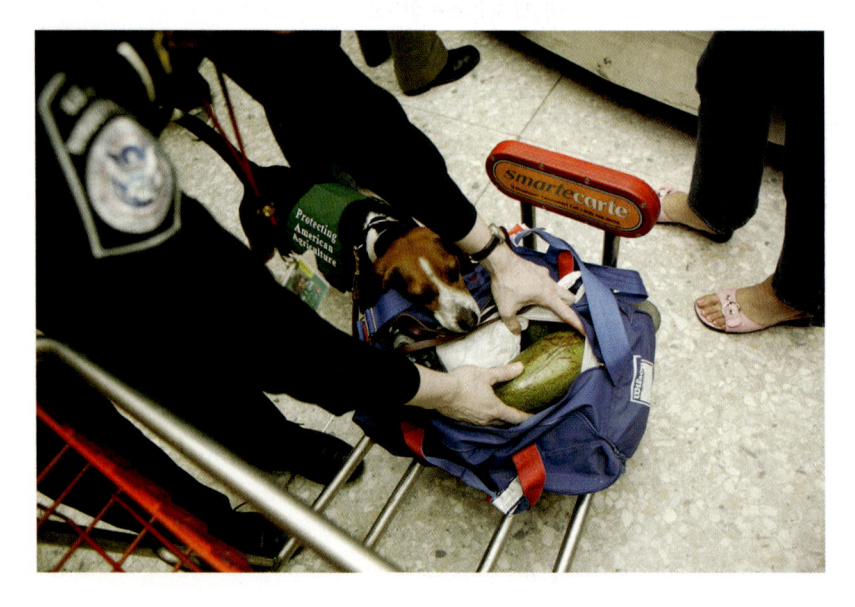

A beagle, working with a U.S. Customs and Border Protection Agricultural Specialist, finds an illegal food product that may contain pests harmful to U.S. agriculture. U.S. CUSTOMS AND BORDER PROTECTION

at a value of $22.9 billion per year in the U.S. by eating bugs that are agricultural pests, as well as mosquitoes." Since 2006, when the first evidence of the fungus was discovered in caves in New Albany, New York, untold millions of bats have died across the United States, making them one of the most endangered species on the continent. Pearson notes that, as of 2014, the loss of bats has resulted in an additional 2,291 tons (2,079 metric tons) of insects each year that are not being controlled by bats. Scientists describe the impact on agricultural yield in the United States as potentially catastrophic, and efforts are underway to add affected species of bats to the federal Endangered Species List. In the meantime, State and National Parks Services agencies across the United States have closed or limited access to caves known to be threatened by White Nose Syndrome in an effort to curtail the spread of the disease and increase national biosecurity.

SEE ALSO Ecosystems; Genetically Modified Organisms (GMOs); Invasive Species; Monoculture; Natural Resources

For more information

PERIODICALS

Garrett, Laurie. "Biology's Brave New World: The Promise and Perils of the Synbio Revolution." *Foreign Affairs* (November/December 2013). Available online at http://www.foreignaffairs.com/articles/140156/laurie-garrett/biologys-brave-new-world (accessed March 18, 2015).

Pearson, Gwen. "The Secret Bataclysm: White Nose Syndrome and Extinction." *Wired* (August 12, 2014). Available online at http://www.wired.com/2014/08/bats-white-nose-syndrome-uv-light/ (accessed April 22, 2014).

WEBSITES

"Biosecurity." U.S. Environmental Protection Agency, June 27, 2012. http://www.epa.gov/agriculture/tbis.html (accessed March 18, 2015).

"Biosecurity in Food and Agriculture." FAO Committee on Agriculture, Seventeenth Session Rome, March 31–April 4, 2003. http://www.fao.org/docrep/MEETING/006/Y8453E.HTM (accessed March 18, 2015).

Cook, R. J., et al. "Crop Biosecurity and Countering Agricultural Bioterrorism: Responses of The American Phytopathological Society." American Phytopathological Society. http://www.apsnet.org/publications/apsnetfeatures/Pages/Bioterrorism.aspx (accessed March 18, 2015).

Tucker, Jonathan B. "Biosecurity: Limiting Terrorist Access to Deadly Pathogens." United States Institute for Peace, November 1, 2003. http://www.usip.org/publications/biosecurity-limiting-terrorist-access-deadly-pathogens (accessed March 18, 2015).

Biotechnology

Biotechnology is technology based on living systems and organisms. Specifically, it is the use of any biological process for agricultural, medical, industrial, or environmental purposes. This includes everything from creating a new variety of apple to developing a vaccine for a deadly disease. Biotechnology can be used to clean up pollution and to make renewable, plant-based fuels to replace nonrenewable fossil fuels. It can also promote sustainability by creating enough food and resources for the planet's inhabitants while preserving biodiversity.

The history of biotechnology

Biotechnology dates back to prehistoric times, when humans first learned to make beer with fermented grain. People soon adapted the natural fermentation process, where yeast converts sugars into carbon dioxide, to make bread. Early farmers used biology to domesticate animals for farm work and as livestock. They chose animals with desirable characteristics and bred them with each other to produce offspring with those same qualities. This is called selective breeding. Farmers also used selective breeding to develop varieties of food that were tasty and easy to grow.

In 1919 Hungarian agronomist, or agricultural scientist, Karoly Ereky (1878–1952) coined the term *biotechnology* to describe how raw materials are turned into useful products through biological processes. In 1928, Scottish scientist Alexander Fleming (1881–1955) used fermentation to produce penicillin, an antibiotic that has saved millions of lives and launched the modern pharmaceutical industry. Genetic engineering, or technologies that modify genes, became possible after the discovery of deoxyribonucleic acid (DNA) in 1953 and the development of recombinant DNA technology in the 1970s. In this process, a section of an organism's DNA, or genetic code, is cut out and transferred to another organism. This recombination of genes gives the second organism the trait associated with that portion of the first organism's genetic code.

Biotechnology in the modern era led to what is known as the Green Revolution. Following World War II (1939–1945), a team of scientists led by American biologist Norman Borlaug (1914–2009) developed new varieties of corn and rice using traditional breeding techniques. These

WORDS TO KNOW

Biofuels: Fuels derived from living biological material, which makes them a renewable resource, unlike fossil fuels.

Bioremediation: Using living organisms to remove pollution from the environment.

Biotechnology: The use of any biological process for agricultural, medical, industrial, or environmental purposes.

Genetic engineering: Changing an organism's genetic material through biotechnology.

Precautionary principle: When there is significant scientific uncertainty about potentially serious harm from chemicals or technologies, decision makers should act to prevent harm to humans and the environment.

---

new crop varieties, when combined with low-cost fertilizers, produced twice as much grain as traditional varieties. This was especially beneficial for countries with growing populations, such as Mexico, India, and Pakistan, which were able to drastically increase their food production in a few short years. In doing so, they avoided the mass starvation that was almost certain to accompany their rapid population growth. While the Green Revolution solved one problem, however, it created another. In establishing monoculture worldwide, which is the practice of growing only one crop over a wide area, it ultimately depleted the soil of nutrients and led to erosion and deforestation. This is an example of biotechnology's unintended consequences. What started out as a way to sustain people ended up being unsustainable for the land.

The precautionary principle

Since the 1970s, biotechnology has become more controversial as scientists pursue stem cell research, cloning, and genetically modified (GM) food. Supporters of biotechnology believe that the field will result in many breakthroughs that will allow people to live longer, healthier lives and solve environmental challenges. Opponents of biotechnology believe it could cause new problems that are worse than the ones it tries to solve. Others are concerned about moral issues.

Scientists and government officials have attempted to address these concerns through the precautionary principle. This is the idea that if a new technique or substance could possibly harm people or the environment, its developers must prove that it is safe before it becomes widely

Biotechnology

used. Several important United Nations sustainability treaties incorporate the precautionary principle, including the Montreal Protocol to limit ozone in the atmosphere, the Rio Declaration to guide sustainable development worldwide, and the Kyoto Protocol to limit climate change.

Biotechnology and agriculture

Many agronomists use biotechnology to discover new ways to efficiently and nutritiously feed people living in poverty. For example, some GM seed varieties are developed to grow in areas with little rainfall. This will help agriculture and conservation of resources in arid, or dry, parts of the world. Other GM seed varieties are biofortified, meaning they are designed to have more nutrients than traditional varieties. They can be grown in areas of the world where poor nutrition leads to high rates of infant mortality and disease. Golden rice is genetically modified with beta carotene, which is a form of vitamin A. About 500,000 children in the developing world each year go blind from a lack of vitamin A, and more than a million people die from it. Substituting traditional rice for this GM variety will prevent many cases of blindness and death.

However, golden rice and other GMOs (genetically modified organisms) are controversial because people are concerned about the effects they could have on the environment and human health. Indian

A researcher takes tissue samples from genetically modified corn plants. The researcher is attempting to create corn that is resistant to the corn rootworm. © BRENT STIRTON/GETTY IMAGES

physicist and environmentalist Vandana Shiva (1952–) is an outspoken opponent of GMOs because of their possible effects on native species of plants and animals that keep ecosystems healthy. She and many others believe that when one or two varieties of GM seeds become the primary source of food worldwide, farmers will be forced to buy their seeds from large corporations, becoming economically dependent on them. This also means that food security worldwide could be jeopardized if a disease or pest becomes specific to those varieties. Ultimately, Shiva says, biotechnology could disrupt the way millions of people have been living off the land for generations. Additionally, many people are concerned that GMOs may not be safe to eat. Scientists are continuing to research these issues. It is too early to know whether GM plants are a sustainable practice.

Bioremediation

Bioremediation is the technique of using living organisms to remove pollution from the environment. The organisms that perform these functions are known as bioremediators. Composting is a type of bioremediation. This is when food and yard waste are collected and allowed to decompose naturally. Bacteria breaks down the organic components until it becomes a nutrient-rich substance that can be used as garden fertilizer. This recycling of nutrients is a sustainable solution to building soil fertility. Bioremediation can also be much more sophisticated. Scientists have developed forms of bacteria that can digest toxic substances from nuclear waste sites or oil spills. Mycoremediation is a subcategory of bioremediation in which mushrooms and other fungi are used to degrade dangerous gases, oils, and pesticides into carbon dioxide and water, which are much less harmful. These fungi can be grown on shorelines that have been damaged by oil spills or on land that has been contaminated by industrial waste.

Algae

Algae are a diverse group of organisms that show great promise in biotechnology. They are easy to grow and can be used to remove toxic substances from sewage, to prevent fertilizer runoff from entering waterways, and even to serve as biofuel for cars. One advantage algae has over other traditional biofuels such as corn or sugarcane is that it does not require farmland to produce. It is easily grown in large, shallow, outdoor ponds or specially designed indoor facilities. A utility company in Sweden has even used algae to absorb greenhouse gas emissions from its power plants.

Several companies are working on growing algae on an industrial scale, and in 2013 one company produced enough jet fuel from algae to fly a passenger airliner over 1,000 miles (1,600 kilometers), from Houston, Texas, to Chicago, Illinois. Researchers are experimenting with genetic modification to produce algae that can either become a fuel source or clean toxins from the environment. However, some scientists who study the energy industry caution that algae research and development is expensive and algae cannot yet be produced on a scale massive enough to make it an affordable replacement for fossil fuels.

Biotechnology and biofuels

Biotechnology is also used to create biofuels, which are fuels derived from plants or algae. Biofuels are a renewable alternative to fossil fuels, which come from buried deposits of carbon-rich material like petroleum and coal. Bioethanol, more commonly known simply as ethanol, is fuel made from corn, soybeans, sugarcane, or other crops. Many vehicles can be adapted to run solely on bioethanol, but it is usually mixed with gasoline or diesel fuel. Brazil is the world leader in adopting bioethanol as a fuel source. Over 80 percent of all vehicles in the country run on it.

A big advantage of biofuels is that they can be carbon neutral. This means that while the crops are growing, they absorb carbon dioxide from the environment. When they are burned, they release it back into the air. There is no excess carbon emitted into the atmosphere like with fossil fuels, which release carbon that has been trapped underground for millions of years. The exception to this is if biofuels are grown on land that has been clearcut, where all or most trees in the area have been removed at one time. Clearcutting and burning is an unsustainable practice that adds greenhouse gases into the atmosphere.

SEE ALSO Biofuel Energy; Biosecurity; Farming, Industrial; Food Security; Genetically Modified Organisms (GMOs); Precautionary Principle; Public Health; Sustainability; United Nations Conference on Environment and Development (UNCED)

For more information

BOOKS

Morris, Jonathan. *The Ethics of Biotechnology.* Biotechnology in the 21st Century series. New York: Chelsea House, 2005.

Renneberg, Reinhard. *Biotechnology for Beginners.* Waltham, MA: Academic Press, 2007.

PERIODICALS

Gunther, Marc. "Will Algae Ever Power Our Cars?" *The Guardian* (October 15, 2012). Available online at http://www.theguardian.com/environment/2012/oct/15/will-algae-ever-power-cars (accessed March 19, 2015).

Mulkern, Anne C. "Algae as Fuel of the Future Faces Great Expectations—and Obstacles." *New York Times* (September 17, 2009). Available online at http://www.nytimes.com/gwire/2009/09/17/17greenwire-algae-as-fuel-of-the-future-faces-great-expect-71147.html (accessed March 19, 2015).

WEBSITES

"The Biotechnology Initiative." United Nations. http://www.un.org/en/globalissues/biotechnology/ (accessed March 18, 2015).

California Center for Algae Biotechnology. http://algae.ucsd.edu/research/ (accessed March 19, 2015).

"What Is Biotechnology?" Biotechnology Industry Organization. https://www.bio.org/articles/what-biotechnology (accessed March 18, 2015).

Brundtland Report

The Brundtland Report refers to the findings of a commission named after former prime minister of Norway, Gro Harlem Brundtland. The commission was asked to examine environmental problems around the world and to propose ways to solve them. The resulting report, which emphasized how these problems must be addressed globally, not just by individual nations, is also known as *Our Common Future*.

In 1983 the General Assembly of the United Nations (UN) authorized the formation of the World Commission on Environment and Development (WCED). The commission was charged with finding ways countries could work together to achieve economic growth, especially in developing countries, without undue harm to the environment. The Secretary General of the United Nations, Javier Pérez de Cuéllar (1920–), a Peruvian diplomat, appointed Gro Harlem Brundtland (1939–), who was Prime Minister of Norway and a champion of environmental issues, to be chairperson of the commission.

The commission held worldwide hearings to gather evidence and recommendations from politicians, professors, experts in ecology and economics, and leaders of industry. In April 1987, the commission issued its report, titled *Report of the World Commission on Environment and Development: Our Common Future*. The General Assembly accepted the report in a resolution that year.

The Brundtland Report addressed many issues that affect global sustainability. Sustainability is the ability of people and the earth's systems to adapt and survive. In the report, commission members addressed the importance of improving social inequality around the world, especially variations in income or prosperity. The report also emphasized sustainable development.

WORDS TO KNOW

Agenda 21: Plan of action for sustainable development from the first Earth Summit in 1992.

Brundtland Report: Authored in 1987 by the United Nations World Commission on Environment and Development (WCED), the report was the first international plan for sustainable development, which it defined as "development that meets the needs of the present without compromising the ability of future generations to meet their own needs."

Earth Summit: Also known as the Rio Summit. A conference held in Rio de Janeiro, Brazil, in 1992. It resulted in numerous documents and international agreements regarding sustainable development, including the Rio Declaration and Agenda 21.

Multilateral: Involving many or all countries in the world.

Rio Declaration: List of principles for sustainable development from the first Earth Summit in 1992, named such because it was held in Rio de Janeiro, Brazil.

Sustainability: The capacity of the earth's natural systems and human cultural systems to survive, flourish, and adapt to changing environmental conditions for many years into the future.

Sustainable development: Development that meets the needs of the present without compromising the ability of future generations to meet their own needs.

World Commission on Environment and Development (WCED): The Brundtland Commission, tasked by the UN to find means of economic growth without environmental harm.

Sustainable development

When looking at the global environment and economy, the Brundtland Commission members considered current and future issues. One of these was how those who set policies in countries, companies, and worldwide organizations could develop systems to promote their peoples' standard of living and meet their basic needs without harming the environment. If a country, or world, overdevelops to improve the economy and resources for one generation, the consequence could be that no resources are left for future generations of humans, plants, and animals. This planning balance is called sustainable development.

A major task for the Brundtland Commission was to define and detail sustainable development. The definition developed by the commission is still widely used today. Before the commission met, the UN and governments around the world considered economic and social development to be a problem that was not related to protection of the environment. The commission's definition emphasized that economic development, social equality, and environmental protection are so interrelated that they cannot be considered separately. Brundtland wrote in her foreword to the report, "The 'environment' is where we live; and development is what we all do in attempting to improve our lot within that abode. The two are inseparable."

The final definition of sustainable development used by the commission: "development that meets the needs of the present without compromising the ability of future generations to meet their own needs, " emphasizes that people must use resources sustainably so that future generations will be able to be sustained. With this definition, the Brundtland Commission opened the new field of sustainable development and made it an important consideration of national governments and world organizations.

Results of the commission's report

The Brundtland Report called for multilateral action to combat poverty, especially in developing nations. At the same time the commission called on all nations to cooperate to find ways to do so that would not destroy the environment for people in the future. Multilateralism is cooperation and mutual effort among many countries, but, at the time, there was little spirit of multilateralism around the world. Another recommendation of the report was to reduce the influence of large multinational corporations on the economic and social policies of governments and to make corporations responsible for damages to the environment. This was also not a high priority of the governments of wealthy countries. Richer countries have gained economically from industrialization and other economic practices that have harmed the environment through increased greenhouse gas emissions, deforestation, overfishing, and other problems affecting poor countries.

Gro Harlem Brundtland

Gro Harlem Brundtland is a Norwegian politician and diplomat. She has a medical degree from the University of Oslo and a Master of Public Health (MPH) degree from Harvard University. She was the first female prime minister of Norway and served three times in that capacity. She is most famous for chairing the World Commission on Environment and Development (WCED), which introduced the concept of sustainable development in its 1987 report to the United Nations, The Brundtland Report.

Gro Harlem Brundtland. © AP IMAGES/JACQUES BRINON

To realize the recommendations of the Brundtland Report, the UN convened a meeting of 172 governments in Rio de Janeiro, Brazil, in 1992. The United Nations Conference on Environment and Development (UNCED), also known as the "Earth Summit," greatly increased multilateral action to promote sustainable development. The conference produced the *Rio Declaration,* a list of twenty-seven principles that the participating countries agreed were necessary for sustainable development. The conference also produced a plan of action for the UN and governments around the world to foster sustainable development. This plan was called *Agenda 21,* with "21" referring to the twenty-first century. This plan has been revised and extended at subsequent UN summit conferences on sustainable development and continues to guide worldwide efforts. For example, in subsequent years, sustainable development has focused on sanitation, water, and human settlements.

The Brundtland Report defined the new field of sustainable development and made it a topic of discussion in international forums and national governments around the world. It focused the world's attention on the need to alleviate poverty but also on the need to protect earth for the future. It called for a new spirit of multilateral cooperation to achieve these goals, bold action to make them possible, and for new thinking about how to do so. The report stated, "The time has come to break out of past patterns. Attempts to maintain social and ecological stability through old approaches to development and environmental protection will increase instability. Security must be sought through change."

PRIMARY SOURCE

Our Common Future (the Brundtland Report), Annex 1

Report (excerpt)

By: World Commission on Environment and Development

Source: World Commission on Environment and Development, 1987. Annex 1: Summary of Proposed Legal Principles for Environmental Protection and Sustainable Development Adopted by the WCED Experts Group on Environmental Law. This report is available online at http://www.un-documents.net/ocf-a1.htm.

About the document: In an annex (a section added at the end of a document) to the full report, eight "General Principles, Rights, and Responsibilities" are set out to guide nations toward carrying out environmental protection and sustainable development.

I. General Principles, Rights, and Responsibilities

Fundamental Human Right

1. All human beings have the fundamental right to an environment adequate for their health and well being.

Inter-Generational Equity

2. States shall conserve and use the environment and natural resources for the benefit of present and future generations.

Conservation and Sustainable Use

3. States shall maintain ecosystems and ecological processes essential for the functioning of the biosphere, shall preserve biological diversity, and shall observe the principle of optimum sustainable yield in the use of living natural resources and ecosystems.

Environmental Standards and Monitoring

4. States shall establish adequate environmental protection standards and monitor changes in and publish relevant data on environmental quality and resource use.

Prior Environmental Assessments

5. States shall make or require prior environmental assessments of proposed activities which may significantly affect the environment or use of a natural resource.

Prior Notification, Access, and Due Process

6. States shall inform in a timely manner all persons likely to be significantly affected by a planned activity and to grant them equal access and due process in administrative and judicial proceedings.

Sustainable Development and Assistance

7. States shall ensure that conservation is treated as an integral part of the planning and implementation of development activities and provide assistance to other States, especially to developing countries, in support of environmental protection and sustainable development.

General Obligation to Cooperate

8. States shall cooperate in good faith with other States in implementing the preceding rights and obligations.

SEE ALSO Sustainability; United Nations Conference on Environment and Development (UNCED)

For more information

BOOKS

World Commission on Environment and Development. *Report of the World Commission on Environment and Development: Our Common Future.* New York: Oxford University Press, April 1987. Available online at http://www.un-documents.net/our-common-future.pdf (accessed March 13, 2015).

PERIODICALS

"Future Doesn't Lie in Developing Coal Plants." *Energy Next* (May 13, 2012). Available online at http://www.energynext.in/dr-gro-harlem-brundtland/ (accessed March 13, 2015).

WEBSITES

Bärlund, Kaj. "Sustainable Development—Concept and Action." United Nations Economic Commission for Europe. http://www.unece.org/oes/nutshell/2004-2005/focus_sustainable_development.html (accessed December 12, 2014).

Brundtland, Gro Harlem. *Report of the World Commission on Environment and Development: Our Common Future, Chairman's Foreword.* UN Documents: Gathering a Body of Global Agreements, April 1987. http://www.un-documents.net/ocf-cf.htm (accessed December 12, 2014).

"Environment for Development." United Nations Environment Programme. http://www.unep.org/geo/geo4/report/01_Environment_for_Development.pdf (accessed December 16, 2014).

Building Design

Building design is the act of planning how a building will be constructed. It involves the fields of architecture and engineering. Building design for sustainable buildings aims to reduce the ecological footprint of buildings by using less energy-intensive materials that may have to be transported long distances to the building site.

Buildings use energy to maintain a comfortable environment for residents or workers; they must be heated or cooled. A building should provide its occupants with water for drinking, cooking, and sanitation. Sustainable buildings are designed to use far less energy and water.

Principles of sustainable design

With all of these considerations, making a sustainable building means that the architects and builders must draw on many technologies and best practices to decrease the effect that the building has on the environment.

Building Design

WORDS TO KNOW

Carbon footprint: The total amount of greenhouse gases produced by human activity. A person's carbon footprint includes, for example, the fuel to power a car or heat a house or cook food and would extend to the power used to produce and transport the goods a person uses.

Energy footprint: A measure of the land required to absorb carbon dioxide emissions.

Gray water: Water that has been used but is not severely contaminated, for example, water used for laundry.

Infrastructure: Basic physical and organizational structures, like buildings and roads, needed for the operation of a society.

Passive cooling: Use of systems that do not require energy to cool buildings.

Passive heating: Use of systems that do not require energy to heat buildings.

Retrofit: Addition of a component or accessory to a product that was not present or available when the product was manufactured.

Solar panel: Panel designed to use the sun's light or heat to create electricity.

Wind turbine: A device that converts energy from the wind into electric power.

Principles of sustainable building are applied to all types of buildings. Giant skyscraper office buildings, factories, apartments, and single-family homes can all be designed to reduce their use of energy, land, and water by including as many appropriate energy, water, and land use techniques as possible; constructing them of renewable resources; and carefully planning for how the building materials will be reused or disposed of when the building is no longer needed.

The U.S. Green Building Council has a program called Leadership in Energy and Environmental Design (LEED) to certify that all types of buildings are constructed with the best available strategies to conserve land, water, and energy, while still providing a safe and healthy environment for the occupants. The International Living Future Institute encourages creation of sustainable buildings around the world with its Living Building Challenge program. The building certification program comprises seven performance categories for sustainability of new and existing structures.

Governments encourage developers to use sustainable practices by offering tax and other incentives to include sustainability features in their buildings. Developers also have a financial incentive to build green buildings, because they can promote to buyers the cost savings from reduced use of water and energy in a well-designed green building.

Minimizing land use

One way to save resources when planning a building is to locate it on the best available site. If many people will be using an office building, choosing a site that is accessible by public transportation will save energy for every occupant who rides rather than drives and reduces the building's commuter carbon footprint, which reduces greenhouse gas emissions. A factory located near a railroad or a harbor saves energy compared with a location where raw materials and products must be shipped by truck and transported by train or ship. A home or apartment complex that is located closer to where its inhabitants work can save energy by reducing the miles people are commuting. Developers and city planners can reduce the energy needs of buildings by locating them where the energy costs of reaching the building are least, which also reduces the land that must be used for transportation infrastructure, such as roads, in the surrounding area.

Sustainable construction

Using material that requires a great deal of energy to produce and that must be transported long distances to a building site increases the energy footprint of the building, making it less sustainable. A sustainable building makes as little use of such materials as possible. Buildings made with materials available at or near the building site reduce the energy needed to transport the construction materials. For example, a designer might prefer a dark wood from another country, but if the builder can find similar wood harvested locally with the same look, it saves transport energy and supports a local business.

Buildings made with resources that can be rapidly renewed, such as bamboo, reduce the demand that construction of the building places on ecosystems. Many building materials can be recycled from used materials, which saves energy and raw materials. Drywall, insulation, and glass tiles are some examples of construction materials that contain recycled content. Some building materials can be reused from other sources rather than discarded. For example, salvage yards often contain light and plumbing fixtures. It may also be more sustainable to reuse an entire existing building, which would otherwise have been torn down, rather than build a new building. Even though the new building would be equipped with technologies that reduce its ecological footprint, reuse of the existing building is more ecologically sound.

Building Design

Careful selection of materials also can help ensure the health of the occupants of a building and the environment. Builders that avoid using materials made with toxic substances or that prevent release of toxic substances into the air of the building after installation can reduce toxins in the environment and improve the health of the people who use the buildings. All materials, especially those in the building's interior, should be carefully chosen to minimize toxins and solvents, and to make the interior of the building as safe as possible for the people who live and work there.

Saving energy

When people work or live inside a building, they need a comfortable air temperature to work in and light to see by. The U.S. Department of Energy says that heating and cooling account for 48 percent of the energy used in a typical U.S. home. There are many technologies available to provide these necessities in new or existing buildings with greatly reduced energy use. Passive heating and cooling help the natural processes of the sun's light heat a building, and breezes to cool the inside air. Some passive strategies are simple. For example, white roofing materials reflect heat, and materials such as stone floors in sunlight absorb heat inside a building to warm it up.

Playgrounds at the energy-efficient K-12 school in Greensburg, Kansas, which opened in 2010. Natural daylighting throughout the building and operable windows in classrooms are just two of the energy-efficient features of the school. PHOTO BY LYNN BILLMAN, NREL 17921

U•X•L Sustainable Living

Building Design

By setting windows at the correct distance inside the walls of a building, by designing overhanging structures above windows, or by using reflective blinds, the heat from the sun can be reflected away from the windows in the summer, keeping the building cool. In winter, when the sun is lower, it shines in the windows and helps warm the building. When as much daylight as possible is let into a building, it reduces the need to use energy to light the interior of the building. Aside from windows, designers might add light wells, which may be placed high on a wall, on a roof, or in any area that would otherwise be dark without artificial lighting. Other technologies use ventilation at night to cool buildings to a comfortable temperature, instead of running air conditioning. Placing plants strategically outside of a building can provide shade from the sun and shelter from the wind.

Where possible, a sustainable building should generate energy. A roof covered by solar panels can lower electric bills by converting the energy from sunlight into electrical power that can be used throughout the building. Some structures or the land around them can also be used to generate wind power with the strategic placement of wind turbines.

Ideally, a building will generate more electricity than it needs from renewable sources and feed the excess energy back to the local or regional power grid to replace other less sustainable sources.

The wetland outside of the environmental studies building at Oberlin College in Ohio was built to collect stormwater.
© JESSICA BETHKE/SHUTTERSTOCK.COM

Saving water

Modern green buildings use water conservation appliances, such as low-flow toilets and showerheads, to reduce the amount their inhabitants consume. Reuse of some or all water provides greater sustainability. The sewage systems of buildings can be designed to divert the gray water, or water that has been used for activities such as washing hands, dishes, or clothes but is not severely contaminated, to other purposes, such as washing cars, cooling systems, or watering gardens and irrigating farms. Sewage can be separated so that the solids are composted for fertilizer and the liquids treated so they too can be used as gray water. The rain that hits a building can also be collected and saved for use as gray water.

Reusing and recycling materials

When a building is ready for demolition, any toxic material should be removed and carefully disposed of. Much of a modern building can be recycled. The steel and glass of a skyscraper can be melted down and reused, which uses less energy than manufacturing new glass and steel. Concrete from demolished buildings can be crushed and repurposed as fill or in paving material. The designer of a green building plans right up to the demolition of the building to reduce toxins in the waste stream and to increase the ease with which the building's materials are recycled or reused.

By making use of the best available technologies and practices from the time a site is chosen until a building is ultimately torn down, developers, architects, and builders can reduce the effects of a building on an ecosystem. It is even possible that a building can benefit the land around it, providing power to surrounding buildings and gray water to local gardens and farms. Designing new buildings in a sustainable fashion, and retrofitting existing structures with sustainable features where possible, reduce the impact of our buildings on the earth.

SEE ALSO Air Pollution; Ecological Footprint; Energy Conservation; Greenhouse Gas Emissions; Solar Power; Waste Management; Water Access and Sanitation; Water Pollution; Wind Power

For more information

BOOKS
Lankford, Ronald D., ed. *Green Cities*. Detroit, MI: Greenhaven Press, 2011.

PERIODICALS
Zubrzycki, Jaclyn. "'Green Schools' Go on National Display" *Education Week* (March 12, 2013). Available online at http://www.edweek.org/ew/articles/2013/03/13/24green_ep.h32.html (accessed March 17, 2015).

WEBSITES
"Certification." United States Green Building Council. http://www.usgbc.org/certification (accessed March 17, 2015).
"Green Building." United States Environmental Protection Agency, October 9, 2014. http://www.epa.gov/greenbuilding/ (accessed March 17, 2015).

"Heating & Cooling." United States Department of Energy. http://energy.gov/public-services/homes/heating-cooling (accessed March 17, 2015).

"Living Building Challenge 3.0." International Living Future Institute. http://living-future.org/lbc/about (accessed March 21, 2015).

Sachs, Harvey M. "9 Ways to Make Your Home More Energy Efficient." Green Home Guide, September 3, 2009. http://greenhomeguide.com/know-how/article/9-ways-to-make-your-home-more-energy-efficient (accessed March 17, 2015).

C

Carbon Cycle

All organisms need the element carbon for life. Carbon is used to make carbohydrates, fats, proteins, DNA, and other organic compounds. The carbon cycle is the movement and exchange of carbon to and from the atmosphere, oceans, soils, vegetation, humans, and other living organisms.

The earth's climate depends on the amount of carbon in the atmosphere. In the atmosphere, carbon joins with oxygen to form carbon dioxide (CO_2). Carbon dioxide is a greenhouse gas that traps heat in the earth's atmosphere. If the carbon cycle removes too much carbon dioxide from the atmosphere, the atmosphere will cool. If the cycle releases too much carbon dioxide into the atmosphere, the atmosphere will warm. As a result, even the smallest changes to the carbon cycle can affect the earth's climate.

Human activities have caused certain parts of the carbon cycle to change in ways that are not beneficial to living organisms and the environment. Activities such as transportation and industry require the burning of fossil fuels, which release large amounts of carbon, in the form of carbon dioxide, into the atmosphere. Deforestation, or the removal of trees over large areas, has reduced the ability of ecosystems to naturally remove carbon dioxide from the atmosphere. These activities have increased carbon dioxide in the atmosphere and have been linked to climate change and global warming.

Carbon cycle steps

Plants (producers) absorb carbon dioxide from the atmosphere. They use carbon dioxide, along with water and sunlight, in the process of photosynthesis and convert it into energy-storing molecules. This energy

WORDS TO KNOW

Aerobic respiration: The breaking down of chemical energy using oxygen.

Anaerobic respiration: The breaking down of chemical energy without the use of oxygen.

Atmosphere: The layer of gases that surrounds the earth's surface and makes life possible.

Carbon: An element that is found in all life on earth.

Carbon dioxide: A greenhouse gas that contains carbon and has been linked to global warming.

Carbon footprint: The total amount of greenhouse gases produced by human activity. A person's carbon footprint includes, for example, the fuel to power a car or heat a house or cook food and would extend to the power used to produce and transport the goods a person uses.

Carbon sequestration: A pollution-control process in which carbon dioxide generated by power plants is pumped underground to be stored indefinitely so it does not contribute to climate change.

Carbon sink: A reservoir that stores carbon over a long period of time. Carbon sinks can be natural or human made.

Climate change: Gradual and enduring changes in weather patterns over the earth that impact numerous ecosystems in different and often dramatic ways.

Emissions: The production and discharge of something, especially gas or radiation.

Fossil fuel: Nonrenewable energy source formed over millions of years through geological processes. Includes coal, oil, and natural gas, which when burned to release energy also emit greenhouse gases that contribute to climate change and air pollution.

Greenhouse gases: Any of the gases in the earth's atmosphere that absorb or reflect back to earth infrared radiation from the sun, thereby trapping heat close to the earth's surface. An increase in greenhouse gases corresponds with climate change. The main greenhouse gases are carbon dioxide, methane, nitrous oxide, and ozone. Clouds and water vapor also function as greenhouse gases.

Industrial Revolution: The period of time between the mid-1700s and the mid-1800s when society transitioned to new manufacturing processes.

Photosynthesis: The process by which plants make food from sunlight.

---

is stored in the form of carbohydrates such as glucose. When animals (consumers) eat plants, glucose moves from the plant to the animal.

In a process called aerobic respiration, plants and animals break down glucose and other organic compounds to produce the energy needed for movement, growth, and reproduction. Aerobic respiration, the production of cellular energy through a process that involves oxygen, also produces carbon dioxide, which is released back into the atmosphere.

Carbon Cycle

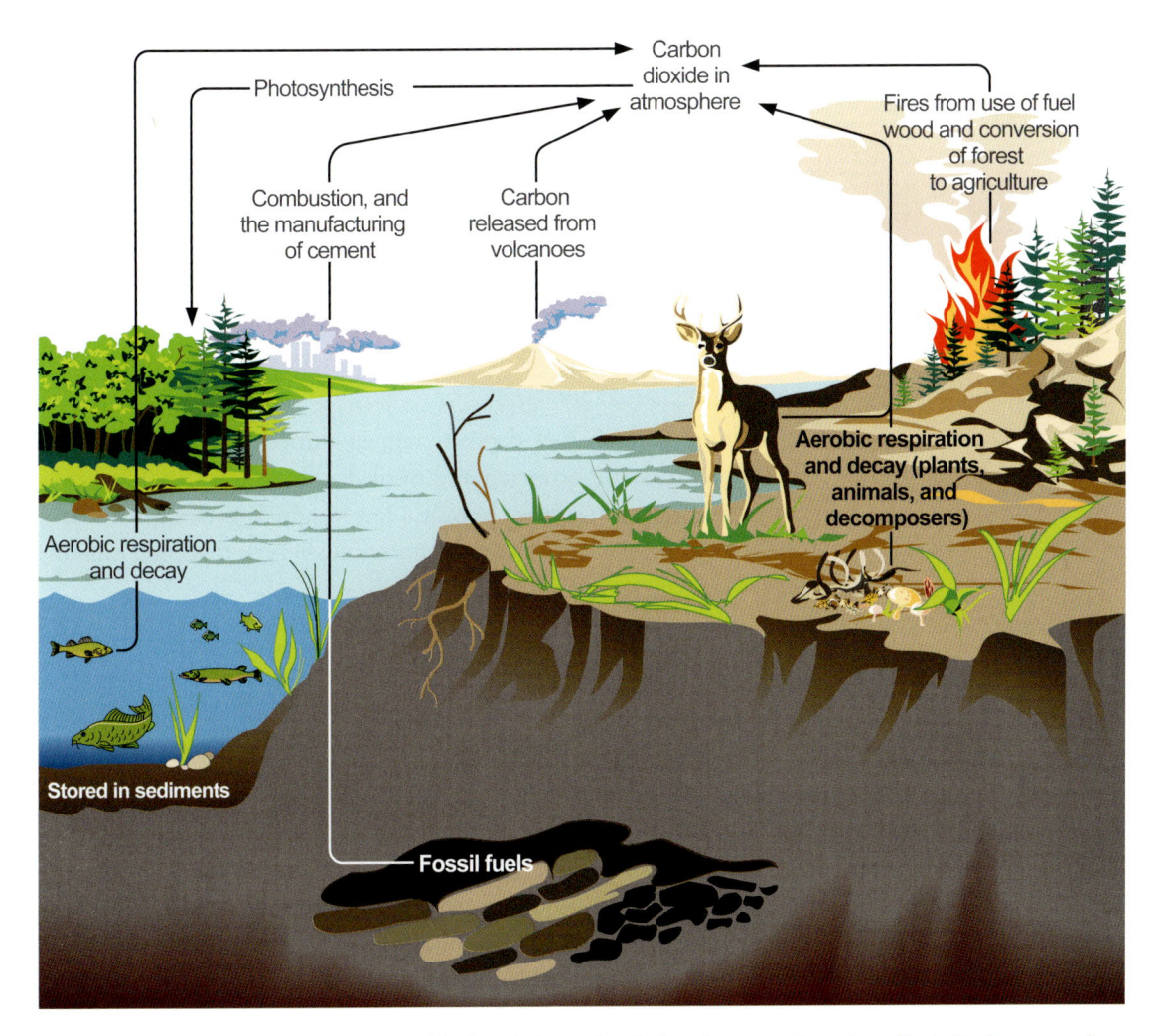

The series of chemical, physical, geological, and biological changes by which carbon moves through earth's air, land, water, and living organisms is called the carbon cycle. © CENGAGE LEARNING

Together, the processes of photosynthesis and aerobic respiration work to cycle carbon through the biosphere.

Carbon dioxide also enters the atmosphere when plants and animals die and decomposers such as bacteria and fungi feed on their remains. Two categories of microorganisms consume and decompose organic matter: those that need oxygen (aerobic) and those that do not (anaerobic).

U•X•L Sustainable Living

Carbon Cycle

Aerobic decomposers extract energy from decomposing organic matter and release carbon dioxide into the atmosphere. Anaerobic decomposers also extract energy, but they release methane gas (CH_4) into the atmosphere.

In some ecosystems, decomposition occurs quickly, and carbon dioxide returns to the atmosphere at a fast rate. In other ecosystems, decomposition occurs more slowly. In places such as bogs and the ocean, organic material of plants and animals may accumulate in layers of carbon-containing sediment, the matter that settles to the bottom of the water. Over millions of years, the layers of sediment compress the buried deposits of dead organic material and bacteria. High pressure and heat convert the organic deposits into carbon-containing fossil fuels, such as oil, coal, and natural gas.

As long as fossil fuel deposits remain buried, they store carbon. When fossil fuels are extracted and burned, the carbon they contain is released into the atmosphere. In only a few hundred years, humans have extracted and burned enormous amounts of fossil fuels that took millions of years to form.

Humans and the carbon cycle

The carbon cycle has occurred naturally for millions of years. Most of the time, the cycle operates in balance. The total amount of carbon dioxide that enters the atmosphere from all sources has been approximately equal to the total amount of carbon dioxide removed by photosynthesis or dissolved in oceans. For much of earth's recent geologic history, the carbon dioxide levels in the atmosphere remained relatively stable at approximately 270 parts per million. On some occasions, natural activity disrupted the carbon cycle. For example, volcanic eruptions release large amounts of carbon dioxide into the atmosphere.

The Industrial Revolution (1760–1840) was a period of rapid industrial growth in Western Europe and other parts of the world, characterized by a shift in focus from agriculture to manufacturing. Since the Industrial Revolution, human activity has altered the carbon cycle, adding increasing amounts of carbon dioxide to the atmosphere. Humans have burned large amounts of carbon-containing fossil fuels stored in the earth in order to generate electricity, power vehicles, run machinery in factories, and heat homes and buildings. Burning fossil fuels releases this ancient stored carbon into the atmosphere. In 2015 global carbon dioxide levels surpassed 400 parts per million.

Humans also alter the carbon cycle through deforestation, the clearing of large areas of plants and trees in forests for lumber or to make way for agriculture or cities. When the land is cleared, most of the carbon stored in the plants and soil is converted into carbon dioxide and released into the atmosphere. Deforestation also reduces the number of plants and trees that absorb carbon dioxide from the atmosphere and act as carbon sinks, a reservoir that stores carbon.

Through these activities, humans are putting more carbon dioxide into the atmosphere than plants can absorb. This has caused the carbon cycle to become unbalanced. It has also affected the earth's climate. Most scientists agree that increasing amounts of carbon dioxide in the atmosphere have caused a rise in global temperatures.

Because balancing the carbon cycle is essential to sustainability and the health of the environment, scientists are looking for ways that humans can reduce the release of carbon dioxide into the atmosphere. They are investigating alternative, non-carbon-containing sources of energy, such as solar power, wind power, and waterpower. People can help sustain the carbon cycle by conserving energy and recycling and by reusing materials to decrease their individual carbon footprint. Carbon sequestration is the capturing of carbon from the atmosphere and from carbon dioxide–generating activities and storing it for a long time. Carbon farming, where farmers change their farming methods to capture and retain more carbon in the soil and in plants, is one way farmers around the globe are working to reduce carbon dioxide levels in the atmosphere. Industries are looking at carbon-capture and carbon-storage methods, where carbon dioxide is pulled from factory emissions and injected into underground storage areas. Many people are calling for government policies that give incentives for businesses and industries to decrease carbon dioxide emissions.

SEE ALSO Agriculture; Biofuel Energy; Climate Change; Energy Conservation; Fossil Fuels; Pollution

For more information

BOOKS

"Carbon Cycle." In *The Gale Encyclopedia of Science.* Edited by K. Lee Lerner and Brenda Wilmoth Lerner. 4th ed. Vol. 1. Detroit, MI: Gale, 2008, 769–771.

"Carbon Cycle." In *Encyclopedia of Biodiversity.* Edited by Stanley A. Rice. New York: Facts on File, 2012, 101–103.

PERIODICALS

Bradford, Alina. "Effects of Global Warming." LiveScience, (December 17, 2014). Available online at http://www.livescience.com/37057-global-warming-effects.html (accessed April 29, 2015).

Lallanila, Marc. "What Is the Greenhouse Effect?" LiveScience, (January 28, 2015). Available online at http://www.livescience.com/37743-greenhouse-effect.html (accessed April 29, 2015).

WEBSITES

"Carbon Cycle Science." Earth System Research Laboratory. http://www.esrl.noaa.gov/research/themes/carbon/ (accessed April 29, 2015).

"The Current and Future Consequences of Global Change." NASA.gov. http://climate.nasa.gov/effects/ (accessed April 29, 2015).

"Overview of Greenhouse Gases." U.S. Environmental Protection Agency, updated July 21, 2015. http://www.epa.gov/climatechange/ghgemissions/gases.html (accessed July 29, 2015).

Carrying Capacity

Carrying capacity describes the number of individuals of a species that can survive in a given environment without depleting the available natural resources or degrading the living standards of the members of the species. Initially a population at less than the carrying capacity increases rapidly. Eventually, as the population approaches the carrying capacity of the habitat, the rate of growth decreases and the death rate increases until the population stabilizes at the carrying capacity. Most nonhuman species will eventually level out if their environment's carrying capacity is exceeded. Humans, however, risk overpopulating far beyond carrying capacity because technology allows us to leverage our resources to survive. For example, large urban centers typically feature tall, vertical housing, which can partially avert the consequences of overdevelopment, while agricultural methods like monoculture allow us to grow large amounts of a single crop rather than relying on naturally available food sources. On the other hand, the human ability to populate beyond carrying capacity can negatively affect both the human and other species.

Population size

The population of a species increases when new individuals are born. This is called the birth rate. It also increases when individuals move in from another area. This is called immigration. For example, when a bird

WORDS TO KNOW

Carrying capacity: The maximum number of one species that can survive in one area at a time.

Emigration: The movement of an individual out of a population.

Immigration: The movement of an individual into a population.

Maximum carrying capacity: A carrying capacity in which the population uses as many resources as are necessary to support the largest possible population.

Optimum carrying capacity: A carrying capacity in which the population only uses resources as quickly as the ecosystem can replace them.

Population: A group of individuals of the same species living in an area.

---

flies from one population to another, this is immigration. Organisms can leave their environment, too. This is called emigration. Emigration and organism death (through starvation, disease, old age, or predation) cause populations to decrease.

Many factors influence the size of a population. A factor that prevents a population from growing is called a limiting factor. Every organism needs resources to live and thrive. Resources include light, food, water, and space. As a population grows, more resources are needed. If resources become scarce, death rates will increase, causing populations to decrease, and organisms may not be able to reproduce if they are lacking resources. This causes the birth rate to decrease. A decrease of birth rates or increase of death rates causes the population to stop increasing or even decrease.

Human carrying capacity

Scientists study the earth's carrying capacity for the human population, which in mid-2015 was about 7.3 billion. The United Nations estimates it will grow to almost 11.2 billion by the year 2100. Estimates of earth's carrying capacity for humans vary widely. Humans consume a large amount of resources, but the human population continues to increase due to technological, medical, and chemical advancements. Modern agriculture has increased the amount of food that humans can produce, and transportation allows food to be moved easily around the world. Medical advances allow humans to live longer, which decreases the death rate. However, these advances also allow humans to alter the ecosystem and displace or eliminate other species, causing imbalances in population rates across species.

Carrying Capacity

Carrying capacity as shown on a graph of population as a function of time. Initially a population at less than the carrying capacity increases rapidly. Eventually, as the population approaches the carrying capacity of the habitat, the rate of growth decreases until the population stabilizes at the carrying capacity. This shape of curve, which begins with exponential growth and levels off as a saturation point is reached is called a sigmoid curve, or S-curve. The population may even briefly exceed the carrying capacity, but will decrease if the carrying capacity is exceeded.
© CENGAGE LEARNING

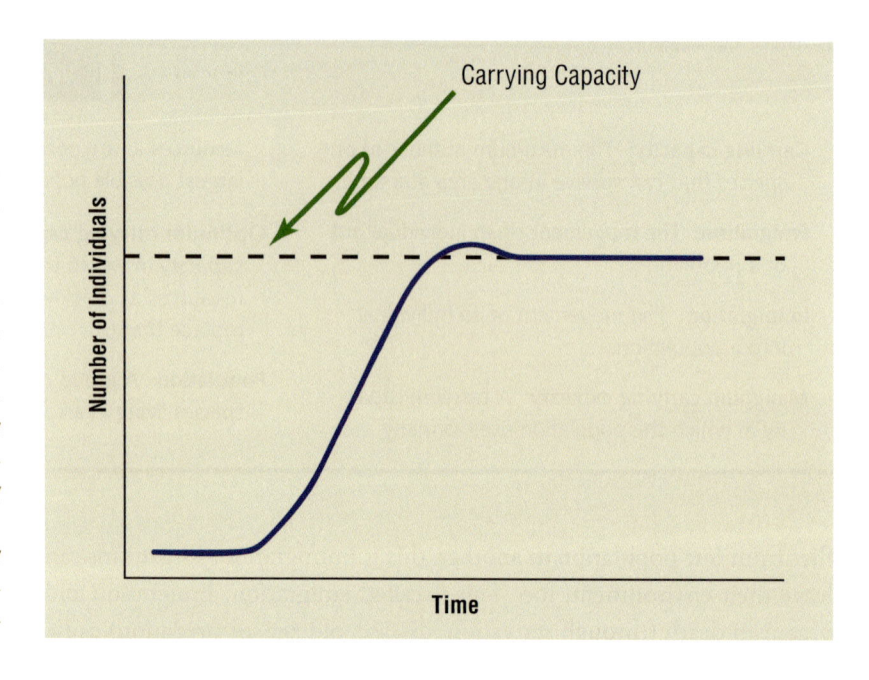

Just because humans can increase in population does not necessarily mean that they should. There is a limit to population growth, called the *maximum carrying capacity* of the planet. At the maximum carrying capacity, resources will be used faster than the ecosystem can replace them, and eventually the maximum carrying capacity will decrease as resources are depleted. The human population is already using many resources faster than they can be replaced and destroying wilderness and species to support the growing population. The *optimum carrying capacity* for humans on earth is likely much smaller. At the optimum carrying capacity, the population only uses resources at a rate that allows the resources to be promptly replaced, so that the population is sustainable from generation to generation.

Human intervention can affect carrying capacity

Because agriculture and technology have allowed human populations to be so mobile and flexible in terms of habitat, it sometimes is considered necessary to relocate other species to or from a human living environment. When human beings develop a piece of land for their habitation, they might remove the nonhuman animal species already living in that ecosystem, or they might let them die out through an altered carrying capacity or emigrate to a new area on their own. In some cases they might choose to bring in one species to prey on another species that has exceeded its carrying capacity due to a lack of natural predators—as was done with the reintroduction of gray wolves to Yellowstone National Park in 1995—or humans might foresee the need for a source of food in a new habitat, as happened at a remote Coast Guard station in Alaska in 1944.

During World War II (1939–1945), the United States Coast Guard (USCG) operated a radio navigation station on St. Matthew Island, Alaska, an island in the Bering Sea. In case the men on the island were cut off from supplies by the enemy or by weather, the USCG released twenty-nine reindeer on the island in 1944 to serve as an emergency food supply for the men operating the station. None of the reindeer were ever shot, and the station was shut down after the war. Otherwise populated only by Arctic fox, sea birds, and voles, and rich in lichen for the reindeer to eat, the island seemed like a good environment for the deer to thrive. But with no natural predators, the deer overpopulated. By 1963, there were 6,000 reindeer on the island and the lichen was becoming sparse. The winter of 1963–1964 was harsh, and by the time it ended only forty-two reindeer, with no breeding males, remained on the island. The rest had starved. Over the next several years, the rest of the deer died off, as no calves were born to replace them.

With no predators or human management of their numbers, the reindeer quickly exceeded the carrying capacity of the island by so much that the lichen, a limiting factor to their growth, was completely used up. Any population, including humans, that overuses a resource to such an extent that it is exhausted risks the same population crash. For a sustainable level of population of any animal, including humans, the necessary resources must be managed or used in such a way that they are replaced and the population does not greatly or more than briefly exceed the carrying capacity of the environment, or population reduction is inevitable.

SEE ALSO Biodiversity; Ecology; Ecosystems; Invasive Species; Monoculture; Population, Human; Wildlife Management

For more information

BOOKS
Krebs, Charles J. *Ecology: The Experimental Analysis of Distribution and Abundance.* 5th ed. San Francisco, CA: Benjamin Cummings, 2001.
Molles, Manuel C., Jr. *Ecology: Concepts and Applications.* 5th ed. Dubuque, IA: McGraw-Hill, 2009.

PERIODICALS

Klein, David R. "The Introduction, Increase, and Crash of Reindeer on St. Matthew Island." *Journal of Wildlife Management* 32 (1968): 350–367.

Sullivan, Colin, and ClimateWire. "Human Population Growth Creeps Back Up." *Scientific American* (June 14, 2013). Available online at http://www.scientificamerican.com/article/human-population-growth-creeps-back-up/ (accessed March 17, 2015).

WEBSITES

"Javan Rhino Conservation Program." International Rhino Foundation. http://www.rhinos.org/javan-rhino-conservation-program (accessed March 17, 2015).

"World Population Prospects: The 2015 Revision." Population Division of the Department of Economic and Social Affairs of the United Nations Secretariat, 2015. http://esa.un.org/unpd/wpp/index.htm (accessed August 12, 2015).

Citizen Science

Citizen science is the involvement of the general public in science inquiry and research. Generally, citizen-science projects involve a large number of volunteers who are recruited to observe or conduct experiments for a project. Then, they share the results with one another and, in many cases, with professional scientists. The Internet is an important tool for organizing citizen-science projects.

History of citizen science

Historically, scientific inquiry was pursued by amateurs because science had not yet evolved into a profession. Most of the well-known names in scientific discovery were private citizens who either had enough personal wealth to pursue science as a hobby or had wealthy benefactors to help support their research. Galileo Galilei (1564–1642) was studying to become a doctor when he began experimenting with physics and mathematics. Benjamin Franklin (1706–1790) was a lifelong scientific hobbyist. And Charles Darwin (1809–1882) had worked as a geologist and planned to become a parson when he undertook his famous voyage on the ship *Beagle* and began formulating his theory of biological evolution.

Birds were the subjects of some of the first citizen-science projects. An American ornithologist named Wells Cooke (1858–1916) organized

Citizen Science

WORDS TO KNOW

Bias: A prejudice for or against a certain idea or result.

Citizen science: The involvement of the general public in science inquiry and research.

Log: A daily record, such as the log of a ship.

Ornithologist: A scientist who studies birds.

a network of volunteers in Iowa to keep track of bird migration in the winter of 1881–1882. He used the data to identify migration patterns and estimate the sizes of bird populations.

Developments in personal technology devices in the 2000s have made citizen science accessible to more people than ever. The Internet by its very nature encourages groups of people with similar interests to come together, and portable computing devices such as smartphones and tablets allow individuals to monitor and record any changes they observe easily, as well as allowing for immediate transmissions of findings.

Advantages and disadvantages of citizen science

Many scientists and researchers welcome and encourage volunteers to contribute to their projects. By using volunteers, the scientists can save both time and money, and then those resources can be devoted to other aspects of the project. They may be able to expand the scope of the project or draw stronger conclusions because of citizen-science volunteers' contributions. But while many citizen-science projects have been successful, in some cases scientists have questioned the accuracy of the data that volunteers gathered. Causes of poor data include incorrect observation techniques, faulty equipment, and bias. Bias is a prejudice in favor of or against a certain idea or result. Monitoring volunteers to ensure accuracy is nearly impossible as well.

High school students help check nets for American eels on the Black Creek in West Park, New York. © AP IMAGES/MIKE GROLL

Citizen Science

Citizen science and sustainability

The use of citizen science helps to stimulate public discussion of sustainability issues. These issues affect large groups of people and the environment. Getting communities of people involved in active projects that study or implement sustainable practices promotes the cause of sustainable living. Wildlife organizations commonly put out calls for project volunteers to observe the flora and fauna surrounding their homes or in their neighborhoods. Many citizen-science projects are sponsored or promoted by an organization called the Citizen Science Alliance.

Here are some of the projects that the Alliance promoted in 2014:

Old Weather: Our Weather's Past, the Climate's Future (www.oldweather.org) Data about the weather of the past may help scientists understand the earth's weather and climate today, and to predict changes to climate in the future.

Bat Detective (www.batdetective.org) Many scientists think that bats indicate the overall health of an ecosystem. In this project, volunteers record bat sounds, listen to the sounds, and then interpret or classify the sounds. Scientists then analyze and interpret the data to draw conclusions about the bat populations of a region.

Plankton Portal (www.planktonportal.org) Plankton are small organisms that drift or float in the water. The plankton that perform photosynthesis provide oxygen to the atmosphere. In this project, volunteers study photos of ocean water. They identify and classify the plankton they see.

SEE ALSO Citizenship

For more information

BOOKS

Landgraf, Greg. *Citizen Science Guide for Families: Taking Part in Real Science.* Chicago: Huron Street Press, 2013.

PERIODICALS

Barbash, Fred. "This Animation of the Wondrous Monarch Butterfly Migration Was the Work of Thousands of Citizen Scientists." *Washington Post* (July 17, 2014). Available online at http://www.washingtonpost.com/news/morning-mix/wp/2014/07/16/this-animation-of-the-migration-of-the-monarch-butterfly-was-the-work-of-thousands-of-citizen-scientists/(accessed March 24, 2015).

WEBSITES

Citizen Science Alliance. http://www.citizensciencealliance.org/ (accessed March 24, 2015).

"Citizen Science." *Scientific American.* http://www.scientificamerican.com/citizen-science/ (accessed March 24, 2015).

Citizenship

Citizenship means having the rights and duties, such as voting, working, and living within the country, of a person recognized by a nation's government. Citizenship also involves engagement in governmental processes and working to improve society. Derived from the Latin word for "city," citizenship as a concept has evolved over time, and the way in which it is commonly used—denoting rights and duties—is generally considered a Western notion usually seen in modern democracies. Citizens can support sustainability both nationally and in their local communities by exercising these rights and duties of citizenship.

Civic engagement is when members of the public—citizens—are involved in the political process and issues that affect them and is a way for all members of a society to contribute to a sustainable society. Some common ways that citizens can be civically engaged are by voting, volunteering, lobbying, working in government, or working in a nongovernmental organization (NGO). Engaging in sustainability decision-making brings together many disciplines, such as architecture, education, political science, science, technology, engineering, and mathematics. Together, everyone can determine what is best for the public good and which policies and issues should be given priority.

Voting

United States citizens over the age of eighteen are eligible to vote in elections. As potential voters, citizens have a duty to become educated on the issues to ensure that their voting decisions are well informed. Each citizen should vote, either for a candidate running for office or on a particular issue, in a manner that represents his or her beliefs. Issues to consider when trying to create a more sustainable community include the environmental and social justice aspects of potential housing developments, the impact of transportation choices on the quality of community living,

WORDS TO KNOW

Citizenship: The rights and duties, such as voting, working, and living within the country, held by a person that is recognized as a citizen by their government.

Civic engagement: The involvement of the public in the political process and the issues that affect the public.

Grassroots organization: A group of ordinary citizens who work toward specific goals driven by a community's politics.

Infrastructure: Basic physical and organizational structures, like buildings and roads, needed for the operation of a society.

Legislation: A law or set of laws made by a government.

Legislator: A person elected to serve as a law maker.

Lobbyist: A representative for an interest group that meets with elected officials to persuade them to act in the interest group's favor.

Petroleum: A thick, blackish liquid created over millions of years through the decay of the remains of plants and animals subjected to heat and pressure beneath the surface of the earth. Also called oil and crude oil.

Pollutant: A substance that has negative effects on the environment (land, water, air, etc.).

---

local job opportunities, energy independence, food security, and issues affecting the quality of air and water. There are many organizations that champion these issues, so it is important that citizens use all available information and viewpoints, as well as each candidate's official position statements, to make their decisions.

Volunteering

An important role for citizens in maintaining a sustainable community is a healthy volunteer force. In local communities, common volunteer opportunities include working at food pantries and homeless shelters, for local conservation organizations and park services, or even doing unpaid internships within local government. Some national and international volunteering options are environmental leadership programs, unpaid internships within national government, involvement in citizen science projects, the Green Corps, and the Peace Corps. Citizens can determine their availability for local or global participation and choose which issues are most important to them to maintain a sustainable community, such as the environment, infrastructure, or human rights. Volunteering is a valuable way to remain engaged in civic issues and build personal skills and a sense of community.

Citizenship

Children assist in a tree planting ceremony at an Arbor Day celebration in Oster Bay, New York. © LITTLENY/SHUTTERSTOCK.COM

Lobbying

A more formal way to influence policy is to become a lobbyist, someone who tries to influence legislation on behalf of a specific interest. Lobbyists can represent large or small organizations, individuals, or the general public. Their main job is to persuade legislators to take action on issues that the lobbyists represent. Lobbyists must be excellent speakers and passionate and knowledgeable about the causes they represent. They must also conduct much research to ensure they know the people whom they are lobbying and tailor their conversations to each legislator. Lobbyists will be important for sustainable communities to ensure that the public's needs are met and their voices are heard within government. Some potential areas for sustainability lobbyists are in the sectors of energy, climate change, agriculture, infrastructure, human rights, and community development.

Citizenship

Grassroots Organizations

There are many grassroots organizations that involve young people in confronting difficult sustainability issues. One of these organizations is 4-H, a nationwide organization run through the Cooperative Extension Program of U.S. land-grant universities. Land-grant universities were funded by the 1862 and 1890 Morrill Acts, which promoted the establishment of institutes of higher learning that focused on agriculture, engineering, and practical sciences. 4-H is the system's youth development program, which champions community involvement, science, citizenship, and healthy living in chapters across the United States that offer clubs, camps, and after-school programs for kids ages eight to eighteen. About six million kids in the United States participate in 4-H programs at any given time, in groups led by adult volunteers and mentors that include the creative arts, agriculture, professional development, good citizenship, nutrition, conflict resolution, and community action. 4-H boasts a network of more than 600,000 volunteers and 25 million alumni and is highly regarded for its success in preparing young people for leadership roles in society.

Working in government

Within the United States government there are many opportunities to cause change and take a leadership role on sustainability issues. Congress and the president can act to reduce carbon emissions and find cleaner energy sources for the country. There are many governmental agencies that are in charge of either developing a plan or enforcing these actions. For example, the Environmental Protection Agency (EPA) sets the standards for, and enforces, safe levels of ozone, carbon dioxide, and other pollutants and greenhouse gases in the atmosphere. The EPA also regulates pollutants in the ground and in the water, ensuring a cleaner and more sustainable future. The Department of Housing and Urban Development (HUD) is responsible for developing plans to make more energy-efficient buildings, both commercial and residential, in order to reduce energy consumption. The Department of Transportation (DOT) both maintains current roads and other infrastructure, and plans for future transportation structures that can increase public transportation use and minimize pollution from cars, trains, and other modes of transportation. Finally, the Department of Energy (DOE) researches alternative energy sources to reduce dependence on carbon-emitting petroleum. When different governmental organizations work together, the United States has the opportunity to be a leader in sustainability.

Working in nongovernmental organizations

Another way for citizens to create change is to work in a nongovernmental organization, or NGO. These organizations fill local, national, or international needs. NGOs, just as the name suggests, are organizations that are not run by any particular government. They typically focus their work on specific issues, such as renewable energy, community access to clean water, or the regulation of hazardous wastes and pollution. NGOs often work to educate governmental officials, but they may also work with businesses or communities to come up with solutions that are environmentally sustainable and positive for the people involved. NGOs often have scientific expertise and operate as independent parties.

It is important for communities to protect and preserve natural resources and ensure social justice. Planning for and working towards a sustainable future is a responsibility that falls on all members of a community. The type and level of involvement may vary, but it is important for all community members to be educated and involved.

SEE ALSO Activism; Citizen Science; Climate Change; Environmental Policy; Nongovernmental Organizations (NGOs); Social Justice

For more information

PERIODICALS

Han, Hahrie. "Engaging Voters Can Kickstart Community Activism." *Washington Post* (November 26, 2014). Available online at http://www.washingtonpost.com/blogs/monkey-cage/wp/2014/11/25/engaging-voters-can-kickstart-community-activism/ (accessed March 24, 2015).

WEBSITES

Americans for Informed Democracy. http://www.aidemocracy.org/ (accessed March 24, 2015).
The Case Foundation. http://www.casefoundation.org (accessed March 24, 2015).
"Civic Engagement." Pew Research Center, April 25, 2013. http://www.pewinternet.org/2013/04/25/civic-engagement/ (accessed March 24, 2015).
4-H. http://www.4-h.org (accessed March 24, 2015).

Climate Change

Climate change is a gradual and enduring change in long-term weather patterns of the planet. Whereas the term *weather* refers to short-term variations in the temperature, rainfall, and wind over a small area, such as a city or state, *climate* refers to long-term averages of those factors over a large area, such as a hemisphere. While weather in any given area may be colder or warmer than normal, overall the climate of the planet is becoming warmer. For this reason, climate change is often called *global warming*. The key factor causing global warming is the greenhouse effect, in which the sun's heat becomes trapped in the atmosphere.

Climate Change

> ### WORDS TO KNOW
>
> **Anthropogenic:** Caused by human activity.
>
> **Climate change:** Gradual and enduring changes in weather patterns over the earth that impact numerous ecosystems in different and often dramatic ways.
>
> **Deforestation:** Removing trees from a forest, especially to the point that the forested area is cleared.
>
> **Developed country:** A country that has developed industries, technology, and a mature economy, as compared to less developed countries. The United States, Canada, and Germany are examples.
>
> **Developing country:** A country that has a low standard of living, including low average annual income per person, high infant mortality rates, widespread poverty, and an underdeveloped economy. Most of these countries are located in Africa, Asia, and Latin America.
>
> **Fossil fuel:** Nonrenewable energy source formed over millions of years through geological processes. Includes coal, oil, and natural gas, which when burned to release energy also emit greenhouse gases that contribute to climate change and air pollution.
>
> **Geoengineering:** The manipulation of the environment to counteract climate change.
>
> **Greenhouse effect:** The process whereby gases in the atmosphere allow sunlight to enter the atmosphere but do not allow its heat to escape.
>
> **Greenhouse gases:** Any of the gases in the earth's atmosphere that absorb or reflect back to earth infrared radiation from the sun, thereby trapping heat close to the earth's surface. An increase in greenhouse gases corresponds with climate change. The main greenhouse gases are carbon dioxide, methane, nitrous oxide, and ozone. Clouds and water vapor also function as greenhouse gases.
>
> **Mitigation:** Measures taken to control, reduce, or halt the impacts of environmental change.
>
> **Weather:** Short-term variations in the temperature, rainfall, and wind over a small area.

Over hundreds of millions of years the earth's climate has swung between glacial and interglacial periods, that is, between long eras of extreme cold, when glaciers cover much of the planet, and long eras when those glaciers retreat and climate is milder. The current interglacial period began about eleven thousand years ago. During this time humans learned to farm, and civilization evolved. The Industrial Revolution (1760–1840), a period of rapid industrial growth in Western Europe and other parts of the world characterized by a shift in focus from agriculture to manufacturing, led to the invention and use of many machines requiring large amounts of fossil fuels to operate.

The fossil fuels coal, oil, and eventually natural gas became sought-after commodities. Mining or drilling for them created enormous environmental

Climate Change

Two photographs of the Muir Glacier in Alaska taken sixty-three years apart. The photo on the left was taken on August 13, 1941; the one of the right August 31, 2004. Muir Glacier has retreated more than 4 miles (6.4 kilometers), the inlet is exposed, and trees and shrubs are growing on the ridge. LEFT: U.S. GEOLOGICAL SURVEY/PHOTO BY ULYSSES WILLIAM O. FIELD; RIGHT: U.S. GEOLOGICAL SURVEY/PHOTO BY BRUCE F. MOLNIA

devastation, and burning them released gases into the air that strengthened the greenhouse effect. With the rise of the automobile came a huge demand for gasoline, a form of refined oil. Burning gasoline released billions of tons of carbon dioxide and other greenhouse gases into the atmosphere within a few decades. Greenhouse gas emissions continue to rise annually as the world's energy demands grow. This has caused the average global temperature to increase much more quickly than it has at any other point in the planet's history. Thus, scientists believe that current climate change is anthropogenic, meaning that it is caused by human activity.

The greenhouse effect

The greenhouse effect refers to the process in which gases in the atmosphere allow sunlight to enter the atmosphere but do not allow its heat to escape. Sunlight hits the earth and is radiated back into the atmosphere as infrared radiation, or heat. Some gases form a barrier that prevents the heat from filtering back through the atmosphere. This warms the atmosphere just like a greenhouse, which allows plants to grow when it is cold outside.

The greenhouse gases

The gases that trap the sun's heat are called greenhouse gases. The three major greenhouse gases are carbon dioxide, methane, and nitrous oxide. Once these gases enter the atmosphere, they can stay there for hundreds of years. Other than common water vapor, which stays in the atmosphere for only a couple of weeks, carbon dioxide is the most common greenhouse gas. It stays in the atmosphere for an average of a hundred years. This means that Ford Model T cars from the early twentieth century are still having an effect on our climate.

Methane is the next most common greenhouse gas. While it stays in the atmosphere for an average of only twelve years, it has twenty-five times more warming potential than carbon dioxide. This means that it takes much less methane than carbon dioxide to warm the atmosphere the same amount. Methane is released when natural gas is burned and as a waste product of the digestive processes of livestock. Landfills are another source of methane, which is produced when garbage decomposes. Additional methane will likely enter the atmosphere as the Arctic permafrost (frozen soil) continues to melt. An amount of methane equal to fifty years' worth of worldwide carbon emissions is locked up in the Arctic land and polar ice that will be released as the land and ice thaw.

Nitrous oxide is the least common of the major greenhouse gases, but its warming potential is three hundred times greater than carbon dioxide's. A little nitrous oxide can do a lot of damage. Some nitrous oxide in the atmosphere, like the other greenhouse gases, is a natural part of life on the earth. But about 40 percent of nitrous oxide emissions are caused by human activity, mainly in the areas of agriculture, transportation, and industry. In agriculture, fertilizer is composed mainly of nitrogen. In the United States, nitrogen fertilizer accounts for about 75 percent of all nitrous oxide emissions.

Of the 7.35 billion tons (6.67 billion metric tons) of greenhouse gases emitted in the United States during 2013, according to the Environmental Protection Agency, carbon dioxide accounted for 82 percent, methane for 10 percent, nitrous oxide for 5 percent, and fluorinated gases (mostly chlorofluorocarbons) for 3 percent. While carbon dioxide occurs naturally in the atmosphere, human activities have increased the amount significantly, from 320 parts per million in the early 1960s to over 400 parts per million in 2015. The burning of fossil fuels for transportation, industry, and generating electricity accounts for this rise.

Causes of climate change

In addition to the greenhouse gases produced by transportation, electricity generation, industry, and agriculture, climate change results from other, often related activities. For example, climate change is already responsible for the melting of Arctic ice and glaciers around the world. Because ice and snow are white, they reflect sunlight away from the earth, making it cooler. When ice and snow melt, they reveal darker-colored land and water. These darker substances absorb sunlight and radiate heat. This becomes a positive feedback loop in which the more snow and ice that melt, the worse climate change becomes, which in turn makes the snow and ice melt even faster.

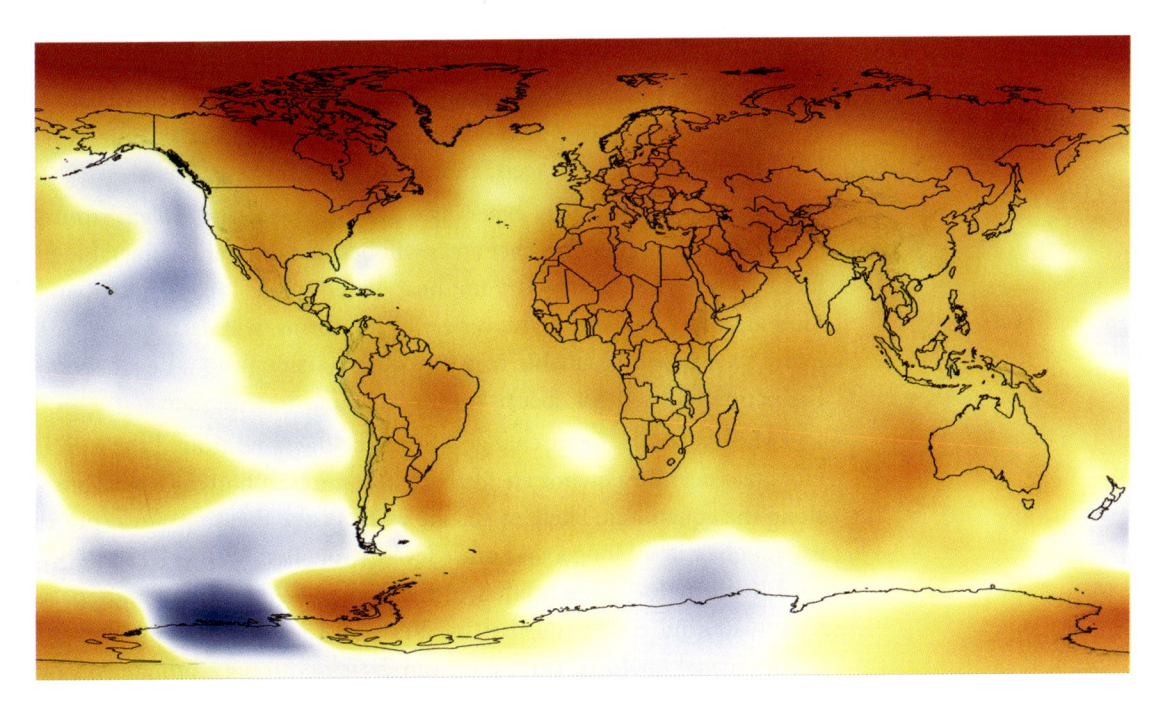

Earth's surface temperature for 2012 compared to the average global temperature from 1951 to 1980. Dark red indicates 2°C higher; dark blue 2°C lower. Note the warmer northern polar region at the top of the map. NASA GODDARD'S SCIENTIFIC Visualization Studio

Climate change is also affected by deforestation. Trees and plants absorb carbon dioxide and emit oxygen. By cutting down trees, people reduce the amount of carbon dioxide that forests naturally remove from the atmosphere. The oceans also absorb carbon dioxide and heat from the atmosphere, but this function is disrupted when the ocean temperature gets too warm. Evidence shows that the oceans have warmed significantly in the past hundred years. This warming coincides with the oceans becoming more acidic. When this happens, the ocean becomes an inhospitable habitat for many marine organisms, especially phytoplankton, microscopic plantlike organisms that are essential in the oceanic food web. This becomes another positive feedback loop that may lead to the extinction of many species of marine life.

The effects of climate change

Climate change has drastically increased the amount of Arctic ice that melts each summer. This increased polar melting will raise the level of the world's oceans and flood many coastal areas. Many of the world's large cities are at risk of disappearing at least partly into the water. Additionally, warmer oceans mean that hurricanes and typhoons are likely to be more frequent and more powerful, which will cause extensive damage along coastal areas. The biodiverse ecosystems in these coastal areas, including wetlands, coral reefs, and deltas, will also be damaged.

While some areas may experience more frequent and violent storms owing to climate change, other areas will become drier and vulnerable to forest fires. Farmland may dry up; heat waves will be longer, hotter, and more deadly. Biodiversity, the variety of life-forms, will decrease because many species will be unable to adapt quickly enough to a new habitat. Extinction of just a few species can upset an entire ecosystem.

The effects of climate change will not be the same around the world. Hot areas near the equator are likely to become even hotter. Coastal areas along the equator are likely to get the worst of the flooding. Areas prone to drought will see longer and more severe droughts. A study by the Goddard Institute for Space Studies of the National Aeronautics and Space Administration concluded that by 2059 up to 45 percent of the land on the planet could be suffering from extreme drought brought on by warmer temperatures that result in greater water evaporation in many areas. As vegetation dies during the drought, less carbon dioxide will be absorbed from the atmosphere, causing the planet to continue to warm.

With damage to farmland, some areas of the world may experience increased food insecurity. Subsistence farmers, those who raise their own food for survival, may be forced to rely on relief supplies and nongovernmental organizations to meet their food needs. This may increase poverty and political instability around the globe. Additionally, prices of commodities such as corn, wheat, rice, and cotton will rise on the world market, leading to more food insecurity even in developed countries. Climate change may also lead to many outbreaks of disease as disease-carrying insects migrate to new habitats, where people have less immunity to them.

One of the effects of a warmer climate is a slowing of the jet stream, the main air currents that circle the globe. When this happens, weather patterns can get stuck. This means that rain, snow, droughts, and heat waves will last longer, making them more severe. Outbreaks of tornadoes and dust storms may increase.

Climate change will cause intensified melting of the glaciers. Glaciers are the major source of freshwater for millions of people on the earth. For example, the Himalayan glaciers are the source for the Ganges, the Yangtze, and the Yellow Rivers, which more than a billion people rely on for water, irrigation, and power. Once these glaciers melt completely, these rivers will dry up.

Addressing climate change: mitigation and adaptation

Climate change is a global problem that requires a global solution, yet few countries have demonstrated the political will to address climate change either on their own or in conjunction with others. The most notable international climate change treaty is the United Nations' Kyoto Protocol, which was adopted in 1997 and entered into force in 2005. The treaty's objective is to reduce greenhouse gases in the atmosphere to levels that will prevent catastrophic change to the planet's climate. As of 2015, 192 countries were parties to the protocol, but the United States had not ratified it, and Canada had withdrawn its support.

The first commitment period of the Kyoto Treaty, from 2008 to 2012, saw mixed results. Sixteen countries, including Canada, Australia, Switzerland, and Japan, failed to meet their goals to reduce emissions. However, twenty countries, including Germany, France, the United Kingdom, Poland, and Russia, did meet their goals to reduce emissions. Notably, both China, the world leader in carbon emissions, and India were exempt from meeting carbon reductions, owing to their status as

The Intergovernmental Panel on Climate Change

In addition to the Kyoto Protocol, the United Nations is also home to the Intergovernmental Panel on Climate Change (IPCC), a group of scientists who interpret international research data on climate change. The IPCC has stated that the "warming of the climate system is unequivocal" and that "atmospheric concentrations of carbon dioxide, methane, and nitrous oxide have increased to levels unprecedented in at least the last 800,000 years." The group has concluded that the areas likely to be most affected by climate change are in developing countries, which lack the resources necessary to deal with it. This means that impoverished people are much more likely to suffer from climate change than wealthier people and those in developed countries. Furthermore, the IPCC states, even if fossil fuels were outlawed tomorrow, climate change would continue to increase for the next hundred years before leveling off. This is the result of the length of time greenhouse gases persist in the atmosphere.

Rajendra Kumar Pachauri, chairman of the Intergovernmental Panel on Climate Change, speaks at the 20th Conference of the Parties (COP 20) of the United Nations Framework Convention on Climate Change (UNFCCC) in Lima, Peru, December 1, 2014.
© XINHUA NEWS AGENCY/XU ZIJIAN/NEWSCOM

developing nations. A second phase of the Kyoto Protocol extends to 2020, but it applies to only a small fraction of the world's total carbon emissions and seems unlikely to stop climate change.

When it comes to individual countries' responses to climate change, the two main options are mitigation and adaptation. Mitigation means slowing climate change as much as possible in order to avoid creating a positive feedback loop, and adaptation means limiting the most harmful effects of climate change. An example of mitigation is enacting a law that raises how many miles per gallon of gasoline cars must achieve. Another example is that cities can pass a law that limits how many automobiles can enter the city center, which will cut down on traffic and carbon emissions.

An example of adaptation is requiring homes built near coastlines to be constructed on stilts so they will not be damaged by storm surges. This recognizes that dangerous storms are inevitable and allows builders and residents to adapt their behavior to try to avoid deadly consequences of climate change. Both mitigation and adaptation require finding ways to make low-carbon energy options attractive and affordable. Alternative energy sources, such as wind and solar, will be part of this strategy if scientists can increase their efficiency and manufacturers can lower their cost.

According to the International Energy Agency, mitigation will require limiting carbon emissions worldwide to no more than 565 gigatons between 2012 and 2050, but as of 2015 the world is on track to surpass this amount by 2030. While growing demand for energy accounts for part of the predicted increase, many large oil companies use their political and economic power to fight legislation that could limit emissions.

According to the U.S. National Academy of Sciences, the four major prevention strategies to reduce greenhouse gas emissions substantially by 2050 are these: (1) reduce the use of fossil fuels, especially coal, and improve energy efficiency of the fossil fuels that are used, especially natural gas; (2) shift from carbon-based fossil fuels to renewable energy based on regional availability; (3) halt clear-cutting of rain forests and institute a massive tree-planting campaign worldwide to absorb carbon dioxide; and (4) shift to sustainable agriculture techniques. Other sources of carbon emissions could be curbed by plugging leaks in natural gas pipelines and trapping methane emissions from landfills, rice paddies, and coal mines.

Limiting soot by making power plants, diesel engines, kilns, and cook stoves more efficient would prevent some melting of polar ice and glaciers. Soot darkens ice and snow, allows them to absorb more solar heat, and makes them melt faster. Other ways to prevent greenhouse gases from entering the atmosphere include making factory owners pay to emit greenhouse gases. This would give polluters an incentive to adopt cleaner technology. Carbon emissions could also be pumped into repositories beneath the ground or ocean, preventing them from reaching the atmosphere. This technique, however, is still in the experimental stage.

Agriculture experts are developing genetically modified crops that need less water than traditional crops and encouraging governments to maintain stockpiles of grain for emergencies caused by drought. Conservationists suggest a more extensive network of wildlife preserves to allow plants to migrate and animals to move freely, without artificial barriers such as roads or towns. Some cities, such as Venice, Italy, and London, England, are building massive flood-control barriers to protect against storm surges and sea-level rise. Projected water shortages may be avoided by building desalination plants, which allow salt to be removed from seawater so it can be used for irrigation and drinking.

Finally, geoengineering is the manipulation of the environment to counteract climate change. These techniques are mostly experimental or theoretical, but they could someday play a role in limiting the effects of greenhouse gases. One geoengineering technique is to genetically modify trees to absorb more carbon than traditional trees. Another is to sprinkle iron pellets in the ocean to promote the growth of organisms that can absorb carbon. Other ideas focus on the atmosphere. Some scientists propose launching giant mirrors into orbit around the planet that would reflect sunlight back into space before it reaches the atmosphere. Airplanes or high-altitude balloons could spray a reflective aerosol into the stratosphere. Seawater could be used to create bright, puffy cumulus clouds, which have better reflective properties than other types of clouds.

PRIMARY SOURCE
Climate Change Impacts in the United States

Report (excerpt)

By: Melillo, Jerry M., Terese (T. C.) Richmond, and Gary W. Yohe, Eds., U.S. Global Change Research Program

Source: Melillo, Jerry M., Terese (T. C.) Richmond, and Gary W. Yohe, Eds. "Climate Change Impacts in the United States: The Third National Climate Assessment." May 2014. This report is available online at http://nca2014.globalchange.gov.

About the document: The following summary identifies climate change as anthropogenic (that is, human-caused) and lists the areas and people in the United States that are already affected. Flooding due to violent storms, deadly heat waves, and massive wildfires all cause millions of dollars worth of damage each year and have wide-ranging economic consequences. If anything, the report states, earlier climate change projections were too cautious. Recent advances in climate science have fine-tuned our prediction abilities, which will help us confront the challenges we face in the near future. What follows is the introduction from the report.

Climate Change and the American People

Climate change, once considered an issue for a distant future, has moved firmly into the present. Corn producers in Iowa, oyster growers in Washington

State, and maple syrup producers in Vermont are all observing climate-related changes that are outside of recent experience. So, too, are coastal planners in Florida, water managers in the arid Southwest, city dwellers from Phoenix to New York, and Native Peoples on tribal lands from Louisiana to Alaska. This National Climate Assessment concludes that the evidence of human-induced climate change continues to strengthen and that impacts are increasing across the country.

Americans are noticing changes all around them. Summers are longer and hotter, and extended periods of unusual heat last longer than any living American has ever experienced. Winters are generally shorter and warmer. Rain comes in heavier downpours. People are seeing changes in the length and severity of seasonal allergies, the plant varieties that thrive in their gardens, and the kinds of birds they see in any particular month in their neighborhoods.

Other changes are even more dramatic. Residents of some coastal cities see their streets flood more regularly during storms and high tides. Inland cities near large rivers also experience more flooding, especially in the Midwest and Northeast. Insurance rates are rising in some vulnerable locations, and insurance is no longer available in others. Hotter and drier weather and earlier snow melt mean that wildfires in the West start earlier in the spring, last later into the fall, and burn more acreage. In Arctic Alaska, the summer sea ice that once protected the coasts has receded, and autumn storms now cause more erosion, threatening many communities with relocation.

Scientists who study climate change confirm that these observations are consistent with significant changes in earth's climatic trends. Long-term, independent records from weather stations, satellites, ocean buoys, tide gauges, and many other data sources all confirm that our nation, like the rest of the world, is warming. Precipitation patterns are changing, sea level is rising, the oceans are becoming more acidic, and the frequency and intensity of some extreme weather events are increasing. Many lines of independent evidence demonstrate that the rapid warming of the past half-century is due primarily to human activities.

The observed warming and other climatic changes are triggering wide-ranging impacts in every region of our country and throughout our economy. Some of these changes can be beneficial over the short run, such as a longer growing season in some regions and a longer shipping season on the Great Lakes. But many more are detrimental, largely because our society and its infrastructure were designed for the climate that we have had, not the rapidly changing climate we now have and can expect in the future. In addition, climate change does not occur in isolation. Rather, it is superimposed on other stresses, which combine to create new challenges.

Climate Change

This National Climate Assessment collects, integrates, and assesses observations and research from around the country, helping us to see what is actually happening and understand what it means for our lives, our livelihoods, and our future. The report includes analyses of impacts on seven sectors—human health, water, energy, transportation, agriculture, forests, and ecosystems—and the interactions among sectors at the national level. The report also assesses key impacts on all U.S. regions: Northeast, Southeast and Caribbean, Midwest, Great Plains, Southwest, Northwest, Alaska, Hawaii and Pacific Islands, as well as the country's coastal areas, oceans, and marine resources.

Over recent decades, climate science has advanced significantly. Increased scrutiny has led to increased certainty that we are now seeing impacts associated with human-induced climate change. With each passing year, the accumulating evidence further expands our understanding and extends the record of observed trends in temperature, precipitation, sea level, ice mass, and many other variables recorded by a variety of measuring systems and analyzed by independent research groups from around the world. It is notable that as these data records have grown longer and climate models have become more comprehensive, earlier predictions have largely been confirmed. The only real surprises have been that some changes, such as sea level rise and Arctic sea ice decline, have outpaced earlier projections.

What is new over the last decade is that we know with increasing certainty that climate change is happening now. While scientists continue to refine projections of the future, observations unequivocally show that climate is changing and that the warming of the past 50 years is primarily due to human-induced emissions of heat-trapping gases. These emissions come mainly from burning coal, oil, and gas, with additional contributions from forest clearing and some agricultural practices.

Global climate is projected to continue to change over this century and beyond, but there is still time to act to limit the amount of change and the extent of damaging impacts.

This report documents the changes already observed and those projected for the future. It is important that these findings and response options be shared broadly to inform citizens and communities across our nation. Climate change presents a major challenge for society. This report advances our understanding of that challenge and the need for the American people to prepare for and respond to its far-reaching implications.

SEE ALSO Agriculture; Air Pollution; Alternative Energy; Automobiles; Biodiversity; Carbon Cycle; Coal; Consumption; Desalination;

Ecological Footprint; Ecosystems; Energy Conservation; Farming, Sustainable; Food Security; Food Systems; Fossil Fuels; Genetically Modified Organisms (GMOs); Geothermal Power; Greenhouse Gas Emissions; Hydraulic Fracturing; Hydropower; Natural Gas; Oil; Polar Melting; Solar Power; Sustainability; Systems and Systems Thinking; Tragedy of the Commons; Transportation; Waste Management; Wind Power

For more information

BOOKS
Nakaya, Andrea C. *Climate Change* Thinking Critically series. San Diego, CA: Referencepoint Press, 2014.

PERIODICALS
Clark, Duncan. "Has the Kyoto Protocol Made Any Difference to Carbon Emissions?" *The Guardian* (November 26, 2012). Available online at http://www.theguardian.com/environment/blog/2012/nov/26/kyoto-protocol-carbon-emissions.

WEBSITES
"Causes of Climate Change." World Meteorological Organization. https://www.wmo.int/pages/themes/climate/causes_of_climate_change.php (accessed March 24, 2015).

"Megadroughts Projected for West." NASA Goddard Institute for Space Studies. http://www.giss.nasa.gov/ (accessed April 1, 2015).

"Overview of Greenhouse Gases." U.S. Environmental Protection Agency, updated July 21, 2015. http://epa.gov/climatechange/ghgemissions/gases.html (accessed July 24, 2015).

Coal

Coal is decayed plant material that has been subjected to heat and pressure from the earth over millions of years and become fossilized. Thus, coal, like natural gas and oil, is a fossil fuel. Burning these fossil fuels releases the energy that the plants absorbed from the sun while they were alive. Coal has been used for thousands of years as a fuel source for heating water and for metallurgy. During the Industrial Revolution (1760–1840) it became the favored fuel for heating water to power steam engines. (The Industrial Revolution was a period of rapid industrial growth in Western Europe and other parts of the world characterized by a shift in focus from agriculture to manufacturing.) Today, coal continues to be a primary energy source for power plants and industry.

WORDS TO KNOW

Biodiversity: The variety of species or organisms in a given environment or ecosystem. A large range of plant and animal life in a given region is symptomatic of its health; a narrow range or declining number of species in a region may indicate environmental damage or stress.

Carbon sequestration: A pollution-control process in which carbon dioxide generated by power plants is pumped underground to be stored indefinitely so it does not contribute to climate change.

Coal: Decayed organic matter that has become fossilized over the course of millions of years from the heat and pressure of the earth.

Fly ash: Toxic matter made up of very small particles that are generated when coal is burned and that will rise into the atmosphere if not trapped by pollution-control devices. It is often mixed with bottom ash, which is heavier and does not enter the atmosphere, and buried or held in slurry ponds.

Greenhouse gas: Any of the gases in the earth's atmosphere that absorb or reflect back to earth infrared radiation from the sun, thereby trapping heat close to the earth's surface. An increase in greenhouse gases corresponds with climate change. The main greenhouse gases are carbon dioxide, methane, nitrous oxide, and ozone. Clouds and water vapor also function as greenhouse gases.

Coal, like all fossil fuels, is a nonrenewable resource. Once earth's supply is used up, it will take millions of years to generate more. According to the World Coal Association, the known coal reserves worldwide will last for 113–134 years at current usage rates. Because it is nonrenewable and because it generates significant air and water pollution when it is mined and burned, coal is considered an unsustainable source of energy.

Coal generates approximately 40 percent of the world's electricity, more than any other single fuel source. It is also a primary fuel for industrial plants that make cement and steel, the raw materials from which much of the world's infrastructure, such as roads and buildings, is constructed. In 2014 coal generated about 39 percent of the electricity in the United States, with natural gas, nuclear power, and hydropower generating most of the rest. However, coal-fired power plants and factories generated 77 percent of all carbon dioxide emissions. Carbon dioxide is the primary greenhouse gas. Greenhouse gases trap heat in the atmosphere, contributing to climate change.

Much of the world's coal supply is located in the United States, China, India, and Indonesia. China is the largest producer and consumer

A coal power plant stands next to a canal in Germany. Coal generates 40 percent of the world's electricity. Because it emits many greenhouse gases and harmful particulates, coal is considered the dirtiest fossil fuel. © GUENTERMANAUS/SHUTTERSTOCK.COM

of coal, using over 46 percent of the world total each year. U.S. coal reserves are concentrated in West Virginia, Kentucky, and Wyoming. Most of this coal is recovered through strip-mining and mountaintop removal, both of which involve clear-cutting forests (entirely removing stands of trees), which disrupts watersheds and ecosystems and results in a loss of biodiversity, the variety of life-forms found on the earth. When all the trees in a forest are felled to recover the coal underneath that ground, all the animals that live in association with the trees are displaced. Topsoil erodes into nearby streams and rivers, killing many of the sensitive organisms in these waterways. It is very difficult, if not impossible, for the ecosystems to recover when the mining operation shuts down.

Kingston Fossil Plant Spill

On December 22, 2008, after several weeks of heavy rains, a dike ruptured at the Kingston Fossil Plant near Knoxville, Tennessee, releasing 5.4 million cubic yards (4.1 million cubic meters) of fly ash slurry into the Emory and Clinch rivers and onto 300 acres of surrounding land. The slurry damaged or destroyed dozens of homes, killed millions of fish, and raised serious questions about the quality of drinking water in the area. It was the largest but by no means the only fly ash release in U.S. history. The plant's ash was known to include toxic and heavy metals such as arsenic, lead, barium, chromium, and manganese. Exposure to these toxins can cause cancer, liver damage, and neurological problems.

The Kingston power plant was built in the 1950s to provide electricity for nearby Oak Ridge. Its ash pond disposal area was found to hold much more slurry than it was designed for. Much of the slurry was decades old. In fact, the ash pond had been built to a height of 55 feet (16.8 meters) above the nearby riverbank. The Environmental Protection Agency had previously recommended that the slurry be disposed of in a permanent lined landfill, but lack of federal oversight had not made this a priority for plant officials. The country's continued reliance on coal as a power source, along with its aging infrastructure, increases the likelihood that tragedies such as the Kingston slurry spill may be repeated in the future.

Dirty coal vs. clean coal

Apart from water and soil pollution caused by coal mining, burning coal generates ash. Some of this ash rises up through smokestacks and enters the atmosphere; this is called fly ash. Ash that remains on the ground when coal is burned is called bottom ash. Fly ash contains various amounts of many hazardous and/or radioactive substances, including silicon dioxide, arsenic, boron, beryllium, strontium, mercury, and vanadium. Release of these substances contributes to acid rain, which harms plants, animals, and aquatic life and can change the chemical makeup of soil. In addition to ash, burning coal also releases greenhouse gases into the air, especially carbon dioxide and sulfur dioxide, which contribute to climate change.

Coal emissions also contain small particles that can become lodged in people's lungs, leading to health problems such as asthma and lung cancer. According to the Clean Air Task Force, roughly thirteen thousand people in the United States die each year from health complications resulting from air pollution linked to coal-burning power plants. In China, hundreds of thousands of people die each year from coal pollution because smokestacks contain few, if any, pollution-control devices and because toxic ash is stored in open and unprotected landfills. In the United States, fly ash is captured and buried in landfills or in abandoned mines or is mixed with water and held in large holding ponds. The ash slurry (a semiliquid mixture) in these holding ponds can drain away or break through a barrier and seep into nearby groundwater, devastating surrounding areas.

The Clean Air Act, enacted in the United States in 1963, has helped limit pollution from coal-fired power plants in the ensuing years; thus, industrial areas are far less covered in soot than they were in the early twentieth century. However, the coal companies and electric utilities have consistently lobbied against stricter pollution-control measures and have blocked attempts to have ash classified as hazardous waste. Since the 1990s the U.S. coal industry has campaigned to position coal as a clean energy source by suggesting that existing power plants can be modified with high-tech air pollution–control devices. Critics argue that this is not a workable solution, because burning coal generates a set amount of ash no matter whether it is emitted into the air or is stored somewhere else.

Clean coal proponents believe that carbon capture and storage technology can eliminate carbon emissions from power plants by pumping carbon dioxide underground, where it can be stored indefinitely. However, carbon storage, or carbon sequestration as it is also known, is still an experimental process. Critics believe it will never become a widespread practice, owing to cost and safety concerns. Not only may trapping large amounts of carbon dioxide and other greenhouse gases underground make certain areas geologically unstable, it could also pollute groundwater supplies. Additionally, it would take a large portion of the plant's generated energy to pump the gas underground. Such technologies would take many billions of dollars and significant political will to develop, making them unlikely. Additionally, mining coal will always be tremendously disruptive to the environment. For these reasons, continued use of coal for power and industry will most likely be unsustainable.

PRIMARY SOURCE

In the Depths of a Coal Mine

Article (excerpt)

By: Stephen Crane

Source: Crane, Stephen. 1894. "In the Depths of a Coal Mine." *McClure's Magazine* (August): 195–209. This document is available online at http://www.unz.org/Pub/McClures-1894aug-00195.

About the document: Stephen Crane (1871–1900) was one of the most celebrated writers of his day. In this magazine article, he paints a portrait of life in a coal mine near Scranton, Pennsylvania. It is a dangerous profession, but one that America's swift industrialization depended on. Children worked alongside men in the mines, which Crane characterizes as unholy places of extraordinary noise, dirt, and danger. While underground mining is much safer today than in the nineteenth century and miners make above average salaries, it is still one of the most dangerous professions.

From this tunnel of our first mine we went with our guide to the foot of the main shaft. Here we were in the most important passage of a mine, the main gangway. The wonder of these avenues is the noise of the crash and clatter of machinery as the elevator speeds upward with the loaded cars and drops thunderingly with the empty ones. The place resounds with the shouts of mule-boys, and there can always be heard the noise of approaching coal-cars, beginning in mild rumbles and then swelling down upon one in a tempest of sound. In the air is the slow painful throb of the pumps working at the water which collects in the depths. There is booming and banging and crashing, until one wonders why the tremendous walls are not wrenched by the force of this uproar. And up and down the tunnel there is a riot of lights, little orange points flickering and flashing. Miners stride in swift and sombre procession. But the meaning of it all is in the deep bass rattle of a blast in some hidden part of the mine. It is war. It is the most savage part of all in the endless battle between man and nature. These miners are grimly in the van. They have carried the war into places where nature has the strength of a million giants. Sometimes their enemy becomes exasperated and snuffs out ten twenty, thirty lives. Usually she remains calm, and takes one at a time with method and precision. She need not hurry. She possesses eternity. After a blast, the smoke, faintly luminous, silvery, floats silently through the adjacent tunnels.

In our first mine we speedily lost all ideas of time, direction, distance. The whole thing was an extraordinary, black puzzle. We were impelled to admire the guide because he knew all the tangled passages. He led us through little tunnels three and four feet wide and with roofs that sometimes made us crawl. At other times we were in avenues twenty feet wide, where double rows of tracks extended. There were stretches of great darkness, majestic silences. The three hundred miners were distributed into all sorts of crevices and corners of the labyrinth, toiling in this city of endless night. At different points one could hear the roar of traffic about the foot of the main shaft, to which flowed all the commerce of the place....

Great and mystically dreadful is the earth from a mine's depth. Man is in the implacable grasp of nature. It has only to tighten slightly, and he is crushed like a bug. His loudest shriek of agony would be as impotent as his final moan to bring help from that fair land that lies, like Heaven, over his head. There is an insidious, silent enemy in the gas. If the huge fan-wheel on the top of the earth should stop for a brief period, there is certain death. If a man escape the gas, the floods, the "squeezes" of falling rock, the cars shooting through little tunnels, the precarious elevators, the hundred perils, there usually comes to him an attack of "miner's asthma" that slowly racks and shakes him into the grave. Meanwhile he gets three dollars per day, and his laborer one dollar and a quarter.

SEE ALSO Fossil Fuels; Greenhouse Gas Emissions; Mining; Natural Gas; Oil

For more information

BOOKS

Espejo, Roman. *Coal.* Opposing Viewpoints series. Farmington Hills, MI: Greenhaven Press, 2011.

Freese, Barbara. *Coal: A Human History.* New York, Penguin, 2004.

PERIODICALS

Dewan, Shaila. "At Plant in Coal Ash Spill, Toxic Deposits by the Ton." *New York Times* (December 29, 2008). Available online at http://www.nytimes.com/2008/12/30/us/30sludge.html (accessed March 9, 2015).

WEBSITES

"Coal Statistics." World Coal Association. http://www.worldcoal.org/resources/coal-statistics/ (accessed March 9, 2015).

"How Coal Works." Union of Concerned Scientists. http://www.ucsusa.org/clean_energy/coalvswind/brief_coal.html (accessed March 12, 2015).

"Learn About Carbon Pollution from Power Plants." United States Environmental Protection Agency, June 2, 2014. http://www2.epa.gov/carbon-pollution-standards/learn-about-carbon-pollution-power-plants (accessed March 9, 2015).

"USGS Compilation of Geographic Information System (GIS) Data Representing Coal Mines and Coal-Bearing Areas in China." United States Geological Survey. http://pubs.usgs.gov/of/2014/1219/pdf/of2014-1219.pdf (accessed March 9, 2015).

Community-Supported Agriculture (CSA)

Community-supported agriculture (CSA) is a system for marketing local farm products in which many people share the risks of farming in return for a share in the rewards. Consumers invest in a CSA farm by buying a share. Shareholders are often called subscribers. Usually, shares are sold and paid for before any crops are planted. Most CSA farms distribute products once per week during the season. Each week's harvest from the

Community-Supported Agriculture (CSA)

WORDS TO KNOW

Carbon footprint: The total amount of greenhouse gases produced by human activity. A person's carbon footprint includes, for example, the fuel to power a car or heat a house or cook food and would extend to the power used to produce and transport the goods a person uses.

Community-supported agriculture (CSA): A farming enterprise that sells shares to individuals and relies on these members to help run the operation. Shareholders receive an amount of produce and goods proportionate to their ownership stake in the farm.

Cover crop: A crop planted to minimize soil erosion and improve its quality and to manage weeds, pests, and diseases.

Distribution: In CSA farming, the produce generally given to each subscriber each week.

Season: In CSA farming, the time during which people owning shares can expect to receive a distribution each week. The season will depend on the local climate and the length of the growing season.

Share: In CSA farming, an investment in a proportion of the production of the farm in return for a proportion of the farm harvest, usually distributed weekly during the season.

Subscriber: In CSA farming, a person who buys a share.

---

farm is divided so that every subscriber gets an equal distribution of the harvested products. Often, depending on how the farmer packages the distribution each week, the distribution to each subscriber might also be called a basket or a box. Some CSA farms also sell half shares, where a subscriber pays less money but also receives less product in each distribution.

How a CSA farm works

A traditional, non-CSA farmer decides which crops to plant, pays for the equipment, seed, and other supplies, then plants, tends, and harvests the crops, and finally seeks a buyer for the product. He or she must sell the crop at whatever the market price is at the time of harvest. A traditional farmer has a large financial risk, since he or she does not know how much product will be harvested and at what price the product can be sold. By harvest time, it is too late to change any decisions about the crop being grown. The investment in what to grow has already been made. CSA farming reduces the risk for the farmer because he or she is paid by subscribers before planting. The farmer knows how much seed, fertilizer, and other supplies to buy because he or she knows how much crop the subscribers expect. The farmer also does not need to worry about

Community-Supported Agriculture (CSA)

finding a buyer for his or her harvest, since the farmer is committed to splitting the product the farm produces equally among the subscribers. The farmer usually charges enough per share to earn an income from the labor of running the farm.

The subscribers take on the risk of a bad harvest or crop damage from weather. If there is a hailstorm that destroys the lettuce in the field, the subscribers will not get any lettuce in their distribution that week. (But a traditional farmer would lose all of the money and labor that he had invested in the lettuce crop.) The reward for the subscribers is that when the farm is productive, they will get larger distributions each week. The consumer also has the knowledge that their share in the farm is helpful in building a sustainable food supply. The food that subscribers receive from a CSA farm is fresh, because it is harvested just before each distribution, and it is locally grown. Subscribers also get the benefit of being part of a community—they feel they are part of the farm and the effort to produce some of the food that they eat.

A typical CSA farm is small and produces fruits, vegetables, and herbs. The farmer aims to make each distribution contain enough different fruits and vegetables to provide the produce that a family of four needs for a week. The farm will have two to five acres planted with garden

Tomato plants and lettuce are examined at a CSA farm in Shelbyville, Illinois. The produce will be distributed to shareholders after it is harvested. © AP IMAGES/JOURNAL GAZETTE, SARAH MILLER

fruits and vegetables and have about the same amount of land that is not in production with a cover crop. Cover crops are planted in fields to prevent erosion and improve the soil. The land not in use might also be used as pasturage for animals. The farm will have at least 80 to 100 full-share subscribers, each of whom pays between $300 and $700 per share, and a smaller number of half-share subscribers, who pay between $150 and $350 for each half-share. If the farm has fewer subscribers than this, the farmer will not be able to earn enough money to make a living wage. The farm will distribute food every week from late spring until the middle of the fall, for a total of between twenty and twenty-five distributions. Farms in climates where the growing season is longer will distribute longer, or even for the entire year, whereas farms in the northern part of the United States might only distribute from early June until early October.

CSA farm hands

CSA farming is labor-intensive. One farmer can usually provide the labor needed for two acres. At a maximum, two acres can grow enough produce for no more than 100 subscribers. If the farmer has more land under production, he or she will need to find help for the additional labor. Some CSA farms require each subscriber to help on the farm for a certain number of hours or offer lower-price subscriptions in return for working on the farm. This lowers the farmer's labor costs. Elderly or infirm subscribers often can fulfill their work requirement by helping with washing and sorting the distributions, while younger and healthier subscribers weed and harvest. If the farm is larger than two acres, the farmer will probably reduce labor cost by using machinery and a small tractor, but the CSA farmer will not have as large a carbon footprint as the traditional farmer who uses an array of powered machinery. On the CSA farm, manual labor is used rather than machinery, reducing the need for fossil fuel use, the farm's carbon footprint, and impacts on climate change.

Rotating crops

The farmer will plant different crops throughout the season in order to have a variety of produce for the subscribers each week. The farmer will also plant the same crop at different times, to ensure that some is ready to distribute throughout the season and ensure that, if one crop fails, there will be other produce to put in the distributions. A farm might have forty different crops over the course of a season and plant some crops as often as every ten days to ensure that the crop can be harvested continuously throughout the season. Many of the crops must be started in a greenhouse and then transplanted. The farmer usually harvests two or three times per week. Subscribers pick up their distributions at the end of the harvesting days after the farmer has cleaned, sorted, and divided the week's harvest. Some CSA farms deliver distributions to their subscribers each week. By raising many different crops and rotating where they are planted, the farmer is using a sustainable practice that preserves and improves the soil and naturally prevents plant diseases and pests, reducing the farmer's need to use manufactured pesticides.

Sustainable farming

Most customers of CSA farms buy their shares in part because they wish to support sustainable farming. Usually, CSA customers want local produce that is grown organically using sustainable practices. Most CSA farms therefore avoid the use of artificial pesticides and chemical fertilizers and use farming techniques that, while usually more expensive and less productive than traditional farms, are more sustainable, and require fewer inputs from outside the farm, such as fuel, fertilizer, and pesticide. Instead, farmers use natural fertilization from compost or manure, weed by hand, and control pests by natural means. Another way that CSA farmers promote sustainable practices is to grow varieties of produce that are not available from traditional farms, such as heirloom tomatoes, preserving genetic variation in food crops.

Part of a CSA farmer's marketing strategy is to build a sense of community around the farm and an understanding among his or her subscribers of what CSA farming entails. While the supermarket has tomatoes for

Typical CSA Products

The contents of a CSA distribution change each week according to the season. Here are examples of what one CSA farm delivered to each subscriber in a June week compared to the same CSA farm in an August week:

June

    1 head broccoli

    1 bunch basil

    2 pounds yellow squash

    1 pound zucchini

    1 bunch Swiss chard

    1 bunch red beets

    1 bunch green onions

    1 head red leaf lettuce

    1 bag salad mix

August

    2 pounds potatoes

    6 heirloom tomatoes

    2 pounds green beans

    2 English cucumbers

    3 red/green bell peppers

    8 ears sweet corn

    1 cantaloupe

    1 pint okra

    1 pint yellow pear tomatoes

sale every day of the year, a CSA farm in the northern United States will only have tomatoes for parts of July and August. New CSA customers may not know how to prepare or cook some of the produce they find in their distributions. Many CSA farms publish a newsletter or regularly email their subscribers with suggestions and recipes for upcoming harvests. The newsletter will also keep the subscribers informed about what is happening around the farm. If subscribers need to do work on the farm, the newsletter will include the work schedule.

CSA farmers can also encourage a sense of community in other ways. Some CSA farms donate part of each week's distribution to local food banks or offer free shares to needy families in return for work on the farm. A farmer might offer extra shares at lower cost if the subscriber donates the share to persons in need or take payments over time instead of all at once from families that cannot afford to pay the whole amount before the growing season. Since many CSA farms are fully organic and use sustainable practices, they host field trips for schools so students can learn about sustainable farming, or the farmer may take on and support an intern or apprentice farmer to teach him or her how to run a sustainable farm. Most CSA farmers encourage their subscribers to spend time on the farm to see their produce growing in the field. It is important for the farmer to talk to and listen to his subscribers, to learn what they want to find in their distributions, and to explain to them that some products are too labor-intensive to put in the distribution every week.

CSA extras

CSA farmers may have other business operations on their farms to supplement their income from the CSA or to offer their customers extra services. If the farmer has an orchard or berry bushes, they may offer you-pick berries and fruit at an extra charge, since normally it takes too much labor to pick a pint of berries for every subscriber. Some CSA farmers branch out from just garden produce and raise chickens for meat and eggs or produce cheese from goat or cow milk. Some keep beehives to help with pollination of the plants and also to provide honey and beeswax for sale. Some sell cut flowers or include them in each week's distribution. Two or more CSA farmers might work together in order to provide their subscribers with a greater variety and quantity of produce with each farmer raising what his or her land is best for growing and sharing with the others. Some CSA farms offer delivery of the weekly distribution for a fee. Some sell bread and baked goods made from their own or other farms' produce. By using a variety of crops and sustainable practices, along with good business sense and public relations, a CSA farm can sustainably produce food for many people from a small amount of land while still providing the farmer with an adequate income.

PRIMARY SOURCE
Defining Community Supported Agriculture

Article (excerpt)

By: Suzanne DeMuth

Source: DeMuth, Suzanne. 1993. "Defining Community Supported Agriculture." In *Community Supported Agriculture (CSA): A Annotated Bibliography and Resource Guide.* Washington, DC: USDA National Agricultural Library. This document is available online at http://www.nal.usda.gov/afsic/pubs/csa/csadef.shtml.

About the document: Suzanne DeMuth explains the CSA concept, which was newly imported to the United States from Europe in the early 1990s. She outlines its many benefits, but she could not have known that just twenty years later that CSAs would be instrumental in the rise of organic food, the locavore movement, and urban farming, all of which benefitted from people's increasing interest in healthy agricultural practices and a rejection of monoculture. She also described the economics of the system, which differ vastly from the traditional system of federal subsidies and reliance on commodity crops.

In basic terms, CSA consists of a community of individuals who pledge support to a farm operation so that the farmland becomes, either legally or spiritually, the community's farm, with the growers and consumers providing mutual support and sharing the risks and benefits of food production. Typically, members or "share-holders" of the farm or garden pledge in advance to cover the anticipated costs of the farm operation and farmer's salary. In return, they receive shares in the farm's bounty throughout the growing season, as well as satisfaction gained from reconnecting to the land and participating directly in food production. Members also share in the risks of farming, including poor harvests due to unfavorable weather or pests. By direct sales to community members, who have provided the farmer with working capital in advance, growers receive better prices for their crops, gain some financial security, and are relieved of much of the burden of marketing.

Although CSAs take many forms, all have at their center a shared commitment to building a more local and equitable agricultural system, one that allows growers to focus on land stewardship and still maintain productive and profitable small farms. As stated by Robyn Van En [1948–1997], a leading CSA advocate, "… the main goal … of these community supported projects is to develop participating farms to their highest ecologic potential and to develop a network that will encourage and allow other farms to become involved." CSA farmers typically use organic or biodynamic farming methods, and strive to provide fresh, high-quality foods. More people participate in the farming operation than on conventional farms, and some projects encourage members to work on the farm in exchange for a portion of the membership costs.

Most CSAs offer a diversity of vegetables, fruits, and herbs in season; some provide a full array of farm produce, including shares in eggs, meat, milk, baked goods, and even firewood. Some farms offer a single commodity, or team up with others so that members receive goods on a more nearly year-round basis. Some are dedicated to serving particular community needs, such as helping to enfranchise homeless persons. Each CSA is structured to meet the needs of the participants, so many variations exist, including the level of financial commitment and active participation by the shareholders; financing, land ownership, and legal form of the farm operation; and details of payment plans and food distribution systems.

CSA is sometimes known as "subscription farming," and the two terms have been used on occasion to convey the same basic principles. In other cases, however, use of the latter term is intended to convey philosophic and practical differences in a given farm operation. Subscription farming (or marketing) arrangements tend to emphasize the economic benefits, for the farmer as well as consumer, of a guaranteed, direct market for farm products, rather than the concept of community-building that is the basis of a true CSA. Growers typically contract directly with customers, who may be called "members," and who have agreed in advance to buy a minimum amount of produce at a fixed price, but who have little or no investment in the farm itself. An example of one kind of subscription farm, which predates the first CSAs in this country, is the clientele membership club. According to this plan, which was promoted by Booker Whatley in the early 1980's, a grower could maintain small farm profits by selling low cost memberships to customers who then were allowed to harvest crops at below-market prices.

SEE ALSO Agriculture; Climate Change; Farming, Sustainable; Food Security; Food Systems

For more information

BOOKS
Dawling, Pam. *Sustainable Market Farming: Intensive Vegetable Production on a Few Acres.* Gabriola Island, BC, Canada: New Society Publishers, 2013.

PERIODICALS
Parsons, Russ. "Extending the Reach of Farmers Markets." *Los Angeles Times* (January 16, 2015). Available online at http://www.latimes.com/food/la-fo-future-markets-20150117-story.html (accessed March 12, 2015).

WEBSITES
"Community Supported Agriculture." LocalHarvest. http://www.localharvest.org/csa (accessed December 2, 2014).

"Community Supported Agriculture." USDA National Agricultural Library. http://www.nal.usda.gov/afsic/pubs/csa/csa.shtml (accessed March 12, 2015).

"Community Supported Agriculture 2015 Season." Elmwood Stock Farm. http://www.elmwoodstockfarm.com/csa.htm (accessed March 12, 2015).

"Community Supported Agriculture: An Introduction to CSA." Biodynamic Association. https://www.biodynamics.com/content/community-supported-agriculture-introduction-csa (accessed March 12, 2015).

"Managing a CSA farm." UW-Madison Center for Integrated Agricultural Systems. http://www.cias.wisc.edu/managing-a-csa-farm-1production-labor-and-land (accessed March 12, 2015).

Composting

Compost is a ground-up mixture of natural materials that have been allowed to decay, such as plant clippings, vegetable scraps, and even some kinds of paper. These wastes are decomposed (broken down) into a fine crumbly material by microorganisms and other organisms. The process of decomposition is part of the cycle of life, and composting is a natural way to recycle materials for a sustainable future.

Composting reduces trash and instead puts waste to good use. Worms, bacteria, and insects turn garbage into a valuable product through composting. Some gardeners call it black gold because of its value in improving garden soil. Typical household garbage is about 20 to 30 percent kitchen scraps and yard trimmings. All this natural plant matter can be turned into compost, an enriched soil-like mixture. Once compost has been prepared, it can be mixed into gardens and spread around the base of plants. It creates a rich soil full of nutrients.

Composting

> ### WORDS TO KNOW
>
> **Compost:** A decayed mixture of plants (such as leaves and grass) that can be used to improve the soil in a garden.
>
> **Ecological footprint:** The measure of human stress on the planet's ecosystems. The footprint considers how much land and water resources a population consumes and the ability of the environment to absorb the population's corresponding waste.
>
> **Microorganism:** An extremely small living thing that can only be seen with a microscope.

Composting can also be done on a larger scale. Residents in some communities are able to bring their grass clippings and leaves to a facility to be composted. The results are often used by the communities to amend soil in parks or other municipal grounds. It may also be made available to residents for use in their own yards or gardens. The largest scale of composting is done by commercial companies that collect organic materials from citizens or other companies.

What goes into a compost pile?

A compost pile is carefully stacked with both fresh and old plant matter. Gardeners and others who compost identify four essential materials—greens, browns, water, and air.

- Greens for nitrogen: Spring/summer leaves, weeds, grass clippings, vegetable and fruit peels and pits, eggshells.
- Browns for carbon: Autumn leaves, hay, dead branches or twigs, paper, sawdust, nutshells, fireplace ashes.
- Water for moisture: Compost piles must be damp. If the materials are too dry they will not break down. If they are too wet the pile becomes mushy and does not become useable compost.
- Air for organisms: The microorganisms and other decomposers must have oxygen to do their jobs. Compost piles need to be turned over several times for air to reach all parts of the mixture.

Make a compost pile A compost pile or bin should be in a dry, partially shady spot. The browns and greens should be stacked in layers, and moistened as they are layered. The best ratio is three parts brown to one part green. Food scraps should be at least 10 inches (25 centimeters) down to avoid attracting unwanted animals. The materials will break down, causing the compost pile to heat up. Sometimes it will even steam in the cold of winter. The mixture can take several months to mature. The compost pile needs to be turned a few times so that it will decompose evenly.

The finished compost will be dark and crumbly when it is ready to use. The compost can be spread thinly over a lawn or mixed into the soil of a garden. It also can be dug into the soil under shrubs and around the base of trees.

Why it matters

There are many benefits to composting. Composted vegetable matter will:

- Enrich the soil, help retain water, and improve root growth in plants.
- Reduce the need for chemical fertilizers and pesticides, thus reducing environmental pollution.
- Keep food scraps and yard waste out of landfills. This uses less space and helps reduce methane gas emissions, which contribute to global warming and climate change.
- Lower your ecological footprint.

Composting is easy if the composter learns to think in greens and browns. A simple way to get started is by recycling leaves and grass clippings. Composting can save money and reduce the amount of waste sent to landfill by converting household waste and food scraps into usable materials.

SEE ALSO Agriculture; Climate Change; Ecological Footprint; Farming, Sustainable; Food Waste; Pesticides; Waste Management

For more information

BOOKS
Appelhof, Mary. *Worms Eat My Garbage: How to Set Up and Maintain a Worm Composting System*, 2nd ed. Illustrated by Mary Frances Fenton. Kalamazoo, MI: Flower Press, 2003.
Pears, Pauline. *The Organic Book of Compost: Easy and Natural Techniques to Feed Your Garden.* Springville, UT: Cedar Fort, 2013.

PERIODICALS

Higgins, Adrian. "How to Compost, and Why It's a Good Idea." *Washington Post* (October 17, 2014). Available online at http://www.washingtonpost.com/lifestyle/home/recycle-autumn-leaves-by-composting/2014/10/15/225e22a0-4f19-11e4-babe-e91da079cb8a_story.html (accessed March 26, 2015).

WEBSITES

"Composting at Home." United States Environmental Protection Agency, October 6, 2014. http://www2.epa.gov/recycle/composting-home (accessed March 26, 2015).

"Small Scale or Backyard Composting." Cornell Waste Management Institute. http://cwmi.css.cornell.edu/smallscale.htm (accessed March 26, 2015).

Comprehensive Environmental Response, Compensation, and Liability Act (CERCLA)

The Comprehensive Environmental Response, Compensation, and Liability Act (CERCLA) of 1980 is the U.S. federal law that requires and regulates the cleanup of hazardous waste sites that have polluted the air, soil, surface water, or groundwater in the surrounding area. More commonly known as the Superfund law, CERCLA is administered by the Environmental Protection Agency (EPA). CERCLA plays an important role in working toward sustainability in the United States by helping to repair and reclaim severely polluted abandoned hazardous waste sites.

Superfund sites are those that have been environmentally degraded through industrial processes or the dumping of toxic waste materials. The soil and water at these sites may be contaminated with chemicals and toxins such as cyanide, lead, arsenic, heavy metals, benzene, xylene, and radioactive substances. Prior to the 1950s, the dangers of many industrial chemicals were not well understood, and, as a result, their disposal was not regulated. The new law provided the legal framework requiring manufacturers or landowners to clean up contaminated sites.

As of 2015 there were 1,368 sites on the EPA's Superfund National Priorities List (NPL), which is the list of hazardous waste sites eligible for Superfund financing for cleanup. Over the years, 1,166 sites have been cleaned up and removed from the list. The EPA identifies the potential

Comprehensive Environmental Response, Compensation, and Liability Act (CERCLA)

WORDS TO KNOW

Bioremediation: Using living organisms to remove pollution from the environment.

CERCLA: Comprehensive Environmental Response, Compensation, and Liability Act, the U.S. federal law that requires and regulates the cleanup of hazardous waste sites. Also known as the Superfund law.

Hazardous waste: Waste that can be solid, liquid, or gas and that is harmful to living things and the environment. Hazardous waste can be discarded commercial products, like cleaning fluids or pesticides, or the by-products of manufacturing processes.

responsible party (PRP) for the contamination and sees that the PRP pays to have the site cleaned up. About 70 percent of Superfund sites have been cleaned up by the PRP. If the PRP no longer exists—for example, if the company has gone out of business—the Superfund program itself may pay the cleanup costs. These government funds have been collected through a tax on the oil and chemical industries.

When a site is brought to the attention of the EPA, it is evaluated according to the Hazard Ranking System to see if it meets the NPL criteria. The rankings range from 0 to 100, and a score of 28.5 or higher will earn the site a spot on the NPL. To meet the criteria, the site's health risks are evaluated. A site that presents an immediate health risk has a good chance of ending up on the NPL.

Cleaning up hazardous waste sites takes two forms: removal of waste and remediation of the land. Removing waste is a time-sensitive action

The town of Picher, Oklahoma, part of the Tar Creek Superfund Site, is seen among huge lead-laced piles of rock on April, 6, 2008. Years of mining led to giant piles of chat mine tailings laced with zinc and lead that blew toxic dust into the air. Heavy metals also seeped into the groundwater. Most residents had left by 2014. © AP IMAGES/CHARLIE RIEDEL

U•X•L Sustainable Living

141

that requires carting away drums of chemicals or other physical waste that immediately threaten the health of those in the area. Remediating the land involves making the site permanently safe by removing contaminants from the soil and making it suitable for new development. Large amounts of soil and contaminated vegetation are often removed and taken to approved hazardous waste sites. The soil is then replaced with clean, nonpolluted soil. Bioremediation, or treatment that uses microorganisms to clean the soil or water, may be done if appropriate.

An important amendment to CERCLA was the 1986 Emergency Planning and Community Right-to-Know Act, which requires manufacturers or any company that uses hazardous substances on the premises to report publically which substances they release into the environment and how much. Citizens can see what is emitted in the environment in their neighborhoods by consulting the EPA's Toxic Release Inventory website.

CERCLA was inspired by a neighborhood in Niagara, New York, called Love Canal. In the 1950s, a school and a neighborhood were unknowingly built on land that had previously been used by a chemical company as a toxic waste dump. By the 1970s many residents were suffering from serious health problems, and an investigation led to the discovery of the toxic waste. The government relocated eight hundred families and bulldozed the town.

SEE ALSO Hazardous Waste; Soil Pollution

For more information

PERIODICALS

Drange, Matt, and Susanne Rust. "Toxic Trail: The Weak Points in the Superfund Waste System." *The Guardian* (March 17, 2014). Available online at http://www.theguardian.com/environment/2014/mar/17/toxic-trail-weak-points-superfund-waste (accessed March 25, 2015).

WEBSITES

"CERCLA Overview." U.S. Environmental Protection Agency, updated December 12, 2011. http://www.epa.gov/superfund/policy/cercla.htm (accessed March 25, 2015).

"National Priorities List (NPL)." U.S. Environmental Protection Agency, updated October 17, 2013. http://www.epa.gov/superfund/sites/npl/ (accessed April 2, 2015).

"Toxic Release Inventory (TRI) Program." U.S. Environmental Protection Agency, updated March 20, 2015. http://www2.epa.gov/toxics-release-inventory-tri-program (accessed March 25, 2015).

Conservation

Conservation is the protection of natural resources. This includes plants and animals, and their habitats. Through conservation, people work to use resources only as needed and prevent the loss of resources and biodiversity. Conservation is similar to preservation. But conservation is about the proper use of nature, and preservation is about protecting nature from use.

Using a resource wisely is conservation. Not using a resource at all is preservation. We conserve water and energy by using it wisely. We preserve national parks by keeping them in their state of natural beauty. Conserving resources is a big part of sustainable development. Only by efficient use of water, land, plants, and animals can we sustain our way of life so future generations can enjoy a similar bounty.

The U.S. conservation movement

In the United States the conservation movement dates back to 1854 with the publication of Henry David Thoreau's *Walden*. Thoreau was a naturalist and philosopher. He believed in living close to nature in a state of simplicity and self-reliance. Thoreau's ideas captured the imagination of the American public.

Dietrich Brandis (1824–1907) was a German botanist who influenced early conservation policy. He developed a systematic way to harvest trees for lumber and paper. His method included replanting forests as they were harvested. This method kept the lumber industry going and avoided deforestation.

Gifford Pinchot (1865–1946) adopted the ideas of Brandis. Pinchot became the first chief of the U.S. Forest Service in 1905. Pinchot coined the term *conservation ethic*. He defined conservation as meaning "the greatest good to the greatest number for the longest time." This included developing the country's natural resources to further its economic growth. Despite Pinchot's important role in forest management and conservation, some of his beliefs would not be considered sustainable today.

The conservation movement continued to grow between 1890 and 1920. This time period is known as the Progressive Era. President Theodore Roosevelt (1858–1919; served 1901–1909) enacted many new policies during this time in an effort to stop the destruction of the country's natural resources. He disliked overhunting of mammals and birds that brought some

Conservation

WORDS TO KNOW

Biodiversity: The variety of species or organisms in a given environment or ecosystem. A large range of plant and animal life in a given region is symptomatic of its health; a narrow range or declining number of species in a region may indicate environmental damage or stress.

Conservation: The protection of natural resources, plants and animals, and their habitats to prevent unnecessary loss of resources or biodiversity.

Deforestation: Removing trees from a forest, especially to the point that the forested area is cleared.

Preservation: The maintenance of wilderness areas in an undisturbed state.

Hikers navigate water and rocks within a canyon called "The Narrows" in Zion National Park, Utah. NATIONAL PARK SERVICE PHOTO/MARC NEIDIG

species to the brink of extinction. Roosevelt outlawed commercial hunting and was a founding member of the Boone and Crockett Club in 1887. This club was named after American frontiersmen Daniel Boone (1734–1820) and Davy Crockett (1786–1836). It was the first organization to seek protection of federal lands from overhunting.

The Boone and Crockett Club also promoted the expansion of the National Park System, the National Forest Service, and the National Wildlife Refuge system. Their collective actions became known as the North American Model of Wildlife Conservation. This system promotes the ideas that wildlife should only be killed for legitimate reasons, not for sport, and that wildlife policy should be guided by science.

The modern conservation movement

Conservation became an important issue in the 1930s during the Great Depression. A serious drought in the Plains states destroyed millions of acres of farmland. Poor farming practices made the situation worse. Thousands of families suffered financial ruin and hunger in what became known as the Dust Bowl. President Franklin Roosevelt created the Civilian Conservation Corps (CCC) in 1933 to address the situation.

The CCC was a work relief program. It employed three million men on federal and state-owned lands to conserve natural resources. Workers planted three billion trees and constructed the foundation for 800 parks across the country.

Aldo Leopold (1887–1948) began his career in game management, and his interest in ecology and conservation grew. Leopold began writing and teaching about the natural world and developed the idea of "land ethic," or the right of nature to continue existing, and the role people play in protecting nature. His most important writing was the 1949 book titled *A Sand County Almanac*. Although the book was not published until after Leopold died, his writing expressed the message of conservation and helped inspire readers to take action. Leopold also helped found the U.S. Wilderness Society, and many people call him the father of U.S. wildlife management.

Conservation efforts took a back seat to other events during and after World War II (1939–1945). Interest in conservation was revived in the 1960s. At this time, leaders of many countries, including the United States, realized that they had high levels of water, soil, and air pollution. The first Earth Day in 1970 raised public awareness and led to an increase in public understanding of acid rain, ozone depletion, and climate change. New laws in the late 1960s and throughout the 1970s established the foundation of the modern U.S. conservation movement. The Clean Air Act was passed in 1963. The Environmental Protection Agency was formed in 1970 and the Clean Water Act was passed in 1972.

Aldo Leopold. © EVERETT COLLECTION HISTORICAL/ ALAMY

Conservation worldwide

One of the most important conservation issues facing the world today is deforestation. Deforestation is the removal of trees from forested areas. This is a very big problem in rain forests, which are the most biodiverse regions on the earth. Conserving the rain forests is important because they are thought to contain more than half of all plant and animal species

Conservation

Conservation vs. Preservation: The Hetch Hetchy Dam

The Hetch Hetchy dam and reservoir in Tuolumne County, California, provides water for the two million people who live in the San Francisco Bay area. In 1919, when the project was proposed, it was controversial because it would disrupt the Tuolumne River in Yosemite National Park. The park was protected in 1864 by President Abraham Lincoln. It had since become the crown jewel of the new National Park System. Conservationists and preservationists debated the merits of building the dam. Conservationists believed the dam was necessary to supply water to the growing population of the Bay Area. Preservationists argued that Yosemite National Park was to be preserved as pristine wilderness and was off limits to development because it was designated as a national park. Ultimately, the conservationists won, and Congress signed an act that allowed construction of the dam on the federally protected Tuolumne River. In the twenty-first century, preservationist groups such as the Sierra Club have advocated for removing the dam to restore the valley to its original state.

The Hetch Hetchy Dam in Yosemite National Park. © RADOSLAW LECYK/SHUTTERSTOCK.COM

on earth. Millions of life forms surviving in rain forests have not yet been classified by scientists.

Millions of acres in the Amazon Rainforest have been clearcut or burned to extend agriculture and grazing land for cattle. The lush canopies of trees hold and store vast quantities of carbon dioxide. When these trees are cut down and burned, the stored carbon dioxide enters the atmosphere, contributes to global warming, and prevents future carbon dioxide from being absorbed.

Global conservation of water is another issue of extreme importance. Most fresh water worldwide is used for agriculture, but households, manufacturing, and energy production also require vast amounts of water. The United Nations sponsors World Water Day each March 22 to raise awareness of water conservation issues. UN-Water is an agency that works with countries to conserve fresh water in both developed and developing countries around the world. Keeping water as a safe resource that people can access is an issue that exemplifies conservation and sustainability. All life requires clean water. The resource needs to be conserved so people today and in future generations continue to have access to it.

PRIMARY SOURCE

Hetch Hetchy Valley

Book chapter (excerpt)

By: John Muir

Source: Muir, John. "Hetch Hetchy Valley." In *The Yosemite.* New York: Century, 1912. This book is available online at https://www.gutenberg.org/files/7091/7091-h/7091-h.htm.

About the document: John Muir (1838–1914) was a naturalist, biologist, and activist and the founder of the Sierra Club, one of the most influential conservation organizations in the United States. In *The Yosemite,* Muir champions the national park that he was instrumental in founding. In this excerpt from Chapter 16, he rails against plans to build a dam on the Tuolumne River in Yosemite's Hetch Hetchy Valley. Nevertheless, the dam was built in 1923 and the valley disappeared beneath the reservoir. The Sierra Club and other conservationists continue to lobby in the twenty-first century to dismantle the dam and restore the valley.

It appears, therefore, that Hetch Hetchy Valley, far from being a plain, common, rock-bound meadow, as many who have not seen it seem to suppose, is a grand landscape garden, one of Nature's rarest and most precious mountain temples. As in Yosemite, the sublime rocks of its walls seem to glow with life, whether leaning back in repose or standing erect in thoughtful attitudes, giving welcome to storms and calms alike, their brows in the sky, their feet set in the groves and gay flowery meadows, while birds, bees, and butterflies help the river and waterfalls to stir all the air into music—things frail and fleeting and types of permanence meeting here and blending, just as they do in Yosemite, to draw her lovers into close and confiding communion with her.

Sad to say, this most precious and sublime feature of the Yosemite National Park, one of the greatest of all our natural resources for the uplifting joy and peace and health of the people, is in danger of being dammed and made into a reservoir to help supply San Francisco with water and light, thus flooding it from wall to wall and burying its gardens and groves one or two hundred feet deep. This grossly destructive commercial scheme has long been planned and urged (though water as pure and abundant can be got from outside of the people's park, in a dozen different places), because of the comparative cheapness of the dam and of the territory which it is sought to divert from the great uses to which it was dedicated in the Act of 1890 establishing the Yosemite National Park….

The most delightful and wonderful camp grounds in the Park are its three great valleys—Yosemite, Hetch Hetchy, and Upper Tuolumne; and they are also the most important places with reference to their positions relative to the other great features—the Merced and Tuolumne Cañons, and the High Sierra peaks and glaciers, etc., at the head of the rivers. The main part of the Tuolumne Valley is a spacious flowery lawn four or five miles long, surrounded by magnificent snowy mountains, slightly separated from other beautiful meadows, which together make a series about twelve miles in length, the highest reaching to the feet of Mount Dana, Mount Gibbs, Mount Lyell and Mount McClure. It is about 8500 feet above the sea, and forms the grand central High Sierra camp ground from which excursions are made to the noble mountains, domes, glaciers, etc.; across the Range to the Mono Lake and volcanoes and down the Tuolumne Cañon to Hetch Hetchy. Should Hetch Hetchy be submerged for a reservoir, as proposed, not only would it be utterly destroyed, but the sublime cañon way to the heart of the High Sierra would be hopelessly blocked and the great camping ground, as the watershed of a city drinking system, virtually would be closed to the public. So far as I have learned, few of all the thousands who have seen the park and seek rest and peace in it are in favor of this outrageous scheme….

That any one would try to destroy such a place seems incredible; but sad experience shows that there are people good enough and bad enough for anything. The proponents of the dam scheme bring forward a lot of bad arguments to prove that the only righteous thing to do with the people's parks is to destroy them bit by bit as they are able. Their arguments are curiously like those of the devil, devised for the destruction of the first garden—so much of the very best Eden fruit going to waste; so much of the best Tuolumne water and Tuolumne scenery going to waste. Few of their statements are even partly true, and all are misleading….

These temple destroyers, devotees of ravaging commercialism, seem to have a perfect contempt for Nature, and, instead of lifting their eyes to the God of the mountains, lift them to the Almighty Dollar.

Dam Hetch Hetchy! As well dam for water-tanks the people's cathedrals and churches, for no holier temple has ever been consecrated by the heart of man.

SEE ALSO Environmental Law; Environmental Policy; Preservation

For more information

BOOKS

Hambler, Clive, and Susan M. Canney. *Conservation.* New York: Cambridge University Press, 2004.

Pinchot, Gifford. *The Fight for Conservation.* Reprint. Whitefish, MT: Kessinger, 2009.

WEBSITES

Conservation Databases. IUCN. http://www.iucn.org/knowledge/tools/databases/ (accessed April 17, 2015).

"Conservation vs Preservation and the National Park Service." National Park Service. http://www.nps.gov/klgo/learn/education/classrooms/conservation-vs-preservation.htm (accessed April 16, 2015).

"The North American Model of Wildlife Conservation." The Wildlife Society. http://joomla.wildlife.org/documents/positionstatements/41-NAModel%20Position%20Statementfinal.pdf (accessed April 16, 2015).

UN Water. http://www.unwater.org/ (accessed April 17, 2015).

Consumption

Consumption is the process of buying new items, using them for a while, and then disposing of the used product. It is related to consumerism, in which a society and its economy are largely ordered around the acquisition of material goods in increasingly greater amounts. Both terms are used in the study of economics to describe the goals and values of market-driven economies (those countries where the economy depends upon people's spending habits). In the sustainability movement, both consumption and consumerism are viewed more negatively because they encourage waste and can become a major focus of people's lives. Advocates of sustainability maintain—and science increasingly agrees—that

Consumption

> ## WORDS TO KNOW
>
> **Consumerism:** The devotion of a great deal of time, energy, resources, and thought to buying more things.
>
> **Ethical:** Following accepted rules of behavior.
>
> **G.I. Bill:** The common name for a bill passed by Congress called the Servicemen's Readjustment Act of 1944. The bill provided government aid to service personnel after World War II (1939–1945).
>
> **Sustainable:** Able to maintain present levels of growth without damage to the environment or people.

consumerism and excess consumption are not only damaging to the earth but also destructive to individual wellbeing.

Background

The second half of the twentieth century is known for producing perhaps the largest consumption economy in history, particularly in the United States. After the Great Depression of the 1930s and the rationing of World War II (1939–1945), Americans were eager to leave behind the hardship they had suffered since the economic crash of 1929. Troops returned home from the war to jobs with high wages, and the G.I. Bill allowed many to finish high school and attend college. Suburban housing developments appeared with affordable single-family homes, all of which had to be furnished and outfitted with the latest technological breakthroughs in cooking, cleaning, and entertainment products. Car sales increased as suburbanites needed to drive from their new homes to their jobs in the city. And the newfound social and consumer optimism lead to an unprecedented increase in the birth rate until about 1957, when births began to taper off. The "Baby Boom" required increased spending, ushering in a new era of the American Dream.

Twentieth-century consumerist culture was shaped by the advertising industry, which reached its high point in the 1950s and 1960s, when televisions became a fixture in the American home. From the start, many television advertisements were aimed at children, a population particularly vulnerable to advertising's consumerist messages. In the early twenty-first century, advertising to children had spread to the Internet and even school cafeterias. According to Lucia Moses of *Adweek,* in 2014 American children ages two to eleven were exposed to 25,600 advertisements annually. Advertisers refer to children as "gatekeepers," meaning that they strongly influence household buying habits because they see more ads than adults and have not yet developed the intellectual discernment to make informed decisions. Psychologists and pediatricians, meanwhile, have raised alarms about the effects of exposure to advertising on children's physical and emotional health.

Since the mid-twentieth century, the world's population has consumed more goods and services than all previous generations of people combined. Even though consumption has promoted economic growth and a better quality of life for many people, it has also contributed to social and environmental problems. Consistently high demand for goods has led corporations to relocate work to countries with few or no labor laws. This keeps prices low so that people in developed countries can continue to buy the products, but it also exploits workers in poorer countries, who earn pennies on the dollar and work in dangerous conditions. Additionally, consumption societies use more resources and cause greater environmental damage than those in which consumption is limited. This inequality has created a divide between developed and developing countries, particularly the United States compared with other nations. According to *Scientific American* magazine, as of 2012, "Americans account for only five percent of the world's population but create half of the globe's solid waste," with an average American consuming about fifty-three times more goods and services than the average citizen of China.

Seafood is for sale at the Tsukiji fish market in Japan. The market is one of the biggest fish markets in the world. Rising human population and consumption put pressure on wildlife and natural resources and lead to many environmental problems. © JEERAWUT RITYAKUL/SHUTTERSTOCK.COM

Consumption

Consumption and sustainability

According to the U.S. Environmental Protection Agency, every person in the United States disposed of about 4.4 pounds (2 kilograms) of garbage per day in 2013, resulting in a total of 254 million tons (226 million metric tons) of waste material for the country's population as a whole. Likewise, the Sierra Club's Dave Tilford says, "A child born in the United States will create thirteen times as much ecological damage over the course of his or her lifetime as a child born in Brazil." This latter figure accounts not just for waste but for total usage of natural resources in products purchased. Earth cannot sustain this consumption lifestyle indefinitely. As other countries around the world are increasingly adopting American consumption habits, resources are running out. People must become aware of how their daily activities impact the world and the environment in which they live. Citizens have a duty to examine the impact of their daily actions on the environment. It is often difficult to see how small actions people do in their everyday life—such as traveling, shopping, technology use, water consumption, and waste disposal—have an immediate impact on the environment, the economy, and society.

Sustainable consumption is the consumption of goods and services that has significantly less impact on the environment and encourages social justice. A sustainable consumption commitment seeks alternative methods for meeting the basic needs of people worldwide and encourages all countries, social classes, and economies to help change the current consumption lifestyle to a more sustainable lifestyle. A sustainability-focused society would embrace a wide range of social, economic, and political practices that would support the reduction of products that damage the environment. This type of society would provide all global citizens with the basic necessities—such as water, health care, food, and shelter—in addition to producing goods and services that promote a better quality of life for everyone. For example, a sustainable society would support the development of energy- and water-efficient appliances and promote public transportation systems. It would also promote lifestyles that value the ethical and just treatment of every citizen, including the diverse cultures and traditions by which they live.

For society to adopt sustainable consumption, it must educate its citizens to be aware and supportive of any new community, government, or industry recommendation that seeks to improve stewardship of the environment and address social-justice issues. Further, it must teach everyone to discard the values of consumption and replace them with values of sustainability in the goods and services purchased. Research has indicated that personal happiness not only is not associated with increased ownership of material goods but can actually be impeded by a lifestyle heavily dependent upon consumption, in part because of a psychological phenomenon called *hedonic adaptation,* which means that once people get used to a new item their happiness and interest in it wears off and they must seek something new to achieve the same feeling of excitement. This cycle of constant novelty-seeking feeds into the consumerist lifestyle and is believed to contribute to a number of social ills, from depression to addiction, in addition to causing damage to the ecosystem.

As awareness of the importance of sustainable consumption grows, consumers are increasingly demanding products with longer lifespans and more environmentally and socially conscious manufacturing methods. They want to be informed of how production affects workers and resources across the globe. In response, many countries including the United States have outlined energy-efficiency standards for household appliances such as refrigerators, air conditioners, washers and dryers, heaters, ovens, and lighting. Standards for lighting efficiency, power savings, and recycling have been introduced into the United States through the Energy Star Program, and there are regulations for new cars to reduce energy use as well as mandatory health labeling on consumer products. The U.S. Food and Drug Administration (FDA) issued a regulation that requires manufacturers to list trans fats, genetically modified ingredients, and organic food claims. Corporations have caught on to the trend toward

The Human Cost of Cheap Products

A culture of consumption demands the constant availability of low-cost items to satisfy the desire for novelty. What is rarely considered, however, is how manufacturers can afford to keep prices so low and still earn a profit. The answer is overseas labor, where labor laws often are nonexistent and human rights routinely violated.

Less than 1 percent of the final cost of a product made offshore is paid to the workers. Those workers make, on average, 15 to 25 cents per hour. If a consumer pays US$50 for an item, workers in another country receive less than 50 cents for producing it, and this amount is far below what they need for even the most basic sustenance. As an example, in the Ocean Sky Apparel factory in El Salvador, women are paid 8 cents for every US$25 National Football League (NFL) T-shirt they sew. The Salvadoran Ministry of the Economy puts the workers' wages (72 cents an hour) at one-quarter of a family's basic needs.

Nearly four in ten clothing and apparel items for sale in the United States and Canada are made in China, where workers who labor in sweatshops are forbidden to organize to improve work conditions. Factories often make use of child and prison labor. Entire generations of families are compromised in these situations.

Typical sweatshop employees, 90 percent women, are young (ages 16 to 25) and uneducated. Eight in ten products purchased by the consumer class (living mainly in North America, Western Europe, Japan, Australia/New Zealand, and affluent Middle East) are made by girls aged twelve to fourteen who are on the assembly line rather than in school.

sustainability and have begun allying themselves with various organizations that promote social and ethical responsibility. Originally intended for coffee, tea, and banana growers, the Fairtrade labeling system has been adopted by the makers of more than two thousand products. Other types of labeling systems, like that of the Rainforest Alliance, identify products that use sustainable forestry practices, preserve biodiversity, and treat workers fairly.

Consumption and citizenship

Citizens have a responsibility to be aware of the potential for environmental improvements through the use of best practices, such as industry standards and mandatory labels, sustainability education, voluntary labeling, and alternative advertising. More important to ensure change, however, is a widespread commitment to action. Through behavior like voting and exercising their purchasing power, citizens can influence public policy and industry methods. Nonprofit organizations like Campaign for a Commercial-Free Childhood offer practical information and advice for families hoping to cut down on their consumption and also lobby for change at the legislative level. In her groundbreaking 2010 book *The Story of Stuff: The Impact of Overconsumption on the Planet, Our Communities, and Our Health—And How We Can Make It Better,* activist Annie Leonard writes: "We need to radically reduce the overall demand for the materials being extracted. We need to increase the efficiency or productivity of resources used and ramp up reuse and recycling programs. Finally, we need to seek out alternative ways to meet our needs, which, for many, means less focus on a constant flow of new Stuff."

SEE ALSO Abundance; Carrying Capacity; Citizenship; Economics; Fair Trade; Green Economy; Local Economy

For more information

BOOKS

Leonard, Annie. *The Story of Stuff: The Impact of Overconsumption on the Planet, Our Communities, and Our Health—And How We Can Make It Better.* New York: Free Press, 2010.

McGregor, Sue L. T. *Consumer Moral Leadership.* Rotterdam, Netherlands, and Boston: Sense Publishers, 2010.

Wright, Erik Olin, and Joel Rogers. *American Society: How it Really Works.* 2nd ed. New York: Norton, 2015.

PERIODICALS

Moses, Lucia. "A Look at Kids' Exposure to Ads." *Adweek* (March 11, 2014). Available online at http://www.adweek.com/news/advertising-branding/look-kids-exposure-ads-156191 (accessed May 7, 2015).

Scheer, Roddy, and Doug Moss. "Use It and Lose It: The Outsize Effect of U.S. Consumption on the Environment." *Scientific American* (September 14, 2012). Available online at http://www.scientificamerican.com/article/american-consumption-habits/ (accessed August 4, 2015).

Watson, Bruce. "The Tricky Business of Advertising to Children." *The Guardian* (February 24, 2014). Available online at http://www.theguardian.com/sustainable-business/advertising-to-children-tricky-business-subway (accessed March 27, 2015).

WEBSITES

Campaign for a Commercial-Free Childhood. http://commercialfreechildhood.org/ (accessed May 7, 2015).

"Municipal Solid Waste." U.S. Environmental Protection Agency. http://www.epa.gov/epawaste/nonhaz/municipal/index.htm (accessed July 20, 2015).

"Promoting Sustainable Consumption: Good Practices in OECD Countries." Organisation for Economic Co-operation and Development, January 1, 2008. http://www.oecd.org/greengrowth/40317373.pdf (accessed December 16, 2014).

"The Rise of American Consumerism." American Experience. http://www.pbs.org/wgbh/americanexperience/features/general-article/tupperware-consumer/ (accessed December 16, 2014).

"Sustainability Concepts: Sustainable Consumption." Global Development Research Center. http://www.gdrc.org/sustdev/concepts/22-s-consume.html (accessed December 16, 2014).

"Youth, Sustainable Consumption Patterns and Life Styles." United Nations Educational, Scientific and Cultural Organization. http://unesdoc.unesco.org/images/0012/001242/124238e.pdf (accessed December 16, 2014).

Coral Reefs

See **Ecosystems.**

Cradle-to-Cradle Design

Cradle-to-cradle design, often called C2C or regenerative design, is the process of manufacturing products in a closed-loop cycle to save natural resources and energy. This eliminates waste and promotes sustainability. Just as the water cycle and the nitrogen cycle are closed-loop systems

Cradle-to-Cradle Design

WORDS TO KNOW

Biological nutrient: An organic, biodegradable material that can be returned to the earth as food for another organism.

Circular economy: A regenerative manufacturing economy in which the material inputs are designed to either flow back into the natural world safely or be reused to create new products indefinitely. Circular economies are prime models of sustainable practices.

Closed-loop system: A system that does not rely on matter exchange from outside the system, instead relying on its output as its input. An example in nature is the water cycle of condensation, evaporation, and precipitation.

Cradle-to-cradle design: The manufacture of products in a closed-loop cycle to save natural resources and energy. All used goods are either broken down into components that are recycled and made into other goods or returned to the earth as food for organisms in the soil.

Regenerative design: Design systems created to restore and/or renew their own sources of materials and energy. Regenerative design is a sustainable design process.

Technical nutrient: A synthetic material that can be continually reused without becoming degraded or entering the waste stream.

---

that sustain life on earth, C2C design works to mimic natural closed-loop processes. C2C is a key concept of the emerging theory of circular economy. Circular economics encourages lengthening the time material products are useful and reusing their materials whenever possible. This limits unsustainable overconsumption of natural resources. C2C design is in contrast to traditional cradle-to-grave design, in which resources are used and then sent to a landfill or incinerator when no longer needed.

The term *cradle-to-cradle* was coined in the 1970s by Walter Stahel (1946–), a Swiss architect and early advocate of sustainability. The C2C design concept was created by William McDonough (1951–), an American architect, and Michael Braungart (1958–), a German chemist. Wide-scale adoption of the process has been slow, but some companies have incorporated elements of it into their manufacturing plans. For instance, one company has created a shoe made of natural materials that are all found within 200 miles (320 kilometers) of the factory. Additionally, no toxic adhesives hold the shoe together, the leather is colored with vegetable dye, and the laces are made of renewable biodegradable hemp. When the buyer is done with the shoes, they can be returned to the manufacturer, which grinds them up and turns them into other products.

Cradle-to-cradle process

In the C2C process, materials are called "nutrients" and are categorized as either technical or biological. A "technical nutrient" is a synthetic material that can be continually reused without becoming degraded or entering the waste stream. Steel is an example of a technical nutrient. A "biological nutrient" is an organic biodegradable material that can be returned to the earth, like wood, which becomes a food source for microbes and improves soil quality. An example of a C2C product is a specially manufactured wool fabric that is grown and dyed organically. The waste trimmings from the wool are used as garden fertilizer. The dye itself is made from organic materials, not toxins. In the C2C process, manufacturing wastes become food for some other form of life.

The C2C process requires consumers to return the used product to the manufacturer so its materials can be disassembled and reused properly. Habits can be hard to change, and this new way of thinking and behaving may take people time to learn. Consumers are accustomed to throwing things away when they are finished with them. Another criticism is that the use of the product needs to be considered in addition to its manufacturing and recycling. For example, a car made of biological and technical nutrients may still burn nonrenewable fossil fuels and contribute to climate change. The car itself is sustainable, but its use is not.

Cradle-to-cradle certification

C2C design is used in urban planning, product packaging, and industrial design. As of 2012, basic, silver, gold, and platinum certifications are awarded through the Cradle to Cradle Products Innovation Institute, a nonprofit organization. In order for a product to be certified, it needs to meet five criteria: (1) materials need to be assessed as being low risk, meaning they do not present a hazard to people or the environment; (2) materials must be able to be recovered and recycled at the end of the product's life; (3) energy required for production of goods should come from renewable sources, such as wind or sun; (4) water used in the manufacturing process should be used sparingly and discharged cleanly; and (5) management must engage in fair labor practices. Products that have earned certification include household paints, cleaning products, building materials, fabrics, and beauty products. Products manufactured using these C2C criteria are sustainably produced.

SEE ALSO Industrial Ecology; Zero Waste

For more information

BOOKS

McDonough, William, and Michael Braungart. *Cradle to Cradle: Remaking the Way We Make Things.* New York: Vintage, 2002.

McDonough, William, and Michael Braungart. *The Upcycle: Beyond Sustainability—Designing for Abundance.* New York: North Point Press, 2013.

PERIODICALS

Sherwin, Chris. "Sustainable Design 2.0: New Models and Methods." *The Guardian* (January 14, 2013). Available online at http://www.theguardian.com/sustainable-business/blog/sustainable-design-models-methods-biomimicry-cradle (accessed March 26, 2015).

WEBSITES

"Ask the Experts: Why Hasn't Cradle-to-Cradle Design Caught on Yet?" Treehugger, April 18, 2012. http://www.treehugger.com/sustainable-product-design/ask-experts-why-hasnt-cradle-to-cradle-design-caught-on-yet.html (accessed March 26, 2015).

"Aveda Sets Groundbreaking Standard in Sustainability for Beauty Industry." PR Newswire. http://www.prnewswire.com/news-releases/aveda-sets-groundbreaking-standard-in-sustainability-for-beauty-industry-62003462.html (accessed April 13, 2015).

"Cradle to Cradle." The Product-Life Institute. http://www.product-life.org/en/cradle-to-cradle (accessed March 26, 2015).

Cradle to Cradle Products Innovation Institute. http://www.c2ccertified.org/ (accessed March 26, 2015).

McDonough, William, and Michael Braungart. "The Cradle-to-Cradle Alternative." William McDonough, 2003. http://www.mcdonough.com/speaking-writing/the-cradle-to-cradle-alternative/#.VRQPdijLLaI (accessed March 26, 2015).

CSA

See **Community-Supported Agriculture (CSA).**

D

Dams
See **Hydropower.**

Deep Ecology

Deep ecology is an environmental philosophy in which the value of human life is no greater than the value of any other organism's life. Stated another way, all life has value, and diversity of life adds to that value. Deep ecologists hold that humans should not be controllers of nature but should understand that they exist as part of nature. They feel that some modern ecologists, who believe that humans must limit their use of ecosystem resources to what the earth can replace while sustaining a high level of human development, do not go far enough. Every organism on earth is important to its ecosystem and contributes to the health of the whole planet; therefore, humans must also contribute to the health of the whole.

Based on the premise that human existence is no more valuable than other life and that humans have no right to harm other life, it follows in deep ecology that there are too many humans on the earth to exist as part of nature. Deep ecologists feel that humans could have flourishing lives and cultures even if there were far fewer humans on earth than currently occupy the planet and that other organisms cannot flourish because there are far too many humans. Accordingly, the basic economic, technological, and ideological underpinnings of human cultures must be changed to reverse this situation. Deep ecologists feel that human culture

WORDS TO KNOW

Deep Ecology: An environmental philosophy in which the value of human life is no greater than the value of any other organism's life.

Ecology: The study of the relations and interactions between organisms and their environment.

Ecosystem: A complete and interdependent system of biotic (living) and abiotic (nonliving) components that cycles matter and transfers energy within a given area. The three major types of ecosystems are freshwater, terrestrial, and marine.

---

has wrongly dominated earth's ecosystems. To deep ecologists, human destruction of any part of an ecosystem diminishes the whole. Humans should live in a way that acknowledges that people are part of their ecosystem, rather than thinking that people live apart from natural processes and attempting to manage them.

Arne Naess (1912–2012), a Norwegian philosopher, first used the term deep ecology. Naess did not accept that humans were different than, or superior to, any other organism. Whether humans could reason, or possessed consciousness, did not matter to Naess, who insisted that all organisms had an equal right to live, whether an organism was a microbe, a plant, an animal, or a human.

Some opinions based on deep ecology are quite radical and suggest that people should drastically reduce human population and abandon development, industrialism, and large organized societies. However, the fundamental beliefs of deep ecology, that people are no more entitled to life or the earth's resources than any other organism, offers a philosophical basis for a sustainable society. In embracing deep ecology, humans should think of themselves as a part of, rather than apart from, nature, and live accordingly.

SEE ALSO Ecology; Ecosystems; Permaculture; Sustainability

For more information

BOOKS

Fox, Warwick. *A Theory of General Ethics: Human Relationships, Nature, and the Built Environment.* Cambridge, MA: The MIT Press, 2006.

WEBSITES

"The Deep Ecology Platform." Foundation for Deep Ecology. http://www.deepecology.org/platform.htm (accessed July 8, 2015).

Harding, Stephan. "What is Deep Ecology?" Schumacher College. https://www.schumachercollege.org.uk/learning-resources/what-is-deep-ecology (accessed July 8, 2015).

Zimmerman, Michael E. "Introduction to Deep Ecology: An Interview with Michael E. Zimmerman." By Alan AtKisson. Context Institute, 1989. http://www.context.org/iclib/ic22/zimmrman/ (accessed July 8, 2015).

Deforestation
See **Carbon Cycle; Climate Change; Conservation.**

Desalination

Desalination is the process of turning saltwater from the ocean into freshwater that can be used for drinking and irrigating crops. As freshwater resources in many areas of the world decline as the result of overuse and climate change, desalination is becoming a partial solution for our increasingly thirsty planet. This is because more than 97 percent of the water on the earth is saltwater; it is a much more abundant resource than freshwater.

Freshwater that all people and land animals and plants rely on for survival comes from lakes, rivers, groundwater, or rain. For thousands of years these resources have been plentiful. With rapid population growth and the increased agriculture required to feed more people, however, the demand for freshwater is starting to exceed supply in some areas of the world, especially the Middle East, Australia, and even California.

For many years desalination has been used on ships and submarines, but it was believed that building plants to generate huge quantities of freshwater for hundreds of thousands of people on land would be too costly. Advances in technology, increased energy efficiency, and the scarcity of freshwater has increasingly made desalination an economical solution for some areas.

Worldwide as of 2014, about three hundred million people rely on desalination plants for their water. Even though a gallon (3.8 liters) of desalinated water costs twice as much as conventional freshwater, it still averages less than a penny a gallon. The largest desalination plant in the world as of 2014 was in Saudi Arabia, but an even larger plant opened near

Desalination

> ### WORDS TO KNOW
>
> **Combined heat and power plant:** A facility that reuses waste heat generated during its processes.
>
> **Desalination:** The process of turning saltwater into freshwater for human consumption and agricultural uses.
>
> **Groundwater:** Freshwater that accumulates underground, usually in aquifers.
>
> **Multistage flash distillation:** A type of desalination in which water is flash-heated into steam in a series of chambers to separate it from the salt, which becomes the waste product brine.
>
> **Reverse osmosis:** A type of desalination in which saltwater is forced through a semipermeable membrane that allows water molecules but not salt molecules to pass through.

San Diego, California, in 2015 to address the state's historic drought. By 2015 Israel received about one-quarter of its freshwater from desalination.

Types of desalination

Most desalination plants work by using reverse osmosis or multistage flash distillation. Reverse osmosis is the process of filtering seawater through a semipermeable membrane that allows water molecules but not salt molecules to pass through. The process also filters out bacteria and unwanted minerals. This process works on an industrial scale in desalination plants, but personal reverse osmosis kits can be used by individuals who lack access to freshwater, as in impoverished or rural areas or following natural disasters, when the usual water supply is unavailable.

Multistage flash distillation is the process of converting intake water to steam in a series of pressurized chambers. By the time the water reaches the final chamber, the brine, or salt, has been removed. About 15 percent of the total water is lost to evaporation through this process. Although distillation requires much energy to generate the heat that converts the water to steam, this heat is recycled. Thus, a multistage flash distillation facility can become a combined heat and power plant, in which energy is reused, thereby increasing its efficiency.

Desalination and sustainability

One possible problem with large-scale desalination plants is their effect on marine life, according to the U.S. Environmental Protection Agency. When large amounts of water are diverted to plants for intake, fish eggs, larva, and crucial microorganisms can be destroyed if proper precautions are not taken. Additionally, according to a report by the Pacific Institute, returning concentrated amounts of salt and other desalination fluids to the ocean may further upset marine life by making the water too salty. Ultimately, some critics argue that building desalination plants to counteract drought is an expensive, permanent solution to a short-term problem. When the drought ends and the rain returns, the plant may no longer be needed, thus representing a huge, long-term investment of money for a short-term solution. This happened during a drought in the 1980s, when California built a $34 million desalination plant in Santa Barbara. It never went into operation and was partially dismantled when the drought ended. Critics also say that existing freshwater supplies are adequate and need to be managed more carefully instead.

Despite these concerns, desalination may prove to be the best way to provide water to growing urban areas in the desert, both in the United States and around the world. To bring down the cost of these plants, research and development at major corporations and universities require funding. Some companies are experimenting with solar-powered desalination plants. This will increase their energy efficiency and eliminate the need to generate steam with fossil fuels, which emit greenhouse gases that trap heat in the atmosphere and contribute to climate change. To see the future of desalination, look to the Middle East, where some of the world's fastest-growing cities, such as Dubai, have built numerous desalination plants that sustain millions of people in the middle of the desert. On a planet with finite freshwater, desalination is a valuable tool to ensure long-term sustainability.

SEE ALSO Agriculture; Drought; Farming, Sustainable; Water Access and Sanitation

For more information

BOOKS
Kallen, Stuart A. *Running Dry: The Global Water Crisis.* Minneapolis, MN: 21st Century, 2015.

PERIODICALS
Gillis, Justin. "For Drinking Water in Drought, California Looks Warily to Sea." *New York Times* (April 11, 2015). Available online at http://www.nytimes.com/2015/04/12/science/drinking-seawater-looks-ever-more-palatable-to-californians.html (accessed May 6, 2015).

Hiltzik, Michael. "Desalination Plants Aren't a Good Solution for California Drought." *Los Angeles Times* (April 24, 2015). Available online at http://www.latimes.com/business/hiltzik/la-fi-hiltzik-20150426-column.html (accessed May 28, 2015).

WEBSITES

Cooley, Heather, Newsha Ajami, and Matthew Heberger. "Key Issues in Seawater: Desalination in California, Marine Impacts." Pacific Institute, December 2013. http://pacinst.org/publication/desal-marine-impacts/ (accessed May 28, 2015).

"Desalination: Option or Distraction for a Thirsty World?" WWF, June 19, 2007. http://wwf.panda.org/index.cfm?uNewsID=106660 (accessed May 6, 2015).

Dove, Laurie. "How Desalination Works." How Stuff Works. http://science.howstuffworks.com/environmental/earth/oceanography/desalination.htm (accessed May 6, 2015).

Harris, Emily. "Israel Bringing Its Years of Desalination Experience To California." *NPR.org*, June 14, 2015. http://www.npr.org/sections/parallels/2015/06/14/413981435/israel-bringing-its-years-of-desalination-experience-to-california (accessed August 4, 2015).

Desertification

Desertification happens when dryland soil becomes degraded and can no longer support the amount and variety of plant and animal life it once did; it becomes like a desert. Desertification can be caused naturally by drought and climate change, but it can also be the result of deforestation and poor agricultural practices. According to a Millennium Ecosystem Assessment report from 2005, 10 to 20 percent of drylands are already degraded. The United Nations estimates that each year about 30 million acres (12 million hectares) of farmland are lost to desertification. Desertification represents a major threat to biodiversity (the variety of life-forms) worldwide and presents a considerable challenge to sustainable development. Climate change is predicted to make droughts more frequent and severe in the coming years. This will increase the threat of desertification in many areas.

Causes of desertification

Human desertification is caused by three main practices. First, clear-cutting forests for timber or strip-mining removes the roots that anchor the fragile topsoil and destroys the ecosystems that provided the nutrients

WORDS TO KNOW

Arable land: Land that can be plowed and used to plant crops.

Desertification: Breakdown of the soil when it becomes increasingly dry and can no longer support the amount and variety of plant and animal life it once did.

Dryland: An area, such as desert, that receives very little rainfall and experiences significant evaporation of moisture.

Erosion: Removal of soil by wind or water, often resulting in desertification.

Evaporation: The process of turning a liquid into a gas.

Farmer-managed natural regeneration (FMNR): A set of practices for planting and farming land that is designed to reverse desertification.

Land degradation: The first step in desertification, when soil becomes dry and depleted of nutrients.

Market valuation: The price that a resource will bring in a regional economy.

Subsistence farming: Farming focused on growing enough food to feed one's family rather than farming to produce food to sell.

Sustainable agriculture: Growing crops using methods that focus on protecting and regenerating the soil and the local environment.

Topsoil: The top layer of soil, which contains the most organic matter and has the most biological activity.

---

that maintained soil health. Without the structure provided by the forest, the topsoil can dry out and blow away in the wind or wash away in the rain. Second, placing too many cattle and livestock in a pasture causes overgrazing. This negatively impacts the ecology of the grassland and prevents new plants from regenerating. The soil dries out, and when the animals loosen the soil with their hooves, it can blow or wash away. Third, intensive farming on sensitive arid land drains away vital nutrients from the soil, preventing new plants from growing. Once again, the thin topsoil dries out and blows or washes away. Intensive farming can include excessive plowing, which disrupts soil and makes it easier to erode, and planting too many crops over too many continuous seasons. When these practices result in a loss of land suitable for growing crops, they are considered unsustainable.

According to Luc Gnacadja, the former executive secretary of the United Nations Convention to Combat Desertification, "desertification, land degradation, and drought is an issue of market failure. The lack of economic market valuation has led to land being perceived as a cheap resource." This shortsighted thinking prevents farmers and industries from considering what will happen to their profits when they can no longer grow crops or raise livestock. A key to sustainability is creating economic systems that will not deplete the environment in such a way that they threaten the economy of a nation or community for future generations. Desertification can lead to economic collapse in a relatively short time.

Desertification leads directly to a loss of biodiversity. When one species disappears, many others that depend on it are also threatened. Soon, an entire ecosystem is disrupted. Desertification can lead directly to malnutrition, food insecurity, and high rates of infant death. Poverty and displacement often follow.

Areas at risk of desertification

The areas most susceptible to desertification are drylands and deserts. A dryland is an area where rainfall is equal to surface evaporation, meaning that very little water trickles down into the soil. Drylands are also called arid lands. The driest drylands are called deserts. About 40 percent of land on the earth is dryland or desert, and the population of these areas exceeds two billion. All continents have substantial dryland areas, but Africa and Asia have the most. With the exception of Antarctica, the world's driest deserts are all in developing countries. Unsustainable agricultural practices in drylands due to rapidly growing populations, marginally productive land, poverty, a lack of infrastructure, and little government oversight threaten many of these areas with desertification. It is important to note that drylands' lack of water does not equate to lack of life. Healthy dryland ecosystems are complex and support many different forms of life that have adapted to harsh conditions, yet these ecosystems are very fragile.

Desertification has affected every country on every inhabited continent. It tends to be concentrated around six of the world's major deserts: the Sahara in northern Africa, the Kalahari in southern Africa, the Gobi in Asia, the Atacama in South America, the Sonora in the United States, and the Great Victoria in Australia. The countries bordering the Sahara to the south and the Central Asian countries of Kazakhstan and its southern neighbors are the hardest hit.

In the United States, 90 percent of the arid land is considered to be degraded by desertification. This land is concentrated in the West and

Midwest, from Canada in the north to Mexico in the south. The main causes are overgrazing by cattle and depletion of groundwater to irrigate crops. The states hardest hit are Nebraska, Texas, Oklahoma, and Kansas. In California and Texas, excessive withdrawal of water from aquifers has led to salinization, or saltiness, of the soil, which makes plants unable to grow. This may prove to have a huge impact on agriculture in California, which produces more of the fruits and vegetables eaten in the country than any other state.

The United Nations Convention to Combat Desertification

The United Nations Convention to Combat Desertification (UNCCD) was established in 1994 following the 1992 Earth Summit in Rio de Janeiro. The summit members acknowledged desertification as a global environmental threat. UNCCD is the only international agreement that seeks to enact environmentally sustainable land management to combat desertification. The convention's ten-year plan, adopted in 2007, aims to "forge a global partnership to reverse and prevent desertification/land degradation and to mitigate the effects of drought in affected areas in order to support poverty reduction and environmental sustainability."

Shifting sand dunes have buried the road and telegraph poles in the Western Desert, Egypt. © ROBERT HARDING PICTURE LIBRARY LTD/ALAMY

According to the UNCCD, 2.6 billion people worldwide rely directly on agriculture in dryland areas for their well-being, and more than half of them are directly affected by land degradation. An overwhelming percentage of these people are poor and live in developing countries, where overpopulation places pressure on the land. When groundwater is depleted in an effort to farm dryland areas and when resources are depleted, people move to urban areas. These urban areas are often ill-equipped to handle the growth. Without jobs and skills, many of these people make their way to ever-expanding slums.

Techniques to reverse desertification

The UNCCD recommends several practices to stop or reverse desertification. The first is planting trees, or reforestation, along with a variety of specialized plants that will increase the fertility of the remaining soil. This technique includes farmer-managed natural regeneration (FMNR), in which farmers promote tree and plant growth by selecting the most promising seedlings from a field and getting rid of the rest. This allows the strongest plants to grow without competing for scarce water and nutrients. Growing a few strong plants and trees is better than growing many weak plants and trees. Strong trees have healthier root systems that are more capable of nourishing and anchoring the soil.

When these healthy trees are big enough, they are carefully pruned to encourage growth and to provide room for smaller plants to grow underneath. Together, this vegetation system works to keep the soil moist. Additionally, FMNR encourages sustainable agricultural practices, such as contour planting, terracing, and no-till planting, to stop the spread of desertification. These practices enable farmers to grow crops without disturbing the soil. FMNR is designed to be easily adopted by low-income subsistence farmers, those who grow food for their own survival, because it does not require expensive technology or equipment.

Another crucial technique for combating desertification is water management. The UNCCD encourages governments to create an infrastructure and guidelines that prevent farmers from depleting the groundwater. Finally, reversing desertification requires that soil be kept in place. Strategically placed fences, rows of trees and bushes as windbreaks, and other barriers can be erected to prevent soil from blowing or washing away.

An excellent example of the use of such a barrier is in China, where the Gobi is swiftly overtaking agricultural and urban areas. In 1978 the government began planting a 3,000-mile (4,828-kilometer) "green wall" of trees called the Three-North Shelter Forest Program, which it hopes to complete by 2050. Each year China loses 1,400 square miles (3,626 square kilometers) of grassland to desertification. It is hoped that this green wall will slow the process of desertification. A similar program to create a green wall along the southern edge of the Sahara in Africa has been talked about for many years, but as of 2015 no trees had been planted.

SEE ALSO Climate Change; Drought; Soil

For more information

BOOKS
Griffith, Brian. *The Gardens of Their Dreams: Desertification and Culture in World History.* London: Zed Books, 2001.

PERIODICALS
Millennium Ecosystem Assessment. *Ecosystems and Human Well-being: Desertification Synthesis.* World Resources Institute (2005). Available online at http://www.millenniumassessment.org/documents/document.355.aspx.pdf (accessed March 27, 2015).

Nuwer, Rachel. "It's Not Genghis Khan's Mongolia." *New York Times* (September 22, 2014). Available online at http://www.nytimes.com/2014/09/23/science/its-not-genghis-khans-mongolia.html (accessed March 27, 2015).

WEBSITES
"Desertification Land Degradation and Drought (DLDD)." United Nations Convention to Combat Desertification. http://www.unccd.int/Lists/SiteDocumentLibrary/WDCD/DLDD%20Facts.pdf (accessed March 27, 2015).

"Drought in the Dust Bowl Years." National Drought Mitigation Center. http://drought.unl.edu/DroughtBasics/DustBowl/DroughtintheDustBowlYears.aspx (accessed March 27, 2015).

King, Ed. "Desertification Crisis Affecting 168 Countries Worldwide." Response to Climate Change, April 18, 2013. http://www.rtcc.org/2013/04/17/desertification-crisis-affecting-168-countries-worldwide/ (accessed March 27, 2015).

Roos, Dave. "How Desertification Works." How Stuff Works. http://science.howstuffworks.com/environmental/conservation/issues/desertification2.htm (accessed March 17, 2015).

United Nations Convention to Combat Desertification. http://www.unccd.int/en (accessed March 27, 2015).

"World Day to Combat Desertification." http://www.un.org/en/events/desertificationday/background.shtml (accessed March 27, 2015).

Deserts

See **Desertification; Ecosystems.**

Drought

A drought is a period of time during which there is a severely reduced amount of precipitation or no precipitation at all. It can last for just a few weeks or can develop over a period of time and last for years. Droughts that last for several weeks or months are considered short-term droughts, while those that last longer are called long-term droughts. The frequency and severity of a drought can have long-lasting and adverse effects on the health and viability of the environment both locally and across a region. Because droughts affect food production and availability and cause other changes to the environment, responding to their effects is an important aspect of sustainability. Human activities can increase the severity of droughts through overuse of water resources and some agricultural practices, and climate scientists agree that human carbon emissions influence the weather patterns that cause drought.

How droughts happen

The key causes of droughts involve changes in atmospheric conditions that affect land and water temperatures, wind patterns, and soil moisture content. Although these may seem to be individual factors, they are all connected and together can create a cycle that leads to drought.

An increase in the surface temperatures of land and water promotes greater rates of evaporation, which moves water into the atmosphere. As the evaporation rate changes, it affects the formation of clouds, leading to changes in local weather patterns. Air currents produced by the uneven heating of the earth's surface can move clouds in different directions. Scientists have discovered that there is a relationship between the changes in ocean surface temperatures and the air circulation patterns in the atmosphere. When the ocean's surface temperature is increased, shifts

WORDS TO KNOW

Evaporation: The process of turning a liquid into a gas.

Gray water: Water that has been used but is not severely contaminated, for example, water used for laundry.

Habitat: The natural environment where a living organism resides.

Mitigation: Measures taken to control, reduce, or halt the impacts of environmental change.

---

in existing wind patterns occur. Ocean air currents that would normally generate moisture-rich air masses, which can move over land and deposit precipitation, are disrupted. This causes some areas to experience greater precipitation than normal while others experience less.

Droughts worsened by human activity

Periodic droughts are natural occurrences, but sometimes human beings increase their devastation through poor farming practices, failing government policies, and activity that contributes to global climate change. A 2015 study by the National Aeronautics and Space Administration (NASA) found that a warmer planet will increase the intensity of droughts by increasing evaporation, which will lead to overly dry and eroded soil conditions as well as drained reservoirs. Additionally, increased rainfall and decreased snowfall will cause areas that depend on reservoirs to go without adequate water during naturally dry seasons because those regions rely on snowpack to melt slowly in order to maintain reservoir levels. According to the study's authors, reducing human carbon emissions is a necessary step toward controlling the severity of droughts.

Drought in California

California is the most populous U.S. state, with 38.8 million residents as of July 2014, and the third-largest by land area. Its temperate Mediterranean-like climate has long been considered ideal for growing crops year-round, and it supplies about 50 percent of the produce sold in the United States. While the state is subject to periodic droughts—having a rainy season and a dry season—the combined effects of drought, population increase, and climate change have led many scientists to declare that the drought that began in 2011 may be the worst the state has seen

The Dust Bowl

In the 1930s, during the Great Depression, a vast stretch of prairie from the border of Canada in the north through Texas in the south suffered from desertification due to severe drought and unsustainable farming practices. Native grass varieties that previously anchored the soil were removed by farmers in favor of shallow-rooted crops such as wheat and corn. Their intensive plowing of fields, made easy owing to new motorized tractors and combines, loosened the soil, making it susceptible to erosion.

When the drought struck after years of deceptively good weather, the prairie soil turned to sand and blew away in massive dust storms called "black blizzards." The area became known as the "Dust Bowl." The sand buried farm equipment and houses and brought economic ruin to roughly a half million people. Many of these destitute families made their way to California, where they became migrant workers.

This was the United States' first wide-scale experience with desertification. In response, President Franklin Roosevelt established the Soil Conservation Service to initiate practices to stop the erosion. In one effort, more than two hundred million trees were planted from Canada to Texas to serve as windbreaks and to hold soil in place as well as to prevent water from evaporating. Farmers were instructed and even paid to employ erosion-prevention techniques such as crop rotation and contour plowing. The Drought Relief Service was created to provide emergency relief to farmers who had lost everything. By the time the drought ended, 75 percent of the topsoil had blown away. Within a generation, however, much of the desertification had been reversed through the practices of the Soil Conservation Service, and the dryland prairie region was once again a major contributor to agriculture in the United States. The Soil Conservation Service is now called the National Resources Conservation Service (NRCS) and still plays a major role in conserving soil throughout the United States.

in recorded history, and possibly the worst in a thousand years. According to Peter Gleick, head of the Pacific Institute in Oakland, California, "The current California drought is bad because for the first time ever, scientists from many different fields see parallel lines of evidence for the influence of human-induced climate changes, including the fingerprints of higher temperatures and changes in the atmospheric circulation patterns. In short, climate change has made the current drought worse."

The severity of drought is measured on a scale of intensity from "abnormally dry" to "exceptional." As of July 2015, two-thirds of California was considered in "extreme" drought and 47 percent in "exceptional,"

California's drought exposes the 180–200-foot (54–60-meter) drop in water levels at the Silverthorn Resort on Shasta Lake near Redding in August 2014. The reservoir is receding at an average of 4.9 inches (12.4 centimeters) per day. © DAVID GREITZER/SHUTTERSTOCK.COM

leading Governor Jerry Brown to order a mandatory 25 percent water use reduction across the state. Green lawns and swimming pools are common in some parts of the arid state, and those features of suburban life have been targeted as wasteful. But many experts maintain that the state's agricultural industry is the worst culprit in water waste, with 40 percent of the state's water going to agriculture and just 10 percent used by people in urban centers (the remaining percentage must stay in rivers and marshes according to the state's environmental policies).

Historically, California law has allowed farmers to tap into groundwater sources to irrigate their crops, but the drought has triggered fears that such underground aquifers will quickly dry up because there is not enough water from melting snowpack to replenish the groundwater. If this water, which lies so deeply underground that it is called "ancient" water, is not replaced, the risk of ground settling and collapse increases. Across the state, reservoirs and even lakes that depend on snowmelt to maintain water levels are shrinking. Critics of the state's drought emergency legislation, which applies to homeowners and businesses but not farmers, have noted that the imbalance between the amount of water consumed by the average California resident and the amount used by the agriculture industry unfairly penalizes citizens while not holding farmers accountable for their considerably larger water usage. Supporters of the new legislation maintain that farmers have already reduced their water use by allowing at least 400,000 acres of land to lie fallow, or unused, during the drought. Richard M. Frank of the *San Francisco Chronicle* sums up the larger issue of water and drought in California: "The fundamental problem is that California's water rights system was created over a century ago, when the population of the entire state was less than three million residents, and relatively stable water supplies were more than adequate to support the agrarian economy of the state at that time."

How drought affects human lives

Droughts not only alter the qualities of ecosystems, they also can cause social and economic turmoil. Droughts have both direct and indirect effects in the communities in which they occur. A direct effect would be poor growing conditions that lead to crop failure. An indirect effect would be the loss of income for people down the economic chain in the agriculture industry. For example, if farmers are experiencing poor growing conditions, they might be less apt to purchase new farming equipment, which would mean lower profits for the people who manufacture and sell the equipment. Likewise, long-lasting droughts usually cause a rise in food prices because, as crops fail, certain foods become scarce during a drought. So, while a drought might be occurring in one part of a country, people living in another area might have to pay significantly more for what they buy at their grocery store. Locally, consequences of drought may come in the form of water rationing and poor water quality in wealthy nations and disease and starvation in poor countries. Citizens in developing countries may not have enough water to give to their livestock, upon which they depend for milk, food, and labor. If the animals die, this puts families who are already poor in dire living situations. When droughts cause wildfires, residents must leave their homes due to the risk of fires spreading to populated areas. Such fires can alter the balance of wildlife populations, destroy old-growth forests, and endanger already tenuous ecosystems as well.

Drought mitigation

Although droughts occur naturally, people can take steps to mitigate, or reduce, their effects. To prepare, some communities have begun to develop drought plans, which include ways to reduce water usage by citizens, monitoring the environment for conditions that might lead to drought, better water and crop management, and raising public awareness. These plans also must include planning in case climate change increases the length, frequency, and/or severity of droughts.

Having suffered the worst drought in its history from 1997 to 2009—in some areas it was not declared over until 2012—Australia is considered a model for instituting drought mitigation policies that include recycling gray water; encouraging and rewarding such home-based conservation efforts as rain barrels, water-efficient bathroom fixtures, and rock gardens; and instituting a water exchange that farmers use like a stock exchange. Australia's Millennium Drought also saw massive investment in and building of desalination plants, which most experts say should be considered only as a last resort due to the financial and environmental costs of the technology.

SEE ALSO Agriculture; Climate Change; Conservation; Desalination; Desertification; Food Security; Soil; Water Access and Sanitation

For more information

BOOKS
Kennedy, Brian, ed. *Water*. Detroit, MI: Greenhaven Press, 2012.

PERIODICALS
Associated Press. "Study Sees Even Bigger Longer Droughts for Much of the US West." *New York Times* (February 12, 2015). Available online at http://www.nytimes.com/aponline/2015/02/12/science/ap-us-sci-worse-droughts.html (accessed March 18, 2015).

Frank, Richard M. "Another Inconvenient Truth: California Water Law Must Change." *San Francisco Chronicle* (April 10, 2015). Available online at http://www.sfchronicle.com/opinion/article/Another-inconvenient-truth-California-water-law-6192703.php (accessed May 12, 2015).

Nuccitelli, Dana. "Nasa Climate Study Warns of Unprecedented North American Drought." *The Guardian* (February 16, 2015). Available online at http://www.theguardian.com/environment/climate-consensus-97-per-cent/2015/feb/16/nasa-climate-study-warns-unprecedented-north-american-drought (accessed May 12, 2015).

WEBSITES
"Drought for Kids." National Drought Mitigation Center. http://drought.unl.edu/DroughtforKids.aspx (accessed March 18, 2015).

"Drought Mitigation." Ojos Negros Research Group. http://threeissues.sdsu.edu/three_issues_droughtfacts04.html (accessed March 18, 2015).

"Drought Termination and Amelioration." NOAA: National Climatic Data Center. http://www.ncdc.noaa.gov/temp-and-precip/drought/recovery.php (accessed March 18, 2015).

Gleick, Peter. "The Growing Influence of Climate Change on the California Drought." *ScienceBlogs* (December 8, 2014). http://scienceblogs.com/significantfigures/index.php/2014/12/08/the-growing-influence-of-climate-change-on-the-california-drought/ (accessed May 12, 2015).

Herring, David. "Dry Times in North America." NASA: Earth Observatory, September 25, 2000. http://earthobservatory.nasa.gov/Features/NAmerDrought/NAmer_drought.php (accessed March 18, 2015).

"Surviving the Dust Bowl: The Drought." American Experience. http://www.pbs.org/wgbh/americanexperience/features/general-article/dustbowl-drought/ (accessed May 12, 2015).

E

Ecological Footprint

Ecological footprint is a term used to measure the consumption of ecological resources by a particular consumer, such as a person, a family, a company, an industry, a country, or the whole world. Measures of ecological footprint compare the resources used by a person or group of people to the ability of the ecosystem to renew or replace those resources. Generally speaking, calculating a population's ecological footprint allows us to know which groups are overusing resources to a point at which earth cannot support them and they must alter their activities or risk exhausting the resources permanently. In other words, it tells us how much demand we put on the natural environment. Ecological footprint can also determine the effect lifestyle choices or activities have on the environment. For example, when a person chooses to use recycled paper instead of new paper, he or she is choosing the option that creates a smaller ecological footprint.

Calculating the ratio of land to people

To calculate ecological footprint, researchers total the amount of land and sea area needed to produce, transport, and use everything that is consumed by the population being studied. The researchers also add the amount of land needed to absorb and recycle, or dispose of, the waste materials that are produced by the population, and the amount of land the population uses for infrastructure. Infrastructure includes the roads, buildings, power supplies, water and sewage systems, and any other physical structures needed to support the activities of a society. The calculation

Ecological Footprint

> ### WORDS TO KNOW
>
> **Agribusiness:** Large-scale corporate farming.
>
> **Biocapacity:** The amount of resources available in an area, or on all of earth, expressed in terms of the area of land needed to produce the resources.
>
> **Carbon footprint:** The total amount of greenhouse gases produced by human activity. A person's carbon footprint includes, for example, the fuel to power a car or heat a house or cook food and would extend to the power used to produce and transport the goods a person uses.
>
> **Developed country:** A country that has developed industries, technology, and a mature economy, as compared to less developed countries. The United States, Canada, and Germany are examples.
>
> **Developing country:** A country that has a low standard of living, including low average annual income per person, high infant mortality rates, widespread poverty, and an underdeveloped economy. Most of these countries are located in Africa, Asia, and Latin America.
>
> **Ecological footprint:** The measure of human stress on the planet's ecosystems. The footprint considers how much land and water resources a population consumes and the ability of the environment to absorb the population's corresponding waste.
>
> **Greenhouse gases:** Any of the gases in the earth's atmosphere that absorb or reflect back to earth infrared radiation from the sun, thereby trapping heat close to the earth's surface. An increase in greenhouse gases corresponds with climate change. The main greenhouse gases are carbon dioxide, methane, nitrous oxide, and ozone. Clouds and water vapor also function as greenhouse gases.
>
> **Hectare:** Metric measurement used for land area, about 2.47 acres. A square 100 meters on each side encloses 1 hectare. A city block is about one hectare.
>
> **Overshoot:** Having a larger ecological footprint than earth can support.
>
> **Per capita:** Per person. *Per capita* is a Latin term that means "for each head."

should also include the land needed to support the wild ecosystems and organisms found on the same land as the population. For example, in considering the development of an area, city planners who are mindful of ecological footprint will want to include ample green space to maintain the existing nonhuman animal and plant populations.

Then, the researchers divide the area of the land needed to support the population by the number of people. This gives the amount of land needed per person, or per capita. Ecological footprint is often stated in hectares per capita. A hectare is a metric unit of area equal to a square 100 meters on a side, or about 2.47 acres. One hectare is roughly the size of a city block, or two and a half football or soccer fields.

An ecological footprint needs to include all the ways a population or activity takes resources from the environment, including how those resources will be replaced, and all the ways that using the resource adds to the waste that the environment must absorb. For example, the footprint for obtaining lumber should not only include the land from which the trees were harvested, but also the amount of land needed to grow new timber at the rate wood is being used. The footprint should include the land needed to produce all the machinery and energy used to cut, transport, and process the lumber. It should include the land resources needed for the environment to reabsorb the waste, including enough land to absorb the greenhouse gases emitted by the machinery and the decomposition of the sawdust and the unused parts of the trees.

Calculations of ecological footprint do not include resources that the ecosystem cannot renew. The metals and petroleum used to construct and provide power for logging machinery cannot be renewed, and are not counted, although the area of land needed to absorb the carbon dioxide produced by the machinery needs to be counted.

The threshold of sustainability

If all the productive land and water on earth's surface is added together, and then divided by the size of the population of earth, the result is the world's biocapacity, or the maximum amount of resources, expressed as land area, that can be used sustainably. If a population has a larger footprint than this threshold, the population is using resources faster than they can be replaced by the ecosystem. Having a larger footprint than biocapacity is called overshoot. A population that overshoots is not sustainable, because the population will consume all the available resources, or the ecosystem will be unable to absorb all the waste generated by the population, or both.

What is the global footprint?

An organization called Global Footprint Network (GFN) collects data on resource use and works to provide policy makers with information about the ecological footprint of activities and populations. The president of the organization is Dr. Mathis Wackernagel, who first started the field of ecological footprint analysis as a PhD student in the early 1990s. GFN estimates that the population of earth began to overshoot in 1975. GFN estimates that the world has 1.78 hectares of productive land per capita, but that each person, on average, uses the resources from 2.70 hectares.

Ecological Footprint

Ecological Footprint

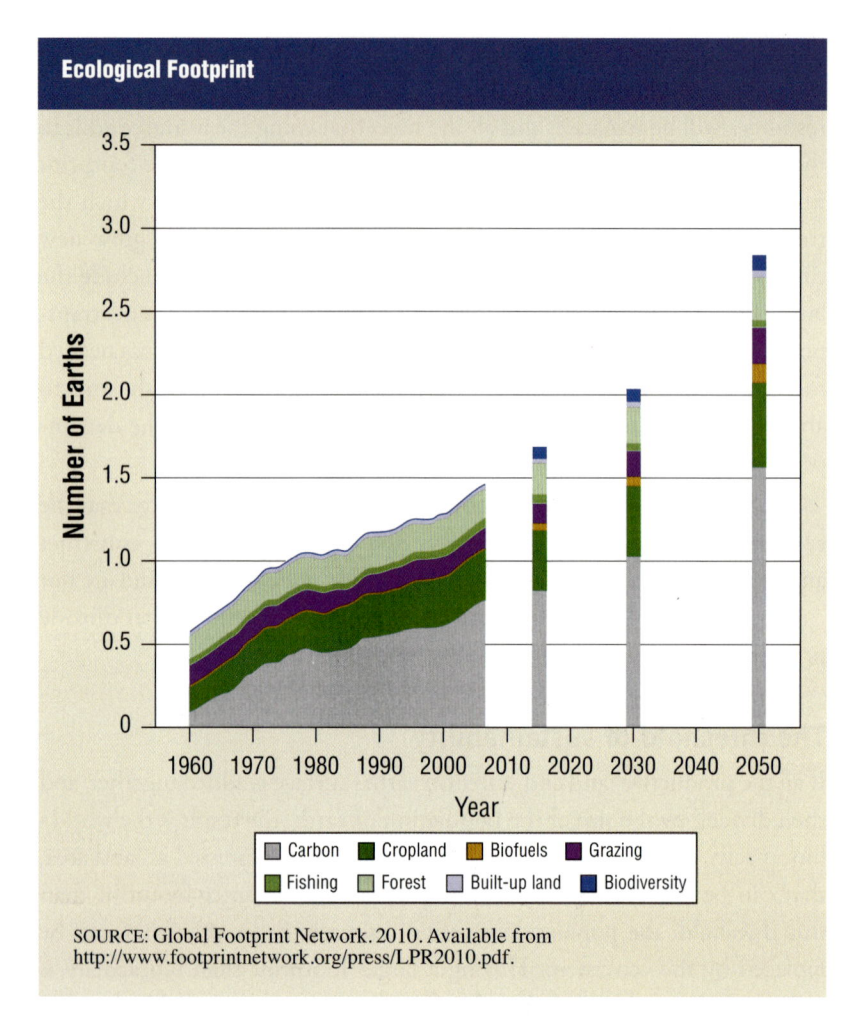

Today, humanity uses the equivalent of 1.5 earths to provide the resources we use and to absorb our waste. This means it now takes earth one year and six months to regenerate what we use in a year. In 1960 humanity needed only 0.5 planets. On a "business as usual" projection we will need nearly three planets by 2050.
© WWF. *LIVING PLANET REPORT 2010.* P. 89 FIGURE 34. WWF. PANDA.ORG. SOME RIGHTS RESERVED.

SOURCE: Global Footprint Network. 2010. Available from http://www.footprintnetwork.org/press/LPR2010.pdf.

This is an overshoot of 51 percent. Put another way, the population needs 1.5 earths to sustain its current rate of resource use. Earth needs a year and six months to replace what the population is using each year. In order to be sustainable, the overshoot must be eliminated. The population has to use less than one earth, or less than 1.78 hectares per capita.

According to GFN, about half the human ecological footprint comes from its carbon footprint. Through deforestation, burning fossil fuels, and raising cattle, people have increased the level of carbon in the atmosphere. Plants on land and in water can remove carbon from the atmosphere to a degree. A hectare of land can remove the carbon from burning about 403 gallons (1,525 liters) of gasoline, but only if that hectare has

Ecological Footprints and Global Development

Some comparisons measure the ecological footprints of countries against their United Nations human development index. The term "development" refers to a country's living conditions, including life expectancy, education, and per-household income. Factors that are also included in measuring development are access to health care, infant and childhood death rates, availability of clean drinking water, employment opportunities, and the threat of crime. Simply put, a country's overall level of development depends upon its citizens quality of life—including whether or not the factors of high quality of life extend across socioeconomic groups; if only a country's wealthiest citizens experience high quality of life while its poorest do not, that country is not considered developed in proper terms.

The countries with the highest level of development tend to have the largest and least sustainable ecological footprints, while those that are less developed tend to have the smallest ecological footprint. This is because development has traditionally required a heavy use of resources and dependence on the use of resources like fossil fuels and large amounts of land for agricultural use. The items that many people in developed countries take for granted as increasing their quality of life, such as individually owned automobiles and single-family houses, require large amounts of resources like water, electricity, and consumer goods to maintain. In less developed countries, on the other hand, most citizens tend to use far fewer resources, sometimes because the resources are too expensive for them to afford and sometimes because they are simply unavailable. In much of the world, for example, meat is a luxury reserved only for the very wealthy or at times for special occasions, so there may be few, if any, large-scale meat-production farms that overuse resources and emit methane and carbon. And in much of the less developed world, single-family homes may not exist, with several generations of families living together in small huts on small plots of land. This kind of lifestyle uses up far fewer resources and has a much smaller ecological footprint.

But the story may be more complex than a developed-versus-less developed narrative suggests. While the overall ecological footprint of developed countries is larger, less developed countries may have lower standards for air and water quality, meaning that pollution may be more of a problem. The tendency of the poor to move to large cities to find work to support their families means that less developed countries might have overpopulated urban centers in which people are forced to live in slums or tent cities, with little or no sanitation. Urban centers around the world generally have an ecological footprint larger than rural areas because they usually are overpopulated and the land areas on which they sit cannot adequately sustain the number of people living in them. Additionally, governments of less developed countries may be less inclined to abide by health and human rights standards or to institute sustainability measures if they will require a greater investment of finances than less sustainable resource management techniques.

Experts agree that the ideal outcome to achieve sustainability for the earth's biocapacity is for developed countries to decrease their ecological footprint through more sensible use of resources while less developed countries increase theirs or distribute their resource use more equally among their citizens.

Ecological Footprint

natural foliage that is available and the land is not being utilized for some other purpose, such as parking lots. If human greenhouse gas emissions were reduced to zero, there would be no global overshoot with earth's present population.

Personal choices

People living primarily in developed countries make lifestyle choices that add to the ecological footprint. The United States and Canada have a large biocapacity compared to their population, 4.9 hectares of productive land per capita. But each person in North America uses, on average, the resources from 7.9 hectares. In North America, just the overshoot, by 3.0 hectares per capita, is greater than the world average ecological footprint. Sixty-nine percent of the North American ecological footprint is its carbon footprint, mainly from transportation and energy use.

By using less transportation and consuming less energy, the population of North America, and elsewhere, can reduce its carbon footprint. By driving smaller, more efficient cars, making fewer driving trips, using public transportation, and conserving electricity or obtaining electricity from carbon-free sources, the ecological footprint of North America could be well below its biocapacity.

Other personal choices affect carbon footprint. Meat and dairy production require more land than other food products. The land used for

Bill Nye watches his meter run backwards as his solar electric panels feed power back into the grid at his home. Nye, the host of the educational series Bill Nye, The Science Guy, *and his neighbor actor Ed Begley Jr. are locked in a friendly but serious eco-battle to see who can leave the smaller ecological footprint.* © AP IMAGES//REED SAXON

182

U•X•L *Sustainable Living*

production of these items must be cleared of naturally existing plant life—mainly forests—in order for large-scale meat and dairy production to take place, particularly when agribusiness overtakes smaller, more ecologically responsible farms. The methane emissions from livestock add to the carbon footprint associated with these food choices. Eating less of these foods reduces carbon footprint and frees up biocapacity that can absorb carbon by leaving more land undeveloped and thereby more plant life available to absorb some of the carbon output.

Many people in developed countries live in large houses on large lots far from where they work. Large homes require more energy to heat and cool and use up land that could add to, rather than take from, earth's biocapacity. Urban sprawl also requires land for the roads and parking lots that allow a commuter lifestyle. People could choose to live in smaller, more efficient homes closer to where they work, homes where they could get to work by walking or using public transportation, reducing their carbon and ecological footprints.

Earth has only a limited capacity to restore the resources that the human population takes from it. As the population grows—estimated at 7.3 billion people in mid-2015—and as the per capita ecological footprint increases, the overshoot of the human race will continue to grow. In order to have a sustainable society within earth's ecosystem, each person, and society as a whole, must reduce its footprint, and in particular its carbon footprint, to a level that earth can sustain on an ongoing basis.

SEE ALSO Carbon Cycle; Climate Change; Consumption; Ecosystems; Land; Natural Resources; Population, Human; Sustainability

For more information

BOOKS

Johnson, Bea. *Zero Waste Home: The Ultimate Guide to Simplifying Your Life by Reducing Your Waste.* New York: Scribner, 2013.

Wackernagel, Mathis, and William E. Rees. *Our Ecological Footprint: Reducing Human Impact on the Earth.* Gabriola Island, BC Canada: New Society Publishers, 1996.

PERIODICALS

Kaplan, Sarah. "Animal Numbers are Shrinking, But Kids Can Help." *Washington Post* (October 13, 2014). Available online at http://www.washingtonpost.com/lifestyle/kidspost/earths-animal-populations-are-shrinking-fast--but-kids-can-take-action-to-help/2014/10/13/061ecb90-4d65-11e4-8c24-487e92bc997b_story.html (accessed March 13, 2015).

WEBSITES

"Ecological Footprint." World Wildlife Fund Global. http://wwf.panda.org/about_our_earth/teacher_resources/webfieldtrips/ecological_balance/eco_footprint/ (accessed December 12, 2014).

"Ecological Footprint FAQ." Earth Day Network. http://www.earthday.org/footprintfaq (accessed December 15, 2014).

Ewing, Brad, David Moore, et al. *Ecological Footprint Atlas 2010*. Oakland CA: Global Footprint Network, 2010. http://www.footprintnetwork.org/en/index.php/GFN/page/ecological_footprint_atlas_2010 (accessed December 15, 2014).

"Footprint Basics—Introduction." Global Footprint Network. http://www.footprintnetwork.org/en/index.php/GFN/page/basics_introduction/ (accessed March 13, 2015).

Ecological Restoration

Around the world, many natural places have been affected or damaged by unsustainable human activity. Ecological restoration, the process of repairing damage caused by humans to ecosystems, can at least partially reverse some of this harm. The goal of ecological restoration is to reestablish ecological balance. Some restoration activities include planting trees, reintroducing native species, eliminating invasive species, removing dams to restore river flows, and reviving grasslands, wetlands, stream banks, and coral reefs.

Ecological restoration does not happen overnight; it takes time to have an effect. Humans have dramatically altered land and ecosystems that took billions of years to form. Although ecological restoration may be able to revive many disturbed areas, it can take a very long time to achieve.

Restoration approaches

Scientists have studied how ecosystems recover naturally in order to develop approaches to ecological restoration projects. Most ecological restoration projects follow four main approaches: restoration, rehabilitation, replacement, or the creation of artificial ecosystems.

Volunteers plant trees during a mangrove restortation project in Thailand. © SURA NUALPRADID/SHUTTERSTOCK.COM

Ecological Restoration

WORDS TO KNOW

Biodiversity: The variety of species or organisms in a given environment or ecosystem. A large range of plant and animal life in a given region is symptomatic of its health; a narrow range or declining number of species in a region may indicate environmental damage or stress.

Ecosystem: A complete and interdependent system of biotic (living) and abiotic (nonliving) components that cycles matter and transfers energy within a given area. The three major types of ecosystems are freshwater, terrestrial, and marine.

Ecosystem restoration: The process of returning a damaged ecosystem to its original condition.

Invasive species: A species that is intentionally or unintentionally introduced to one part of the world from another that causes harm in the new area. Invasive species may become competitors, predators, or parasites of native species.

Native species: The species of organisms normally found in a given habitat.

Scavenger: An organism that feeds on dead animal and plant material.

Toxic: Poisonous.

Restoration projects aim to return a damaged habitat or ecosystem to a condition that is as similar as possible to its original state. Some difficulties arise when scientists do not know what the area's original state was like. Additionally, restoration to a natural state can be impossible in some cases where environmental conditions have changed.

Other ecological restoration projects take a rehabilitation approach. Rehabilitation turns a damaged ecosystem into a functioning and useful ecosystem. It does not necessarily restore the ecosystem to its original state. Instead, it attempts to repair damage into order to make the environment healthy. For example, restoration projects may remove pollutants from abandoned mines or replant trees to reduce soil erosion.

A third approach to ecological restoration is replacement. Replacement projects replace a damaged ecosystem with another type of ecosystem. Replacement projects are common in areas with surface mines and lands severely damaged by cities and industrial activity. For example, a forested area that was cleared and mined may be turned into a lake.

In other cases, artificial ecosystems are created to restore damaged areas. Artificial ecosystems are made and controlled by humans to mimic natural ecosystems. For example, an artificial wetland can be introduced to an area in order to reduce flooding and to filter water. Artificial reefs can be used to stabilize areas degraded by blast fishing, the process of using explosives to stun or kill schools of fish for easy collection.

Ecological Restoration

Kissimmee River Restoration

The Kissimmee River is a large river that flows from north to south in Florida. It flows into Lake Okeechobee, which is located in a large system of Florida wetlands called the Everglades. From 1961 to 1971, the Kissimmee River was altered. Through dams and straightening projects, the river is no longer in its natural channel. This straightening project has had many unforeseen consequences. Water quality has diminished in Florida, because the river no longer slowly winds through wetlands that filtered nutrients and pollutants from the water. Natural ecosystems were destroyed, harming native species. Waterfowl populations have declined 90 percent. Water quality in the Everglades has also been decreasing.

In 1992 the U.S. Congress authorized the Water Resources Development Act to implement the Kissimmee River Restoration Project. The U.S. government and Florida government have partnered to fund this project. The project will restore the original meandering pattern of the river for over 40 square miles (103 square kilometers) of the river and floodplain ecosystem, including more than 12,000 acres (4,856.2 hectares) of wetlands. To date, plant and animal species that were disrupted have returned in great numbers and are thriving in the restored system. The project is expected to be completed in 2019.

The natural flow of the Kissimmee River in central Florida, which has been restored, can be seen in the foreground with the straightened section in the background. © KRT/MARK RANDALL/NEWSCOM

Four-step restoration strategy

For most ecological restoration projects, scientists recommend a four-step strategy based on science. The first step of any ecological restoration project is to identify the causes of the area's damage. Causes of damage can include human activities such as farming or mining; damage also may be the result of livestock overgrazing, pollution, or the introduction of an invasive species.

After the causes of the damage are identified, the second step is to eliminate these causes or significantly minimize their impact in order to prevent further damage. Workers may remove toxic soil pollutants and add nutrients and new topsoil to improve soil quality. Ecological damage can also be reduced by controlling or eliminating nonnative, invasive species. For example, a large number of forest ecosystems in southeastern North America have been damaged by a plant known as Japanese honeysuckle (*Lonicera japonica*). Brought to the United States from Asia, the Japanese honeysuckle quickly began to spread and displaced natural plants in forest ecosystems. In order to restore these damaged ecosystems, the honeysuckle plant is removed.

A third step, if needed, is to reintroduce key native species to an area in order to restore its natural ecological processes. For example, the gray wolf is an important predator in parts of the western United States. The wolves hunt bison, elk, moose, and mule deer, keeping the herd populations at manageable levels. They also keep the coyote population under control and provide food for scavengers such as raven, bald eagles, and foxes by leaving some of their kills partially uneaten. When wolf populations declined in Yellowstone National Park in the mid-1900s, their absence had a significant effect on the park's ecosystem. The numbers of elk, moose, and mule deer grew. They devastated vegetation, which increased soil erosion and harmed the populations of other species that ate the vegetation, such as beaver. In turn, this affected species that depended on wetlands created by the beavers. To revive the ecosystem, federal officials reintroduced gray wolves from Canada into Yellowstone National Park in 1995 and 1996. Scientists studying the effects of reintroducing the gray wolves say that it has restored the area's natural ecosystem processes and helped it to regain some of its original biodiversity (variety of life-forms).

The fourth and final critical step in an ecological restoration project is to protect the revitalized area from future damage. For example, in the 1980s, cattle grazing and movement degraded the vegetation and soil on the banks of the San Pedro River in Arizona. In order to protect and restore the area, officials banned cattle grazing and off-road vehicle use. Over ten years, secondary ecological succession, the process of regrowth after a destructive event, naturally restored the area.

Unsustainable human activities have caused damage to ecosystems around the world. Through ecological restoration, these areas can be repaired and renewed. At the same time, adopting sustainable policies and practices that protect the environment from additional harm are an important part of sustainable living.

SEE ALSO Biodiversity; Conservation; Ecology; Ecosystems; Invasive Species; Preservation; Wildlife Management

For more information

BOOKS

Galatowitsch, Susan M. *Ecological Restoration.* Sunderland, MA: Sinauer Associates, 2012.

PERIODICALS

Conniff, Richard. "Rebuilding the Natural World: A Shift in Ecological Restoration." *Environment 360* (March 17, 2014). Available online at http://e360.yale.edu/feature/rebuilding_the_natural_world_a_shift_in_ecological_restoration/2747/ (accessed May 3, 2015).

Schierenbeck, Kristina A. "Japanese Honeysuckle (*Lonicera japonica*) as an Invasive Species; History, Ecology, and Context." *Critical Reviews in Plant Sciences* 23, no. 5, (2004): 391–400.

WEBSITES

"Ecological Restoration." Nature.com. http://www.nature.com/scitable/knowledge/library/restoration-ecology-13339059 (accessed May 3, 2015).

"Kissimmee River Restoration." Florida Center for Environmental Studies. http://www.ces.fau.edu/riverwoods/kissimmee.php (accessed May 3, 2015).

"Restoring the Kissimmee River." South Florida Water Management Department. http://my.sfwmd.gov/portal/page/portal/xweb%20protecting%20and%20restoring/kissimmee%20river (accessed May 3, 2015).

Society for Ecological Restoration. http://www.ser.org/ (accessed May 3, 2015).

Ecology

Ecology is the study of interactions between organisms and their physical environment. Ecologists, scientists who study these interactions, often can help scientists predict the cause and effect of human impacts on the environment as well as provide information about how people can live

WORDS TO KNOW

Ecology: The study of the relations and interactions between organisms and their environment.

Evolution: The change and adaptation of organisms to their environments.

Law of Conservation of Matter: The natural law that states that in chemical reactions matter cannot be created or destroyed.

Natural selection: Evolution that occurs through an organism's interactions with the natural world.

Population: A group of individuals of the same species living in an area.

Thermodynamics, First Law of: The natural law that states that in any physical or chemical change, matter is neither created nor destroyed but merely changed from one form to another.

Thermodynamics, Second Law of: The natural law that states that energy always changes from a more useful, more highly organized form to a less useful, less organized form.

---

more sustainably. Understanding how society is a part of the ecological balance of earth is one of the keys to sustainable development.

As a scientific discipline, ecology is fairly new. However, it is thought that human societies have been using principles of ecology as far back as 500,000 BCE. Throughout history, many principles of ecology were understood, but German biologist Ernst Haeckel (1834–1919) first used the term *ecology* in 1866. In 1963 American ecologist Eugene Odum (1913–2002) introduced the idea that ecosystems have both structure and function. It was at this time that ecology became a more widely practiced science.

In the 1960s people began to notice that pollution was having a negative impact on ecosystems. In 1962, American biologist Rachel Carson's (1907–1964) book, *Silent Spring*, was published. Carson brought to people's attention the impacts that pesticide use was having on ecosystems and human health. Since then, scientists have used ecology to determine human impacts on the environment.

A combination of many sciences

Ecology is a multidisciplinary field of study. That means that an ecologist must have some knowledge from many fields. Biology is obviously important, but an ecologist must also understand facets of chemistry, physics, geology, and other sciences. The ways in which organisms interact with each other and their physical environment are ultimately controlled by the laws of physics and chemistry. The chemist's Law of Conservation of Matter is crucial to understanding how organisms interact with the environment. In chemical reactions, which drive all life, matter cannot be created or destroyed. Another way of looking at this is to say that the number of atoms in a chemical reaction never changes; the atoms are simply rearranged into different substances. The cycling of matter through ecosystems in matter cycles, such as the carbon and nitrogen cycles, relies on the Law of Conservation of Matter.

The physics and chemistry concepts that arise from thermodynamics, the study of how energy is transferred, are key to understanding ecosystems. The First Law of Thermodynamics can be stated, as in Brian J. Skinner and Barbara W. Murck's *The Blue Planet*, in these terms: "In any physical or chemical change, matter is neither created or destroyed, but merely changed from one form to another." Consider a pan on a hot stove. Energy from the stove is transferred to the pan, and energy from the pan is transferred to the food in the pan and the air around the stove. The energy entering the pan is equal to the energy that leaves the pan, plus any energy that remains in the pan as the pan becomes hot.

The Second Law of Thermodynamics can be defined (also from *The Blue Planet*) in this way: "Energy always changes from a more useful, more highly organized form, to a less useful, less organized form." All processes in an ecosystem must also conform to these two laws of thermodynamics. If the pan in the previous example is taken from the stove and placed on a cool countertop, the pan contains a concentration of energy because it is hot. The pan will cool because its energy spreads out to the countertop, but some heat also escapes to the air in the kitchen, warming the countertop and the air slightly while the pan cools. The energy concentrated in the pan spreads out until the entire system reaches the same temperature. The Second Law has many implications for all sciences, but two important ones are that energy always moves from hot to cold, never the reverse, and that some energy is always lost as energy is transferred.

The sun is the source of the energy in ecological systems and is controlled by the laws of thermodynamics. When sunlight strikes a plant, a tiny fraction (up to 3 percent) of the energy in the sunlight is captured by photosynthesis and stored as sugars. (Averaged over all of earth, only about 0.05 percent of sunlight is converted to biological energy.) The rest of the

Ecology

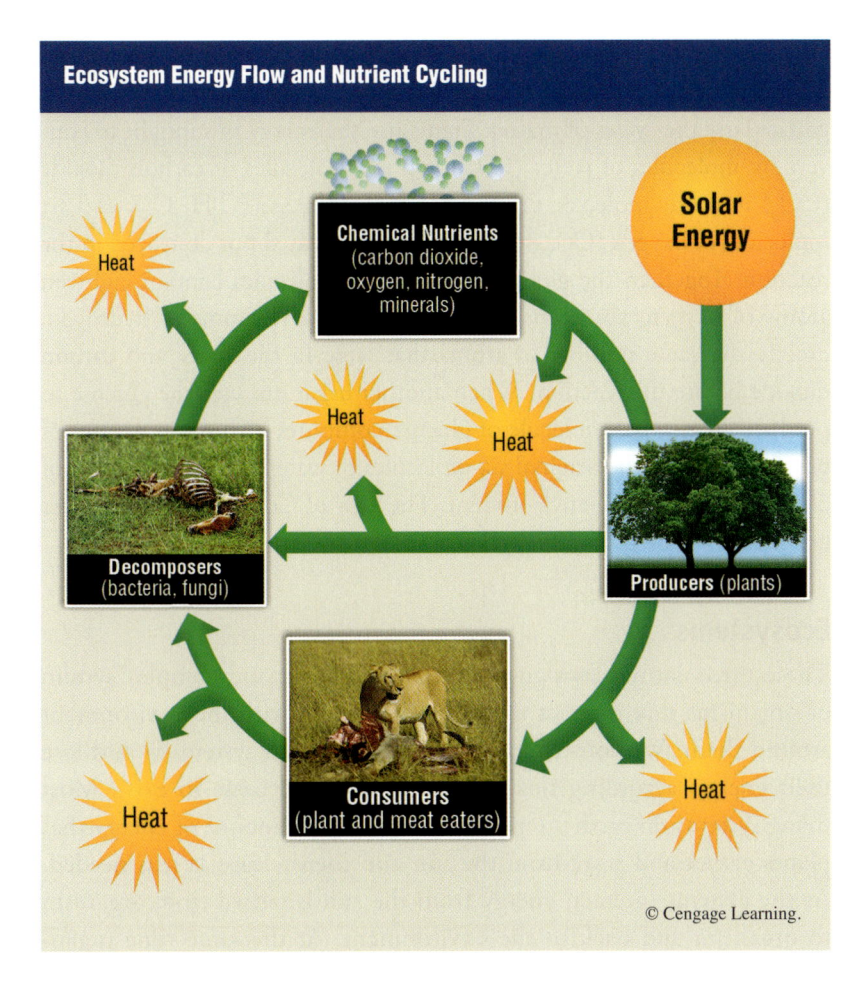

Ecosystem Energy Flow and Nutrient Cycling

Within ecosystems, plants capture energy from the sun and store it as chemical energy. Soil, water, and air provide the matter (the chemicals) that store the energy. Animals must eat either plants or other animals to acquire energy to live. As energy moves through the system, much of it is lost as heat (The Second Law of Thermodynamics.) Matter is never lost. Decomposers return the chemicals to the system to be used again. LEFT: BLACK SHEEP MEDIA/SHUTTERSTOCK.COM. MIDDLE: ANA GRAM/SHUTTERSTOCK.COM. RIGHT: DEBRA MILLET/SHUTTERSTOCK.COM.

sunlight warms the environment and keeps it at a temperature at which the chemical reactions needed for life are possible. As other organisms consume the plants, they use the energy stored in the sugars, but most of the energy is lost as it travels through the environment as heat. When another animal eats the animal that ate the plant, much of the stored energy is again lost to the environment, according to the Second Law. Thus, each trophic level in an ecosystem contains only about 10 percent of the energy found at the previous level. The trophic level is the position an organism occupies in a food chain. According to the First Law, at each trophic level, the energy not passed to the next level is not destroyed but is released into the environment. Eventually, the lost energy escapes to space as heat, because the whole earth system must also obey the First Law.

The Law of Conservation of Matter affects photosynthesis and all other biological processes as organisms interact with the environment, particularly the cycles of matter. Plants use the energy in sunlight to convert six molecules of water (H_2O) and six molecules of carbon dioxide (CO_2) into one molecule of a simple sugar, glucose ($C_6H_{12}O_6$), and six molecules of oxygen (O_2). Atoms are neither created nor destroyed in the reaction. Together, the glucose and oxygen molecules contain eighteen atoms of oxygen, six atoms of carbon, and twelve atoms of hydrogen, exactly the same number of atoms that were in the water and carbon dioxide before the reaction. When another organism uses the glucose to produce energy, the molecule of glucose combines with six molecules of oxygen to return the original six molecules of water and six molecules of carbon dioxide to the environment. The Law of Conservation of Matter governs all of the ecological cycles of matter.

Ecosystems

These three natural laws govern a vast, dynamic, and complex system of organisms that interact with each other and with the environment around them. Without energy from the sun, such systems would lose their energy, according to the Second Law, and cease to exist. Most living systems on earth are powered by the tiny amount of energy that plants gather and store from the sun and then release as it is needed. As the systems interact, energy from the sun is passed from organism to organism and back to the environment. At the same time organisms take atoms from the environment, use them for a time, and then return them to the environment. The atoms are endlessly recycled, and the sun continuously provides the energy needed to organize them. These systems, whether for a small region or for all of earth, are called ecosystems.

However, these systems and cycles are delicately balanced and easily disturbed. Each organism in a system has a function to perform, and disrupting a single part of the system can disturb or destroy the entire system. If only one organism performs a function in an ecosystem, loss of that species can destroy the entire ecosystem. As a simple example, consider a prairie ecosystem having only one species of grass and few or no other plants to capture solar energy and take carbon from the atmosphere. If a disease killed all of the grass, there would be no energy input into the system, and the whole system would be destroyed.

On a larger scale, the First Law says that the energy entering the whole ecosystem of earth must be equal to the energy leaving the system, plus any energy change in the system. Carbon dioxide in the atmosphere decreases the rate at which energy can leave the system. This means there is a positive energy change in the system. Earth must heat up, because the energy leaving is not equal to the energy entering. The result of even this tiny change, a hundred or so more carbon dioxide molecules per billion molecules in the air, will cause the temperature of earth to rise.

Systems thinking and ecology

Places in a system where small changes to one part can greatly affect the whole system, according to the discipline of systems thinking, are called leverage points. As human activity affects ecosystems and the ecology of earth, ecologists must find either the leverage points that are the cause of the damage from human activity or the leverage points that will allow the ecosystem to be restored to normal functioning in order for humans to exist sustainably within the ecosystem.

Human societies are embedded in the whole-earth ecosystem. Their cultural and social values drive their economic systems, their economic systems depend on the resources of the ecosystem to function, and their wastes are released into the ecosystem. When ecologists study the whole of the planet as an ecosystem, they must also account for the effects of humans on the system. By doing so, ecologists can identify the human activities that cause the greatest environmental damage (the bad leverage points), so that those activities can be modified or entirely stopped, to lessen or eliminate the environmental damage they cause. At the same time, ecologists may be able to identify good leverage points that will reverse environmental damage that human activity has already caused. An ecologist must view the environment as a system, not as its individual parts, so that pathways to more sustainable societies can be identified and achieved.

Basic and applied ecology

Ecological research can be basic or applied. The goal of basic research is to learn more about ecosystems. For example, in 1953 Canadian-born American ecologist Robert MacArthur (1930–1972) studied a group of birds that live together in northeastern North America. All of the birds live in the same ecosystem, and each of them eats insects. He found that each kind of bird fed from a different part of each tree. One species found insects inside the trees. Another fed low on the tree, close to the ground. Yet another fed mainly near the top of the tree, and so on. This study helped explain how similar species can live in the same place without depleting the food supply. This type of research is important because it increases the amount of scientific knowledge available. Before the whole of a system can be understood, the role of each element of the system must be known, and the functioning of each cycle and the means by which energy is passed from one trophic level to the next must be understood.

Applied ecology attempts to solve a problem or discover human impacts on ecosystems. For example, Lake Erie has experienced harmful algae blooms. Algae are aquatic organisms that can create food by photosynthesis. Algae blooms occur when the algae living in a body of water reproduce too quickly. Some of these organisms release toxins into the water. The city of Toledo, Ohio, had a drinking water ban for several days in 2014 because of toxins in the water. Applied ecologists are studying the ecology of Lake Erie to determine how to prevent future blooms. Applied ecology, which finds ways to use the science of ecology to enact real-world environmental solutions, is becoming increasingly important as humans continue to determine their impacts on the environment and try to find ways to lessen their negative impacts. A sustainable culture must live within an ecosystem without causing permanent harm to the system.

Ecology is the science that attempts to understand the functioning of organisms and the environment as an entire system. Basic ecology is pure science, while applied ecology attempts to solve a problem. Ecology can be studied in the lab and the field. It is essential that people understand ecology, because to live sustainably humans must abide by natural laws and ecological principles. An ecologist applies knowledge from the fields of biology, chemistry, physics, geology, and many other disciplines to discover the web of relationships between organisms and between organisms and their environments. A better knowledge of the web of relationships can help to identify where the web is broken or weak. The knowledge gained by studying ecology is a key part of identifying how humans can exist in harmony with earth's ecosystem. With such knowledge, humans can develop socially and economically on earth with a minimal level of environmental harm, so that such development can be sustained indefinitely.

Ecology

PRIMARY SOURCE

The "Blue Marble"

Photograph

By: Crew of the *Apollo 17* spacecraft.

Source: NASA. Available online at http://grin.hq.nasa.gov/ABSTRACTS/GPN-2000-001138.html.

About the photograph: The first full-color image of planet Earth was taken on December 7, 1972, by the crew of the Apollo 17 space mission as they headed toward the Moon. The "Blue Marble," as the photo came to be known, is one of the most famous photos ever taken. The photo shows Africa and Antarctica with the earth fully illuminated, because the Sun was behind the spacecraft when the photo was taken. For the first time, the people of earth could see an image of their planet as a whole. The photo helped people realize that the earth is tiny and fragile compared with the endless blackness of space. This new perspective of earth became a unifying symbol for the growing environmental movement of the 1970s, ushering in the "age of ecology."

SEE ALSO Biodiversity; Biomimicry; Carbon Cycle; Carrying Capacity; Ecological Restoration; Ecosystems; Food Web; Nitrogen Cycle; Systems and Systems Thinking; Water Cycle

For more information

BOOKS

Molles, Manuel C., Jr. *Ecology: Concepts and Applications*. 5th ed. Dubuque, IA: McGraw-Hill, 2009.

Skinner, Brian J., and Barbara W. Murck. *The Blue Planet: An Introduction to Earth System Science*. 3rd ed. Hoboken, NJ: Wiley, 2011.

Withgott, Jay H., and Scott R. Brennan. *Environment: the Science Behind the Stories*. 2nd ed. Reading, MA: Benjamin Cummings, 2006.

WEBSITES

Lee, Jane J. "Driven by Climate Change, Algae Blooms Behind Ohio Water Scare Are New Normal." National Geographic, August 6, 2014. http://news.nationalgeographic.com/news/2014/08/140804-harmful-algal-bloom-lake-erie-climate-change-science/ (accessed March 17, 2015).

"The Flow of Energy: Primary Production to Higher Trophic Levels." Introduction to Global Change, October 31, 2008. http://www.globalchange.umich.edu/globalchange1/current/lectures/kling/energyflow/energyflow.html (accessed March 17, 2015).

Morris, Christopher. "Milestones in Ecology." Princeton University Press. http://press.princeton.edu/chapters/s9_m8879.pdf (accessed March 17, 2015).

Economics

Economics is the study of the relationship between money and the production and consumption of goods, services, and resources within a society. Common types of economic systems in the twenty-first century include socialism, communism, and capitalism. Many countries have a mixed economy that includes elements of more than one system. Socialism and communism are forms of planned economies in which the government makes all major decisions about how goods and services are produced and provided on behalf of the citizens. In theory, the citizens jointly own all the factories and property, but the government controls prices and access. In a capitalist economic system, private citizens own factories and property and the cost of goods and services is based on the law of supply and

WORDS TO KNOW

Cost-benefit analysis: An economic tool that helps businesses determine if the benefits of a new product or service will outweigh its costs. In traditional economics, this process usually fails to accurately assess ecosystem services or natural capital.

Ecological economics: A part of economics that promotes sustainability by valuing ecosystems as a whole, rather than simply as land from which natural resources can be taken. It applies market-based principles to the environment to boost the perceived worth of natural resources.

Economics: The study of the relationship between money and the production and consumption of goods, services, and resources within a society.

Ecosystem services: The benefits people obtain from the environment.

Externality: A cost or benefit that affects someone who did not pay for or choose to receive it. Pollution is a common negative externality that affects people who did not cause it.

Free-market system: An economic system in which prices for goods and services are determined by supply and demand.

Natural capital: Any natural resource that can be used to create a good or service. This includes obvious substances such as minerals and water, as well as less obvious things such as pollination or biodiversity hotspots.

Nitrogen fixation: A process that frees the nitrogen in the atmosphere, changing it into a form that can be used by plants to help them grow. Nitrogen compounds are then held in the roots of plants and are released into the soil when a plant dies, fertilizing the soil.

Perverse subsidy: A payment or incentive that encourages a business or industry to continue using environmentally damaging or unsustainable practices.

Subsidy: A sum of money granted by the government to assist a business.

Sustainability: The capacity of the earth's natural systems and human cultural systems to survive, flourish, and adapt to changing environmental conditions for many years into the future.

Sustainable development: Development that meets the needs of the present without compromising the ability of future generations to meet their own needs.

---

demand; this is also called a free-market system. For example, the price of oil on the world market rises and falls depending on how many people want to buy it at a given time. When supply is low and demand is high, a barrel of oil costs more than when demand is low and supply is high.

In the ideal free-market system, consumers benefit from competition because companies try to create a better product at a lower price so their sales will go up. The world economy today is focused on economic growth, which means that each country strives to produce more goods and services at a lower cost and higher profit than it did the previous year. Economic growth is frequently at odds with sustainable development because it undervalues the true costs of using up natural resources, especially those that are nonrenewable. Economics is an essential part of sustainability, because governments and companies must allow people today to meet their needs for goods and services without using up natural resources and making it too difficult for future generations to meet their own needs for goods and services.

Ecological economics

Ecological economics combines ideas from economics, ecology, anthropology, and other fields. It promotes sustainability by valuing ecosystems as a whole, rather than simply as places from which natural resources can be taken. Ecological economics applies market-based principles to the environment to increase the perceived worth of natural resources. For example, in traditional economics, fossil fuels are a natural resource, but the ecosystem from which they are extracted is not valued. Thus, strip mining for coal damages land, pollutes water, and ruins the ecosystem. The land is not valued as much as the coal. In ecological economics, the land and the coal may be equally valued, recognizing that systems such as forests and grasslands have ongoing worth.

The field of ecological economics arose in the late 1980s as a way to promote sustainable development. Two concepts central to ecological economics are natural capital and ecosystem services. Natural capital is any natural resource that can be used to create a good or service. This includes air, land, soil, plants, animals, minerals, energy, natural water purification processes, and nutrient cycling. Natural capital is used to create goods and services, but using them can also generate excess heat, leading to climate change and depleted natural resources, and create pollution and solid waste. Water is a natural resource vital for most manufacturing processes. Soil is a natural resource required for agriculture, and even bees are a natural resource necessary for the pollination and reproduction of many plants. According to ecological economics, these and other sources of natural capital should be valued financially and conserved to promote sustainability.

Ecosystem services are the benefits people gain from the environment. Some of the most important ecosystem services are the geochemical cycles upon which all life on earth depends. This includes the nitrogen, water, carbon, and oxygen cycles. All of these cycles require functioning ecosystems, and all are necessary to produce the food, water, and air we all need to survive. Ecological economics places a monetary value on these processes in an effort to prevent corporations from wasting them. For example, the air we breathe is free, but an ecological economics system would charge a fine to corporations who pollute it. This money would then be used to clean the pollution so the air remains safe to breathe.

A landmark study published in *Ecological Economics* in 1998 divided the earth into terrestrial ecosystems (wetlands, forests, grasslands, rangelands, and croplands) and aquatic ecosystems (coastal waters, open ocean, lakes, and rivers). The researchers found that the annual average value of all major ecosystem services on the planet was 33 trillion U.S. dollars, which is almost double the total value of the global economy. Forest ecosystems alone were estimated to be worth 4.7 trillion dollars annually because the trees remove carbon dioxide (a greenhouse gas) from the air, cycle nitrogen through the soil to help plants grow and then decompose, and add water to the atmosphere through photosynthesis as part of the water cycle. Nothing on earth can accomplish these tasks as efficiently as trees. However, these essential services are not factored into the price of the lumber created by cutting down forest trees. If it were, then the owners of the land would have an incentive to keep the trees intact because they would be worth more alive than they are as lumber.

Perverse subsidies

In a free-market system, consumers reward businesses by paying for their products or services. But this straightforward process can be complicated by subsidies. A subsidy is financial help or a tax break given to a business. Many governments offer subsidies to certain industries. Subsidies can give these industries an unfair advantage over other industries. For example, the U.S. government heavily subsidizes the agriculture, fossil fuels, transportation, water, fisheries, and forestry industries. This encourages these industries to continue operating in sometimes wasteful ways to receive their subsidy rather than adopting new, sustainable tactics that the consumer marketplace might reward. Because of this, these are called perverse subsidies.

Examples of perverse subsidies include paying loggers to cut timber on public land and helping farmers to irrigate their crops with low-cost water. Norman Myers, the environmental scientist who coined the phrase *perverse subsidy,* calculated that these subsidies total about 2 trillion dollars each year, or more than $2,000 for every U.S. taxpayer. These subsidies

Economics

Cost-Benefit Analysis

A cost-benefit analysis is a tool that helps businesses determine if the benefits of a new product or service will outweigh its costs. Analysts add together all the costs, including labor and materials, and subtract the total from how much they think they can sell the new product or service for and how many units they expect to sell. The result is the profit. If this number is high enough, it will make sense for the company to move forward with the project. In ecological economics, however, the cost-benefit analysis technique is used to measure slightly different factors. For instance, the benefits of building a dam, namely the electricity it generates, may or may not be greater than the cost of the dam's effects on the river's ecosystem. Determining cost vs. benefit requires assigning a dollar value to ecosystem services, which is hard to do.

Often, when corporations are asked to conduct a cost-benefit analysis regarding the environment, they overestimate the costs associated with cleaning up or preventing pollution. For example, one U.S. industry organization estimated that the cost of complying with new regulations to protect workers from the negative health effects of vinyl chloride, a cancer-causing gas used to make plastic, would be between 65 and 90 billion dollars. In the end, compliance cost under one billion dollars. The high estimate was essentially a scare tactic used to try to stop the government from enacting any standards that would force the industry to make changes at their own expense. A good cost-benefit analysis outlines all ecosystem services affected along with all short-term and long-term benefits for all populations. It also acknowledges and considers several alternative courses of action.

are difficult to stop because the industries that receive them lobby politicians to continue them. The result is that as long as oil companies receive incentives and subsidies to remove nonrenewable fossil fuels from the earth, it will be difficult for renewable energy companies to compete in the marketplace. Not all subsidies are perverse. The U.S. Department of Energy continues to subsidize the oil industry, but also has provided some subsidies to wind and solar energy companies, for example.

Externalities

An externality is a cost or benefit affecting someone who did not pay for or choose to receive it. Pollution is a common negative externality, because it can affect people who did not cause it. Companies that cause pollution negatively affect an entire society, because the society is responsible for cleaning up the pollution or suffering its effects. Those who live in a neighborhood with air polluted by a nearby factory are forced to breathe unhealthy air. They may have poor health because of this and be forced to spend their income on medication and visits to doctors. This is an externality caused by the company but suffered by residents who had no say in the matter.

Likewise, carbon emissions from motor vehicles that lead to climate change are an externality; everyone is affected by climate change whether they drive a vehicle or not. Measuring externalities is extremely difficult, which makes it nearly impossible to charge consumers or corporations the right amount for them. What is the price tag for reversing climate change and how much should each person pay? Economists try to solve these externalities by making the company account for the effects.

The three pillars of sustainability

The economy is one of the three pillars of sustainability, along with society and the environment. If one pillar fails, a system is unsustainable. Any contribution to sustainability needs to consider all three aspects. This three-pillar concept was introduced at the United Nations' 2005 World Summit on Social Development, one of the largest gatherings of world leaders in history, which focused on creating a holistic solution to the most pressing problems the world faces in the twenty-first century. In the years since, these three pillars have become the basis for various sustainability certification programs, such as those for organic food and fair trade. An economic system needs to take into account social equity—meaning treating all people with respect and fairness—as well as environmental factors that will allow it to continue to provide goods and services for future generations.

PRIMARY SOURCE
Agenda 21

Plan of Action (excerpt)

By: United Nations Division for Sustainable Development

Source: United Nations Division for Sustainable Development, 1992. *Agenda 21*. This document is available online at https://sustainabledevelopment.un.org/content/documents/Agenda21.pdf.

About the document: Agenda 21 is an action plan that provides guidelines for local, state, and national governments and organizations looking to implement sustainable development. This influential document debuted at the 1992 Earth Summit in Rio de Janeiro. Its forty chapters are divided into four sections that concentrate on economics, conservation, stakeholders, and implementation. This excerpt from Chapter 2 acknowledges the global nature of economics and states that sustainable development requires countries to adopt long-term economic policies based on international cooperation, especially between developed and developing countries.

INTERNATIONAL COOPERATION TO ACCELERATE SUSTAINABLE DEVELOPMENT IN DEVELOPING COUNTRIES AND RELATED DOMESTIC POLICIES

2.1 In order to meet the challenges of environment and development, States have decided to establish a new global partnership. This partnership commits all States to engage in a continuous and constructive dialogue, inspired by the need to achieve a more efficient and equitable world economy, keeping in view the increasing interdependence of the community of nations and that sustainable development should become a priority item on the agenda of the international community. It is recognized that, for the success of this new partnership, it is important to overcome confrontation and to foster a climate of genuine cooperation and solidarity. It is equally important to strengthen national and international policies and multinational cooperation to adapt to the new realities.

2.2 Economic policies of individual countries and international economic relations both have great relevance to sustainable development. The reactivation and acceleration of development requires both a dynamic and a supportive international economic environment and determined policies at the national level. It will be frustrated in the absence of either of these requirements. A supportive external economic environment is crucial. The development process will not gather momentum if the global economy lacks dynamism and stability and is beset with uncertainties. Neither will it gather momentum if the developing countries are weighted down by external indebtedness, if development finance is inadequate, if barriers restrict access to markets and if commodity prices and the terms of trade of developing countries remain depressed. The record of the 1980s was essentially negative on each of these counts and needs to be reversed. The policies and measures needed to create an international environment that is strongly supportive of national development efforts are thus vital. International cooperation in this area should be designed to complement and support—not to diminish or subsume—sound domestic economic policies, in both developed and developing countries, if global progress towards sustainable development is to be achieved....

2.5 An open, equitable, secure, non-discriminatory and predictable multilateral trading system that is consistent with the goals of sustainable development and leads to the optimal distribution of global production in accordance with comparative advantage is of benefit to all trading partners. Moreover, improved market access for developing countries' exports in conjunction with sound macroeconomic and environmental policies would have a positive environmental impact and therefore make an important contribution towards sustainable development....

2.8 The international trading environment has been affected by a number of developments that have created new challenges and opportunities and have made multilateral economic cooperation of even greater importance. World trade has continued to grow faster than world output in recent years. However, the expansion of world trade has been unevenly spread, and only a limited number of developing countries have been capable of achieving appreciable growth in their exports. Protectionist pressures and unilateral policy actions continue to endanger the functioning of an open multilateral trading system, affecting particularly the export interests of developing countries. Economic integration processes have intensified in recent years and should impart dynamism to global trade and enhance the trade and development possibilities for developing countries.

SEE ALSO Abundance; Alternative Energy; Biodiversity; Carbon Cycle; Climate Change; Coal; Conservation; Consumption; Fair Trade; Fossil Fuels; Free Trade; Globalization; Green Economy; Jobs; Local Economy; Natural Gas; Natural Resources; Nitrogen Cycle; Oil; Pollution; Soil; Soil Pollution; Solar Power; Sustainability; Waste Management; Water Cycle; Water Pollution; Wind Power

For more information

BOOKS
Ikerd, John. *The Essentials of Economic Sustainability.* Boulder, CO: Kumarian Press, 2012.
Myers, Norman, and Jennifer Kent. *Perverse Subsidies: How Misused Tax Dollars Harm the Environment and the Economy.* Washington, DC: Island Press, 2001.

PERIODICALS
Costanza, Robert, et al. "The Value of the World's Ecosystem Services and Natural Capital." *Ecological Economics* 25, no. 1 (1998): 3–15.

WEBSITES
"Benefit-Cost Analysis." U.S. Environmental Protection Agency, June 24, 2014. http://www.epa.gov/sustainability/analytics/benefit-cost.htm (accessed April 15, 2015).
"What Is Ecological Economics?" Yale Insights, May 2010. http://insights.som.yale.edu/insights/what-ecological-economics (accessed April 13, 2015).

Ecosystems

An ecosystem is a community of living organisms interacting with each other and with the nonliving elements of a specific physical environment. The living organisms in an ecosystem are called biotic elements; these consist of plants, animals, fungi, and bacteria. The nonliving elements of an ecosystem are called abiotic elements; these include the soil, water, rocks, sand, sunlight, air, nutrients, and minerals. Each biotic organism in an ecosystem functions as a producer, consumer, or recycler. Some fill more

Ecosystems

> ## WORDS TO KNOW
>
> **Abiotic:** Not involving living organisms. Nonliving components in an ecosystem include air, sunlight, minerals, and water.
>
> **Biodiversity:** The variety of species or organisms in a given environment or ecosystem. A large range of plant and animal life in a given region is symptomatic of its health; a narrow range or declining number of species in a region may indicate environmental damage or stress.
>
> **Biome:** A habitat consisting of a community of naturally occurring plants and animals that may consist of many ecosystems.
>
> **Biotic:** Describing a living organism. Living components in an ecosystem include bacteria, animals, plants, and fungi.
>
> **Carbon sink:** A reservoir that stores carbon over a long period of time. Carbon sinks can be natural or human made.
>
> **Cellular respiration:** The entire process by which organisms combine oxygen with food molecules, using the chemical energy for life-sustaining processes and casting off carbon dioxide and water as waste products.
>
> **Coniferous forest:** A forest with trees whose leaves are small and needlelike and which stay green year-round.
>
> **Deciduous forest:** A forest whose trees have leaves that change with the four seasons, turning color in the fall, falling off in the winter, and growing back in the spring.
>
> **Ecosystem:** A complete and interdependent system of biotic (living) and abiotic (nonliving) components that cycles matter and transfers energy within a given area. The three major types of ecosystems are freshwater, terrestrial, and marine.
>
> **Ecosystem services:** The benefits an ecosystem provides to humankind. The four main categories are provisioning, regulating, supporting, and cultural.

than one role. These functions are all necessary to continue the cycles that allow the ecosystem to thrive. An ecosystem functions to harness and distribute energy and to cycle elements such as carbon, nitrogen, and phosphorus throughout the environment so they can be used by plants and animals. Ecosystems can range in size from microscopic to hundreds of miles wide. Almost all ecosystems on the earth utilize energy from the sun.

Ecosystems and biomes

A biome is a group of ecosystems in a specific geographic location with similar weather patterns, climate, plants, and animals. Biomes are defined by the types of plants and animals that live in them. Many ecosystems may be present in a single biome. Examples of biomes are the tundra, which is characterized by cold weather and lack of trees; the tropical rain forest, characterized by abundant biodiversity (variety of life-forms),

Estuary: The body of water that forms when the freshwater of rivers and lakes flows into the ocean, mixing with saltwater.

Intertidal zone: An area that is above water at low tide and under water at high tide.

Lagoon: A shallow saltwater area that is close to the sea but separated from it by sandbars, islands, or coral reefs.

Lichen: An organism that is a combination of alga and fungus living in a relationship that benefits them both.

Matter cycling: The movement of matter between abiotic (nonliving) and biotic (living) components of an ecosystem.

Prairie: An ecosystem of grasses and shrubs with a mild climate and moderate rainfall.

Rainforest: A temperate or tropical forest with tall, broad-leaved trees which require a humid climate and a large amount of precipitation.

Savanna: A tropical grassland ecosystem with shrubs and only a few trees, characterized by a very long dry season followed by an extremely wet season.

Sustainability: The capacity of the earth's natural systems and human cultural systems to survive, flourish, and adapt to changing environmental conditions for many years into the future.

Taiga: A subarctic forest region (just south of the Arctic Circle) composed of trees such as spruce, pine, and fir, which have needles instead of broad leaves.

Transfer of energy: The process of energy exchange from one form to another within an ecosystem. For example, photosynthesis transfers energy from the sun into carbohydrates.

Tundra: A region with extremely low temperatures, little diversity of life-forms, and a short growing season.

lush vegetation, and wet weather; and grasslands, characterized by fertile grasses and few trees. Thus, a biome is a large area defined by weather and biota (the flora and fauna of a region). Ecosystems are defined by their ability to cycle and distribute nutrients and energy throughout the environment. The earth has only a handful of agreed-upon biomes but many thousands of ecosystems.

Ecosystem services

Ecosystems provide ecosystem services; these are the benefits humankind receives from an ecosystem. These services are divided into four main categories: provisioning, regulating, supporting, and cultural. A provisioning service is any product that people can take from nature, that is, a provision. These provisions include food, water, lumber, fossil fuels, and plants that can be used for medicine and textiles. A regulating service is the benefit that an ecosystem provides through regulation of a natural phenomenon that people count on. For example, bees pollinate plants so that the plants can reproduce and continue providing us with food. Ecosystems aid the decomposition of dead plants and animals so their remains can nourish the soil and help new plants grow. Many wetlands ecosystems are crucial for preventing floods and soil erosion that could cause damage to buildings and roads. Two of the most important regulating ecosystem services are the control of climate and the storage of carbon so our atmosphere remains temperate and able to sustain life.

Cultural services refer to the advantages people gain from interacting with the environment. People who enjoy hiking, surfing, swimming, rock climbing, camping, and numerous other activities are taking advantage of an ecosystem's cultural services. Additionally, cultural services refer to the ways an ecosystem has affected the development of a group of people. For instance, civilizations that evolved along the Nile in Egypt, where the annual flooding of the river regulated their agricultural and social activities, benefited from different cultural services than did the nearby desert-dwelling Bedouin tribes, who stayed on the move because of lack of water. Finally, supporting services refer to the fundamental processes that allow life to continue to thrive on the earth. Without supporting services, none of the other ecosystem services would exist. For example, the supporting service of photosynthesis, which is how plants use chlorophyll to turn light energy into chemical energy, releases oxygen as a waste product. This oxygen is what people and animals breathe to live. The water cycle and the nitrogen cycle are two other supporting services that are crucial to sustain life.

A major issue in sustainability is learning how to protect ecosystems so all life can continue to benefit from ecosystem services. What nature provides for free needs to be preserved.

Matter cycling and energy transfer

The two major functions of an ecosystem are to cycle matter and to transfer energy. An example of matter cycling is the carbon cycle. Plants, which are biotic, absorb carbon dioxide, which is abiotic, from the air and turn it into carbohydrates through photosynthesis. Animals eat the plants to gain the energy from the plants' carbohydrates. Thus, the carbon molecules are absorbed by the animals. The animals access the energy in the carbohydrates during the process of cellular respiration. Through the process of cellular respiration, carbohydrates are broken down into molecules of carbon dioxide and water. Animals breathe out carbon dioxide, and it once again enters the atmosphere. Plants then reabsorb the carbon dioxide, and the cycle continues.

Matter cycling in ecosystems obeys the law of the conservation of mass. This law states that matter can be neither created nor destroyed. That means a carbon atom in your body today could be the very same carbon atom that was part of a dinosaur's tail more than sixty-five million years ago. This is why conservation is so important to sustainability; human beings cannot simply make more carbon, oxygen, or nitrogen whenever they want. People need to ensure that these elements remain where they can do more good than harm. For example, when carbon is inside plants helping them grow, it is more useful then when billions of plants are burned (as in clear-cutting the rain forest) and excess carbon is released into the atmosphere, where it contributes to climate change.

Energy transfer is when energy is exchanged between one system and another. For instance, photosynthesis is the process whereby energy from the sun is transferred to a plant by conversion into carbohydrates. When plants are eaten by animals, the plants' energy is transferred to the animals. In a functioning ecosystem, the energy transfers from animals to plants to microorganisms in the soil.

Types of ecosystems

Ecosystems are divided into three major categories: freshwater, marine, and terrestrial. Freshwater ecosystems include lakes, ponds, rivers, and wetlands; they differ from marine ecosystems in that they have a lower salt content. Freshwater ecosystems cover only about 1.8 percent of the earth's surface, but they support a wide variety of plant and animal life. Freshwater ecosystems are further defined by whether or not their water is primarily still (a lentic ecosystem) or flowing (a lotic ecosystem). Ponds and wetlands are usually lentic, and rivers and streams are usually lotic. The important abiotic factors in freshwater ecosystems are light, temperature, wind, substrate (the earthy material at the bottom), and chemistry. Estuary ecosystems occur where rivers or streams are connected to the open sea. They are one of the most biodiverse ecosystems.

Marine ecosystems have a significant salt content and cover more area on the earth than freshwater and terrestrial ecosystems combined.

Ecosystems

A coral reef ecosystem off the coast of Indonesia. Coral reefs represent some of the oldest and most complex communities of plants and animals on the earth. © ETHAN DANIELS/SHUTTERSTOCK.COM

They include oceans, saltwater marshes, intertidal zones, estuaries, lagoons, coral reefs, the deep sea, and the sea floor. Marine ecosystems have remarkable biodiversity, and their health is important to terrestrial ecosystems because they produce oxygen, absorb carbon dioxide, and affect the climate for the rest of the planet. Marsh ecosystems are also very biodiverse and play an important role during storms. They absorb flooding and storm water, thereby forming a protective buffer between the ocean and inland ecosystems. A coral reef is an underwater marine ecosystem made of layers of calcium carbonate that are grown by corals, tiny animals that attach themselves to solid surfaces. Coral forms the basis of a biodiverse ecosystem that includes many varieties of aquatic life, from sponges and mollusks to fish and dolphins.

The six major forms of terrestrial, or land-based, ecosystems include the tundra, taiga, deciduous forest, rain forest, grassland, and desert.

A tundra ecosystem is characterized by extremely cold temperatures, low relative humidity, short growing seasons, and few trees. This is the predominant ecosystem near the North and South Poles. Plant species are small and include shrubs, grasses, mosses, and lichens. The soil is usually permanently frozen. Because of these harsh conditions, the tundra supports few mammals, although birds may be numerous. People who populate the tundra tend to live in small communities that are scattered far apart so they do not exhaust the ecosystem's limited resources.

The taiga is an ecosystem found in northern latitudes but south of the tundra. Sometimes called the boreal forest, the taiga is the world's largest terrestrial ecosystem, representing 29 percent of the earth's land. It is characterized by harsh winters and coniferous trees, which are evergreen trees that reproduce through seeds held in pinecones. Most of Canada and Russia are a taiga ecosystem.

Deciduous forests are composed of trees and plants that lose their leaves in autumn. This ecosystem is common throughout the eastern half of the United States, most of Europe, and portions of China. It is characterized by mild temperatures and between 30 and 60 inches (76 and 152 centimeters) of rainfall per year.

A rainforest is a lush forest with tall, broad-leaved trees. Rainforests typically are found in wet tropical regions around the Equator. They may be tropical or temperate, but tropical rainforests are more common. Tropical rainforests have very warm and wet climates; annual rainfall may exceed 70 inches (177 centimeters). Rainforests are important because they provide oxygen, act as carbon sinks (reservoirs to store carbon), and help regulate weather patterns for much of the planet.

Grassland ecosystems occur on all continents except Antarctica. They include savannas and prairies and usually have less rainfall than deciduous forests. Soil is held in place by the grass roots, and if the grass is disturbed, the soil quickly erodes, or wears away. Grasslands are often used as pastures for livestock.

Desert ecosystems have small amounts of rainfall. Soil tends to be sandy and supports little vegetation or animal life. Because there is little plant life to absorb sunlight, the temperature can fall drastically at night and be unbearably hot during the day. Plants and animals in the desert have adapted to conserve water. While some deserts, such as the Sahara in Africa and the Arabian in the Middle East, have large sand dunes, the biggest deserts in the world are actually the cold deserts of Antarctica and the Arctic.

Ecosystem Restoration

Ecosystem restoration, sometimes called ecological remediation, is the process of restoring an ecosystem to its original state after it has suffered damage. The goal is to make the ecosystem as resilient, or strong, as it used to be. It takes time to restore an ecosystem, as well as the cooperation of many people who all agree that the ecosystem should be returned to its natural state. It may also take a lot of money, especially if the ecosystem was damaged by the dumping of toxic waste or through the activities of a mining operation or some other form of heavy industry.

One of the largest ecosystem restoration projects undertaken in U.S. history is taking place in Florida's Everglades. The Everglades ecosystem is a tropical wetland and saw grass prairie that is sometimes called "a river of grass." It is home to many species of animals that are rare elsewhere in the United States, such as alligators and crocodiles, bald eagles, many species of salamanders, and the Florida panther. Beginning in the 1950s, over 1,000 miles (about 1,609 kilometers) of canals and levies were built to divert much of the Everglade's water to areas that were undergoing economic development. As a result, water quality and animal habitats in the Everglades were harmed by rising levels of phosphorus and mercury. State and federal authorities launched the Comprehensive Everglades Restoration Plan in 2000 to return the Everglades to its pre-1950s state. The plan covers 18,000 square miles (about 28,968 square kilometers) and is estimated to cost billions of dollars and take thirty years to complete.

The plan involves redirecting freshwater that now flows to the Atlantic and Gulf of Mexico to the areas in the river of grass that need it. This calls for deconstructing many of the canals and dams that were built to redirect the water in the first place. The hope is that when the water returns, so will the plants and animals that are native to the area. Much progress has been made in revitalizing the ecosystem, but much more work needs to be done.

Threats to ecosystems

Ecosystems are threatened when their processes become unbalanced. Most threats are anthropogenic, meaning they are caused by humans. When too many biotic or abiotic materials are taken from an ecosystem without being replaced, it becomes damaged. When it is damaged to the point that it cannot recover on its own, the ecosystem becomes unsustainable and can collapse.

Deforestation, or the clear-cutting of trees, harms boreal and rainforest ecosystems. The Amazon rainforest ecosystem has been greatly damaged by deforestation. Millions of acres of trees have been cut down since the 1970s so the land can be farmed or become pasture for cattle. Removing the trees reduces the amount of carbon dioxide the ecosystem can

The Cononaco River in the Ecuadorian Amazon rainforest. © DR. MORLEY READ/SHUTTERSTOCK.COM

absorb. Allowing carbon to be released into the atmosphere is believed to contribute to climate change. By destroying their habitat, deforestation leads to the extinction of millions of biotic species before scientists can even discover them.

Other specific threats to ecosystems include overfishing of lakes and marine ecosystems. Many ecosystems are contaminated with poisonous substances, such as pesticides and animal waste from farms or heavy metals from industry. Invasive species that people have introduced to an area choke out species of plants and animals that are native to the area. Ocean ecosystems are threatened by acidification. This happens when carbon dioxide in the atmosphere dissolves into water and forms carbonic acid. This acidification kills coral reefs and weakens the shells of many ocean animals.

Biodiversity within ecosystems is essential for sustainability. A multitude of biotic and abiotic components allows an ecosystem to cycle matter and transfer energy in many ways; this makes it strong. When ecosystems are strong and protected from damage, they can continue providing us with ecosystem services that are essential for life on the earth.

SEE ALSO Biodiversity; Carbon Cycle; Ecological Restoration; Ecology; Nitrogen Cycle; Soil; Sustainability; Water Cycle

For more information

BOOKS

Burk, Sandy. *Let the River Run Silver Again! How One School Helped Return the American Shad to the Potomac River and How You Too Can Help Protect and Restore Our Living Waters.* Newark, OH: MacDonald and Woodward, 2005.

Davis, Barbara J. *Biomes and Ecosystems.* New York: Gareth Stevens, 2007.

Lundgren, Julie K. *How Ecosystems Work.* Vero Beach, FL: Rourke Publishing, 2012.

WEBSITES

"Ecosystem Services." National Wildlife Federation. http://www.nwf.org/Wildlife/Wildlife-Conservation/Ecosystem-Services.aspx (accessed June 3, 2015).

"Ecosystems." NatureWorks. New Hampshire Public Television, 2015. http://www.nhptv.org/natureworks/nwepecosystems.htm (accessed April 28, 2015).

"Energy Transfer in Ecosystems." SchoolTube, 2013. https://www.schooltube.com/video/610451f165de8f639c66/ (accessed April 28, 2015).

"Progress Toward Restoring the Everglades." The National Academy of Sciences. 2008. http://dels.nas.edu/resources/static-assets/materials-based-on-reports/reports-in-brief/everglades_brief_final.pdf (accessed June 3, 2015).

"Terrestrial Ecosystems." United Nations Environment Programme. http://www.unep.org/ecosystemmanagement/UNEPsWork/TerrestrialEcosystems/tabid/436/Default.aspx (accessed April 27, 2015).

Ecotourism

Ecotourism, or ecological tourism, is a combination of vacation travel and educational experience with a little bit of adventure. Travelers interested in nature go to exotic locations to see extraordinary plants or animals. Tourists interested in history go to distant sites of historical interest. Visitors interested cultures go to interact with local people and experience their ways of life.

Ecotourism promotes personal growth and knowledge building. It also may boost learning about sustainable ways for all of us to live on earth. Ecotourism may be a vacation, but it is also about education and sometimes action.

Visiting fragile environments

Tourism is one of the world's largest industries. More people can travel farther and go to more places than ever before. People travel for a variety of reasons. Some like to see new environments. Others want to experience different cultures. Also, travelers want to have fun. Ecotourism can

> **WORDS TO KNOW**
>
> **Cultural heritage:** Refers to parts of culture you can see and touch (for example, artifacts, buildings, and monuments) as well as things that you can't see or touch (for example, traditions, languages, and rituals).
>
> **Developing country:** A country that has a low standard of living, including low average annual income per person, high infant mortality rates, widespread poverty, and an underdeveloped economy. Most of these countries are located in Africa, Asia, and Latin America.
>
> **Ecosystem:** A complete and interdependent system of biotic (living) and abiotic (nonliving) components that cycles matter and transfers energy within a given area. The three major types of ecosystems are freshwater, terrestrial, and marine.
>
> **Ecotourism:** The practice of traveling to beautiful natural places for pleasure in a way that does not damage the environment there.
>
> **Exploit:** To take unfair advantage of, usually for personal gain.
>
> **Low-impact:** With little harmful effect.

satisfy all of these desires. Most importantly, it can do it in environmentally responsible, culturally sensitive, and economically sustainable ways.

Ecotourism usually involves travel to places of natural beauty. The main attractions may be unusual landscapes or rare plants and animals. Ecotourists often also have interest in visiting with local people. Unfortunately, many ecotourism destinations are in fragile environments. Ecotourism strives to go beyond simply looking at nature. It seeks to protect these vulnerable places and sustain them. At the same time, ecotourism can provide local people with income.

The goals of ecotourism

Delicate natural places can be at risk. If too many people visit, fragile environments may be damaged. Ideally, these places can be preserved for future generations. The main goal of sustainable tourism is to provide long-term, ongoing benefits.

Ecotourism is responsible tourism, meaning that ecotourists share a concern for the environment and support local cultures. Most ecotours have these goals:

- To encourage low-impact travel to natural areas.
- To raise environmental awareness that protects fragile ecosystems.
- To support local residents and improve their quality of life.
- To provide educational opportunities for both the visitor and residents.

Ecotourism

Sequoia National Park in California contains big trees (such as these giant sequoias thought to be between 1,800 and 2,700 years old), high peaks, and deep canyons. It attracts over one million visitors every year. © GARY SAXE/SHUTTERSTOCK.COM

Ecotourism benefits and costs

Benefits for travelers Many travelers are eager for ecotourism trips. They like to learn while they travel. Such visitors even have a chance to do volunteer work. They truly enjoy meeting local people. These active travelers often become enthusiastic promoters of conservation.

Benefits for host countries Ecotourism also benefits the local people. It helps their economy, and it can help to protect and even improve the environment. Local people gain by operating small businesses and having jobs related to tourism. These are important economic opportunities:

- Ecotours involve only small investments by local people, yet they can dramatically improve the nation's economic base.
- Tour profits can help to finance protection of fragile natural areas.
- Educational ecotourism can fund research programs.

In developing countries there may not be many ways to make money. Successful ecotourism relies on keeping ecosystems healthy. Thus locals also want keep the areas natural and undamaged. Destructive practices like poaching or burning forests may be reduced if ecotourism is a priority for a community. Revenue from visitors helps to fund national parks and reserves, which creates jobs for local residents. They can work as wildlife guides, park rangers, or service workers in the tourist hotels and restaurants. People are motivated to care for the land when it means earning money from tourism.

Dangers to the environment Ecotourism may not be good in every case. Some areas are just too ecologically sensitive to be visited by tourists. If not handled in a sustainable way, there can be damage to or even extinction of some plants and animals. The increase of tourist hotels may cause too much building or construction in fragile areas.

Disadvantages for locals Care must be taken to ensure that ecotourism does not exploit, or take advantage of, local people. Hotels, parks, and shops must benefit all of the community and not just the owners and tourists. There is a tendency for profits to end up with just a few individuals, rather than shared among members of the community. In addition, local economies may end up over-dependent on tourism that may not last.

Ecotourism is about travelers from other parts of the world and other cultures meeting local people. Unfortunately, when cultures meet, local people tend to be the ones that change their way of life. They are more likely to adopt the visitors' lifestyle rather than preserve their own cultural practices. All ecotourists should respect cultural heritage. Cultural heritage is made up of things you can see and touch: for example, paintings, drawings, monuments, and buildings; as well as things that you can't: for example, traditions, oral histories, languages, and rituals that are passed down from generation to generation.

Ecotour locations

Ecotours can take place anywhere in the world. There are major ecotourism programs in South America, Central America, Africa, Southeast Asia, and the Pacific Islands. These areas all have large areas of land that are still in their natural state. Sustainable ecotourism seeks to keep theses areas unspoiled and protected. However, ecotourism does not always involve traveling to far away

Ecotourism

> ### Samples of Ecotours
>
> Visit an elephant sanctuary in Cambodia.
>
> Observe blue-footed boobies in the Galapagos Islands.
>
> Zip-line through a canopy of orchids in a rainforest.
>
> Go snorkeling with sea lions.
>
> Kayak through coastal cave environments in Thailand.
>
> Tour the rain forests of the Amazon.
>
> Take a safari to photograph wildlife in Kenya.
>
> Dive through a coral reef in Australia.
>
> Find colorful rainforest birds in Costa Rica.
>
> Help protect endangered sea turtles.

or exotic places. There may be ecotourism locations in a European city or in the United States.

The United States has a large national park system. Several states have ecotourism programs in place. Alaska has stunningly beautiful natural areas in Denali, Tongass, Glacier Bay, and Ketamai National Parks. There are wildlife reserves for animals such as caribou, bears, muskoxen, and sea lions. Hawaii is a tropical paradise with native plants, animals, and volcanic activity. Rocky Mountain National Park in Colorado, the Grand Canyon in Arizona, and Yellowstone National Park all offer ecotourism programs for visitors, and there are many others.

Sustainable ecotourism

Sustainable ecotourism protects ecosystems. It is an opportunity to experience plants, animals, and natural wonders. There is lasting value in travel that lets you live or view life the way that people do in diverse parts of the world. Travel adventures and unusual experiences sometimes awaken special passions that may influence people's career and life choices so that they live more sustainably in the future.

SEE ALSO Activism; Biodiversity; Ecological Footprint; Economics; Ecosystems; Ecovillages

For more information

BOOKS

Honey, Martha. *Ecotourism and Sustainable Development: Who Owns Paradise?* 2nd ed. Washington, DC: Island Press, 2008.

Wearing, Stephen, and John Neil. *Ecotourism: Impacts, Potentials, and Possibilities.* New York: Routledge, 2009.

PERIODICALS

Carpenter, Susan. "In Panama, a Taste of the Tropics and a New State of Mind." *Los Angeles Times* (February 28, 2010). Available online at http://www.latimes.com/travel/la-tr-panama-20100228-story.html (accessed March 18, 2015).

WEBSITES

"Defining Eco-Tourism." The Global Development Research Center. http://www.gdrc.org/uem/eco-tour/etour-define.html (accessed March 18, 2015).

Gordon, David G. "Ecotourism: World Travel Goes Green." Scholastic.com .http://www.scholastic.com/teachers/article/ecotourism-world-travel-goes-green (accessed March 18, 2015).

Whelan, Court. "Spotlight on Sustainability: Why is Ecotourism Special?" WWF.org, September 24, 2013. http://www.worldwildlife.org/blogs/good-nature-travel/posts/spotlight-on-sustainability-why-is-ecotourism-special (accessed November 13, 2014).

Ecovillages

Ecovillages are communities of individuals who choose to live together with the shared goal of living in a way that is more environmentally friendly and sustainable, while having a smaller ecological impact. Each person who joins an ecovillage must be committed to the concept of community living, and work with the other members to realize the goals of the community. In order to be self-sufficient, an ecovillage needs members with a wide variety of skills that complement the skills of the other members. All the skills needed to support the community must be present within the population. The scale of the population of an ecovillage is deliberately kept small, so that every member of the community can know and interact with every other member.

Ecovillages can be intentional communities, where individuals choose to be members of the village and the village chooses who can live there, or they can be the result of a traditional community attempting to improve their livelihood while adopting more eco-friendly patterns. In resource-poor, developing countries, for instance, indigenous communities may develop into ecovillages as a way to lessen their ecological footprint, or impact on the environment, while increasing their wealth and resources. According to the Global Ecovillage Network database, as of June 2015, there were over one thousand ecovillages worldwide, on every continent except Antarctica.

Low ecological footprint community

The infrastructure of an ecovillage is deliberately built with the goal of living with the smallest possible ecological footprint. Homes are built with local materials, so that a minimum of fossil fuel is used to transport them. Solar or wind power generators within the ecovillage supply residents with electricity, and excess green energy may be sold to the

Ecovillages

WORDS TO KNOW

Consensus government: Government by obtaining the agreement of all, or by minimizing the objections of as many as possible.

Digesters: A device that uses bacteria to convert organic waste to methane.

Ecological footprint: The measure of human stress on the planet's ecosystems. The footprint considers how much land and water resources a population consumes and the ability of the environment to absorb the population's corresponding waste.

Intentional community: Planned neighborhood or village where all of the people in the community choose to live and work together for a common purpose.

---

local utility company, so that it can be used to supply energy to other areas. The village is kept small so that no transportation other than walking and/or biking is needed. Buildings are designed to require as little heating and cooling as possible, to reduce their energy footprint. For the same reason, homes are usually smaller than typical homes, and heavily insulated.

An ecovillage community often uses ecologically sound methods to purify and distribute its own water and processes its own wastewater. The gardens use sewage and kitchen waste as compost for fertilizer. Wastewater that would ordinarily go to a sewage treatment facility is instead reused.

Members of the ecovillage "Grishino" and others gather during a festival. The main activity of this Russian ecovillage is the preservation and restoration of the surrounding forest. © DE VISU/SHUTTERSTOCK.COM

Garden and sewer waste can also be collected in containers called digesters, where bacteria can convert it into methane gas. The methane can then be used for cooking or heating.

Ecovillages generally produce all or almost all of their own food. The food produced on ecovillage farms and gardens is raised organically, without chemical fertilizers and pesticides. Many ecovillages use organic agriculture as a source of income. Food raised in the ecovillage is sold through community-supported agriculture (CSA) markets or farmers' markets to produce income for the ecovillage. This incoming money also pays for the small amount of fuel used by farming equipment and trucks to bring the produce to market.

Laboratory for sustainability

The land on which an ecovillage is built is usually owned by the community and shared by members in a communal or cooperative manner. Members pay a share into a trust, or lease part of the land to build their homes. These funds are placed in a trust that is managed by all of the members of the community, or a group elected by the community. Most ecovillages have building and farming equipment, storage buildings, and cars or trucks that are shared. Many have a large common building that is shared by all of the members. This large building can be used as a meeting hall, a schoolhouse, a general store, and for community-wide social events.

Members of ecovillages join not only in order to reduce their own ecological footprint, but also to show others that living in a more sustainable way *can* be done. As more and more people live in low footprint homes and communities, the members of an ecovillage gain valuable experience and learn better ways to live sustainably. Ecovillages often have tours that show people outside the community how they are living in a more sustainable manner. Ecovillages also host educational programs, such as workshops and classes, that teach people about sustainability subjects such as organic agriculture and/or

The Ecovillage Model

Starting in 2012, Habitat for Humanity, a nonprofit organization that uses volunteer labor and donations to construct homes for needy families, began building an ecovillage in River Falls, Wisconsin. The goal of this project is to apply the best practices for community planning and management to create a self-sufficient, sustainable community lifestyle. The completed project will have eighteen homes, built in part by their new occupants and in part by volunteers. The community will contain shared services, such as renewable energy systems and outdoor spaces for community gardens. The goal of the ecovillage is to be a model for future investors by demonstrating a positive investment return, while illustrating the viability of sustainable living design.

permaculture (agricultural ecosystems designed to be sustainable and self-sufficient), low-impact building, low-polluting industries, and natural waste treatment.

Community decisions

Since ecovillages tend to be small, every villager usually knows all of the other villagers. When choices have to be made, ecovillages typically use a consensus method of government, instead of electing leaders. Alternatives are discussed and changed until all members agree that an option is desirable. Under consensus decision-making, proposals are changed until no serious objections to the proposal remain. Another popular way of making decisions is that committees of members who are knowledgeable about a given aspect of village life, such as the sewer system, and how that system impacts the community and the environment, make decisions related to their area of expertise.

Low footprint economy

Since ecovillages produce almost all of what they need themselves, they generally do not need to buy much from outside of the village except when starting up. When an ecovillage is first established, solar power equipment, tractors, and many other items that the villagers cannot make themselves need to be purchased. All members pay a share of these costs, or they are taken from community income. Once an ecovillage is running, it buys very little from outside its community. Often though, a member or members will have low-footprint businesses, often farming or crafts, that sell to people outside of the community to provide some income. Within an ecovillage, members will trade with each other, using barter or some local currency developed inside and for the village economy. If villagers have nothing else to trade, they always have their labor, which is valuable.

For those who are willing to give up some comfort and material wealth, and who are willing to do some hard work, an ecovillage offers a rewarding way of life that reduces their impact on the environment and leads the way to a more sustainable future. In an ecovillage, members cause as little harm as possible to the environment and live with a high level of social equality. The members of ecovillages are developing the means to live sustainably and independently, and offer an example to others of ways to pursue more eco-friendly living.

SEE ALSO Alternative Energy; Building Design; Ecological Footprint; Farming, Sustainable; Sustainability; Transition Towns Movement

For more information

BOOKS
Litfin, Karen T. *Ecovillages: Lessons for Sustainable Community.* Malden, MA: Polity Press, 2014.

PERIODICALS
Brown, Kassandra. "Moving to an Ecovillage." *Natural Life Magazine* (Nov.–Dec. 2013). Available online at http://www.life.ca/naturallife/1312/moving-to-an-ecovillage.htm (accessed March 13, 2015).

McAteer, M. J. "Where We Live: Loudoun's Environmentally Conscious Eco Village." *Washington Post* (December 28, 2011). Available online at http://www.washingtonpost.com/realestate/where-we-live-loudouns-environmentally-conscious-ecovillage/2011/12/19/gIQAoCPLMP_story.html (accessed March 13, 2015).

WEBSITES
"Ecovillage." Berea College. http://www.berea.edu/sens/ecovillage/ (accessed December 16, 2014).

"Farming and Food." Ecovillage Ithaca. http://ecovillageithaca.org/grow/farming-and-food/ (accessed December 16, 2014).

"GEN db." Database of the Global Ecovillage Network. http://db.ecovillage.org/en (accessed June 2, 2015).

Gilman, Robert. "The Eco-village Challenge." Context Institute. http://www.context.org/iclib/ic29/gilman1/ (accessed December 16, 2014).

"Starting a Residential Intentional Community." Ecovillage Education US. http://www.ecovillageeducation.com/startingintentionalcommunityworkshop (accessed December 16, 2014).

"What is an Ecovillage?" Global Ecovillage Network. http://gen.ecovillage.org/en/article/what-ecovillage (accessed August 11, 2015).

Endangered and Threatened Species

When no living members of a species can be found anywhere on earth, the species is considered extinct. Since life appeared on earth, numerous plant and animal species have become extinct. There have been between three and five mass extinctions, which are periods when unusually large numbers of species die out, in earth's history. Scientists believe that these rare mass extinctions were caused by catastrophic environmental events,

WORDS TO KNOW

Aquatic: Having to do with water, such as a species that lives in water.

Biodiversity: The variety of species or organisms in a given environment or ecosystem. A large range of plant and animal life in a given region is symptomatic of its health; a narrow range or declining number of species in a region may indicate environmental damage or stress.

Ecosystem: A complete and interdependent system of biotic (living) and abiotic (nonliving) components that cycles matter and transfers energy within a given area. The three major types of ecosystems are freshwater, terrestrial, and marine.

Endangered: At high risk of extinction.

Extinct: No longer in existence.

Habitat: The natural environment where a living organism lives.

Poacher: A person who illegally kills protected animals.

Threatened: Species that are considered critically endangered, endangered, or vulnerable.

Vulnerable: Species that face a possibility of extinction in the world, but are less likely to become extinct than those considered to be endangered.

---

such as ice ages or asteroids from outer space crashing on the earth. Although fossils and other scientific evidence indicate that all species eventually become extinct, the process is usually gradual and involves small numbers of species at a time.

Scientists believe the earth is currently undergoing another mass extinction as a result of human population growth. Species are now becoming extinct one hundred to one thousand times faster than they did before humans evolved. Scientists theorize that human activities such as excessive depletion of natural resources; overhunting of wild animals for meat and other products; destruction of habitats; and the effects of human activities, such as air, water, and ground pollution, and climate change; are the cause of this mass extinction. Many environmental scientists predict that by the end of the twenty-first century, up to half of the world's known species will be extinct and many species, such as elephants, chimpanzees, and tigers, will only exist in zoos and wildlife preserves.

Extinction risks

The International Union for Conservation of Nature (IUCN), which monitors and classifies species' risks of extinction, classifies these risks into several categories. Under the IUCN system, species are ranked and listed as extinct, critically endangered, endangered, vulnerable, or threatened, based on the number of existing individuals. These classifications are used to determine the level of protection needed for each species. Although some species have been removed from these lists due to conservation efforts, the lists are growing.

Scientists are unsure of how many species there are on earth. Estimates range from two million to one hundred million. It is known that populations of the approximately two million identified plant and animal species on earth are decreasing to different degrees. Several factors influence their susceptibility to extinction. Species able to thrive under extreme conditions such as hot or cold climates are less likely to become extinct. Species that can eat a variety of foods are also at less risk of extinction. Those with more limited diets, such as giant pandas, which exclusively eat bamboo, are at a higher extinction risk. As American biodiversity expert Edward O. Wilson (1929–) states, "The first animal species to go are the big, the slow, the tasty, and those with valuable parts."

Biodiversity is important

Extinction does not just affect individual species. The process threatens biodiversity, which is the variety of life and ecosystems on earth. An ecosystem, which is the community of living organisms and nonliving components of the environment, provides natural services, such as air and water purification, pollination of plants, and natural pest control. Without diverse species and environments, or biodiversity, these natural services disappear, along with the ability of ecosystems to function and sustain themselves. Without biodiversity, ecosystems cannot adapt to changing environmental conditions, such as drought or insect infestations. In diverse ecosystems, each species has a different method of adapting to changes. This variety of survival strategies increases the system's chance of enduring the changes. One example of the

Classifications of Endangered Species

The International Union for Conservation of Nature (IUCN) classifications for species' risks of extinction use complex criteria to rate the severity of extinction risk. A species is considered to be *extinct* when the last individual is confirmed to be dead. A similar category is called *extinct in the wild,* meaning that the species is only known to survive in captivity (as in a zoo or preserve). *Critically endangered* means that a species faces an extremely high risk of extinction in the wild, and *endangered* means a species has a very high risk of extinction in the wild. The *vulnerable* category applies to species that face a high risk of extinction in the wild, and the *threatened* category applies to species that are critically endangered, endangered, or vulnerable. These categories are determined by biologists' best estimates of the number of mature surviving organisms of a particular species. With so many species endangered, vulnerable, and threatened, biodiversity scientists fear that life on earth will no longer be sustainable unless people take drastic measures to restore biodiversity.

dire consequences of a lack of biodiversity occurred in the 1800s in Ireland during what is known as the Irish Potato Famine. About a million people died of starvation and another million left Ireland between 1845 and 1852 because they relied completely on one crop, potatoes. The potato crop was devastated by a disease called potato blight during the 1850s.

Today, the large amount of endangered and extinct species is creating severe ripple effects on ecosystems worldwide. For example, when frogs become extinct, the insects they typically eat instead grow in population and overrun certain ecosystems. Reptiles and birds that feed on frogs can face food shortages that affect their survivability. These effects proceed up the food chain.

What to do?

Scientists agree that ongoing threats to biodiversity are not environmentally or physically sustainable and that people must act immediately to reverse these losses. Global efforts to address the problems include international treaties and conventions to protect endangered and threatened species, such as the 1975 Convention on International Trade in Endangered Species (CITES), which was signed by 178 countries and bans hunting, capturing, or selling threatened or endangered species. CITES has reduced international trade in animals, but a lack of uniform enforcement in various countries has limited its effectiveness. In the United States, the Endangered Species Act of 1973, amended in 1982, 1985, and 1988, protects endangered species and imposes fines of up to $100,000 and prison terms for violations. However, people who violate this law are rarely caught.

Other efforts by conservation groups such as the World Wildlife Fund are making slow, but constant, headway. These programs involve protected areas worldwide and captive breeding programs at zoos and wildlife preserves to restore endangered populations and release them into the wild. Progress has been slow because of these animals' low reproduction and survival rates. Still, captive breeding programs in places like the San Diego Zoo Safari Park have saved species like the California condor, peregrine falcon, Arabian oryx, black-footed ferret, and golden lion tamarin from extinction. The expansion of aquaculture, or fish farming, has also helped restore some aquatic species because it satisfies some of the demand for seafood and cuts down on the amount of overfishing of wild species that has significantly diminished aquatic populations.

Endangered and Threatened Species

Teenagers in Thailand release young endangered sea turtles into the sea. © PORNCHAI KITTIWONGSAKUL/AFP/GETTY IMAGES

Along with these efforts, environmental scientists are applying what are known as the principles of sustainability to saving species and ecosystems. These principles include teaching people to respect biodiversity and to understand how sustaining biodiversity helps combat many serious problems that diminish the ability of all life forms to adapt to environmental changes.

Integrated approaches

The principles of sustainability are being incorporated into the growing trend of emphasizing an ecosystem approach, which focuses on preserving ecosystems rather than simply protecting individual endangered species. Many biologists believe an ecosystem approach will prove to be a better way of addressing the extinction crisis.

One successful ecosystem restoration project illustrates how such programs work. In 1987 the U.S. Fish and Wildlife Service (USFWS) introduced thirty-one endangered gray wolves into Yellowstone National Park to help restore its damaged ecosystem. By 1997 there were ninety-seven wolves in the park. With their return, the wolves reduced an overabundance of elk. Birds such as eagles and ravens thrived by eating leftover elk carcasses after the wolves finished eating. After many native populations were restored, soil erosion around streams and rivers decreased. More trees grew to shade the water, which allowed fish populations to recover. Beavers returned to river areas to build their dams, which helped other wetland species thrive. Scientists note that this ecosystem was restored to a sustainable level, and in 2013 the USFWS considered the wolf reintroduction "one of the world's greatest conservation successes."

Coping with the biological, environmental, political, cultural, and social aspects of species and ecosystem endangerment takes tremendous investments of time, money, and effort. However, environmental scientists believe these commitments are essential to stem the tide of massive extinctions before it is too late to reverse the trend.

SEE ALSO Biodiversity; Conservation; Ecosystems; Environmental Law; Food Web; Wildlife Management

For more information

BOOKS

Friedman, Lauri. *Endangered Species.* Farmington Hills, MI: Greenhaven Press, 2011.

Maczulak, Anne. *Biodiversity: Conserving Endangered Species.* New York: Facts on File, 2009.

Sheehan, Steve. *Endangered Species.* New York: Gareth Stevens Publishing, 2009.

PERIODICALS

Associated Press. "Draft Rule Ends Protections for Gray Wolves." *USA Today* (April 26, 2013). Available online at http://www.usatoday.com/story/news/nation/2013/04/26/protections-gray-wolves/2116657/ (accessed March 25, 2015).

Giller, Geoffrey. "Are We Any Closer to Knowing How Many Species There Are on Earth?" *Scientific American* (April 8, 2014). Available online at http://www.scientificamerican.com/article/are-we-any-closer-to-knowing-how-many-species-there-are-on-earth/ (accessed June 1, 2015).

International Union for the Conservation of Nature. "A World Without Biodiversity." *World Conservation* (January 2008). Available online at http://cmsdata.iucn.org/downloads/00_world_conservation_2008_01.pdf (accessed March 12, 2015).

WEBSITES

"About Biodiversity." International Union for the Conservation of Nature. http://www.iucn.org/what/biodiversity/about/ (accessed March 25, 2015).

"IUCN Red List Categories and Criteria" Version 3.1, Second edition (2012). International Union for the Conservation of Nature. http://jr.iucnredlist.org/documents/redlist_cats_crit_en.pdf (accessed June 1, 2015).

Energy Conservation

Energy conservation means saving energy—in the form of electricity and fuel—by using less of it or using alternative sources such as solar and wind power. Energy can be conserved either by reducing the amount of energy-consuming activities a person or business engages in or by using more efficient ways of accomplishing the same activities, which is called "energy efficiency." An example of reducing energy consumption by reducing use is to drive a car fewer miles every month, while reducing energy use through increased energy efficiency is to drive the same number of miles each month in a car that uses less fuel per mile driven. Individuals, businesses, and governments can all save energy by practicing energy conservation. Reducing energy consumption conserves resources, reduces the need for producing energy, reduces pollution released into the environment, and saves money.

Benefits of conserving energy

Producing energy for human use can be harmful to the environment and is expensive. Therefore, saving energy through conservation has two major benefits: reducing environmental impacts and saving money. Major sources of energy are petroleum (oil), natural gas, coal, nuclear fission, and renewable energy sources such as ethanol, solar power, and wind power. Oil, natural gas, and coal are called fossil fuels because natural processes produced these sources of energy millions of years ago. They are nonrenewable because they cannot be replaced after they are extracted. When they have been burned, they are gone.

Burning fossil fuels not only pollutes the environment and causes climate change but also uses up the limited amount of these resources that

Energy Conservation

WORDS TO KNOW

CAFE (Corporate Average Fuel Economy) standards: A regulation from the Environmental Protection Agency that requires car makers selling cars in the United States to have all cars sold achieve a given level of fuel economy.

Carpool: The practice of commuters riding together in one car instead of separately in different cars.

Energy audit: An inspection of a building or facility by a professional who is trained to locate areas where the use of energy can be made more efficient, or areas where the greatest amount of energy is being wasted.

Energy efficiency: Using less energy to accomplish the same task, for example using fluorescent instead of incandescent light bulbs to produce the same amount of light.

Fossil fuels: Nonrenewable energy source formed over millions of years through geological processes. Includes coal, oil, and natural gas, which when burned to release energy also emit greenhouse gases that contribute to climate change and air pollution.

Greenhouse gases: Any of the gases in the earth's atmosphere that absorb or reflect back to earth infrared radiation from the sun, thereby trapping heat close to the earth's surface. An increase in greenhouse gases corresponds with climate change. The main greenhouse gases are carbon dioxide, methane, nitrous oxide, and ozone. Clouds and water vapor also function as greenhouse gases.

Insulation: Material such as foam or fiberglass sheeting that is placed between walls in houses and other buildings to maintain energy efficiency.

LED light bulb: A type of light bulb and lamp that give light with light-emitting diodes with greater energy efficiency and longer lifespan.

LEED standards: A set of voluntary standards that show a building or factory exhibits Leadership in Energy and Environmental Design (LEED), awarded by the U.S. Green Building Council.

Politicize: To relate an issue or idea to politics in a way that makes people less likely to agree.

---

are available. Mining coal and drilling for oil and natural gas and then transporting the fuel to the user can also harm the environment through spills and habitat destruction. Energy conservation reduces environmental damage and allows for more prolonged use of fossil fuel energy by reducing the amount of fuel used.

The production of energy also requires huge amounts of water. Water is used to cool power plants, and an enormous amount is used in extracting and processing fuel for use in power plants. When a person or business conserves energy, they are also conserving water to help build a more sustainable way of life.

Unlike fossil fuels, electricity is a secondary energy source, meaning that other types of energy called primary sources must be used to produce electricity. According to the U.S. Energy Information Administration, in 2014 coal accounted for 39 percent of all electricity generated in the United States, with natural gas at 27 percent, nuclear power at 19 percent, hydropower at 6 percent, and all renewable sources (wind, solar, geothermal, and biomass) combined at 7 percent. Reducing electricity consumption can likewise help to reduce consumption of fossil fuels and thereby also reduce the release of greenhouse gases into the atmosphere, cutting down on global climate change.

While energy conservation saves money in the long term, many alternative forms of energy require an up-front investment. Installing solar energy panels, for example, is particularly costly in the United States, in part because the technology is complex and not in high demand by consumers. According to Energy Informative, installation of solar panels on the average American single-family home in 2015 varied from $15,000 to $40,000. The savings on energy bills over a twenty-year span, however, can range from $10,000 to $64,000 depending on the amount of daily sunlight a state or region tends to experience. A smaller example is the LED (light-emitting diode) light bulb. While a single LED bulb can cost as much as $11—versus about a dollar for an incandescent bulb—LED bulbs typically last about 22,000 hours and cost about $1.32 annually in electricity. Incandescent bulbs, on the other hand, last about 1,200 hours and cost about $7.21 a year in electricity. During the lifetime of just one LED bulb, an incandescent bulb may need to be replaced eighteen times, so in addition to an annual savings in electricity of $5.89 per year, the user of one LED bulb will also save $18 in replacement costs over two and a half years.

Despite their high initial cost, energy-conserving technologies can earn consumers tax credits and rebates that may add significantly to their appeal. In the United States, consumers who install solar energy, solar water heating, fuel cells, small wind-energy, or geothermal heat pump systems into their residences can qualify to receive a tax rebate amounting to 30 percent of their final investment cost. Businesses that install solar energy panels can also earn a 30 percent tax credit, meaning that they will be able to deduct 30 percent of the cost of the panels from their total tax bill. Additionally, the U.S. government offers the Production Tax Credit to businesses that research, develop, and manufacture energy conservation technologies, and there are numerous credits, grants, and incentives available at both the federal and state level for individuals, businesses, and communities to use alternative energy sources.

Energy conservation in the home

There are many ways that electricity can be conserved by individuals in their homes. The simplest is to not turn on lights and appliances unless they are being used and to turn them off when they are not being used. Of course, people can change light bulbs from incandescents to LEDs, too. Kitchen and laundry appliances use large amounts of electricity or natural gas. Dishwashers, washing machines, dryers, and water heaters use more than half of an average U.S. house's energy. The U.S. government has a program called Energy Star to encourage the use of high-efficiency appliances. High-efficiency appliances are marked with the Energy Star logo so buyers can see which appliances meet government standards for efficiency. Additionally, many states and power companies offer rebates, tax discounts, or other incentives similar to those mentioned above to buy Energy Star appliances. This makes it more attractive for the buyer to spend extra money to get high-efficiency appliances.

Houses also use, on average, about 40 percent of total energy for heating and cooling, which can be reduced to taking simple steps. By setting the thermostat lower in the winter and higher in the summer, less energy is used for heating and air conditioning. The government Energy Star program also rates furnaces, boilers, and air conditioners, so homeowners can choose the most efficient equipment to heat and cool their homes. Homes that have "leaks" around windows and doors as well as from attics that let allow heat to leave the house in the winter and cold air in the summer, or homes that are not well insulated to keep in the heat and cold, can also waste energy. Sealing leaks and insulating reduces energy use.

A homeowner can have an energy conservation expert come to the home and perform an energy audit. The auditor will test the house for leaks, inspect insulation and heating equipment, and measure how much energy each appliance is using. When the auditor is done, he or she will prepare a report for the homeowner that shows what steps can be taken to save energy. The auditor will also report which steps will save the owner the most energy and money, such as insulating the attic or buying an Energy Star refrigerator. Then the homeowner has knowledge to help make the best decisions on what to buy and how to improve the energy efficiency of his or her home.

Architects can design buildings that save energy by naturally staying cooler in the summer and warmer in the winter. Even planting

A high school student puts the finishing touches on a home in Idaho—the first student-built home to qualify for the LEED environmental stamp.
© SHAWN RAECKE/IDAHO STATESMAN/MCT/NEWSCOM

trees and shrubs in strategic places around buildings and homes will help the buildings use less energy. Architects can design roofs and window openings on new buildings so that a minimum of heat enters the building in summer and leaves the building in winter. Buildings can also be designed to take advantage of natural lighting with the installation of strategically placed windows, atriums, and light wells, reducing the need for electric lighting. A building that meets high standards for energy efficiency can apply to the U.S. Green Building Council to be certified as showing Leadership in Energy and Environmental Design (LEED).

Energy conservation and business

Businesses also stand to gain by saving energy. Although businesspeople usually try to make their businesses more profitable by increasing revenue (the amount of money their company takes in), they can also make their businesses more profitable by reducing their expenses. By installing energy-efficient equipment, reducing lighting, and shipping goods by efficient transportation, a business can reduce expenses, make more profit, and help build a sustainable energy program by using less energy.

Energy Conservation

> ### Bicycles and Sustainable Energy
>
> In cities around the world, bicycles are being incorporated into urban transportation planning as a way to cut down on fossil fuel use. In addition to encouraging residents to ride their own bicycles for traveling to work and errands, some cities have initiated bike share programs. These are networks of automated stations that house bicycles for public use. Commuters can access the bikes by paying membership fees or by the hour, day, or month, and some can be used with applications on phones and other hand-held devices. The most energy-efficient means of travel invented by humans, bicycles contribute no pollution to the air or water, are fueled only by physical effort, are far less costly and easier to manufacture than any other means of transportation, reduce traffic congestion, offer the potential for more social rides to and from destinations, and result in healthier commuters.

Energy conservation and transportation

After electrical generation, the next largest use of energy in the United States is for transportation. People travel around the country in cars and airplanes. Goods are moved in trucks, trains, airplanes, and ships. The first and easiest way to conserve energy that is used for transportation is to travel less and ship less. Travelers can combine trips so that they use their cars less. For example, rather than making separate trips to buy groceries, go to the park, and go to an appointment all in one town, these three activities could be done in one trip. Also, people can share rides to work (called carpooling) or use public transportation, such as buses or trains. Public transportation can use much less energy than personal cars. A full subway train can carry hundreds of people, who each might otherwise be driving alone in a car.

Fuel is a big expense for airlines, trucking, and railroad companies. By decreasing the amount of fuel they use, they consume fewer resources, pollute less, and save money, and are able to offer lower fares and shipping rates to their customers. At the same time, they can increase their profits,. Because transportation companies can save money by using less energy, the companies that make trucks, trains, and airplanes compete for business by continually making their vehicles more fuel-efficient. Transportation companies can also conserve fuel and energy by carefully planning the routes and loading of their vehicles. Vehicles that are fully loaded and take the shortest route will use less energy than a larger number of lightly loaded vehicles on longer trips.

Energy conservation is an important step on the path to achieving sustainability that can be achieved by reducing traditional energy usage in addition to developing new alternative energy technologies and encouraging consumers to use those alternatives that are already available, such as wind and solar power. In terms of the rate of progress being made to integrate renewable energy sources into existing systems, countries in the

European Union (EU) are moving far ahead of the United States. EU member countries set a goal in 2010 of reducing reliance on fossil fuels by producing 20 percent of their energy from renewable energy sources by 2020. As of 2015, Sweden, Bulgaria, Lithuania, and Estonia had already achieved or exceeded their targets, while twelve other countries were within a few percentage points of reaching theirs. With an especially large target of 67.5 percent, Norway was producing 65.5 percent of its energy from alternative sources in 2015. Other EU countries are running far below their target percentages, though, and the EU average as of 2015 was at 15 percent. In the United States, meanwhile, 10 percent of primary energy used comes from renewable energy sources, with 13.1 percent of electricity generated through renewable sources. In 2014 Stanford University scientist Mark Jacobson publicized a plan that would convert all fifty states to 100 percent renewable energy usage in the form of wind, water, and solar power by 2050. Such programs require strong state and federal support, however, and the issues of climate change and sustainability have become highly politicized, with some U.S. elected officials refusing to pass legislation, claiming human-caused climate change is a hoax.

PRIMARY SOURCE

The President's Proposed Energy Policy

Speech (excerpt)

By: President Jimmy Carter

Source: Carter, Jimmy. 1977. "The President's Proposed Energy Policy." In *Vital Speeches of the Day* (May 1, 1977): 418–420. This document is available online at http://www.pbs.org/wgbh/americanexperience/features/primary-resources/carter-energy/.

About the document: President Carter (1924– ; served 1977–1981) gave this televised speech shortly after taking office, when the 1973 OPEC oil crisis was still fresh in people's minds. Carter recognized the need to conserve nonrenewable fossil fuels and find new sources of clean energy, but many citizens resented his call for energy conservation, considering it a hindrance to economic growth and power. Several months later, Carter formed the Department of Energy by consolidating several existing agencies, which established America's first national energy policy. Ultimately, however, new sources of energy were developed and the country's energy consumption continued to rise instead of fall.

I know that some of you may doubt that we face real energy shortages. The 1973 gasoline lines are gone, and our homes are warm again. But our energy problem is worse tonight than it was in 1973 or a few weeks ago in the dead of winter. It is worse because more waste has occurred, and more time has passed by without our planning for the future. And it will get worse every day until we act.

The oil and natural gas we rely on for 75 percent of our energy are running out. In spite of increased effort, domestic production has been dropping steadily at about six percent a year. Imports have doubled in the last five years. Our nation's independence of economic and political action is becoming increasingly constrained. Unless profound changes are made to lower oil consumption, we now believe that early in the 1980s the world will be demanding more oil that it can produce.

The world now uses about 60 million barrels of oil a day and demand increases each year about five percent. This means that just to stay even we need the production of a new Texas every year, an Alaskan North Slope every nine months, or a new Saudi Arabia every three years. Obviously, this cannot continue....

The world has not prepared for the future. During the 1950s, people used twice as much oil as during the 1940s. During the 1960s, we used twice as much as during the 1950s. And in each of those decades, more oil was consumed than in all of mankind's previous history....

Each new inventory of world oil reserves has been more disturbing than the last. World oil production can probably keep going up for another six or eight years. But some time in the 1980s it can't go up much more. Demand will overtake production. We have no choice about that.

But we do have a choice about how we will spend the next few years. Each American uses the energy equivalent of 60 barrels of oil per person each year. Ours is the most wasteful nation on earth. We waste more energy than we import. With about the same standard of living, we use twice as much energy per person as do other countries like Germany, Japan, and Sweden.

One choice is to continue doing what we have been doing before. We can drift along for a few more years.

Our consumption of oil would keep going up every year. Our cars would continue to be too large and inefficient. Three-quarters of them would continue to carry only one person—the driver—while our public transportation system continues to decline. We can delay insulating our houses, and they will continue to lose about 50 percent of their heat in waste....

We will not be ready to keep our transportation system running with smaller, more efficient cars and a better network of buses, trains and public transportation.

We will feel mounting pressure to plunder the environment. We will have a crash program to build more nuclear plants, strip-mine and burn more coal, and drill more offshore wells than we will need if we begin to conserve now. Inflation will soar, production will go down, people will lose their jobs. Intense competition will build up among nations and among the different regions within our own country.

If we fail to act soon, we will face an economic, social and political crisis that will threaten our free institutions.

But we still have another choice. We can begin to prepare right now. We can decide to act while there is time.

SEE ALSO Alternative Energy; Automobiles; Biofuel Energy; Building Design; Climate Change; Coal; Conservation; Ecological Footprint; Geothermal Power; Hydropower; Industrial Ecology; Mass Transit; Natural Gas; Nuclear Power; Oil; Solar Power; Transportation; Water Access and Sanitation; Water Pollution; Wind Power

For more information

BOOKS
Haugen, David, Susan Musser, and Ross M. Berger, eds. *The U.S. Energy Grid.* Detroit, MI: Greenhaven Press, 2012.

PERIODICALS
"The Elusive Negawatt." *The Economist* (May 8, 2008). Available online at http://www.economist.com/node/11326549 (accessed July 8, 2015).

Glick, Daniel, and The Daily Climate. "How Saving Energy Means Conserving Water in U.S. West." *Scientific American* (August 1, 2011). Available online at http://www.scientificamerican.com/article/how-saving-energy-means-conserving-water/ (accessed July 8, 2015).

Kisner, Corinne. *Integrating Bike Share Programs into a Sustainable Transportation System.* National League of Cities Center for Research and Innovation (February 2011). Available online at http://www.nlc.org/documents/Find%20City%20Solutions/Research%20Innovation/Sustainability/integrating-bike-share-programs-into-sustainable-transportation-system-cpb-feb11.pdf (accessed July 8, 2015).

Lovins, Amory. "Amory Lovins, Efficiency Advocate: Interview with Amory Lovins." By Michelle Nijhuis. *National Geographic.* Available online at http://ngm.nationalgeographic.com/2009/03/energy-issue/lovins-field-notes (accessed March 18, 2015).

Mascaro, Lisa. "'Climate Change is Real and Not a Hoax,' Senate Overwhelmingly Decides." *Los Angeles Times* (January 21, 2015). Available online at http://www.latimes.com/nation/politics/politicsnow/la-pn-senate-climate-hoax-20150121-story.html (accessed July 8, 2015).

Rosner, Sean. "10 Easy Ways to Save on Energy at Home." *Mother Earth News* (July 21, 2009). Available online at http://www.motherearthnews.com/renewable-energy/save-money-on-energy.aspx#axzz3K0v7wEDt (accessed July 8, 2015).

Schwartz, Mark. "Stanford Scientist Unveils 50-State Plan to Transform U.S. to Renewable Energy." *Stanford News* (February 26, 2014). Available online at http://news.stanford.edu/news/2014/february/fifty-states-renewables-022414.html (accessed July 8, 2015).

Werber, Cassie. "Three European Countries Have Already Hit Their 2020 Renewable Energy Goals." *Quartz* (March 10, 2015). Available online at http://qz.com/359415/three-european-countries-have-already-hit-their-2020-renewable-energy-goals/ (accessed July 8, 2015).

WEBSITES

"Embodied Energy and Carbon—The ICE database." Circular Ecology. http://www.circularecology.com/embodied-energy-and-carbon-footprint-database.html (accessed March 18, 2015).

"Energy Conservation." U.S. Environmental Protection Agency, November 5, 2012. http://www.epa.gov/greeningepa/energy/ (accessed July 8, 2015).

"Energy Star." U.S. Environmental Protection Agency. http://www.energystar.gov (accessed July 8, 2015).

"Human Power." The Exploratorium's Science of Cycling. http://www.exploratorium.edu/cycling/humanpower1.html (accessed July 8, 2015).

Sustainable Energy For All. http://www.se4all.org (accessed July 8, 2015).

U.S. Energy Information Administration. http://www.eia.gov (accessed July 8, 2015).

Environmental Justice

The U.S. Environmental Protection Agency (EPA) defines environmental justice as the fair treatment and meaningful involvement of all people regardless of race, color, national origin, or income with respect to the development, implementation, and enforcement of environmental laws, regulations, and policies. So, it means that every person has the right to be treated equally to the benefits of a healthy environment and the right to be involved in decisions concerning what happens to that environment.

Examples of environmental justice

Environmental justice is a part of a larger social movement that addresses environmental issues, including those affecting people. The beginnings of the environmental justice movement in the United States might be

Environmental Justice

WORDS TO KNOW

Activists: A person or group who uses actions or writings to produce political change.

CERCLA (Comprehensive Environmental Response, Compensation, and Liability Act of 1980): Law in the United States that provided funding to clean up severely polluted industrial sites, commonly known as the Superfund law.

Ecosystem: A complete and interdependent system of biotic (living) and abiotic (nonliving) components that cycles matter and transfers energy within a given area. The three major types of ecosystems are freshwater, terrestrial, and marine.

Hazardous waste: Waste that can be solid, liquid, or gas and that is harmful to living things and the environment. Hazardous waste can be discarded commercial products, like cleaning fluids or pesticides, or the by-products of manufacturing processes.

Landfill: A site where solid waste (the garbage of a particular community) is buried.

Polychlorinated biphenyls (PCB): Refers to a broad group of chlorinated hydrocarbons, man-made organic chemicals, which vary in complexity and toxicity.

---

seen as protests led by Lois Gibbs (1951–), a housewife and mother of two, in 1978 over the environmental contamination of a neighborhood known as "Love Canal" in upstate New York. Gibbs and other families complained that their children had become sick due to the toxic waste buried under their town in the 1950s. Activists called on the government to address the issues of pollution in the environment, mostly focusing on stopping corporations from dumping hazardous wastes in local communities. Various industries dumped hazardous waste into local ecosystems in different ways, including releasing substances into rivers, burying waste in the ground, and releasing it into the air. Activists realized that this pollution was causing health problems to the people who lived in or near these areas and began to protest as a way to get the government to take action. The efforts of Gibbs and her neighbors led to the creation of the Comprehensive Response, Compensation, and Liability Act of 1980 (CERLCA, or Superfund), which allowed the U.S. government to collect millions of dollars from those responsible for the pollution.

In September 1982, the state government of North Carolina decided to dump 6,000 tons (5,443 metric tons) of soil contaminated with polychlorinated biphenyls (PCBs) into a newly built landfill in Afton, a section of the town of Shocco, in Warren County. PCBs are a human-made chemical proven to cause cancer. They are used in electrical transformers and to cool machine tools because they slow down the spread of fires. The Ward Transformers Company used PCBs in their transformers, and in 1973 dumped 31,000 gallons of the chemical onto the side of a road. The PCBs entered the soil, and the government of North Carolina decided to remove all contaminated soil and deposit it into a landfill. As the soil was being transported by dump trucks to the disposal site, protesters began lying in the street to prevent the trucks from passing. The protesters were citizens from the town who believed that the harmful chemicals would leach into their water supply and cause health problems for themselves, their pets, and their livestock. Leaching is the process where contaminants become absorbed or dissolved by rainwater as it percolates through the soil. This contaminated water then gets into the groundwater, which can be consumed by humans or animals. For six weeks people held nonviolent protests, but in the end they did not succeed. The government prevailed and the soil was dumped into the landfill. Even though this can be seen as a defeat, it drew national attention through the media's coverage of the protests. While there were a few instances before the Warren County incident that highlighted environmental injustice, this incident was one of the first to use the media to ask for support from the nation. This created a shift in the public's attitude, from "Not in my backyard" to "Not in anyone's backyard," thereby solidifying the importance of the environmental justice movement.

The Warren County protest did have a positive outcome. It provided the inspiration for groups to create studies that proved minorities and the communities they lived in were receiving hazardous wastes more frequently than other communities. In 1987, one study, called "Toxic Waste and Race in the United States," demonstrated that race was a significant factor for determining where to dispose of toxic wastes. It showed that three out of every five African American and Hispanic people lived in a community that had a hazardous waste site. The report was the first national study to link the disposal sites of hazardous wastes to race.

In 1990 the environmental justice movement was further promoted through two key events. First, the book *Dumping in Dixie: Race, Class, and Environmental Quality* was published. Written by American sociologist Robert Bullard (1946–), it told specific stories demonstrating the connection between waste that was being dumped and race and/or economic class. The book described incidents where toxic waste was being dumped into lower-class neighborhoods where predominantly

Global Environmental Justice Efforts

Global attention on the impact of the disposal of hazardous wastes in local communities lagged behind its initial rise in the United States. Its growth and prominence rose as the increased enforcement of toxic waste disposal regulations made companies look elsewhere for less expensive alternatives. These alternatives sometimes included corporations taking advantage of weaker regulations and governmental supervision in less developed countries around the globe. Three major worldwide events brought attention to this growing trend.

United Nations Conference on Environment and Development (UNCED) Rio Earth Summit (1992)—the focus of the summit was to address the condition of the global environment and to use a political context to help define the relationships between science, the environment and the economic impact they shared for all of the 105 participating countries. One if its most noteworthy accomplishments was the drafting of a document called Agenda 21 that identified basic problems with resource degradation, need for quality of life improvements and management of industrial and chemical wastes.

Johannesburg World Summit on Sustainable Development (2002)—organized by the United Nations Commission on Sustainable Development, its focus was to bring together governments, corporations and NGOs (non-governmental organizations) to call attention to and direct a response towards the challenges of improving the environment and in conserving natural resources in a world faced with a growing population which would require more food, water, sanitation and services. Its main outcome was the Johannesburg Declaration, a collection of policy statements affirming future collaboration of its members in areas of concern such as combatting world poverty and maintaining biodiversity.

Rio Conference on Sustainable Development (2012)—also called Rio +20, it was organized by the UNCED and its goal was to align the needs of protecting the environment with the economic challenges faced by many of its member organizations. It sought to gain political commitments of continuing efforts towards sustainable practices and "green economy" policies, including the reduction of hazardous wastes.

---

people of color lived. The second key event was the challenge to the "Group of Ten." Environmental justice leaders sent a letter to the top ten environmental groups stating that they were not doing enough for the environmental justice movement and that they needed to help because they were in positions of power. This letter was signed by leaders of the environmental justice movement from the Southwest Organizing Project (SWOP). This organization still works today to improve communities in New Mexico by generating data on air quality and community action to improve air quality. They also provide healthy food to people in low-income communities and sponsor other social justice projects. The letter was significant because it called attention to the lack of social advocacy in the existing policies of the major environmental organizations that were viewed as environmental advocates. It did get a few of the groups, such as Greenpeace and Earth Island Institute, to start incorporating environmental justice into their organizational policies.

In 1991 there was a summit in Washington, D.C., that brought together people from all parts of the United States. It was called the First National People of Color Environmental Leadership Summit and it created a document called Principles of Environmental Justice. The document outlined how to organize and solve environmental justice issues within a community, as well as how to get other people involved and raise the issue to a national level of awareness. Success came under the Clinton Administration. In 1994 President Bill Clinton (1946– ; served 1993–2001) signed into action Executive Order 12898—Federal Actions to Address Environmental Justice in Minority Populations and Low-Income Populations, which forced all branches of the federal government to include environmental justice in their policies and programs. This effectively prevented incidents similar to the Warren County episode from ever happening again in the United States because it prevents the government from dumping hazardous waste in low-income neighborhoods and forces those responsible for the waste to find safer alternative solutions.

Environmental justice is essential to sustainability because it addresses how people are affected by decisions made about environmental issues by considering connections between those decisions and their impacts on the members of the communities affected. Today, the environmental justice movement is a global movement that recognizes the threats to humans in the improper disposal of hazardous wastes, particularly in developing countries where education and environmental policies are lacking.

SEE ALSO Activism; Citizenship; Comprehensive Environmental Response, Compensation, and Liability Act (CERCLA); Environmental Law; Fair Trade; Food Security; Hazardous Waste; Human Rights; Pollution; Public Health; United Nations Conference on Environment and Development (UNCED)

For more information
BOOKS
Bullard, Robert D. *Dumping in Dixie: Race, Class, and Environmental Quality,* 3rd ed. Boulder, CO: Westview Press, 2000.

Gibbs, Lois, and Murray Levine. *Love Canal: My Story.* Albany: State University of New York Press, 1982.

PERIODICALS

Mock, Brentin. "Robert Bullard, Pioneer in Environmental Justice, is Honored by the Sierra Club." *Washington Post* (September 25, 2013). Available online at http://www.washingtonpost.com/lifestyle/style/robert-bullard-pioneer-in-environmental-justice-is-honored-by-the-sierra-club/2013/09/24/88e0e882-251c-11e3-b3e9-d97fb087acd6_story.html (accessed March 19, 2015).

WEBSITES

"Environmental Justice." U.S. Environmental Protection Agency, May 24, 2012. http://www.epa.gov/environmentaljustice/basics/ejbackground.html (accessed March 19, 2015).

"Environmental Justice History." U.S. Department of Energy: Office of Legacy Management. http://energy.gov/lm/services/environmental-justice/environmental-justice-history (accessed March 19, 2015).

Gibbs, Lois Marie. "History: Love Canal: The Start of a Movement." Boston University School of Public Health, updated 2002. http://www.bu.edu/lovecanal/canal/ (accessed March 19, 2015).

Skelton, Renee, and Vernice Miller. "The Environmental Justice Movement." Natural Resources Defense Council, October 12, 2006. http://www.nrdc.org/ej/history/hej.asp (accessed March 19, 2015).

"Southwest Organizing Project History." Southwest Organizing Project. http://www.swop.net/about-swop/timeline/ (accessed March 19, 2015).

Environmental Law

Environmental law consists of treaties, laws, regulations, and agreements between state, federal, and international organizations that focus on issues relating to the environment and the protection of natural resources. Some issues environmental laws address are soil, air, and water pollution; global warming; and declining amounts of natural resources, such as oil, coal, and clean water. Some main aims of environmental law are controlling pollution, developing ways to clean up polluted areas, protecting wildlife, and conserving natural resources.

These laws are used to encourage sustainability by protecting and restoring the ecological balance of ecosystems throughout the world. Environmental law provides a legal framework for the development of global sustainability so that humans can live and prosper in nature without damaging or destroying it. These laws can allow government agencies, environmental organizations, and private individuals to take legal

WORDS TO KNOW

Biosphere: The part of the earth in which life can exist.

Conservation: The protection of natural resources, plants and animals, and their habitats to prevent unnecessary loss of resources or biodiversity.

Deforestation: Removing trees from a forest, especially to the point that the forested area is cleared.

Developing country: A country that has a low standard of living, including low average annual income per person, high infant mortality rates, widespread poverty, and an underdeveloped economy. Most of these countries are located in Africa, Asia, and Latin America.

Embargo: Legal prohibition or restriction of trade.

Environmental Protection Agency (EPA): An agency of the U.S. federal government whose mission is to protect human and environmental health.

Environmental sustainability: The ability to satisfy current and future needs without exhausting natural resources or degrading environmental quality.

Sanction: An action taken to enforce a law or rule.

Treaty: An agreement or arrangement made by negotiation, especially one between two or more states or rulers.

---

action against companies or individuals whose practices are causing harm to the environment. Environmental court cases often seek to stop industrial pollution or ensure that companies are held liable, or responsible, for the damage that they have caused. Because of the possible economic effects of halting production and difficulty estimating environmental impact, these cases are often decided in favor of companies and their rights, except where human health is affected. While environmental law is a key part of achieving sustainability, additional tools and practices need to be developed and put into action for the laws to be effective.

History of environmental law

Before the mid-twentieth century, laws regulating the environment were mostly concerned with protecting human health and comfort, by lessening environmental pollution and contamination and by controlling land use. For instance, as early as the first century BCE, Rome's government passed legislation protecting the city's clean bathing and drinking water. In England nuisance laws have been recorded since the twelfth century, and they protect people from having their neighbors develop or build on certain pieces of land considered rural, agricultural, or conservation land. These laws could be used to combat any practice that prevented enjoyment of someone's land, including pollution of the surrounding environment. The Rivers and Harbors Act of 1899 is the oldest federal environmental law in the United States. The U.S. Congress enacted the law to prevent pollution of waterways, which were essential for trade and transportation, and to protect natural resources.

The concept of creating laws specifically to protect the environment and natural resources was not common before the 1960s, when environmental scientists studying ecosystems around the world began to draw attention to how the actions of humans can affect and damage the biosphere, or the part of earth where life exists. These scientific findings and some ecological disasters, such as oil spills, smog events, and heavily polluted rivers and lakes, helped governments, educators, and the public realize the severity of the damage to the air, water, and land that was caused by human actions. This realization brought people together to take unified action.

The concept of legally protecting the air, water, soil, and ecosystems, such as those found in wetlands, forest, deserts, and oceans, quickly spread in the United States, Europe, Australia, and New Zealand before expanding to other parts of the world. Environmental laws have become an essential part of many nations' legal systems, including those of many developing countries. Because the impact of environmental law is global, the practice of environmental law plays an important role in international law. Nations that fail to establish and uphold environmental laws are often sanctioned by other countries through penalties like trade limits or embargos that stop trade until environmental laws are passed and enforced. One example of this is the United States's decision in 1994 to restrict imports from Taiwan because of the country's trade in tigers and rhinoceroses, both endangered animals.

In the United States, environmental law is sometimes used in court cases involving lawsuits, where one party is charged with causing damage to another party. These cases can be nuisance suits or can claim negligence on the part of the defendant, where damage is caused because the defendant acted in a deliberately unlawful or unreasonable way. These lawsuits are difficult to win, but a notable exception is the case *Anderson v. Pacific Gas & Electric Co.*, made famous by the movie *Erin Brockovich*. Residents of the town of Hinkley, California, charged that the Pacific Gas & Electric Co. knew that harmful chemicals they used were contaminating the town's groundwater and soil and affecting the health of inhabitants. The case ran from 1993 to 1996, and ultimately the company was ordered to pay $333 million, clean any polluted sites, and discontinue use of the chemical, Chromium VI.

Current issues and trends

The United States Environmental Protection Agency (EPA) is a part of the U.S. government that protects the health of Americans and the environment in the United States. It works to enforce federal environmental laws such as the Clean Water Act of 1972, the Oil Pollution Act of 1990, and the Food Quality Protection Act of 1996. It also works with other nations to protect the environment globally. While the states within the United States uphold federal environmental laws, many have their own organizations focused on environmental issues specific to the state's needs. A few examples of state organizations are the New York State Department of Environmental Conservation (DEC), the California Environmental Protection Agency (EPA), and Texas's Commission of Environmental Quality (CEQ). New York's DEC may focus on coastal water pollution or damage caused by hurricanes along New York's coastline, California's EPA on drought in southern California and landslides in the Sierra Nevada mountains, and Texas's CEQ on air and water quality throughout the state, while all manage the oversight of natural resources within their state.

There are many environmental organizations and groups in the world, from the United Nations, to science-based organizations such as the American Academy of Environmental Engineers & Scientists (AAEES), to people in small towns in developing countries. With so many groups influencing environmental laws and the numerous regulations they create, it can be difficult to identify issues and solutions and to enforce the laws. Scientific knowledge continues to increase and identify new environmental concerns in addition to the environmental issues that already exist.

Violations of environmental laws can result in a person or a company being fined or even imprisoned. Proving a person's innocence or guilt with regard to an environmental law can be difficult especially if the extent of the damage to the environment will not be measurable for years to come. At times it can be difficult to determine which environmental law was violated and who is responsible for bringing legal action against the violator because state, federal, and international laws overlap in many areas. This makes environmental law costly and complicated for all involved. Many developing nations have established environmental laws but do not have the necessary money, technology, processes, or professionals to

Major Environmental Laws and Treaties

- Rivers and Harbors Act (1899, United States)—Prohibited the dumping of waste in navigable waters.
- Non-Proliferation Treaty (1968, international)—Aimed to control the spread of nuclear weapons.
- National Environmental Policy Act (1969, United States)—Created the Environmental Protection Agency (EPA) and required that all major federal actions provide environmental impact statements.
- Clean Air Act (1970, United States)—Imposed national air quality standards.
- Clean Water Act (1972, United States)—Limited emissions of pollutants onto surface waters.
- Endangered Species Act (1973, United States)—Designed to protect endangered and threatened species and their habitats.
- Resource Conservation and Recovery Act (1976, United States)—Set standards for the management of hazardous waste.
- Toxic Substances Control Act (1976, United States)—Authorized the EPA to set controls on toxic chemicals.
- Montreal Protocol (1987, international)—Limited the production of substances that harm the ozone layer.
- Oil Pollution Act (1990, United States)—Required oil storage facilities and transporters to develop spill-response plans and increased polluters' liability in the case of an oil spill.
- Food Quality Protection Act (1996, United States)—Governed the EPA's regulation of pesticide residue in food.
- The Kyoto Protocol (1997, international)—Set binding limits on greenhouse gas emissions to combat global climate change.

implement the laws. In some developing countries, the people causing the damage may not even be aware of the environmental laws. Without a way to monitor if the environmental laws are being followed or to enforce the laws, they will be less effective and destruction will continue, despite the best intentions of the government and the people of the nation.

At times, environmentally destructive methods are ignored by governments because of the amount of money that is made by using or damaging natural resources, regardless of the destruction to the ecosystem. This is true of fishing practices in the Philippines in the 1960s, where dynamite and sodium cyanide, a type of poison, were commonly used to stun and then catch fish. Other examples are the destruction of coral reefs and marine ecosystems, and the slash-and-burn deforestation used by farmers in developing countries, which destroyed large portions of the Amazon Rainforest in South America.

While the intentions of many of these organizations are worthy and honorable, it is still a challenge to keep up with scientific research and findings about the environment and how best to protect it. Without the ability and processes in place to enforce environmental law, many violations go unrecognized and unpunished. State, federal, and international environmental law organizations throughout the world still struggle to come together in a way that benefits environments globally. For instance the Kyoto Protocol of 1997, an international agreement aimed at lowering greenhouse gas emissions in an effort to combat global climate change, failed to gain complete support, as the United States and Canada ultimately withdrew from the treaty. Improved methods of education, communication, and funding associated with environmental law are needed to simplify processes and reduce the cost of protecting all environments and natural resources.

SEE ALSO Activism; Ecosystems; Environmental Justice; Farm Bill, U.S.; Hazardous Waste; Pollution

For more information

PERIODICALS

Dernbach, John C., and Joel A. Mintz. "Environmental Laws and Sustainability: An Introduction." *Sustainability* 3, no. 3 (March 23, 2011): 531–540. Available online at http://www.mdpi.com/2071-1050/3/3/531/htm (accessed March 18, 2015).

WEBSITES

"Environment and Health in Developing Countries." The Health and Environment Linkages Initiative (HELI), World Health Organization. http://www.who.int/heli/risks/ehindevcoun/en/ (accessed March 18, 2015).

"Environmental Science Jobs." Naturejobs.com. http://www.nature.com/naturejobs/science/jobs/environmental-science (accessed March 18, 2015).

"History of Environmental Law." National Registry of Environmental Professionals. https://www.nrep.org/history.php (accessed December 21, 2014).

"Laws & Regulations." U.S. Environmental Protection Agency, December 24, 2014. http://www2.epa.gov/laws-regulations (accessed March 18, 2015).

Pearce, Fred. "Cyanide: An Easy But Deadly Way To Catch Fish." WWF.org, January 23, 2003. http://wwf.panda.org/wwf_news/?5563/Cyanide-an-easy-but-deadly-way-to-catch-fish (accessed March 18, 2015).

Environmental Policy

Environmental policy refers to the laws, regulations, and programs that are designed, funded, and enforced by government agencies to protect the environment. Policy refers to the actions a government takes, such as laws passed and programs funded. Politics is the process by which individuals and groups try to influence this process. Policies are enacted at various levels of government—local, state, national, and international. The policy life cycle consists of four stages: problem recognition, policy formulation, policy implementation, and policy adjustment. Each of these steps requires an action before moving to the next step. For example, recognizing a problem might produce research about the problem. Once a government forms a policy, it must create a budget to pay for it, and when a policy is implemented, governments must monitor the policy's effectiveness. Effective environmental policy promotes sustainability.

The executive, legislative, and judicial branches of the U.S. federal government work together to enact and oversee environmental policy for the nation. The major environmental legislative acts include the Clean Water Act, the Clean Air Act, the Wilderness Act, the Endangered Species Act, and the Comprehensive Environmental Response, Compensation, and Liability Act (CERCLA), also known as the Superfund. All of these are administered by the Environmental Protection Agency, which was formed in 1970.

How lobbyists influence policy

The policy life cycle involves many individuals and groups, sometimes working together and sometimes working against each other, depending on their interests. In a democracy, policies are recognized, formed, implemented, and adjusted by a committee of elected officials. The action steps—research, budgeting, monitoring, and evaluation—often involve lobbyists, interest groups, citizen groups, and nongovernmental organizations (NGOs) that try to influence the process. A lobbyist is a representative for an interest group that meets with elected officials to persuade them to act in the interest group's favor.

Here is an example of how lobbying works: a congressional committee is deciding whether to approve a thousand-mile-long oil pipeline

Environmental Policy

WORDS TO KNOW

Environmental justice principle: Ensuring that no person or group suffers unfairly from environmental laws or policies.

Environmental policy: The laws, regulations, and programs that are designed, funded, and enforced by government agencies to protect public health and natural resources.

Lobbyist: A representative for an interest group that meets with elected officials to persuade them to act in the interest group's favor.

Politics: The process by which individuals and groups try to influence government policies and processes, such as environmental policy and programs.

Polluter pays principle: The notion that any individual or corporation who pollutes the environment must pay to clean it up.

Precautionary principle: When there is significant scientific uncertainty about potentially serious harm from chemicals or technologies, decision makers should act to prevent harm to humans and the environment.

Prevention principle: Ensuring that elected officials make decisions that prevent environmental problems from occurring.

Reversibility principle: The notion that governments should avoid making harmful environmental decisions that cannot be reversed.

Subsidies: Money granted by a government to an industry or company to help keep the price of a product or service low.

Tax breaks: Deductions, credits, and other reductions in or exemptions from taxes awarded by governments to individuals and corporations, often to encourage a certain behavior.

---

so shale oil can reach a refinery. Lobbyists representing the oil industry tell the committee that the pipeline is essential for maintaining a steady supply of domestic oil in the United States. They say that domestic oil is less expensive and more reliable than importing oil from unstable regions around the world. Additionally, the pipeline will provide jobs and benefit both the economy and consumers.

Conversely, a nature conservation organization lobbies in front of the committee that, according to their research, the pipeline will cross a vital nesting area for an endangered species of bird and cause many other habitat disruptions that could negatively affect biodiversity and drastically increase the risk of dangerous oil spills. They also argue that the amount of oil carried by the pipeline could easily be transported by existing rail or highway networks at a much lower cost than constructing a new pipeline. It is then the committee's job to see which research seems more accurate and to make a decision based on their findings.

Sustainability, special interests, and policy

A high-functioning democracy requires that politicians take the best interests of the people they represent into account in their decisions, without being bribed or accepting favors from those trying to influence the process. Forming policy around sustainability issues can be difficult, because corporations have more money to lobby elected officials than do conservation and citizen groups.

Both corporations and conservation groups are types of special-interest groups. Special-interest groups lobby for laws, subsidies, tax breaks, and regulations favorable to their cause while trying to weaken laws, subsidies, tax breaks, and regulations unfavorable to their cause. The two major categories of special interest groups are corporations and NGOs. NGOs include nonprofit organizations such as labor unions, professional organizations, and conservation groups.

When it comes to major sustainability issues, such as climate change and loss of biodiversity, solutions are complex, long-term, and time-consuming. The democratic policy-making process is often better at short-term issues, because politicians want to make the popular choice that will ensure their re-election. It may take many years for people to see the benefits of long-term policy decisions, so politicians often shy away from issues that require long-term solutions.

Another hurdle to overcome with sustainability issues is education. Many politicians are unfamiliar with the earth sciences and the chemical cycles on which all life depends. Understanding environmental issues requires knowledge of biology, geology, chemistry, meteorology, agronomy, and other sciences, which few politicians have. Some lobbyists capitalize on this lack of knowledge and provide lawmakers with information that advances their agenda but may not be scientifically accurate or widely accepted by scientists. Many politicians then come to believe that

> ### The Natural Resources Defense Council
>
> The Natural Resources Defense Council (NRDC) is an international environmental action group with 500 scientists and legal experts and 1.4 million members and online activists that has programs for every aspect of environmental sustainability. Its mission is broad: "To safeguard the earth—its people, its plants and animals, and the natural systems on which all life depends." It works to establish sustainable environmental policy at the state and federal levels in the United States and internationally through its advocacy and lobbying work.
>
> The NRDC helps enforce the Clean Air Act and the Clean Water Act, works to slow climate change, raises awareness of the dangers of nuclear weapon stockpiles, and promotes the use of renewable energy. Internationally, the organization works to preserve rain forests, promote biodiversity, and protect marine habitats. In an effort to influence policy, analysts for the NRDC meet with legislators, testify before congressional committees, and publish issue papers and legislative analyses, all of which are available on their website.

the science about a particular issue, especially climate change, is open to debate, when in fact it is not.

Sustainability principles of environmental policy

Environmental policy is guided by several principles that promote sustainability. These include the reversibility principle, the precautionary principle, the prevention principle, the polluter pays principle, and the environmental justice principle. The reversibility principle holds that decisions that are irreversible should be avoided. This is the reasoning behind the ban on building nuclear power plants in many countries. The plants generate radioactive waste that is extremely difficult to contain, lasts for long periods of time (thousands of years), and can cause accidents that may have disastrous consequences.

The precautionary principle states that unless there is scientific consensus that a policy will not cause harm to the public or the environment, the policy makers must prove that it is not harmful. For example, the United Nations' Cartagena Protocol on Biosafety uses the precautionary principle. It states that countries can ban genetically modified organisms (GMOs) if they believe the scientific evidence does not prove they are safe. For this reason, all GMOs, including most crops grown in the United States for trade with other nations, must be labeled as GMOs when shipped internationally. Policy makers in the United States, however, believe the precautionary principle has been met with regard to GMOs and do not require any package labeling. As of summer 2015, more than seventy bills had been introduced in thirty states that would require GMO labeling, but none had passed.

The prevention principle states that elected officials should make decisions that prevent problems from occurring, rather than fix problems after they happen. For example, scientific evidence suggests that disposal wells associated with hydraulic fracturing can cause earthquakes. These disposal wells hold polluted water that is injected with great force into the ground, which destabilizes the earth's rock layer. If the prevention principle were applied, policy makers would prohibit this practice to prevent the damage that these earthquakes can cause.

The polluter pays principle states that those who pollute the environment are to be taxed the amount it will cost to clean up the pollution. This is also the concept of full-cost pricing. In the United States, CERCLA requires those who generate hazardous waste to clean it up at their own expense.

The environmental justice principle states that no group of people should suffer from an unfair burden of pollution. For example, a company that dumps its toxic waste in a marshy area near a poor neighborhood is violating the environmental justice principle by affecting the health of everyone in the neighborhood and lowering their property values.

Enacting these principles in environmental policy requires that all those involved in the process understand a number of scientific issues and are willing to look beyond strictly financial issues when making decisions. When these ideals are not enacted, it is often because lobbyists for corporations have influenced policy makers in an effort to limit the legal responsibility of corporations and increase their profits.

SEE ALSO Air Pollution; Biodiversity; Climate Change; Comprehensive Environmental Response, Compensation, and Liability Act (CERCLA); Endangered and Threatened Species; Environmental Law; Farm Bill, U.S.; Genetically Modified Organisms (GMOs); Hazardous Waste; Hydraulic Fracturing; Nongovernmental Organizations; Precautionary Principle; Water Pollution

For more information

BOOKS

Vig, Norman J., and Michael E. Kraft. *Environmental Policy: New Directions for the Twenty-First Century.* 8th ed. Los Angeles: Sage, 2012.

WEBSITES

"National Environmental Policy Act (NEPA)." U.S. Environmental Protection Agency, updated February 3, 2015. http://www.epa.gov/compliance/nepa/ (accessed April 14, 2015).

"The NRDC Story." Natural Resources Defense Council. http://www.nrdc.org/about/nrdc-story.asp (accessed April 14, 2015).

Where to Learn More

Books

Bane, Peter. *The Permaculture Handbook: Garden Farming for Town and Country.* Gabriola Island, BC: New Society Publishers, 2012.

Benyus, Janine. *Biomimicry: Innovation Inspired by Nature.* New York: William Morrow, 1997.

Black, William R. *Sustainable Transportation: Problems and Solutions.* New York: Guilford Press, 2010.

Bloom, Jonathan. *American Wasteland: How America Throws Away Nearly Half of Its Food (and What We Can Do about It).* Cambridge, MA: Lifelong/Da Capo, 2011.

Brown, Robert C., and Tristan R. Brown. *Why Are We Producing Biofuels?* Ames, IA: Brownia, 2012.

Caradonna, Jeremy L. *Sustainability: A History.* New York: Oxford University Press, 2014.

Connett, Paul. *The Zero Waste Solution: Untrashing the Planet One Community at a Time.* White River Junction, VT: Chelsea Green, 2013.

Fox, Thomas. *Urban Farming: Sustainable City Living in Your Backyard, in Your Community, and in the World.* Irvine, CA: Bowtie Press, 2011.

Freinkel, Susan. *Plastic: A Toxic Love Story.* Boston: Houghton Mifflin Harcourt, 2011.

Gibbs, Lois, and Murray Levine. *Love Canal: My Story.* Albany: State University of New York Press, 1982.

Ikerd, John. *The Essentials of Economic Sustainability.* Boulder, CO: Kumarian Press, 2012.

Kallen, Stuart A. *Running Dry: The Global Water Crisis.* Minneapolis, MN: Twenty-first Century, 2015.

Kleppel, Gary. *The Emergent Economy: Farming, Sustainability and the Return of the Local Economy.* Gabriola Island, BC: New Society Publishers, 2014.

Landgraf, Greg. *Citizen Science Guide for Families: Taking Part in Real Science.* Chicago: Huron Street Press, 2013.

Lappe, Frances. *Diet for a Small Planet: Twentieth Anniversary Edition.* New York: Ballantine Books, 2011.

Leahy, Stephen. *Your Water Footprint: The Shocking Facts About How Much Water We Use to Make Everyday Products.* Richmond, Ontario: Firefly Books, 2014.

Leonard, Annie. *The Story of Stuff: The Impact of Overconsumption on the Planet, Our Communities, and Our Health—And How We Can Make It Better.* New York: Free Press, 2010

Litfin, Karen T. *Ecovillages: Lessons for Sustainable Community.* Malden, MA: Polity Press, 2014.

Lundgren, Julie K. *How Ecosystems Work.* Vero Beach, FL: Rourke Publishing, 2012.

Maczulak, Anne. *Biodiversity: Conserving Endangered Species.* New York: Facts on File, 2009.

McDonough, William, and Michael Braungart. *Cradle to Cradle: Remaking the Way We Make Things.* New York: Vintage, 2002.

McDonough, William, and Michael Braungart. *The Upcycle: Beyond Sustainability—Designing for Abundance.* New York: North Point Press, 2013.

Minter, Adam. *Junkyard Planet: Travels in the Billion-Dollar Trash Trade.* New York: Bloomsbury Press, 2013.

Newman, Peter, and Jeffrey Kenworthy. *The End of Automobile Dependence: How Cities Are Moving Beyond Car-Based Planning.* Washington, DC: Island Press, 2015.

Owings, Lisa. *Sustainable Agriculture.* Innovative Technologies series. Minneapolis, MN: Abdo Publishing, 2013.

Pears, Pauline. *The Organic Book of Compost: Easy and Natural Techniques to Feed Your Garden.* Springville, UT: Cedar Fort, Inc., 2013.

Renneberg, Reinhard. *Biotechnology for Beginners.* Waltham, MA: Academic Press, 2007.

Ross, Andrew. *Bird on Fire: Lessons from the World's Least Sustainable City.* New York: Oxford University Press, 2011.

Schanbacher, William D. *The Global Food System: Issues and Solutions.* Santa Barbara, CA: Praeger, 2014.

Stickner, Robert R. *Aquaculture: An Introductory Text* Second Edition, Oxfordshire, UK: CABI, 2009.

Strauss, Rochelle. *Tree of Life: The Incredible Biodiversity of Life on Earth.* Illus. Margot Thompson. Tonawanda, NY: CitizenKid, 2013.

Thayer, Robert L. *Lifeplace: Bioregional Thought and Practice.* Berkeley: University of California Press, 2003.

Where to Learn More

World Commission on Environment and Development. *Report of the World Commission on Environment and Development: Our Common Future.* New York: Oxford University Press, April 1987. Available online at http://www.un-documents.net/our-common-future.pdf (accessed March 13, 2015).

Websites

"Acid Rain." U.S. Environmental Protection Agency. http://www.epa.gov/acidrain/index.html (accessed August 10, 2015).

Arsenault, Chris. "One Million Green Jobs Projected by 2030 in China, EU and U.S.–Experts." *Reuters.com,* March 30, 2015. Available online at http://www.reuters.com/article/2015/03/31/us-climatechange-science-economy-idUSKBN0MR00B20150331 (accessed August 31, 2015).

"Biosecurity." U.S. Environmental Protection Agency, June 27, 2012. http://www.epa.gov/agriculture/tbis.html (accessed August 10, 2015).

"The Biotechnology Initiative." United Nations. http://www.un.org/en/globalissues/biotechnology/ (accessed March 18, 2015).

Brundtland, Gro Harlem. *Report of the World Commission on Environment and Development: Our Common Future, Chairman's Foreword.* UN Documents: Gathering a Body of Global Agreements, April 1987. http://www.un-documents.net/ocf-cf.htm (accessed August 10, 2015).

"Causes of Climate Change." World Meteorological Organization. https://www.wmo.int/pages/themes/climate/causes_of_climate_change.php (accessed August 10, 2015).

"CERCLA Overview." U.S. Environmental Protection Agency, updated December 12, 2011. http://www.epa.gov/superfund/policy/cercla.htm (accessed August 10, 2015).

Citizen Science Alliance. http://www.citizensciencealliance.org/ (accessed August 10, 2015).

"Climate Change." U.S. Environmental Protection Agency. http://www.epa.gov/climatechange/ (accessed August 10, 2015).

"Community Supported Agriculture: An Introduction to CSA." Biodynamic Association. https://www.biodynamics.com/content/community-supported-agriculture-introduction-csa (accessed August 10, 2015).

"Conservation Databases." IUCN. http://www.iucn.org/knowledge/tools/databases/ (accessed August 10, 2015).

"The Deep Ecology Platform." Foundation for Deep Ecology. http://www.deepecology.org/platform.htm (accessed August 10, 2015).

"Drought for Kids." National Drought Mitigation Center. http://drought.unl.edu/DroughtforKids.aspx (accessed August 10, 2015).

"Ecological Footprint." World Wildlife Fund Global. http://wwf.panda.org/about_our_earth/teacher_resources/webfieldtrips/ecological_balance/eco_footprint/ (accessed August 10, 2015).

"Ecosystem Services." National Wildlife Federation. http://www.nwf.org/Wildlife/Wildlife-Conservation/Ecosystem-Services.aspx (accessed August 10, 2015).

"The Extinction Crisis." Center for Biological Diversity. http://www.biologicaldiversity.org/programs/biodiversity/elements_of_biodiversity/extinction_crisis/ (accessed August 10, 2015).

"Food security statistics." Food and Agriculture Organization of the United Nations. http://www.fao.org/economic/ess/ess-fs/en/ (accessed August 10, 2015).

"Global Climate Change: Vital Signs of the Planet." NASA. http://climate.nasa.gov/400ppmquotes/ (accessed August 10, 2015).

"Green Building." United States Environmental Protection Agency, October 9, 2014. http://www.epa.gov/greenbuilding/ (accessed August 10, 2015).

"Green Jobs: Towards Decent Work in a Sustainable, Low-Carbon World—Real Potential, Formidable Challenges." United Nations Environment Programme. http://www.unep.org/civil-society/Implementation/GreenJobs/tabid/104810/Default.aspx (accessed August 10, 2015).

"History of Globalization." Yale Global Online. Yale University. http://yaleglobal.yale.edu/about/history.jsp (accessed August 10, 2015).

"How Can Batteries Help Sustainable Development Worldwide?" Association of European Automotive and Industrial Battery Manufacturers. http://www.eurobat.org/sites/default/files/eurobat_poster_-_iarc_2011_budapest_0.pdf (accessed August 10, 2015).

"How Much Water Goes into a Burger?" U.S. Geological Survey (updated August 7, 2015). Available online at http://water.usgs.gov/edu/activity-watercontent.html (accessed August 10, 2015).

"Hydraulic Fracturing." United States Environmental Protection Agency, August 11, 2014. http://www2.epa.gov/hydraulicfracturing/process-hydraulic-fracturing (accessed August 10, 2015).

"Introduction to Activism." Permanent Culture Now. http://www.permanentculturenow.com/what-is-activism (accessed August 10, 2015).

"Invasive Species." National Wildlife Federation. http://www.nwf.org/wildlife/threats-to-wildlife/invasive-species.aspx (accessed August 10, 2015).

"Living Planet Index" WWF.com. Available online at http://wwf.panda.org/about_our_earth/all_publications/living_planet_report/living_planet_index2/ (accessed August 10, 2015).

"Municipal Solid Waste." U.S. Environmental Protection Agency. http://www.epa.gov/epawaste/nonhaz/municipal/index.htm (accessed August 10, 2015).

"National Organic Program." U.S. Department of Agriculture. http://www.ams.usda.gov/about-ams/programs-offices/national-organic-program (accessed August 10, 2015).

"Noise Pollution." U.S. Environmental Protection Agency. http://www.epa.gov/air/noise.html (accessed August 10, 2015).

"Overview of Greenhouse Gases." U.S. Environmental Protection Agency. http://www.epa.gov/climatechange/ghgemissions/gases.html (accessed August 10, 2015).

"Post-2015 Development Agenda." Sustainable Development Knowledge Platform. https://sustainabledevelopment.un.org/post2015 (accessed August 10, 2015).

"Poverty Overview." World Bank, updated April 6, 2015. http://www.worldbank.org/en/topic/poverty/overview (accessed August 10, 2015).

Society for Ecological Restoration. http://www.ser.org/ (accessed August 10, 2015).

"Staple Foods: What Do People Eat?" Food and Agriculture Organization. http://www.fao.org/docrep/u8480e/u8480e07.htm (accessed August 10, 2015).

"Stratospheric Ozone Layer Depletion and Recovery." Earth System Research Laboratory. http://www.esrl.noaa.gov/research/themes/o3/ (accessed August 10, 2015).

"Transition 101." Transition United States. http://transitionus.org/transition-101 (accessed August 10, 2015).

"U.S. and World Population Clock." United States Census Bureau. http://www.census.gov/popclock/ (accessed August 10, 2015).

"United Nations Conference on Environment and Development, Rio+20" United Nations Department of Economic and Social Affairs. https://sustainabledevelopment.un.org/rio20 (accessed August 10, 2015).

United Nations Convention to Combat Desertification. http://www.unccd.int/en (accessed August 10, 2015).

"Wastes—Hazardous Wastes." U.S. Environmental Protection Agency. http://www.epa.gov/waste/hazard/index.htm (accessed August 10, 2015).

Whelan, Court. "Spotlight on Sustainability: Why is Ecotourism Special?" WWF.org, September 24, 2013. http://www.worldwildlife.org/blogs/good-nature-travel/posts/spotlight-on-sustainability-why-is-ecotourism-special (accessed August 10, 2015).

"What is a Pesticide?" U.S. Environmental Protection Agency, updated August 5, 2014. http://www.epa.gov/pesticides/about/index.htm (accessed August 10, 2015).

"What is an Ecovillage?" Global Ecovillage Network. http://gen.ecovillage.org/en/article/what-ecovillage (accessed August 10, 2015).

"What is Biomimicry?" Biomimicry Institute. http://biomimicry.org/what-is-biomimicry/ (accessed August 10, 2015).

"World Population Prospects: The 2015 Revision." Population Division of the Department of Economic and Social Affairs of the United Nations Secretariat, 2015. http://esa.un.org/unpd/wpp/index.htm (accessed August 10, 2015).

List of Organizations

AMP Global Youth
1220 L Street N.W., Suite 100-161
Washington, D.C. 20005
USA
E-mail: info@aidemocracy
Internet: www.ampglobalyouth.org

Center for Ecoliteracy
The David Brower Center
2150 Allston Way, Suite 270
Berkeley, California 94704-1377
USA
Phone: 510-845-4595
E-mail: info@ecoliteracy.org
Internet: www.ecoliteracy.org

Convention on Biological Diversity
413, Saint Jacques Street, Suite 800
Montreal QC H2Y 1N9
Canada
Phone: +1 514-288-2220
E-mail: secretariat@cbd.int
Internet: www.cbd.int

Earth Day Network
1616 P Street, N.W., Suite 340
Washington, D.C. 20036
USA
Phone: 202-518-0044
E-mail: info@earthday.org
Internet: www.earthday.org

Environmental Defense Fund
1875 Connecticut Avenue, N.W., Suite 600
Washington, D.C. 20009
USA
Phone: 800-684-3322
Internet: www.edf.org

Environmental Justice Foundation
EJF, 1 Amwell Street
London, EC1R 1UL
United Kingdom
Phone: +44 (0) 207 239 3310
E-mail: info@ejfoundation.org
Internet: www.ejfoundation.org

Facing the Future
220 2nd Avenue S #106
Seattle, Washington 98104
USA
Phone: 206-264-1503
E-mail: office@facingthefuture.org
Internet: www.facingthefuture.org

Free the Children
233 Carlton Street
Toronto, Ontario M5A 2L2
Canada
Phone: 416-925-5894
Internet: www.freethechildren.com

List of Organizations

Global Footprint Network
312 Clay Street, Suite 300
Oakland, California 94607-3510
USA
Phone: 510-839-8879
Internet: www.footprintnetwork.org

Global Sustainable Tourism Council
E-mail: info@gstcouncil.org
Internet: www.gstcouncil.org/en/

Green America
1612 K Street N.W., Suite 600
Washington, D.C. 20006
USA
Phone: 800-584-7336
E-mail: info@greenamerica.org
Internet: www.greenamerica.org

Greenpeace International
Ottho Heldringstraat 5
1066 AZ Amsterdam
The Netherlands
Phone: +31 (0) 20 718 20 00
Internet: www.greenpeace.org

Greenpeace USA
702 H Street, N.W., Suite 300
Washington, D.C. 20001
USA
Phone: 800-722-6995
E-mail: info@wdc.greenpeace.org
Internet: www.greenpeace.org/usa/

Hunger Project
5 Union Square West, 7th Floor
New York, New York 10003
USA
Phone: 212-251-9100
E-mail: info@thp.org
Internet: www.thp.org

Intergovernmental Panel on Climate Change (IPCC)
7bis Avenue de la Paix, C.P. 2300
CH-1211 Geneva 2
Switzerland
Phone: +41 22-730-8208/54/84
E-mail: IPCC-Sec@wmo.int
Internet: www.ipcc.ch

International Union for Conservation of Nature (IUCN) Red List of Threatened Species
IUCN UK Office, Sheraton House, Castle Park, Cambridge CB3 0AX
United Kingdom
Phone: +44 (0) 1223 370 031
E-mail: redlist@iucn.org
Internet: www.iucnredlist.org

Local Harvest
PO Box 1292
Santa Cruz, California 95061
USA
Phone: 831-515-5602
Internet: www.localharvest.org

National Sustainable Agriculture Coalition
110 Maryland Avenue, N.E., Suite 209
Washington, D.C. 20002
USA
Phone: 202-547-5754
E-mail: info@sustainableagriculture.net
Internet: www.sustainableagriculture.net

Natural Resources Defense Council
40 West 20th Street
New York, New York 10011
USA
Phone: 212-727-2700
E-mail: nrdcinfo@nrdc.org
Internet: www.nrdc.org

Nature Conservancy
4245 North Fairfax Drive, Suite 100
Arlington, Virginia 22203-1606
USA
E-mail: 703-874-5300
Internet: www.nature.org

List of Organizations

Royal Botanic Gardens Millennium Seed Bank
Wakehurst Place, Ardingly,
Haywards Heath
West Sussex RH17 6TN
United Kingdom
Phone: 01444 894100
E-mail: msbsci@kew.org
Internet: www.kew.org/science-conservation
/collections/millennium-seed-bank

Sierra Club
85 Second Street, 2nd Floor
San Francisco, California 94105
USA
Phone: 415-977-5500
E-mail: information@sierraclub.org
Internet: www.sierraclub.org

Story of Stuff Project
1442 A Walnut Street, # 272
Berkeley, California 94709
USA
Phone: 510-883-1055
E-mail: info@storyofstuff.org
Internet: www.storyofstuff.org

350.org
20 Jay Street, Suite 732
Brooklyn, New York 11201
USA
Phone: 518-635-0350
E-mail: team@350.org
Internet: www.350.org

Transition Network
43 Fore Street
Totnes TQ9 5HN
United Kingdom
Phone: +44 (0) 1803 865 669
Internet: www.transitionnetwork.org

Trees, Water, and People
633 Remington Street
Fort Collins, Colorado 80524
USA
Phone: 877-606-4897
E-mail: info@treeswaterpeople.org
Internet: www.treeswaterpeople.org

United Nations Development Programme (UNDP)
One United Nations Plaza
New York, New York 10017
USA
Internet: www.undp.org

United Nations Environment Programme (UNEP)
United Nations Avenue,
Gigiri, PO Box 30552, 00100
Nairobi, Kenya
Phone: (254-20) 7621234
E-mail: unepinfo@unep.org
Internet: www.unep.org

United Nations High Commissioner for Human Rights
Palais des Nations
CH-1211 Geneva 10
Switzerland
Phone: +41 22 917 9220
E-mail: InfoDesk@ohchr.org
Internet: http://www.ohchr.org/EN/Pages/WelcomePage.aspx

US Agency for International Development (USAID)
1200 Pennsylvania Avenue, N.W.
Washington, D.C. 20460
USA
Phone: 888-782-7937
Internet: www.usaid.gov

US Environmental Protection Agency's Energy Star Program
1200 Pennsylvania Avenue, N.W.
Washington, D.C. 20460
USA
Phone: 888-782-7937
Internet: www.energystar.gov

List of Organizations

US Partnership for Education for Sustainable Development
E-mail: uspesd@gmail.com
Internet: www.uspartnership.org

WaterAid
315 Madison Avenue,
Suite 2301
New York, New York 10017
USA
Phone: 212-683-0430
Internet: www.wateraid.org

World Health Organization (WHO)
Avenue Appia 20
1211 Geneva 27
Switzerland
Phone: +41 22 791 21 11
Internet: www.who.int

World Wildlife Fund (WWF)
1250 24th Street, N.W.
Washington, D.C. 20037-1193
USA
Phone: 202-293-4800
Internet: www.worldwildlife.org

Index

Italic type indicates volume numbers; **boldface** indicates main entries. Illustrations are marked by (ill.)

A

Abu Dhabi, United Arab Emirates, *3:* 612
Abundance, *1:* **1–3**
Accounting, *2:* 317–318
Acid mine drainage, *2:* 411
Acid rain, *1:* **3–7**, 5 (ill.)
    air pollution, *1:* 20–21
    EPA Acid Rain Program, *1:* 23
    fossil fuels, *2:* 296
Active solar heating, *3:* 563
Activism, *1:* **7–11**, 8 (ill.)
    alter-globalization movement, *1:* 24, 26–29, 26 (ill.)
    environmental justice, *1:* 237–240
    nongovernmental organizations, *2:* 442
Adams, William Gryllis, *3:* 562
Adaptation to climate change, *1:* 119–120
Advertising, *1:* 150–151, 154
Aerobic decomposers, *1:* 97–98
Aerobic respiration, *1:* 96–97
Africa, *2:* 381–382; *3:* 518
Age distribution of human population, *3:* 503–504
Agenda 21, *1:* 86, 201–203, 239; *3:* 600–601
Agent Orange, *3:* 616–617
Agribusiness. *See* Industrial farming
Agricultural Act of 2014. *See* Farm Bill, U.S.
Agricultural Adjustment Act, *2:* 391
Agriculture, *1:* **11–17**, 14 (ill.). *See also* Community-supported agriculture; Pesticides

algae blooms and dead zones, *3:* 639–640
alter-globalization movement, *1:* 27, 28
biofuels, *1:* 44, 62–65, 82
biosecurity, *1:* 75–76
biotechnology, *1:* 78–79, 80–81
carbon cycle, *1:* 99
climate change, *1:* 117, 119–120
community-based natural resource management, *2:* 430
desertification, *1:* 165, 168
drought, *1:* 173–174
Dust Bowl, *1:* 172
ecovillages, *1:* 219
erosion, *2:* 379
fair trade, *2:* 312
Farm Bill, *2:* 257–259
food security, *2:* 272–273, 274–277
food systems, *2:* 278–283
food waste, *2:* 284
free trade, *2:* 299–300
genetically modified organisms, *2:* 303–305
Green Belt Movement, *2:* 381–382
habitat destruction, *1:* 53
individual *vs.* communal rights, *2:* 335–336
industrial farming, *2:* 260–265
livestock farming, *1:* 69
local economy, *2:* 387
locavores and the local food movement, *2:* 391–394
monoculture, *2:* 414–418

lxiii

Agriculture (*Continued*)
   nitrogen cycle, *2:* 435–436
   permaculture, *3:* 475, 476–477
   seed banks, *3:* 545–548
   soil, effects on, *3:* 555
   soil pollution, *3:* 559
   sustainable farming, *2:* 266–271
   tragedy of the commons, *3:* 586–587
   Transition Towns movement, *3:* 592
   urban farming, *3:* 605–607
   water pollution, *3:* 639, 641–642
Agriculture Department, U.S. *See* Department of Agriculture, U.S.
Agronomy
   biotechnology, *1:* 80–81
   food supply, *2:* 268
   food systems, *2:* 283
   Green Revolution, *1:* 13–14
Aid for Trade program, *2:* 301
AIDS, *2:* 404; *3:* 518–519
Air pollution, *1:* **17–24**, 19 (ill.). *See also* Greenhouse gas emissions
   acid rain, *1:* 3–7
   automobiles, *1:* 42
   biodiversity threats, *1:* 54
   China, *2:* 337
   coal, *1:* 126–127; *2:* 293
   environmental law, *1:* 245
   fertilizer, *2:* 436
   fossil fuels, *1:* 61
   greenhouse gas emissions, *2:* 319
   hydraulic fracturing, *2:* 342
   treaties, *3:* 498–499
   war, *3:* 618, 619
   wildlife, effects on, *3:* 646–647
Airlines, *2:* 400, 439
Alberta, Canada, *3:* 465
Algae
   algal blooms, *1:* 194; *2:* 436; *3:* 639–640
   biodiversity, *1:* 54
   biofuels, *1:* 81
Alley cropping, *2:* 268–269
Alter-globalization movement, *1:* **24–29**, 26 (ill.)
Alternative energy, *1:* **29–32**
   alternative fuel vehicles, *1:* 43–44, 43 (ill.), 45
   batteries as, *1:* 48–49

   biofuel, *1:* 60–65, 63 (ill.)
   biogas, *2:* 422
   biomimicry, *1:* 67
   biotechnology, *1:* 81, 82
   building design, *1:* 92
   Bureau of Land Management, *2:* 428–429
   carbon cycle, *1:* 99
   costs, *1:* 229
   geothermal power, *2:* 306–309, 307 (ill.)
   green jobs, *2:* 367, 369
   hydropower, *2:* 346–349, 348 (ill.)
   Japan, *2:* 336
   Masdar City, *3:* 612
   mining, *2:* 413
   solar power, *3:* 561–567, 563 (ill.)
   tidal power, *3:* 584–586
   transportation, *1:* 232–233; *3:* 594–595
   wind power, *3:* 648–650
Alternative food systems, *2:* 280–281
Aluminum, *1:* 5
Amazon Rainforest, *1:* 15–16, 15 (ill.), 210–211, 211 (ill.)
American Public Transportation Association, *2:* 397–398
Amnesty International, *2:* 336
Amu Darya river, *2:* 265
Anaerobic decomposers, *1:* 97–98
Anderson v. Pacific Gas & Electric Co., *1:* 243–244
Animals
   acid rain, *1:* 4–5, 21
   automobile collisions, *1:* 43
   biomimicry, *1:* 67 (ill.), 68, 69
   biosecurity, *1:* 76–77
   carbon cycle, *1:* 96
   carrying capacity, *1:* 102–103
   ecological restoration, *1:* 187
   ecology, *1:* 191
   ecosystems, *1:* 204–205
   food web, *2:* 289
   invasive species, *2:* 263
   matter cycling and energy transfer, *1:* 206–207
   noise pollution, *2:* 437–438
   ozone depletion effects, *3:* 471
   polar melting, *3:* 491
   wild horses and burros, *2:* 428, 429 (ill.)

Antarctica, *3:* 491–492
Anthropocentrism, *2:* 428–429
Antibiotics, *1:* 35
Appalachia, *2:* 410; *3:* 632
Apparel industry, *1:* 153
Aquaculture, *1:* 11, **32–37**, 34 (ill.), 37 (ill.), 224
Aquatic ecosystems. *See also* Marine ecosystems; Water pollution
    acid rain, *1:* 5, 6, 21
    ecosystem types, *1:* 207
    hydropower, *2:* 348–349
    invasive species, *3:* 538
    threats, *1:* 211
    water cycle, *3:* 633–634
Aquifers, *1:* **38–40**, 173; *2:* 283
Aral Sea, *2:* 265, 377
Architecture. *See* Building design
Arctic Circle ecosystem, *3:* 499
Arctic Sea ice melt, *3:* 490, 490 (ill.), 491
Arizona, *1:* 187–188
Army Corps of Engineers, U.S., *3:* 538
Arrhenius, Svante, *2:* 319
Artificial ecosystems, *1:* 185
Asia
    atmospheric brown cloud, *1:* 20, 21 (ill.)
    irrigation, *2:* 265
    Millennium Development Goals, *2:* 404–405
Asian carp, *2:* 362
Assessment of the Potential Impacts of Hydraulic Fracturing or Oil and Gas on Drinking Water Resources (EPA), *2:* 343–345
Atmospheric brown cloud, *1:* 20, 21 (ill.)
ATTAC (Association for the Taxation of Financial Transactions and Aid to Citizens), *1:* 28
Australia
    atmospheric brown cloud, *1:* 20
    drought, *1:* 175
    Millennium Seed Bank Project, *3:* 547
Automobiles, *1:* **40–46**, 43 (ill.)
    alternative energy, *3:* 595
    battery-operated vehicles, *1:* 48–49
    biofuels, *1:* 62, 63, 82
    natural gas, *2:* 421
    United States, *2:* 399
    World Solar Challenge, *3:* 564–565

B-corporations, *2:* 317
Ballast water, *2:* 360
Bangladesh, *3:* 506 (ill.), 640–641
Barents Sea, *2:* 293 (ill.)
Barriers, soil, *1:* 168–169
Bartering, *1:* 220; *2:* 388; *3:* 592
Basel Convention, *2:* 331; *3:* 533
Bats, *1:* 76–77, 106
Batteries, *1:* **47–50**, 49 (ill.); *2:* 353; *3:* 567
Becquerel, Alexandre-Edmond, *3:* 561–562
Bell Labs, *3:* 562
Benefit corporations, *2:* 317
Benyus, Janine, *1:* 66, 68
Berkeley Pit, *2:* 410–411
Bicycles, *1:* 45, 232; *3:* 596–597, 596 (ill.)
Bill and Melinda Gates Foundation, *3:* 519
Bioaccumulation, *2:* 329
Biocapacity, *1:* 179, 181, 182–183
Biodegradability. *See* Decomposition
Biodiesel, *1:* 63
Biodiversity, *1:* **50–60**, 55 (ill.)
    agriculture, *1:* 15–16
    biosecurity, *1:* 75
    Brundtland Report, *1:* 87
    climate change effects, *1:* 116
    conservation, *1:* 145–147
    conservation biology, *1:* 52–53
    Convention on Biological Diversity, *1:* 55–56, 57–59
    desertification, *1:* 166
    economic value of, *1:* 56–57
    ecosystems, *1:* 50–52, 211
    endangered species, *1:* 223–224
    free trade, *2:* 300
    genetically modified organisms, *2:* 305
    invasive species prevention, *2:* 364
    monoculture, *2:* 270
    pesticides, *3:* 481
    thermal pollution, *3:* 582
    threats to, *1:* 53–54

Index

Biofuel energy, *1:* 60–66, 63 (ill.)
   algae, *1:* 81
   automobiles, *1:* 44
   biotechnology, *1:* 82
   transportation, *3:* 595
Biogas, *2:* 422
Biological pest control, *3:* 483–484
Biological weapons, *1:* 76; *2:* 378
Biomagnification, *2:* 329
Biomass energy, *1:* 30, 62
Biomes, *1:* 204–205
Biomimicry, *1:* 66–70, 67 (ill.)
Bioplastics, *3:* 488
Bioprospecting, *2:* 300
Bioregionalism, *1:* 70–73, 72 (ill.); *2:* 377
Bioremediation, *1:* 81, 142
Biosecurity, *1:* 74–77, 76 (ill.)
Biota, *1:* 204–205
Biotechnology, *1:* 78–83, 80 (ill.)
Birth control pill, *3:* 504–505
Birth rates, *3:* 503
Bisphenol A, *3:* 487
Blair Ventilated Improved Pit Latrine, *3:* 631
"The Blue Marble" (NASA photograph), *1:* 194 (ill.)
Bluefin tuna, *1:* 36–37, 37 (ill.)
Boone and Crockett Club, *1:* 144
Borlaug, Norman, *1:* 13–14, 78–79; *2:* 268, 274–275
Borneo Island, *2:* 445–446, 445 (ill.)
Bosch, Carl, *2:* 261, 274, 435
Bottle-deposit laws, *3:* 532
Boulding, Kenneth, *2:* 316
Boycotts, *1:* 8
BP oil spill. *See* Deepwater Horizon oil spill
Brandis, Dietrich, *1:* 143
Braungart, Michael, *1:* 156
Brazil, *1:* 15–16, 15 (ill.), 27, 82
Bretton Woods Conference, *1:* 25
British Columbia, *2:* 417
Brittany, France, *3:* 585–586
Bromine, *3:* 471
Brown, Jerry, *1:* 173
Brown, Lester, *3:* 567
Brown marmorated stink bugs, *2:* 362

Brownsfields Redevelopment, *2:* 378–379
Brundtland, Gro Harlem, *1:* 83, 85, 85 (ill.)
Brundtland Report, *1:* 83–88; *2:* 430; *3:* 571–572
Building design, *1:* 88–94, 91 (ill.), 92 (ill.)
   energy conservation, *1:* 230–231, 231 (ill.)
   noise pollution, *2:* 439
   thermal pollution, *3:* 583
Buildings and acid rain, *1:* 6
Bureau of Labor Statistics, U.S., *2:* 368, 369
Bureau of Land Management, U.S., *2:* 427–429
Business
   activism, *1:* 9
   alter-globalization movement, *1:* 24–29
   consumption, *1:* 150–151, 153–154
   cost-benefit analysis, *1:* 200
   energy conservation, *1:* 229, 231
   environmental policy, *1:* 247–248, 249
   fair trade, *2:* 254–256
   globalization, *2:* 310–312
   green economy, *2:* 316–318
   green jobs, *2:* 370
   local economy, *2:* 386–389
   microloans, *3:* 551
   nongovernmental organizations, *2:* 443
   palm oil plantations, *2:* 445–446
Butte, Montana, *2:* 410–411
"Buy local" programs, *2:* 387
Byler, Edna Ruth, *2:* 253–254

C

C2C design. *See* Cradle-to-cradle design
California
   desalination, *1:* 162–163
   drought, *1:* 171–174, 173 (ill.)
   Electronic Waste Recycling Act, *3:* 533
   food system, *2:* 283
   fuel cell vehicles, *1:* 45
   geothermal energy, *2:* 309
   solar power, *3:* 567
   water shortage, *3:* 630
Calories, *2:* 456, 458
Campaign for a Commercial-Free Childhood, *1:* 154

Canada
    bioregionalism, *1:* 71
    hydraulic fracturing, *2:* 342–343
    Kyoto Protocol, *1:* 246
    North American Free Trade Agreement, *2:* 299
    tar sands, *3:* 465
Cap and trade laws, *2:* 425
Capitalism, *1:* 196–198; *2:* 315–316
Captive breeding, *1:* 224
Carbohydrates, *2:* 454
Carbon and biofuels, *1:* 82
Carbon cycle, *1:* **95–100**, 97 (ill.), 206–207
Carbon dioxide
    carbon cycle, *1:* 95, 97
    climate change, *1:* 114–115
    fossil fuels, *1:* 18; *2:* 296
    greenhouse gas emissions, *2:* 320–323
    human activity, *1:* 98
    industrial farming, *2:* 264
    Keeling Curve, *2:* 324–325, 324 (ill.)
    natural gas, *2:* 420, 423
    population, *3:* 505, 506
    recycling, *3:* 530
    transportation, *3:* 593
    war, *3:* 619
Carbon footprint, *1:* 180, 182–183
Carbon sequestration, *1:* 99, 127
Carbon sinks, *1:* 16, 99
Carcinogens, *2:* 265
Carpooling, *1:* 232
Carrying capacity, *1:* **100–104**, 102 (ill.)
Carson, Rachel, *1:* 189; *3:* 482–483, 484–485
Cartagena Protocol, *1:* 55–56, 250
Carter, Jimmy, *1:* 233–235
Cascadia, *1:* 71
Cellular respiration, *1:* 207
Cellulose biofuels, *1:* 63–64; *3:* 595
Centers for Disease Control and Prevention, U.S., *3:* 487
Central America free trade, *2:* 300
CERCLA. *See* Comprehensive Environmental Response, Compensation, and Liability Act
Chapin, Daryl, *3:* 562
Charity Navigator, *2:* 444
Charter of Fair Trade Principles, *2:* 255–256

Chavez, Cesar, *3:* 549
Chemical fertilizers. *See* Fertilizers
Chemistry and ecology, *1:* 190
Chernobyl nuclear power accident, *2:* 450; *3:* 499
Children and infants
    advertising, *1:* 150–151, 154
    child labor, *2:* 412; *3:* 496, 533
    farm to school movement, *2:* 393
    malnutrition, *2:* 457
    Millennium Development Goals, *2:* 403–404
    mortality, *2:* 403, 406
China
    atmospheric brown cloud, *1:* 20, 21 (ill.)
    coal, *1:* 124–125, 126
    coal mining, *2:* 292
    desertification, *1:* 169
    greenhouse gas emissions, *2:* 324
    human rights, *2:* 337
    population policies, *3:* 504
    recycling, *3:* 534
    soil pollution, *3:* 559
    sweatshops, *1:* 153
Chisso Corporation, *2:* 329
Chlorine, *3:* 470–471
Chlorofluorocarbons, *1:* 19–20, 23; *2:* 312; *3:* 470–471
Circular economy, *1:* 1–2, 156; *2:* 316
Cities. *See* Urban areas
Citizen science, *1:* **104–107**, 105 (ill.)
Citizenship, *1:* **107–111**, 109 (ill.), 154
Civilian Conservation Corps, *1:* 144–145
Clean Air Act, *1:* 6–7, 23, 245; *3:* 497
Clean coal, *1:* 126–127
Clean energy. *See* Alternative energy
Clean Water Act, *1:* 245; *3:* 497, 632
Cleanup. *See* Remediation
Clear-cutting
    agriculture, *1:* 15–16
    biodiversity threats, *1:* 53
    biofuels, *1:* 82
    carbon cycle, *1:* 99
    coal mining, *1:* 125
    ecosystem threats, *1:* 210–211

Index

Climate
  carbon cycle, *1:* 95, 99
  food production, *2:* 272
Climate change, *1:* **111–123**, 113 (ill.), 115 (ill.)
  abundance, threats to, *1:* 2–3
  agriculture, *2:* 277
  air pollution, *1:* 18–19, 22
  alter-globalization movement, *1:* 28
  atmospheric brown cloud, *1:* 20
  biodiversity threats, *1:* 53–54
  causes, *1:* 115–116
  clear-cutting, *1:* 16
  drought, *1:* 171
  effects, *1:* 116–117
  environmental law, *1:* 245
  food systems, *2:* 283
  fossil fuels, *2:* 296
  globalization, *2:* 312
  greenhouse effect, *1:* 113–114
  greenhouse gas emissions, *2:* 322, 323
  history, *1:* 112–113
  industrial farming, *2:* 264
  invasive species, *2:* 361
  mitigation and adaptation, *1:* 117–120
  Montreal Protocol, *1:* 23
  oil, *3:* 466
  polar melting, *3:* 490–491
  population, *3:* 505
  public health, *3:* 518
  sustainability challenges, *3:* 575
  terminology, *1:* 111
  tragedy of the commons, *3:* 588
  urbanization, *3:* 611
  water cycle, *3:* 634, 636
Climate Change Impacts in the United States (Melillo, Terese, & Yohe), *1:* 120–122
Clinton, Bill, *1:* 240
Coal, *1:* **123–129**, 125 (ill.)
  China, *2:* 337
  fossil fuels, *2:* 292–293
  industrial ecosystems, *2:* 354
  mining, *2:* 412
  pollution, *2:* 296
Cogeneration, power, *3:* 583
Cogongrass, *2:* 362

Colorado River, *2:* 265; *3:* 630
Common law, *2:* 424
Communal rights, *2:* 335–336
Communism, *1:* 196
Community issues. *See* Local and community issues
Community-supported agriculture, *1:* **129–137**, 131 (ill.); *2:* 280, 280 (ill.)
  "Defining Community Supported Agriculture" (DeMuth), *1:* 135–136
  extras, *1:* 134–135
  how CSAs work, *1:* 130–132
  labor, *1:* 132
  local economy, *2:* 387
  locavores and the local food movement, *2:* 392–393
  rotating crops, *1:* 132–133
  shares, *1:* 129–130
  sustainable farming, *1:* 133–134
  Transition Towns movement, *3:* 592
  urban farming, *3:* 606
Companion plants, *3:* 483
Composting, *1:* **137–140**
  bioplastics, *3:* 488
  food waste, *2:* 286
  permaculture, *3:* 477
  recycling, *3:* 529–530
  waste management, *3:* 624
Comprehensive Environmental Response, Compensation, and Liability Act, *1:* **140–142**
  environmental justice, *1:* 237
  hazardous waste, *2:* 331–332
  land restoration, *2:* 378
Comprehensive Everglades Restoration Plan, *1:* 210
Comte, Auguste, *2:* 424
Concentrated Animal Feeding Operations, *2:* 415, 458
Conference on the Human Environment, *2:* 337
Conoaco River, *1:* 211 (ill.)
Conservation, *1:* **143–149**, 144 (ill.). *See also* Energy conservation; Preservation
  biodiversity, *1:* 55–59
  Brundtland Report, *1:* 87
  climate change adaptation, *1:* 119–120
  drought, *1:* 174–175
  endangered species, *1:* 224–225

Index

green jobs, *2:* 369
Masdar City, *3:* 612
nongovernmental organizations, *2:* 443–444
tilling, *2:* 269
Conservation International, *2:* 443
Conservation of matter, *1:* 190, 192, 207
Conservation Reserve Program, *1:* 56–57
Conspicuous consumption, *2:* 359
Construction, *1:* 90–91
Construction and demolition materials, *3:* 532
Consumer product noise pollution, *2:* 439
Consumer recycling, *3:* 529, 530–532
Consumerism. *See* Consumption
Consumers, food web, *2:* 289
Consumption, *1:* **149–155**, 151 (ill.)
  fair trade, *2:* 256
  green economy, *2:* 314–315
  hazardous waste management, *2:* 330
  intergenerational responsibility, *2:* 355–359
  local economy, *2:* 386–387
  waste, *2:* 352; *3:* 625
  zero waste, *3:* 654–655
Contour plowing, *2:* 268
Contraceptives, *3:* 504–505, 520
Convention on Biological Diversity, *1:* 55–56, 57–59
Convention on International Trade in Endangered Species, *1:* 224
Cook stoves, solar-powered, *3:* 567
Cooke, Wells, *1:* 104–105
Cooking, *1:* 22
Cooling. *See* Heating and cooling
Cooling ponds, *3:* 583
Coote, Anna, *3:* 550
Coral reefs, *1:* 208, 208 (ill.), 211
Corn, *1:* 62, 65
Corporate Average Fuel Economy standards, *1:* 43
Corporations. *See* Business
Cost-benefit analysis, *1:* 200
Costs and prices
  community-supported agriculture, *1:* 132
  consumption, *1:* 151, 153
  desalination, *1:* 163
  drought, effects of, *1:* 174

food, *2:* 273
fossil fuels, *2:* 295
hazardous waste remediation, *2:* 332
industrial ecology, *2:* 353, 354
local economy, *2:* 386, 387
nuclear power, *2:* 449–450
oil, *3:* 462–463
solar power, *3:* 566, 567
Yucca Mountain nuclear waste site, *2:* 452
Court cases, *1:* 243–244
Cover crops, *2:* 261, 417; *3:* 555
Coyotes, *2:* 363
Crabs, *2:* 362
Cradle-to-cradle design, *1:* 2, **155–158**; *3:* 625, 655
Crop rotation, *1:* 132–133; *2:* 269, 417
Cropland agriculture. *See* Agriculture
Crude oil, *3:* 461
Cultural services, ecosystem, *1:* 206
Culture and bioregionalism, *1:* 73
Culver City, CA, *2:* 378–379
Cyclones, *1:* 20

D

Daiichi nuclear power plant accident. *See* Fukushima nuclear power accident
Dams, *1:* 31; *2:* 347–349
Dan River, *2:* 293
Darfur region, Sudan, *3:* 630–631
Darwin, Charles, *1:* 104
Data, citizen science, *1:* 105, 106
Day, Richard Evans, *3:* 562
DDT, *2:* 444; *3:* 482–485, 539
Dead zones, *1:* 54, 62; *2:* 416, 436; *3:* 638–639
Deciduous forest ecosystems, *1:* 209
Decomposition
  bioplastics, *3:* 488
  carbon cycle, *1:* 97–98
  composting, *1:* 137
  ecosystem services, *1:* 206
  food web, *2:* 289
Deep ecology, *1:* **159–161**

Index

"Deep Water" (National Commission on the BP/Deepwater Horizon Oil Spill and Offshore Drilling), *3:* 540–542
Deepwater Horizon oil spill, *2:* 294; *3:* 466–467, 496 (ill.), 540–542
"Defining Community Supported Agriculture" (DeMuth), *1:* 135–136
Deforestation, *2:* 445 (ill.)
    abundance, threats to, *1:* 2
    carbon cycle, *1:* 99
    climate change, *1:* 116
    conservation, *1:* 145
    ecosystem threats, *1:* 210–211
    Green Belt Movement, *2:* 381–382
    palm oil plantations, *2:* 445–446
Deitche, Scott M., *2:* 367–368
Denitrifying bacteria, *2:* 434
Department of Agriculture, U.S.
    food security, *2:* 276–277
    invasive species prevention, *2:* 363–364
    Office of Economic Ornithology and Mammalogy, *3:* 645
    soil pollution, *3:* 559
Department of Energy, U.S., *1:* 110; *2:* 448
Department of Housing and Urban Development, U.S., *1:* 110
Department of Labor, U.S., *2:* 412
Department of the Interior, U.S., *3:* 542
Department of Transportation, U.S., *1:* 110
Depleted uranium weapons, *3:* 619
Desalination, *1:* **161–164**
Desert ecosystems, *1:* 209
Desertification, *1:* **164–170**, 167 (ill.)
    abundance, threats to, *1:* 2
    Dust Bowl, *1:* 172
    food systems, *2:* 283
    livestock farming, *1:* 69
Desiccation, *2:* 377
Design, building. *See* Building design
Developed countries
    aging population, *3:* 504
    Brundtland Report, *1:* 85
    chlorofluorocarbons, *3:* 471
    consumption, *1:* 151–152
    ecological footprint, *1:* 181
    fair trade, *2:* 256
    food systems, *2:* 281–282
    hazardous waste, *2:* 330
    intergenerational responsibility, *2:* 357, 358–359
    monoculture, *1:* 14–15
    pollution, *3:* 496, 497–498
    population, *3:* 505
    waste exports, *3:* 624–625
Developing countries
    Agenda 21, *1:* 201–203
    biodiversity, *1:* 59
    Brundtland Report, *1:* 85
    climate change, *1:* 118
    desertification, *1:* 168
    drought, *1:* 174
    ecological footprint, *1:* 181
    ecotourism, *1:* 215
    electronic waste, *3:* 533
    environmental justice, *1:* 239
    environmental law, *1:* 244–245
    fair trade, *2:* 253–256
    free trade, *2:* 298–301
    Green Revolution, *1:* 13–14
    hazardous waste, *2:* 330–331
    human rights, *2:* 336–337
    industrial farming, *2:* 262–263
    intergenerational responsibility, *2:* 356, 357
    Millennium Development Goals, *2:* 404–405
    natural resources, *2:* 429–430
    pollution, *3:* 494, 496, 498
    population, *3:* 503, 505–506
    public health, *3:* 517–518, 518–521
    resource distribution, *2:* 431–432
    solar power, *3:* 566, 567
    subsistence farming, *2:* 270
    sustainable farming, *2:* 268
    waste exports to, *3:* 624–625
    water pollution, *3:* 640–641
    waterborne diseases, *3:* 638–639
    worker exploitation, *1:* 151, 153
Diamond, Jared, *1:* 13
Diamond mines, *2:* 412
Dingell-Johnson Act, *3:* 646
Dioxin, *3:* 487
Dirty coal, *1:* 126
Disposal, waste. *See* Waste management
Distribution of food, *2:* 273

Doha Development Agenda, *2:* 300–301
Dominican Republic-Central American Free Trade Agreement, *2:* 300
Draft Declaration of Principles on Human Rights and the Environment, *2:* 337
Drinking water. *See* Water access and sanitation; Water pollution
Drip irrigation, *2:* 269
Drought, *1:* **170–176**, 173 (ill.)
    climate change effects, *1:* 116
    desalination, *1:* 162–163
    food systems, *2:* 283
Drought Relief Service, *1:* 172
Dry steam plants, *2:* 307
Drylands. *See* Desertification
Duke Energy, *2:* 293
Dust Bowl, *1:* 56–57, 144–145, 172; *2:* 379
Dutch elm disease, *2:* 362
Dzerzhinsk, Russia, *3:* 499

E

Earth, *1:* 194 (ill.)
Earth Charter, *3:* 572
Earth Day, *1:* 145; *2:* 357 (ill.)
Earth Summit. *See* United Nations Conference on Environment and Development
Earthquakes, *3:* 554
Eco-industrial parks, *2:* 353–354
Ecocentrism, *2:* 428–429
Ecological economics, *1:* 198–199
Ecological footprint, *1:* **177–184**, 180 (ill.), 217–219, 220
Ecological restoration, *1:* **184–188**, 184 (ill.), 186 (ill.)
    ecosystems, *1:* 210
    endangered species, *1:* 226
    Superfund and Brownfields Redevelopment, *2:* 378–379
    systems and systems thinking, *3:* 579
Ecological risk assessment, *3:* 538–539
Ecology, *1:* **188–196**, 191 (ill.), 195 (ill.)
    basic and applied ecology, *1:* 193–194
    deep ecology, *1:* 159–160
    ecosystems, *1:* 192–193

    multidisciplinarity of, *1:* 189–192
    systems and systems thinking, *1:* 57, 193
Economic development. *See also* Sustainable development
    free trade, *2:* 301
    globalization, *2:* 311–312
    Millennium Development Goals, *2:* 404
    natural resources, *2:* 432
    steady-state economy, *2:* 315
Economic multiplier effect, *2:* 388
Economics, *1:* **196–203**
    alter-globalization movement, *1:* 24–29
    alternative energy, *1:* 229
    bats and white nose syndrome, *1:* 76–77
    of biodiversity, *1:* 56–57
    Brundtland Report, *1:* 83–87; *2:* 430
    circular economy, *1:* 1–2
    consumption, *1:* 150
    cradle-to-cradle design, *1:* 156
    desalination, *1:* 163
    desertification, *1:* 165–166
    drought, *1:* 174
    ecological economics, *1:* 198–199
    ecological footprint, *1:* 181
    ecotourism, *1:* 214–215
    ecovillages, *1:* 220
    environmental law, *1:* 245
    externalities, *1:* 200
    fair trade, *2:* 253–256
    food systems, *2:* 282
    fossil fuels, *2:* 295–296
    free trade, *2:* 298–301
    globalization, *2:* 310–312
    green economy, *2:* 313–318
    human rights, *2:* 334–337
    local economy, *2:* 385–389
    microloans, *3:* 551
    natural resources, *2:* 430–432
    perverse subsidies, *1:* 199–200
    public health, *3:* 520
    quality of life indicators, *3:* 524, 525, 526
    sustainability, history of, *3:* 572–573
    systems and systems thinking, *3:* 577–578
    three pillars of sustainability, *1:* 201; *3:* 569–570
    types of economies, *1:* 196–198
    Yasuni National Park, *1:* 55

Index

"The Economics of the Coming Spaceship Earth" (Boulding), *2:* 316
Ecosystems, *1:* **203–212**
    biodiversity, *1:* 50–51, 53–54
    biomes, *1:* 204–205
    biomimicry, *1:* 68
    bioregionalism, *1:* 70–73
    biosecurity, *1:* 74
    carbon cycle, *1:* 97 (ill.), 98
    ecological restoration, *1:* 184–188
    ecology, *1:* 192–193
    economics, *1:* 198–199
    ecosystem services, *1:* 56–57, 205–206
    endangered species, *1:* 223–224, 226
    energy, *1:* 191 (ill.)
    food web, *2:* 287–290, 288 (ill.)
    genetically modified organisms, *2:* 305
    greenhouse gas emissions, *2:* 323
    hydropower, *2:* 348–349
    industrial ecosystems, *2:* 353–354
    intergenerational responsibility, *2:* 356
    invasive species, *2:* 361, 363–364
    matter cycling and energy transfer, *1:* 206–207
    natural gas pipelines, *2:* 422
    Nature Conservancy, *2:* 444
    permaculture, *3:* 477
    risk assessment, *3:* 538
    sustainable farming, *2:* 266–267
    sustaining land, *2:* 380
    systems and systems thinking, *3:* 576–577
    thermal pollution, *3:* 581, 583
    threats, *1:* 210–211
    types, *1:* 207–209
Ecotourism, *1:* **212–217**
Ecovillages, *1:* **217–221**, 218 (ill.)
Ecuador, *1:* 55, 55 (ill.)
Education
    environmental policy, *1:* 249–250
    farm to school movement, *2:* 393, 393 (ill.)
    intergenerational responsibility, *2:* 358
    Millennium Development Goals, *2:* 403, 405
Eisler, Peter, *3:* 558
El Salvador, *1:* 153
Elderly persons, *3:* 504
Electric vehicles, *1:* 43–44, 43 (ill.)

Electricity
    alternative energy, *1:* 29–32
    batteries, *1:* 47–50
    building design, *1:* 92
    coal, *1:* 123–124, 125 (ill.), 126–127; *2:* 293
    energy conservation, *1:* 228–229, 230
    fossil fuels, *2:* 292
    geothermal power, *2:* 307–308, 307 (ill.), 309
    hydropower, *2:* 346–349, 348 (ill.)
    natural gas, *2:* 419–420
    nuclear power, *2:* 447–453
    solar power, *3:* 561, 562–567, 563 (ill.)
    thermal pollution from power plants, *3:* 581, 583
    tidal power, *3:* 584–586
    wind power, *3:* 648–650
Electronic waste
    hazardous waste, *2:* 330
    recycling, *3:* 533
    solar power, *3:* 566
    waste management, *3:* 625
Electronic Waste Recycling Act (California), *3:* 533
Elkington, John, *2:* 317
Emergency Planning and Community Right-to-Know Act, *1:* 142
Emory River, *2:* 293
Endangered and threatened species, *1:* **221–227**, 225 (ill.)
    bats, *1:* 76–77
    environmental law, *1:* 245
    food web, *2:* 289–290
Endangered Species Act, *1:* 224, 245; *3:* 646
Energy, *3:* 563 (ill.)
    abundance, threats to, *1:* 2–3
    alternative energy, *1:* 29–32
    batteries, *1:* 47–50
    biofuel, *1:* 60–65, 81
    coal, *1:* 123–129
    ecological footprint, *1:* 182, 183
    ecology, *1:* 190–191, 191 (ill.), 192, 193
    ecosystems, *1:* 206–207
    food web, *2:* 287–289
    geothermal power, *2:* 306–309
    green economy, *2:* 315
    hydropower, *2:* 346–349
    nuclear power, *2:* 447–453
    oil, *3:* 461–467

quality of life indicators, *3:* 525–526
recycling, *3:* 530–531
solar power, *3:* 561–567
tidal power, *3:* 584–586
wasted energy, *2:* 383
wind power, *3:* 648–650
Energy conservation, *1:* **227–236**, 231 (ill.); *2:* 315 (ill.)
 automobile fuel efficiency, *1:* 43
 benefits, *1:* 227–229
 building design, *1:* 90–93
 businesses, *1:* 231
 green economy, *2:* 315
 green jobs, *2:* 369
 homes, *1:* 230–231
 intergenerational responsibility, *2:* 357–358
 "President's Proposed Energy Policy" (Carter), *1:* 233–235
 solar power, *3:* 565–566
 transportation, *1:* 232–233
Energy Department, U.S. *See* Department of Energy, U.S.
Energy Information Administration, U.S., *2:* 343; *3:* 567
Enforcement of environmental law, *1:* 245–246
England. *See* United Kingdom
Environmental Defense Fund, *1:* 9; *2:* 444
Environmental justice, *1:* **236–241**, 251
Environmental law, *1:* **241–246**. *See also* Comprehensive Environmental Response, Compensation, and Liability Act; Treaties and international agreements
 air pollution, *1:* 22–23
 Brundtland Report, *1:* 87
 Clean Air Act, *1:* 6–7, 23; *3:* 497
 Clean Water Act, *3:* 632
 climate change, *1:* 117–119
 coal, *1:* 126–127
 conservation, *1:* 145
 consumption, *1:* 153
 cost-benefit analysis, *1:* 200
 drought regulations, *1:* 173–174
 Endangered Species Act, *1:* 224; *3:* 646
 environmental justice, *1:* 239–240
 Federal Aid in Sport Fish Restoration Act, *3:* 646
 Federal Aid in Wildlife Restoration Act, *3:* 646
 Federal Insecticide, Fungicide, and Rodenticide Act, *3:* 479–480
 globalization, *2:* 312
 greenhouse gas emissions, *2:* 323–324
 intergenerational responsibility, *2:* 357–358
 Massachusetts Toxics Use Reduction Act, *3:* 510
 Migratory Bird Treaty Act, *3:* 646
 natural law theory, *2:* 424, 425
 Noise Control Act, *2:* 439
 noise pollution, *2:* 439
 pesticides, *3:* 479–480
 pollution, *3:* 497–498
 precautionary principle, *3:* 508–509, 510
 preservation, *3:* 512
 Ramsar Convention, *3:* 579
 recycling, *3:* 532, 533
 Resource Conservation and Recovery Act, *3:* 533
 risk assessment, *3:* 541–542
 Safe Drinking Water Act, *3:* 632
 Senator Paul Simon Water for the Poor Act, *3:* 632
 soil pollution, *3:* 560
 Surface Mining Control and Reclamation Act, *2:* 412
 tragedy of the commons, *3:* 588
 water pollution prevention, *3:* 641
 Water Resources Development Act, *1:* 186
 Wild and Free-Roaming Horses and Burros Act, *2:* 428
 Wilderness Act, *3:* 513–514
 wildlife management, *3:* 645–646
Environmental Modification Convention, *3:* 618
Environmental noise, *2:* 438
Environmental policy, *1:* 239–240, **247–251**
Environmental Protection Agency, U.S.
 air pollution regulations, *1:* 23
 Clean Air Act, *1:* 6–7
 Comprehensive Environmental Response, Compensation, and Liability Act, *1:* 140–142
 employment, *1:* 110
 environmental justice, *1:* 236
 environmental law, *1:* 244, 245
 fuel-economy standards, *1:* 43
 hazardous waste, *2:* 327, 331–332, 343–345
 hydraulic fracturing, impact of, *2:* 341

Index

Environmental Protection Agency, U.S. (*Continued*)
   municipal solid waste, *3:* 625
   ozone depletion, *3:* 471
   recycling, *3:* 529
   risk assessment, *3:* 538–539, 540
   soil pollution, *3:* 558, 560
   solid waste, *3:* 494
   Three Mile Island nuclear accident, *2:* 450
   transportation, *3:* 593
   vinyl chloride risk assessment, *3:* 537–538
Ereky, Karoly, *1:* 78
Erin Brockovich (movie), *1:* 243
Erosion
   land, *2:* 379–380
   mining, *2:* 413
   monoculture, *2:* 416
   sustainable farming, *2:* 268–269
Ethanol, *1:* 62–65, 82; *3:* 595
Europe, air pollution in, *3:* 647
European Food Safety Authority, *3:* 540
European green crabs, *2:* 362
European Union, *1:* 233; *2:* 323–324
Eutrophication, *2:* 264–265; *3:* 640
Evaporation, *3:* 636
Everglades, *1:* 210
Executive Order 12898, *1:* 240
Exploitation, worker, *1:* 151
Exporting waste, *3:* 624–625
Externalities, economic, *1:* 200
Extinction
   biodiversity, *1:* 52, 53–54
   food web, *2:* 289
   invasive species, impact of, *2:* 363
   mass extinctions, *1:* 221–222
Extraction, fossil fuel, *2:* 378; *3:* 465–466, 540–542. *See also* Hydraulic fracturing; Mining
Exxon Valdez, *2:* 294

F

Fabrics, *1:* 68
Factory farming. *See* Industrial farming
Fair trade, *1:* 154; **2: 253–257**, 312
Fairtrade Labelling Organizations International, *2:* 255–256

Family planning, *3:* 504–505, 520
Farm Bill, U.S., 2: 257–259
Farm to school movement, *2:* 393, 393 (ill.)
Farmed fish. *See* Aquaculture
Farmer-managed natural regeneration, *1:* 168
Farmers' markets, *2:* 387 (ill.)
   local economy, *2:* 387
   locavores and the local food movement, *2:* 392–393
   Transition Towns movement, *3:* 592
Farming. *See* Agriculture; Community-supported agriculture; Industrial farming; Subsistence farming; Sustainable farming
Fats, *2:* 454
Federal Aid in Sport Fish Restoration Act, *3:* 646
Federal Aid in Wildlife Restoration Act, *3:* 646
Federal Council for Sustainable Development, *2:* 281
Federal Insecticide, Fungicide, and Rodenticide Act, *3:* 479–480
Feral pigs, *2:* 362
Fertilizers
   algae blooms and dead zones, *3:* 639–640
   community-supported agriculture, *1:* 133
   food security, *2:* 274, 277
   industrial farming, *2:* 261–262, 264–265
   monoculture, *2:* 270
   nitrogen cycle, *2:* 435–436
   water pollution prevention, *3:* 641–642
First National People of Color Environmental Leadership Summit, *1:* 240
Fish
   acid rain, *1:* 5
   aquaculture, *1:* 32–37
   bioaccumulation and biomagnification, *2:* 329
   hydropower, *2:* 348, 349
   invasive species, *2:* 362
   tragedy of the commons, *3:* 587
   wildlife management, *3:* 646
Fish and Wildlife Service, U.S., *3:* 644, 646
Fleming, Alexander, *1:* 78
Flooding
   climate change, *1:* 116, 121
   flood-control, *1:* 120
   land and ocean borders, *2:* 377

polar melting, *3:* 492
systems thinking, *3:* 579
Florida, *1:* 186, 186 (ill.), 210
Fly ash, *1:* 126; *2:* 293
Food. *See also* Agriculture
    aquaculture, *1:* 32–37
    bioaccumulation and biomagnification, *2:* 329
    ecological footprint, *1:* 182–183
    environmental law, *1:* 245
    locavores and the local food movement, *2:* 389–394
    risk assessment, *3:* 540
    sustainability challenges, *3:* 573–574
Food and Agriculture Organization, UN
    biosecurity, *1:* 75
    food security, *2:* 271–272, 273, 276, 277
    food waste, *2:* 284
Food chain. *See* Food web
Food deserts, *3:* 607
Food Quality Protection Act, *1:* 245
Food security, **2: 271–278**, 277 (ill.)
    free trade, *2:* 300
    Great Irish potato famine, *2:* 417
    Millennium Development Goals, *2:* 402
    sustainable food systems, *2:* 280–281, 281–282
    urban farming, *3:* 607
Food sheds, *2:* 392–393
Food systems, **2: 278–284**, 280 (ill.), 393–394, 459–460
Food waste, **2: 284–287**, 304; *3:* 529–530
Food web, **2: 287–290**, 288 (ill.)
    acid rain, *1:* 5
    aquaculture, *1:* 35
    bioaccumulation and biomagnification, *2:* 329
    ecology, *1:* 191
    endangered species, *1:* 224
    Great Pacific Garbage Patch, *3:* 642
    industrial farming, *2:* 265
    thermal pollution, *3:* 582
Forest management, *3:* 601
Forest Service, U.S., *1:* 143; *3:* 512
Fossil fuels, **2: 290–297**. *See also* Hydraulic fracturing; specific fuels
    abundance, threats to, *1:* 2–3
    acid rain, *1:* 3–4, 6, 20–21
    air pollution, *1:* 17–18
    automobiles, *1:* 40–41
    biofuel compared to, *1:* 60–62
    biofuel production, use in, *1:* 62, 65
    carbon cycle, *1:* 98
    climate change, *1:* 112–113
    energy conservation, *1:* 227–228, 232–235
    extraction and land damage, *2:* 378
    free trade, *2:* 300
    green economy, *2:* 314
    greenhouse gas emissions, *2:* 321, 322
    industrial farming, *2:* 264
    nuclear power compared to, *2:* 448
    organic farms, *2:* 271
    polar melting, *3:* 492–493
    population, *3:* 505
    transportation, *3:* 593
    war, *3:* 618–619
4-H organization, *1:* 110
Fracking. *See* Hydraulic fracturing
Franklin, Benjamin, *1:* 104
Free market economics, *1:* 197–198
Free trade, *1:* 25–26; **2: 298–301**
Frogs, *1:* 5
Fuel cell vehicles, *1:* 45; *3:* 595
Fuel efficiency. *See* Energy conservation
Fukushima nuclear power accident, *2:* 336, 449, 450; *3:* 537, 558 (ill.)
Full-cost pricing, *1:* 44–45
Fuller, Calvin, *3:* 562
Fungal diseases, *3:* 546
Fungi and mycoremediation, *1:* 81

G

Galilei, Galileo, *1:* 104
Gandhi, Mahatma, *3:* 549
Ganges River, *3:* 640–641
Gardens
    composting, *1:* 137–139
    integrated pest management, *3:* 483–484
    locavores and the local food movement, *2:* 393–394
    urban farming, *3:* 605–607

Index

Garzweiler lignite mine, *2:* 409–410
Gasoline. *See* Oil
Gates Foundation, *3:* 519
Gender equality, *2:* 403
General Agreement on Tariffs and Trade, *2:* 298
General Motors, *2:* 353
Generational issues. *See* Intergenerational responsibility
Generators, solar power, *3:* 564–565
Genetically modified organisms, *1:* 80 (ill.); *2:* **303–306**
   biodiversity, *1:* 56
   biotechnology, *1:* 80–81
   climate change adaptations, *1:* 120
   conventional food systems, *2:* 280
   environmental policy, *1:* 250
   food security, *2:* 274–276
   food supply, *2:* 268
   industrial farming, *2:* 262–263
   risk assessment, *3:* 540
Genetics
   biotechnology, *1:* 78
   diversity, *2:* 275, 276; *3:* 545, 546
   invasive species, *2:* 361, 363
   resistance, *3:* 481
   seed banks, *3:* 545, 546
Geoengineering, *1:* 120
Geological Survey, U.S., *2:* 342
Georgia Organics, *2:* 393
Geothermal power, *1:* 31–32; *2:* **306–310**, 307 (ill.)
Germany
   Garzweiler lignite mine, *2:* 409–410
   precautionary principle, *3:* 508
   recycling, *3:* 534
Geysers geothermal system, *2:* 309
Gibbons, Jim, *2:* 451–453
Gibbs, Lois, *1:* 10, 237
Glacier melt. *See* Polar melting
Gleaning programs, *2:* 286
Global footprint, *1:* 179–181
Global Fund to Fight AIDS, Tuberculosis and Malaria, *3:* 519
Global surface temperatures, *1:* 115 (ill.)
Global Trade Watch, *1:* 28
Global warming. *See* Climate change

Global Water Partnership, *2:* 442
Globalization, *2:* **310–313**
   alter-globalization movement, *1:* 24–29
   invasive species, *2:* 360–361
   poverty and human rights, *2:* 334
Glyphosate, *3:* 481
Gnacadja, Luc, *1:* 165
Gobi desert, *1:* 169
Golden rice, *1:* 80
Golden Rule, *3:* 549
Government employment, *1:* 110
Government policy. *See also* Environmental policy
   food security, *2:* 276–277
   population policies, *3:* 504
Government subsidies. *See* Subsidies
Grant, Ulysses S., *3:* 512
Grassland ecosystems, *1:* 209
Grassroots activism, *1:* 110; *2:* 442
Gray water, *1:* 92–93, 175
Gray wolves, *1:* 187, 226
Grazing, *1:* 187–188; *3:* 586–587
Great Depression, *1:* 56–57, 172; *2:* 257, 391
Great Irish potato famine, *2:* 417
"The Great Lakes and Mississippi River Interbasin Study" (U.S. Army Corps of Engineers), *3:* 538
Great Lakes Region, *3:* 509
Great Pacific Garbage Patch, *3:* 642, 643 (ill.)
Green Belt Movement, *2:* 381
Green Building Council, *1:* 89, 231
Green economy, *2:* **313–318**, 315 (ill.)
Green jobs, *2:* 367–370, 368 (ill.)
Green Revolution
   agriculture, *1:* 13–14
   biotechnology, *1:* 78–79
   food security, *2:* 274–276
   food supply, *2:* 268
   industrial farming, *2:* 262–263
Green River shale rock formation, *3:* 465
Greenhouse effect
   air pollution, *1:* 18–19, 22
   climate change, *1:* 113–114
   polar melting, *3:* 489
Greenhouse gas emissions, *2:* **319–326**, 321 (ill.), 324 (ill.)
   abundance, threats to, *1:* 2–3
   agriculture, *2:* 277

Index

air pollution, *1:* 19, 22
alter-globalization movement, *1:* 28
bioplastics, *3:* 488
carbon dioxide, *1:* 95
climate change, *1:* 114–115, 118, 119
fossil fuels, *2:* 296
hydraulic fracturing, *2:* 342
industrial farming, *2:* 264
Montreal Protocol, *1:* 23; *2:* 312; *3:* 498–499
natural gas, *2:* 420, 423
oil, *3:* 466
ozone depletion, *3:* 471
polar melting, *3:* 492–493
population, *3:* 505, 506
precautionary principle, *3:* 510
recycling, *3:* 530
solar power, *3:* 566
transportation, *3:* 593
war, *3:* 619
Greenland, *3:* 491, 492
Greenpeace, *2:* 443, 445–446, 445 (ill.)
Grocers and food waste, *2:* 285, 286
Gross domestic product, *3:* 524
Groundwater
aquifers, *1:* 38–39
environmental law, *1:* 243–244
hydraulic fracturing, *2:* 341
nuclear power, *2:* 450
water cycle, *3:* 636–637
Group of 7, *2:* 296
"Group of Ten," *1:* 239
Guatemala, *2:* 310–311, 312
Gulf of Mexico, *2:* 436; *3:* 466–467, 640
Gulf Stream, *3:* 492
Gypsy moths, *3:* 484
Gyres, *3:* 642

H

Haber, Fritz, *2:* 261, 274, 435
Haber Process. *See* Fertilizers
Habitat restoration. *See* Ecological restoration

Habitats
biodiversity, *1:* 53
food web, *2:* 289–290
invasive species, *2:* 361, 363–364
wildlife management, *3:* 646
Haeckel, Ernst, *1:* 189
Hague Institute for Global Justice, *2:* 432
Hamm, Michael W., *2:* 282
Happy Planet Index, *3:* 526
Hardin, Garrett, *3:* 586, 589
Hawaii, *3:* 554
Hawken, Paul, *2:* 316
Hazard Ranking System, *1:* 141
Hazardous waste, *2:* **327–333**, 330 (ill.)
coal, *2:* 292–293
Comprehensive Environmental Response, Compensation, and Liability Act, *1:* 140–142
electronic waste, *3:* 533
environmental justice, *1:* 237–240
environmental law, *1:* 245
environmental policy, *1:* 250
former Soviet Union, *3:* 499
Love Canal, *1:* 10
mining, *2:* 410–411
persistent organic pollutants, *3:* 499–500
Resource Conservation and Recovery Act, *3:* 533
solar power, *3:* 566
Tar Creek Superfund Site, *1:* 141 (ill.)
Health issues
acid rain, *1:* 6
agriculture, *1:* 13
air pollution, *1:* 19
atmospheric brown cloud, *1:* 20
automobiles, *1:* 42
biomimicry, *1:* 68
biosecurity, *1:* 76
biotechnology, *1:* 80–81
building design, *1:* 91
coal, *1:* 126, 127–129; *2:* 292
food insecurity, *2:* 274
food systems, *2:* 282
fossil fuels, *2:* 295
genetically modified organisms, *2:* 305
indoor air pollution, *1:* 22

Index

Health issues (*Continued*)
   Millennium Development Goals, *2:* 403–404, 406
   mining, *2:* 410, 411–412
   noise pollution, *2:* 438
   nutrition, *2:* 454–460
   pesticides, *3:* 480
   plastics, *3:* 487
   pollution, *3:* 494, 496, 498, 499
   population, *3:* 501–502
   public health, *3:* 516–521
   quality of life indicators, *3:* 524–525
   risk assessment, *3:* 537–538, 539–540
   undernourished people, *2:* 277, 277 (ill.)
   water pollution, *3:* 638–639, 641
Hearing, *2:* 437–438
Heating and cooling
   building design, *1:* 91–92
   fossil fuels, *2:* 295
   geothermal power, *2:* 308–309
   homes, *1:* 230
   solar power, *3:* 563
Heavy metals, *2:* 329–330; *3:* 499
Hedonic adaptation, *1:* 153
Herbicides, *1:* 15; *3:* 616–617, 618
Hetch Hetchy Dam, *1:* 146, 146 (ill.)
"Hetch Hetchy Valley" (Muir), *1:* 147–149
High-intensity farming. *See* Industrial farming
High-speed rails, *2:* 400–401
Himalayan Mountains, *1:* 20, 21 (ill.)
Hiroshima, *3:* 617
HIV/AIDS, *2:* 404; *3:* 518–519
Holistic approach to systems, *3:* 577
Holmgren, David, *3:* 475
Homes
   ecological footprint, *1:* 183
   energy conservation, *1:* 230–231, 231 (ill.)
   geothermal power, *2:* 308–309
Horses, wild, *2:* 428, 429 (ill.)
Housing and Urban Development Department. *See* Department of Housing and Urban Development, U.S.
Hubbert, M. King, *3:* 464
Human Development Index, *3:* 525
Human population. *See* Population, human

Human rights, *2:* **333–338**
   alter-globalization movement, *1:* 24, 26, 27
   food security as a right, *2:* 280
   quality of life indicators, *3:* 526
   social justice, *3:* 548, 550
Human Rights Watch, *2:* 336
Humans
   animal carrying capacity, *1:* 102–103
   carrying capacity, *1:* 101–102
   deep ecology, *1:* 159–160
   desertification, *1:* 164–166
   ecological footprint, *1:* 177–184
   ecology, *1:* 193
Hunger. *See* Food security; Nutrition
Hunter-gatherers, *1:* 13; *2:* 458
Hunting, *1:* 143–144; *3:* 645
Hurricane Katrina, *2:* 377
Hybrid vehicles, *1:* 44; *3:* 595
Hydraulic fracturing, *2:* **338–345**, 340 (ill.)
   controversy, *2:* 341–343
   fossil fuels, *2:* 294–295
   future of, *2:* 343
   natural gas, *2:* 420, 422
   precautionary principle, *3:* 510
   process, *2:* 339–341
Hydrofluorocarbons
   air pollution, *1:* 19–20
   greenhouse gas emissions, *2:* 321
   Montreal Protocol, *1:* 23
   ozone depletion, *3:* 470–471
Hydrogen-powered vehicles, *1:* 45; *3:* 595
Hydrological cycle. *See* Water cycle
Hydropower, *1:* 31; *2:* **346–350**, 348 (ill.)

I

Imports, food, *2:* 392
"In the Depths of a Coal Mine" (Crane), *1:* 127–129
Income and wages, *2:* 299; *3:* 525
India
   air pollution, *1:* 19 (ill.)
   atmospheric brown cloud, *1:* 20, 21 (ill.)
   biotechnology, *1:* 80–81

Index

diamond mines, *2:* 412
food security, *2:* 275
recycling, *3:* 534
water pollution, *3:* 640–641
Indigenous people
   biodiversity, *1:* 58
   bioregionalism, *1:* 73
   free trade, *2:* 300
   hydraulic fracturing, *2:* 342–343
Individual *vs.* communal rights, *2:* 335–336, 337
Indonesia, *2:* 445–446
Indoor air pollution, *1:* 22; *3:* 498
Industrial ecology, *2:* **351–355**, 352 (ill.)
Industrial farming, *2:* **260–266**, 263 (ill.)
   alter-globalization movement, *1:* 27
   biodiversity threats, *1:* 53
   conventional food systems, *2:* 279–280
   food security, *2:* 277
   food systems, *2:* 281
   free trade, *2:* 300
   genetic diversity, *3:* 546
   locavores and the local food movement, *2:* 391
   monoculture, *1:* 14–15; *2:* 415–416
   nutrition, *2:* 458
   organic farming, *2:* 271
   subsidies, *2:* 270
Industrial Revolution
   carbon cycle, *1:* 98
   coal, *1:* 123
   population, *3:* 501–502
   social justice, *3:* 548–549
Industry and manufacturing
   acid rain, *1:* 3–4
   automobiles, *1:* 42
   carbon cycle, *1:* 99
   coal, *1:* 123–124
   Comprehensive Environmental Response, Compensation, and Liability Act, *1:* 140–142
   cradle-to-cradle design, *1:* 155–157
   fair trade, *2:* 254
   fossil fuels, *2:* 295
   hazardous waste, *2:* 327–332
   industrial ecology, *2:* 351–354
   pollution prevention and control, *3:* 497
   recycling, *3:* 532–533
   soil pollution, *3:* 558–559

   waste management, *3:* 623
   water pollution, *3:* 642
   zero waste, *3:* 625–626, 654
Infants. *See* Children and infants
Infectious diseases, *3:* 518
Insect invasive species, *2:* 362
Integrated pest management, *3:* 481, 483–484
Integrated Risk Information System, *3:* 539
Intensive farming. *See* Industrial farming
Intentional communities, *1:* 217
Interbreeding and invasive species, *2:* 361, 363
Intercropping, *2:* 269
Interdependency and systems thinking, *3:* 578–579
Intergenerational responsibility, *2:* **355–359**, 357 (ill.)
Intergovernmental Panel on Climate Change, *1:* 118; *3:* 492
Interior Department, U.S. *See* Department of the Interior, U.S.
International Action Center, *3:* 619
International agreements. *See* Treaties and international agreements
International Conference on Chemicals Management, *2:* 331
International Energy Agency, *2:* 420; *3:* 463
International Hydropower Association, *2:* 349
International issues
   acid rain, *1:* 6
   activism, *1:* 9
   air pollution treaties, *1:* 23
   alter-globalization movement, *1:* 24–29
   biodiversity, *1:* 55–56
   biological diversity, *1:* 57–59
   climate change, *1:* 117–118
   desertification, *1:* 167
   economic and social development, *1:* 201–203
   electronic waste, *3:* 533
   environmental justice, *1:* 239
   environmental law, *1:* 243, 244–246
   food systems, *2:* 278–279
   fossil fuels, *2:* 296
   free trade, *2:* 298–301
   hazardous waste, *2:* 330–331
   human rights, *2:* 334–337
   hydraulic fracturing, *2:* 341
   hydropower, *2:* 347

Index

International issues (*Continued*)
   natural gas, *2:* 420–421
   natural resources, *2:* 430–432
   nongovernmental organizations, *2:* 440–446
   nuclear power, *2:* 451
   oil, *3:* 463
   ozone depletion, *3:* 471–472
   pesticides, *3:* 480
   polar melting, *3:* 492–493
   pollution control treaties, *3:* 498–500
   population, *3:* 501, 502–503, 503 (ill.)
   preservation, *3:* 512–513
   public health, *3:* 517–519
   recycling, *3:* 534
   slums, *3:* 610
   sustainability challenges, *3:* 573–575
   transportation, *3:* 594
   undernourished people, *2:* 277 (ill.)
   United Nations Conference on Environment and Development, *3:* 600–601
   waste exports, *3:* 624–625
   water access and sanitation, *3:* 627
   World Solar Challenge, *3:* 564–565
International Monetary Fund, *1:* 25
International Renewable Energy Agency, *3:* 612
International Union for Conservation of Nature, *1:* 222–223
Internet
   citizen science, *1:* 105
   green jobs, *2:* 370
Introduced species. *See* Invasive species
Invasive species, *2:* **359–365**, 363 (ill.)
   biodiversity, *1:* 54
   biosecurity, *1:* 74, 75
   ecological restoration, *1:* 187
   ecosystem threats, *1:* 211
   monoculture, *2:* 416–417
   risk assessment, *3:* 538
Iodine, *2:* 455–456
Iraq, *2:* 378; *3:* 615, 619
Irish Potato Famine, *1:* 224
Irrigation
   farming, industrial, *2:* 265
   food systems, *2:* 283
   sustainable farming, *2:* 269
Italy, *1:* 71, 73

J

Jackson, Wes, *2:* 268
Jacobson, Mark, *1:* 233
Japan. *See also* Fukushima nuclear power accident
   bluefin tuna aquaculture, *1:* 36–37
   Hiroshima and Nagasaki, *3:* 617
   mercury poisoning, *2:* 329
Japanese honeysuckle, *1:* 187
Jenner, Edward, *3:* 501–502
Jobs, *2:* **367–371**
Johannesburg Declaration, *1:* 239
John (king of England), *2:* 333
Johnson, Lyndon B., *3:* 513
Justice. *See* Social justice

K

Kalundborg, Denmark, *2:* 353–354
Kansas, *3:* 491
Keeling, Charles David, *2:* 324–325
Keeling Curve, *2:* 324–325, 324 (ill.)
Keene, New Hampshire, *3:* 592
Kentucky, *2:* 411
Kenya, *2:* 381
"Keynote Address during the 2nd World Congress of Agroforestry" (Maathai), *2:* 380–382
Kimberley Process Certification Scheme, *2:* 412
Kindling Trust, *1:* 9
King, Martin Luther, Jr., *3:* 549
Kingston Fossil Plant spill, *1:* 126; *2:* 293
Kissimmee River restoration, *1:* 186, 186 (ill.)
Kristianstad Vattenrike, Sweden, *3:* 579
Kyoto Protocol, *1:* 117–118, 245, 246; *3:* 498–499

L

La Via Campesina, *1:* 26, 27, 28
Labeling
   consumption, *1:* 153, 154
   environmental policy, *1:* 250
   fair trade, *2:* 255–256

Index

Labor Department, U.S. *See* Department of Labor, U.S.
Labor issues
    child labor, *3:* 496
    Civilian Conservation Corps, *1:* 144–145
    community-supported agriculture, *1:* 132
    cradle-to-cradle design, *1:* 156
    fair trade, *2:* 253–256
    free trade, *2:* 299–300
    mining, *2:* 410, 411–412
    noise pollution, *2:* 438
    pesticides, *3:* 480
    worker exploitation, *1:* 151, 153
Lacey Act, *3:* 645
Lake Erie, *1:* 194
Lake Karachay, *3:* 499
Lake Mead, *2:* 378 (ill.)
Land, *2:* **375–382**, 378 (ill.), 379 (ill.)
    alter-globalization movement, *1:* 27
    building design, *1:* 90
    Bureau of Land Management, *2:* 427–428
    ecological footprint, *1:* 177–184
    livestock, *2:* 459
    preservation, *3:* 511–516
    thermal pollution, *3:* 581
Land ethic, *1:* 145
Land Institute, *2:* 268
Landfills
    bioplastics, *3:* 488
    food waste, *2:* 286
    landfill gas, *1:* 64
Latin America alter-globalization movement, *1:* 27, 29
Law of Conservation of Matter, *1:* 190, 192
Laws and regulations. *See* Environmental law; Treaties and international agreements
Lead, *2:* 353; *3:* 558–559
Leadership in Energy and Environmental Design, *1:* 89, 231, 231 (ill.)
"Leave No Trace" ethic, *3:* 514
LED light bulbs, *1:* 229, 230
Legislation. *See* Environmental law; Treaties and international agreements
Leonard, Annie, *1:* 154
Leopold, Aldo, *1:* 145, 145 (ill.); *3:* 514, 515–516

Leverage points, *3:* 578–580
Lewes, England, *3:* 592
Life expectancy, *3:* 499, 501, 504
Light bulbs, *1:* 229, 230
Light pollution, *2:* **383–384;** *3:* 647
Light-rail trains, *2:* 399
Light-Water Reactor Sustainability program, *2:* 451
Lightning and nitrogen release, *2:* 433–434
Lincoln, Abraham, *1:* 146
Linear economy, *2:* 316, 352
Listed wastes, *2:* 327
Livestock
    agriculture, *1:* 11, 16
    biomimicry, *1:* 69
    ecological footprint, *1:* 182–183
    greenhouse gases, *2:* 264
    inefficiency, *2:* 459
    monoculture, *2:* 415–416
    nutrition, *2:* 458
    tragedy of the commons, *3:* 586–587
Living Building Challenge program, *1:* 89
Living Planet Index, *3:* 526
Living Waters for the World, *3:* 632
Lobbyists, *1:* 109, 247–248
Local and community issues
    activism, *1:* 8
    bioregionalism, *1:* 70–73
    building design, *1:* 90
    community activism, *1:* 8
    community-supported agriculture, *1:* 133–134
    ecotourism, *1:* 214, 215
    ecovillages, *1:* 217–220
    fair trade, *2:* 312
    food systems, *2:* 280
    free trade, *2:* 300
    grassroots activism, *2:* 442
    natural resource management, *2:* 429–430
    noise, *2:* 439
    right to know, *3:* 509
    sustainable farming, *2:* 271
    sustainable food systems, *2:* 282
    Transition Towns movement, *3:* 590–592
Local economy, *2:* **385–389**, 387 (ill.)
Locavores and the local food movement, *2:* **389–395**, 390 (ill.); *3:* 606

Index

London Olympics, *3:* 656
Long-distance mass transit, *2:* 400–401
Love Canal
    activism, *1:* 10
    Comprehensive Environmental Response, Compensation, and Liability Act, *1:* 142
    environmental justice, *1:* 237
    hazardous waste, *2:* 331–332
Lovings, Amory, *2:* 316
Lovins, Hunter, *2:* 316
Low-income people. *See* Poverty

M

Maathai, Wangari, *2:* 380–382
MacArthur, Robert, *1:* 193–194
Magna Carta, *2:* 333
Magnusson, Sven-Erik, *3:* 579
Malaria, *2:* 404, 406; *3:* 482, 483
Malathion, *3:* 483
Malnutrition, *2:* 277, 277 (ill.), 457
Mandela, Nelson, *3:* 549
Manufacturing. *See* Industry and manufacturing
Manure, *2:* 264
Marine ecosystems
    desalination effects, *1:* 162
    ecosystem types, *1:* 207–208
    greenhouse gas emissions, *2:* 323
    monoculture, *2:* 416
    ozone depletion, *3:* 469–470
    threats, *1:* 211
Marsh ecosystems, *1:* 208
Martin County Coal Corporation, *2:* 411
Masdar City, *3:* 612
Mass extinctions, *1:* 221–222
Mass transit, *1:* 232; *2:* **397–401**, 398 (ill.); *3:* 595–596
Massachusetts Toxics Use Reduction Act, *3:* 510
Materials, building, *1:* 90–91, 93
Materials management, *3:* 623, 625
Maternal mortality, *2:* 403–404
Matter, conservation of, *1:* 190, 192
Matter cycling, *1:* 206–207
Mauna Loa Observatory, *2:* 322, 324–325

Max Havelaar Foundation, *2:* 253
Maximum carrying capacity, *1:* 102
Maya Fish company, *1:* 35
Mayflies, *1:* 5
McClymont, Gordon, *2:* 267
McDonough, William, *1:* 156
Meat. *See* Livestock
Megacities, *3:* 520, 610
Melting of glaciers. *See* Polar melting
Mercury, *2:* 329–330
Methane
    biofuel energy, *1:* 64
    food waste, *2:* 286
    greenhouse gas emissions, *1:* 114; *2:* 321, 322
    hydraulic fracturing, *2:* 342
    hydropower, *2:* 348
    industrial farming, *2:* 264
    natural gas, *2:* 294, 423
Mexico
    aquaculture, *1:* 35
    bioregionalism, *1:* 71
    food security, *2:* 274–275
    North American Free Trade Agreement, *2:* 299–300
Micro-scale hydropower, *2:* 349
Microbes, invasive species, *2:* 363
Microloans, *3:* 551
Middle East and the alter-globalization movement, *1:* 27, 29
Migratory Bird Treaty Act, *3:* 646
Millennium Development Goals, *2:* **402–407**; *3:* 629–630
Millennium Seed Bank, *2:* 275; *3:* 547
Minamata Bay, Japan, *2:* 329
Minerals (nutrition), *2:* 454–456
Minerals Management Service, U.S., *3:* 541
Mining, *2:* **407–414**, 409 (ill.). *See also* Extraction
    coal, *1:* 125, 127–129; *2:* 292
    pollution, *3:* 498, 499
    Tar Creek Superfund Site, *1:* 141 (ill.)
    uranium, *2:* 447, 450
Minorities and environmental justice, *1:* 238–239
Mississippi River, *3:* 538, 639–640
Mitigation
    climate change, *1:* 117–119

drought, *1:* 174–175
polar melting, *3:* 493
Mixed economies, *1:* 196
Mixed wastes, *2:* 328–329
Mollison, Bill, *3:* 475
Money, velocity of, *2:* 388
Monoculture, *2:* **414–418**, 416 (ill.)
    agriculture, *1:* 14–15
    alter-globalization movement, *1:* 27
    biodiversity threats, *1:* 53
    biofuels, *1:* 44
    biosecurity, *1:* 75
    biotechnology, *1:* 79
    conventional food systems, *2:* 279–280
    disadvantages of, *2:* 270
    food supply, *2:* 268
    food systems, *2:* 281
    industrial farming, *2:* 262
    organic farming, *2:* 271
    vs. permaculture, *3:* 476
Monongah, West Virginia, *2:* 412
Monsoons, *1:* 20
Montreal Protocol
    air pollution, *1:* 23
    environmental law, *1:* 245
    intergenerational responsibility, *2:* 357
    ozone depletion, *3:* 471–472
    pollution control treaties, *3:* 498–499
Morgan, Peter, *3:* 631
Mortality
    air pollution-related deaths, *1:* 19
    coal mining, *2:* 292
    indoor air pollution, *1:* 22
    Millennium Development Goals, *2:* 403–404, 406
    mining, *2:* 412
    pesticides, *3:* 480
    pollution, *3:* 494, 496
    waterborne diseases, *3:* 638–639
Mosquitoes, *2:* 362; *3:* 482
Mountaintop removal mining, *1:* 125; *2:* 410, 413
Muir, John, *1:* 147–149; *2:* 442; *3:* 511–512
Muir Glacier, AK, *1:* 113 (ill.)
Müller, Paul, *3:* 482

Multinational corporations, *2:* 310–312
Multistage flash distillation, *1:* 162
Municipal solid waste, *3:* 529–530, 531 (ill.), 622 (ill.), 625, 626
Mussels, *2:* 362
Mycoremediation, *1:* 81
Myers, Norman, *1:* 199–200

N

Naess, Arne, *1:* 160
Nagasaki, *3:* 617
Nagoya Protocol, *1:* 56
National Academy of Sciences, *3:* 538–539
National Aeronautics and Space Administration, *3:* 490, 491, 492
National Commission on the BP/Deepwater Horizon Oil Spill and Offshore Drilling, *3:* 540–542
National Environmental Policy Act, *1:* 245
National Forum on BioDiversity, *1:* 52
National Highway Transportation and Safety Administration, U.S., *1:* 43
National parks, *1:* 144 (ill.). *See also* specific parks
    conservation, *1:* 144
    ecotourism, *1:* 216
    preservation, *3:* 511–514
National Resources Conservation Services, U.S., *1:* 172
National Wilderness Preservation System, *3:* 513–514
National Wildlife Refuge System, *1:* 144
Native Americans, *1:* 73; *2:* 342–343
Native species reintroduction, *1:* 187
Natural capitalism, *2:* 315–316
Natural disasters
    invasive species, *2:* 361
    ocean borders, *2:* 377
    soil, *3:* 554
    urbanization, *3:* 611
    water access and sanitation, *3:* 631
Natural gas, *2:* 294–295, **419–423**, 421 (ill.). *See also* Hydraulic fracturing
Natural law theory, *2:* **424–426**

Index

Natural resources, *2:* **426–433**, 426 (ill.)
  abundance, *1:* 1–3
  bioregionalism, *1:* 70–73
  carrying capacity, *1:* 100–104
  conservation, *1:* 143–149
  consumption, *1:* 152
  ecological economics, *1:* 198–199
  ecological footprint, *1:* 177–184
  fossil fuels, *2:* 290–296
  green economy, *2:* 314–315
  industrial ecology, *2:* 351–352
  intergenerational responsibility, *2:* 355–359
  livestock, *2:* 459
  mining, *2:* 407–413
  permaculture, *3:* 475, 476
  population, *3:* 506
  preservation, *3:* 511–516
  sustainability, *3:* 573
  sustainable farming, *1:* 16
  sustainable food systems, *2:* 282
  tragedy of the commons, *3:* 586–589
  urbanization, *3:* 611
Natural Resources Defense Council, *2:* 444
Natural Step Framework, *2:* 316–317
Natural systems, *3:* 568, 575, 577, 580
Nature as model and teacher. *See* Biomimicry
Nature Conservancy, *1:* 57; *2:* 444
Negative externalities, *1:* 200
Neoliberal economics, *1:* 24, 25
Netherlands, *2:* 376–377
New Delhi, India, *1:* 19 (ill.)
New Economics Foundation, *3:* 550
New Orleans, LA, *2:* 377
New Urbanism, *3:* 612
New York City, *2:* 399; *3:* 596, 610
NGOs. *See* Nongovernmental organizations
Niches and invasive species, *2:* 361, 363–364
Niger, *2:* 430
Nigeria, *2:* 431–432
Nitrates, *1:* 6
Nitrogen cycle, *2:* **433–437**, 435 (ill.)
Nitrogen pollution
  acid rain, *1:* 4, 6, 20–21
  climate change, *1:* 114
  greenhouse gas emissions, *2:* 322–323

  industrial farming, *2:* 264
  wildlife, effects on, *3:* 647
"No-deforestation policy," *2:* 445–446
No-till farming, *2:* 269
Nobel Prize
  Borlaug, Norman, *1:* 14; *2:* 275
  Haber, Fritz, *2:* 274
  Maathai, Wangari, *2:* 381
  Müller, Paul, *3:* 482
  Yunus, Muhammad, *3:* 551
Noise Control Act, *2:* 439
Noise pollution, *2:* **437–440**; *3:* 647
Non-Proliferation Treaty, *1:* 245
Nongovernmental organizations, *2:* **440–446**. *See also* specific organizations
  biodiversity, *1:* 57
  consumption, *1:* 154
  environmental justice, *1:* 239–240
  environmental law, *1:* 244
  environmental policy, *1:* 247, 249
  food security, *2:* 277
  green jobs, *2:* 370
  water access and sanitation, *3:* 631–632
  working in, *1:* 110–111
Nonnative species. *See* Invasive species
Nonpoint source pollution, *3:* 496, 637–638, 641–642
Nonprofit organizations. *See* Nongovernmental organizations
Nonrenewable resources, *2:* 427
Norilsk, Siberia, *3:* 499
North American Model of Wildlife Conservation, *1:* 144
North Carolina, *2:* 293
"Not in my backyard," *1:* 238
Novo Nordisk, *2:* 352 (ill.)
Nuclear power, *2:* **447–453**
  alternative energy, *1:* 30
  Chernobyl nuclear power accident, *3:* 499
  Fukushima nuclear disaster, *2:* 336
  risk assessment, *3:* 537
Nuclear Regulatory Commission, U.S., *2:* 448–449; *3:* 537
Nuclear weapons, *1:* 245; *3:* 617, 618
Nuisance laws, *1:* 242–243

Nutrients, soil, *2:* 268, 416; *3:* 555
Nutrition, *2:* **454–460**, 455 (ill.)
Nye, Bill, *1:* 182 (ill.)

O

Obesity, *2:* 456
Occupy Movement, *1:* 27
Ocean Sky Apparel factory, *1:* 153
Ocean surface temperature, *1:* 170–171
Oceans. *See also* Marine ecosystems
    Great Pacific Garbage Patch, *3:* 642, 643 (ill.)
    hydropower, *2:* 349
    land borders, *2:* 376–377
    noise pollution, *2:* 438
    open-ocean aquaculture, *1:* 35
    plastics, *3:* 486–487
    temperatures, *1:* 116; *3:* 490–491
    tidal power, *3:* 584–586
    wave power, *1:* 31
Odum, Eugene, *1:* 189
Office of Nuclear Energy, U.S., *2:* 451
Offshore drilling, *3:* 540–542
Ogallala Aquifer, *1:* 39
Ohio State University, *3:* 656
Oil, *2:* 293 (ill.); *3:* **461–468**. *See also* Hydraulic fracturing
    automobiles, *1:* 41–42
    economics, *2:* 295–296
    energy conservation, *1:* 227–228, 232, 234–235
    environmental law, *1:* 245
    fossil fuels, *2:* 293–294
    oil spills, *2:* 294; *3:* 496 (ill.), 540–542
    transportation, *3:* 593
    Yasuni National Park, *1:* 55
Oil Pollution Act, *1:* 245
Old Weather project, *1:* 106
Open-ocean aquaculture, *1:* 35
Open-pit mining, *2:* 409, 409 (ill.), 412–413
Oposa v. Factoran, *2:* 358
Optimum carrying capacity, *1:* 102
Organic farming, *1:* 16; *2:* 270–271, 280
Our Common Future. *See* Brundtland Report

Overexploitation
    aquaculture, *1:* 32
    biodiversity threats, *1:* 54
    ecosystem threats, *1:* 211
    hunting, *1:* 143–144
Overnutrition, *2:* 456
Ozone depletion, *1:* 19–20; *3:* **468–473**, 470 (ill.)

P

Pachauri, Rajendra Kumar, *1:* 118 (ill.)
Pakistan, *1:* 20; *2:* 275
Paleo diet, *2:* 458–459
Palm oil plantations, *2:* 445–446
Palmer, Paul, *3:* 655
Particulate pollution, *1:* 22, 126; *3:* 618
Passive heating and cooling, *1:* 91–92; *3:* 563
Patel, Harish, *1:* 9
Payment for ecosystem services, *1:* 56
Peak oil, *3:* 464
Pearson, Gerald, *3:* 562
Pennsylvania, *2:* 422, 450
Pensacola Beach, FL, *3:* 496
Pérez de Cuéllar, Javier, *1:* 83
Permaculture, *3:* **475–478**, 606–607
Persian Gulf War, *3:* 615
Persistent organic pollutants, *3:* 499–500
Peru, *2:* 412
Pesticides, *3:* **478–486**, 480 (ill.)
    advantages and disadvantages, *3:* 478–479, 480–482
    biosecurity, *1:* 75–76
    community-supported agriculture, *1:* 133
    DDT, *3:* 482–483
    free trade, *2:* 300
    industrial farming, *2:* 265, 277
    integrated pest management, *3:* 483–484
    monoculture, *1:* 15; *2:* 270
    regulations, *3:* 479–480
    risk assessment, *3:* 540
    Silent Spring excerpt (Carson), *3:* 484–485
Pests and monoculture, *2:* 414–415
Petroleum. *See* Oil
Pharmaceutical companies, *2:* 300
Philippines, *2:* 358

Philosophy
    intergenerational responsibility, 2: 358–359
    land ethic, 1: 145
    natural law theory, 2: 424–426
Photosynthesis
    carbon cycle, 1: 95–96
    ecology, 1: 190, 192
    food web, 2: 288
    matter cycling and energy transfer, 1: 206–207
Photovoltaic cells, 3: 563–564, 567
Physics and ecology, 1: 190–191
Picher, OK, 1: 141 (ill.)
Pigs, feral, 2: 362
Pinchot, Gifford, 1: 143; 3: 511
Pipelines, natural gas, 2: 422
Pittman-Robertson Act, 3: 646
Plankton, 1: 106; 3: 487
Plants
    acid rain, 1: 4–5, 21
    biomimicry, 1: 67
    carbon cycle, 1: 95–96
    ecology, 1: 190–192
    ecosystems, 1: 204–205
    food web, 2: 287–288
    invasive species, 2: 362
    matter cycling and energy transfer, 1: 206–207
    nitrogen, 2: 433
    permaculture, 3: 477
    seed banks, 3: 545–548
Plastics, 3: **486–489**, 487 (ill.), 537–538, 642
Po River Valley, 1: 71, 73
Point source pollution, 3: 496, 637, 642
Polar bears, 3: 491
Polar melting, 3: **489–494**, 490 (ill.)
    air pollution, 1: 22
    atmospheric brown cloud, 1: 20
    climate change, 1: 115, 116, 117, 121, 122
    prevention, 1: 119
    water cycle, 3: 634
Political systems, 3: 578
Politics
    environmental policy, 1: 247–251
    fossil fuels, 2: 296
Polluter pays principle, 1: 250–251; 2: 425
Pollution, 3: **494–500**, 496 (ill.). *See also* Air pollution; Soil pollution; Water pollution
    biodiversity threats, 1: 54
    bioremediation, 1: 81
    coal, 1: 126–127
    Comprehensive Environmental Response, Compensation, and Liability Act, 1: 140–142
    environmental law, 1: 241–246
    fossil fuels, 1: 61; 2: 296
    human rights, 2: 337
    hydraulic fracturing, 2: 341–342
    industrial farming, 2: 264–265
    land, 2: 378–379
    light pollution, 2: 383–384
    noise pollution, 2: 437–439; 3: 647
    nuclear power, 2: 448
    pesticides, 3: 482
    thermal pollution, 3: 581–583
    wildlife, effects on, 3: 646–647
Polyaquaculture, 1: 35
Polychlorinated biphenyls, 1: 237–238
Polyculture, 1: 16; 2: 269, 414–415, 417–418
Polyvinyl chloride, 3: 487
Population, human, 3: **501–507**, 503 (ill.), 506 (ill.)
    carrying capacity, 1: 100–103
    ecological footprint, 1: 177–180, 182, 183
    Green Revolution, 1: 79
    nutrition, 2: 460
    pollution, 3: 494
    sustainability challenges, 3: 574–575
    transportation, 3: 594
    urbanization, 3: 608
Positivism, 2: 424
Postconsumer recycled content, 3: 532
Potential responsible parties, 1: 140–141
Poverty, 2: 335 (ill.)
    environmental justice, 1: 237, 238–239
    food insecurity, 2: 273
    human rights, 2: 334–335
    Millennium Development Goals, 2: 402, 405
    natural resources, 2: 432
    public health, 3: 520–521
    solar power, 3: 567
    sustainability challenges, 3: 573–574
Power plants. *See* Electricity
Precautionary principle, 1: 79–80, 250; 2: 425; 3: **507–511**

Precipitation
    climate change, *1:* 121
    thermal pollution, *3:* 583
    water cycle, *3:* 636
Predators and prey, *2:* 363; *3:* 481
Preservation, *3:* **511–516**, 513 (ill.). *See also* Conservation
"President's Proposed Energy Policy" (Carter), *1:* 233–235
Prevention principle, *1:* 250
Prices. *See* Costs and prices
Primitive diet, *2:* 458–459
Principles of Environmental Justice, *1:* 240
Processed foods, *2:* 458
Procter & Gamble, *2:* 445–446
Producers, food web, *2:* 287–288
Product life cycles, *3:* 623
Production Tax Credit, *1:* 229
Progressive Era, *1:* 143–144
Proteins, *2:* 454
Protests. *See* Activism
Provision services, ecosystem, *1:* 205–206
Public health, *3:* **516–521**, 520 (ill.), 539–540
Public lands, *2:* 427–429; *3:* 513–514
Public policy and nongovernmental organizations, *2:* 442–443
Public transportation. *See* Mass transit
Puerto Rico, *2:* 253–254
Putney, VT, *3:* 592

Q

Quality of life indicators, *3:* **523–527**

R

Race/ethnicity, *1:* 238–239
Radiation
    nuclear power, *2:* 449, 450
    ozone depletion, *3:* 468–469, 471
    soil pollution, *3:* 558 (ill.)
Radioactive waste, *2:* 328–329, 330 (ill.), 450–451, 452–453; *3:* 499

Radon, *2:* 423
Rain gardens, *2:* 380
Rainfall. *See* Precipitation
Rainforest Alliance, *1:* 154
Rainforests, *1:* 211 (ill.)
    agriculture, *1:* 15–16, 15 (ill.)
    conservation, *1:* 145–147
    ecosystem threats, *1:* 210–211
    ecosystem types, *1:* 209
    intergenerational responsibility, *2:* 358
    nongovernmental organizations, *2:* 445–446
Rainwater harvesting, *1:* 38
Rajasthan, India, *3:* 631
Ramsar Convention, *3:* 579
Rare earth metals, *3:* 498
Rasmussen Report (U.S. Nuclear Regulatory Commission), *3:* 537
Reagan, Ronald, *1:* 25
Rechargeable batteries, *1:* 48
Recovery, waste, *3:* 624
Recycling, *3:* **529–535**, 531 (ill.). *See also* Composting
    batteries, *1:* 49–50
    building design, *1:* 90, 93
    cradle-to-cradle design, *1:* 156–157
    electronic waste, *2:* 330
    industrial ecology, *2:* 353–354
    metals, *2:* 413
    plastics, *3:* 487–488
    San Francisco, CA, *3:* 626
    upcycling, *3:* 603–604
    waste management, *3:* 624
    zero waste, *3:* 654–655, 656
Red Book (National Academy of Sciences), *3:* 538–539
Reducing waste, *3:* 623
Reforestation, *1:* 168; *2:* 413
Regenerative design. *See* Cradle-to-cradle design
Regulations. *See* Environmental law
Rehabilitation, ecological, *1:* 185
Reindeer, *1:* 103
Reintroduction of species, *1:* 187, 226
Remediation, *1:* 142; *2:* 331–332; *3:* 560
Removal, hazardous waste, *1:* 141–142
Renewable energy. *See* Alternative energy
Renewable Energy Policy Network, *2:* 442–443

Replacement, ecological, *1:* 185
Report of the World Commission on Environment and Development. See Brundtland Report
Resistance, pesticide, *3:* 481
Resource Conservation and Recovery Act, *1:* 245; *3:* 533
Resource distribution, *2:* 431–432
Respiration, *1:* 96–97, 207
Restaurants and food waste, *2:* 285, 286
Restoration, ecological. *See* Ecological restoration
Reuse, *1:* 90, 93, 156–157; *3:* 623–624
Reverse osmosis, *1:* 162
Reversibility principle, *1:* 250
Right to know, *3:* 509
Rignot, Eric, *3:* 492
Rio Conference. *See* United Nations Conference on Environment and Development
Rio Declaration, *1:* 86; *3:* 508–509, 601
Rio+20 Conference on Sustainable Development
    environmental justice, *1:* 239
    human rights, *2:* 336
    social justice, *3:* 551
    sustainability, history of, *3:* 572–573
Risk assessment, *3:* **535–543**
Risk Assessment in the Federal Government (National Academy of Sciences), *3:* 538–539
Rivers and Harbors Act, *1:* 243, 245
Robèrt, Karl-Henrik, *2:* 317
Rome, ancient, *1:* 242
Rooftop gardens, *2:* 394; *3:* 606
Rooftop solar units, *3:* 567
Roosevelt, Franklin D., *1:* 144; *3:* 646
Roosevelt, Theodore, *1:* 143–144; *3:* 512
Rotating crops. *See* Crop rotation
Roundup, *3:* 481
Russia, *2:* 293 (ill.); *3:* 499

S

Safe Drinking Water Act, *3:* 632
Safety, *2:* 448–450; *3:* 526
St. Matthew Island, AK, *1:* 103
Salinization of water, *1:* 38–39
San Francisco, CA, *3:* 554, 626, 655

San Pedro River banks, *1:* 187–188
A Sand County Almanac (Leopold), *1:* 145; *3:* 515–516
Sanitation. *See* Water access and sanitation
Savory, Allan, *1:* 69
Saw grass prairies, *1:* 210
Schmitt, Otto, *1:* 66
Schumacher, E. F., *2:* 313–314
Science, citizen. *See* Citizen science
Sea levels
    climate change, *1:* 116, 121, 122
    polar melting, *3:* 492–494
    water cycle, *3:* 634
Sea turtles, *1:* 225 (ill.)
Seed banks, *2:* 275, 275 (ill.), 276; *3:* **545–548**
Seismic activity and hydraulic fracturing, *2:* 342
Selective breeding, *2:* 262, 274–276
Self-determination, *2:* 336–337
Senator Paul Simon Water for the Poor Act, *3:* 632
Senge, Peter, *2:* 317
Sequoia National Park, *3:* 511
Sewage. *See* Water access and sanitation
Shale rock, *3:* 464–465
Shiva, Vandana, *1:* 81; *2:* 276, 276 (ill.); *3:* 549
Siberia, *3:* 499
Sierra Club, *1:* 57; *2:* 442
Silent Spring (Carson), *1:* 189; *3:* 483, 484–485
Singh, Rajendra, *3:* 631
Slash-and-burn agriculture, *1:* 15–16, 15 (ill.)
Sludge, oil refining, *2:* 294
Slums, *3:* 610
Slurry, *2:* 292
Small Is Beautiful (Schumacher), *2:* 313–314
Smog, *1:* 20
Snakehead fish, *2:* 363 (ill.)
Social change, *1:* 7–10
Social development, *1:* 201–203; *3:* 550
Social issues
    biosecurity, *1:* 76–77
    three pillars of sustainability, *3:* 570
Social justice, *3:* **548–552**, 550 (ill.)
    alter-globalization movement, *1:* 24
    consumption, *1:* 152
    natural resources, *2:* 432
    three pillars of sustainability, *3:* 570

Social systems, *3:* 578
Socialism, *1:* 196
Society for Organizational Learning, *2:* 317
Soil, *3:* **552–557**, 554 (ill.)
 agriculture, *1:* 16
 biomimicry, *1:* 69
 cellulosic ethanol, *1:* 64
 Conservation Reserve Program, *1:* 56–57
 desertification, *1:* 2, 164–169
 Dust Bowl, *1:* 172
 erosion, *2:* 379–380
 food systems, *2:* 283
 industrial farming, *2:* 261–262, 263–264
 monoculture, *2:* 416
 nitrogen cycle, *2:* 434
 sustainable farming, *2:* 268–269
 urban farming, *3:* 607
Soil pollution, *3:* **557–561**, 558 (ill.)
 acid rain, *1:* 5, 21
 biodiversity threats, *1:* 54
 environmental justice, *1:* 237–238
 environmental law, *1:* 243–244
Solar Energy Industries Association, *3:* 567
Solar power, *3:* **561–568**, 563 (ill.)
 alternative energy types, *1:* 30–31
 batteries, *1:* 48–49
 biomimicry, *1:* 67
 building design, *1:* 92
 costs, *1:* 229
 green jobs, *2:* 368 (ill.)
Solid waste. *See* Waste management
Sonoran Desert, *1:* 71, 73
Source reduction, *3:* 497
South Asia, *1:* 20, 21 (ill.)
Southwest Organizing Project, *1:* 239–240
Soviet Union, former, *2:* 377; *3:* 499
Special interests, *1:* 247–251
Species biodiversity. *See* Biodiversity
Spider silk, *1:* 68
Spoilage, food, *2:* 286
Sports stadiums, *3:* 656
Stahel, Walter, *1:* 156
Standard American Diet, *2:* 458
Stansfield, Stephen, *2:* 438
Statement of forest principles, *3:* 601

States
 environmental law, *1:* 244
 green jobs, *2:* 369
 recycling, *3:* 532
Steady-state economy, *2:* 314–315
Stink bugs, *2:* 362
Stockholm Convention on Persistent Organic Pollutants, *3:* 499–500
Stockholm Water Prize, *3:* 631
The Story of Stuff (Leonard), *1:* 154
Strategic Approach to International Chemicals Management, *2:* 331
Strip-mining, *1:* 125; *2:* 409–410
Subscription farming. *See* Community-supported agriculture
Subsidies
 agriculture, *2:* 391
 economics, *1:* 199–200
 Farm Bill, U.S., *2:* 257–259
 food systems, *2:* 281
 fossil fuels, *2:* 295
 industrial farming, *2:* 270
Subsistence farming
 agriculture, *1:* 15
 alter-globalization movement, *1:* 27
 free trade, *2:* 300
 Green Belt Movement, *2:* 381–382
 locavores and the local food movement, *2:* 390–391
 sustainable farming, *2:* 270
Subsurface mining. *See* Underground mining
Suburbs, *2:* 379 (ill.), 399; *3:* 505
Subways, *2:* 399
Sudan, *3:* 630–631
Sugarcane, *1:* 62, 63 (ill.)
Sulfates, *1:* 6
Sulfur dioxide, *1:* 4, 6, 20–21
Superfund law. *See* Comprehensive Environmental Response, Compensation, and Liability Act
Superweeds, *2:* 416–417; *3:* 481
Supplemental Nutrition Assistance Program, *2:* 258
Supporting services, ecosystem, *1:* 206
Surface mining, *2:* 408–409
Surface Mining Control and Reclamation Act, *2:* 412

Index

Surface temperatures, Earth's, *1:* 115 (ill.)
Sustainability, *3:* **568–576**, 570 (ill.), 571 (ill.)
    abundance, *1:* 1
    achieving sustainabilty, *3:* 575
    acid rain, *1:* 4–6
    activism, *1:* 8–9
    aquaculture, *1:* 34, 35
    automobiles, *1:* 42–43
    biofuels, *1:* 62, 64–65
    biomimicry, *1:* 66, 69
    bioregionalism, *1:* 70, 71, 73
    challenges, *3:* 573–575
    citizen science, *1:* 106
    consumption, *1:* 152–153
    desalination, *1:* 162–163
    ecological footprint, *1:* 179
    ecotourism, *1:* 216
    ecovillages, *1:* 219
    endangered species, saving, *1:* 225–226
    environmental justice, *1:* 240
    environmental policy, *1:* 250–251
    fair trade, *2:* 254–255
    food, *2:* 459–460
    food web, *2:* 289
    free trade, *2:* 298–299
    geothermal power, *2:* 309
    greenhouse gas emissions, *2:* 323–324
    groundwater, *3:* 636–637
    history, *3:* 571–573
    human rights, *2:* 336–337
    hydropower, *2:* 348–349
    mass transit, *2:* 397–398
    Millennium Development Goals, *2:* 404
    natural gas, *2:* 422–423
    nitrogen cycle, *2:* 436
    nongovernmental organizations, *2:* 443–444
    nuclear power, *2:* 451
    oil, *3:* 467
    population, *3:* 505–506
    public health, *3:* 519–520
    risk assessment, *3:* 540
    seed banks, *3:* 546–547
    social justice, *3:* 548, 551–552
    soil, *3:* 554–555, 556
    solar power, *3:* 566–567
    three pillars of, *1:* 201; *3:* 569–571
    transportation, *3:* 593–594
    urban farming, *3:* 606–607
    vs. sustainable development, *3:* 573
    water, *3:* 643
    zero waste, *3:* 656
Sustainable development
    Agenda 21, *1:* 201–203
    Brundtland Report, *1:* 84–87; *2:* 430
    economics, *1:* 197–198
    environmental justice, *1:* 239
    globalization, *2:* 311–312
    human rights, *2:* 335–337
    Millennium Development Goals, *2:* 406
    Rio Declaration, *3:* 601
    sustainability, history of, *3:* 572
    sustainability *vs.*, *3:* 573
    transportation, *3:* 594
    water access and sanitation, *3:* 627
Sustainable farming, *2:* **266–271**, 267 (ill.)
    agriculture, *1:* 16
    alter-globalization movement, *1:* 27, 28
    community-supported agriculture, *1:* 133–134
    Farm Bill, U.S., *2:* 259
    food systems, *2:* 282–283
    three pillars of sustainability, *3:* 571
Sustainable food systems, *2:* 280–283
Sustainable materials management, *3:* 625
Sustainable mining, *2:* 412–413
Sustainable polycultures, *2:* 417–418
Sweatshops, *1:* 153
Switchgrass, *1:* 63–64
Synergies, *2:* 353
Syria, *3:* 617 (ill.)
Systems and systems thinking, *1:* 193; *2:* 317; *3:* **576–580**

T

Taiga ecosystems, *1:* 209
Tailings, mine, *2:* 411, 450
Taparelli D'Azeglio, Luigi, *3:* 548–549
Tar Creek Superfund Site, *1:* 141 (ill.)
Tar sands, *3:* 465
Taxes and tax credits, *1:* 45, 229

Technology
  agriculture, *1:* 13–14
  biomimicry, *1:* 66–69
  biotechnology, *1:* 78–82
  citizen science, *1:* 105
  coal, *1:* 127
  industrial farming, *2:* 260–262
  light pollution, *2:* 384
  solar power, *3:* 567
  Stockholm Water Prize, *3:* 631
  transportation, *3:* 595
  water desalination, *1:* 162
Television, *1:* 150–151
Ten Thousand Villages, *2:* 254
Tennessee, *1:* 126; *2:* 293
Terracing, *2:* 268
Terrestrial ecosystems, *1:* 208–209
Texas Transportation Institute, *2:* 399
Thailand, *1:* 63 (ill.)
Thatcher, Margaret, *1:* 25
Thermal electric energy, *3:* 564–565
Thermal pollution, *3:* **581–584**
Thermodynamics, *1:* 190–191, 193
Thoreau, Henry David, *1:* 143
Threatened species. *See* Endangered and threatened species
350.org, *1:* 9
Three Mile Island nuclear accident, *2:* 450
Three-North Shelter Forest Program, *1:* 169
Three pillars of sustainability, *3:* 569–571, 570 (ill.), 571 (ill.)
Three Rs, *2:* 330, *3:* 623–624
Tidal power, *1:* 31; *3:* **584–586**
Tilling, *2:* 260–261, 263–264, 268–269; *3:* 555
Time banking, *2:* 388; *3:* 592
Times Beach, *2:* 332
Totnes, England, *3:* 592
Tourism, ecological. *See* Ecotourism
Toxic Release Inventory website, *1:* 142
Toxic Substances Control Act, *1:* 245
Toxic waste. *See* Hazardous waste
Toxics Use Reduction Act (Massachusetts), *3:* 510
Trade, *1:* 25–26, 202–203; *2:* 298–301
Tragedy of the commons, *3:* **586–590**
"The Tragedy of the Commons" (Hardin), *3:* 589
Transition Towns movement, *3:* **590–592**, 612

Transnational Institute, *1:* 28
Transportation, *3:* 593–598, 596 (ill.). *See also* Automobiles
  acid rain, *1:* 3–4
  energy conservation, *1:* 232–234
  food security, *2:* 273
  food systems, *2:* 280
  greenhouse gas emissions, *2:* 322
  invasive species, *2:* 360–361
  locavores and the local food movement, *2:* 391–392
  Masdar City, *3:* 612
  mass transit, *2:* 397–401
  oil, *2:* 294
  organic farming, *2:* 271
  urban sprawl, *3:* 611
  war, *3:* 618–619
  World Solar Challenge, *3:* 564–565
Transportation Department, U.S. *See* Department of Transportation, U.S.
Travel, *1:* 212–217
Treaties and international agreements. *See also* Environmental law
  Basel Convention, *2:* 331; *3:* 533
  Cartagena Protocol on Biosafety, *1:* 250
  Convention on Biological Diversity, *1:* 55–56, 57–59
  Convention on International Trade in Endangered Species, *1:* 224
  Environmental Modification Convention, *3:* 618
  free trade, *2:* 300–301
  General Agreement on Tariffs and Trade, *2:* 298
  human rights, *2:* 333–334
  intergenerational responsibility, *2:* 357
  Kyoto Protocol, *1:* 117–118
  Montreal Protocol, *1:* 23, 245; *2:* 357; *3:* 471–472
  natural law theory, *2:* 424, 425
  polar melting, *3:* 493
  pollution control treaties, *3:* 498–500
  Ramsar Convention, *3:* 579
  United Nations Convention to Combat Desertification, *1:* 167–168
  United Nations Framework Convention on Climate Change, *2:* 324

Index

Trees
    acid rain, *1:* 5, 5 (ill.), 21
    Green Belt Movement, *2:* 381–382
    permaculture, *3:* 477
    Transition Towns movement, *3:* 592
Triple bottom line accounting, *2:* 317–318
Trophic levels, *2:* 289
Tropical rainforests. *See* Rainforests
Tropical wetlands, *1:* 210
Tuberculosis, *3:* 519
Tuna, *1:* 36–37, 37 (ill.)
Tundra ecosystems, *1:* 209
Tuolumne River, *1:* 146, 148

U

Ug99 (fungal disease), *3:* 546
Ukraine, *2:* 450; *3:* 499
Ultraviolet radiation, *3:* 468–470
Underground mining, *2:* 410, 411–412
Undernourished people, *2:* 277, 277 (ill.)
Undernutrition, *2:* 457
UNICEF, *3:* 631–632
Unintended consequences
    biofuel energy, *1:* 64
    biotechnology, *1:* 79
    industrial farming, *2:* 262
United Kingdom
    coal mining, *2:* 292
    environmental law, *1:* 242
    Magna Carta, *2:* 333
    Millennium Seed Bank Project, *3:* 547
    seed bank, *2:* 275
    Transition Towns movement, *3:* 592
United Nations. *See also* World Health Organization
    Environmental Modification Convention, *3:* 618
    founding, *2:* 440–441
    free trade, *2:* 298
    global environmental problems, *2:* 312
    Human Development Index, *3:* 525
    Kimberley Process Certification Scheme, *2:* 412
    Millennium Development Goals, *2:* 402
    Montreal Protocol, *3:* 471–472
    pollution control treaties, *3:* 498–500
    population, *3:* 502–503
    public health, *3:* 520–521
    Universal Declaration of Human Rights, *2:* 333–334
    water access and sanitation, *3:* 627
    World Day of Social Justice, *3:* 550
    World Economic and Social Survey, *3:* 573
    World Water Day, *1:* 147
United Nations Commission on Sustainable Development, *1:* 239
United Nations Conference on Environment and Development, *3:* **599–602**
    Agenda 21, *1:* 201–203
    biodiversity, *1:* 57–59
    Brundtland Report, *1:* 86
    Convention on Biological Diversity, *1:* 55–56
    environmental justice, *1:* 239
    invasive species, *2:* 364
    precautionary principle, *3:* 508–509
    sustainability, history of, *3:* 572
United Nations Convention to Combat Desertification, *1:* 167–168
United Nations Division for Sustainable Development, *1:* 201
United Nations Educational, Scientific and Cultural Organization, *3:* 512–513
United Nations Environment Commissions, *3:* 571–572
United Nations Environment Programme, *2:* 367; *3:* 640
United Nations Framework Convention on Climate Change, *2:* 324
United Nations Sustainable Development Goals, *3:* 630
United States
    acid rain, *1:* 4, 6–7
    Agent Orange, use of, *3:* 616–617
    air pollution, *1:* 22, 23
    algae blooms and dead zones, *3:* 639–640
    alter-globalization movement, *1:* 27
    alternative energy, *1:* 31, 229
    aquaculture, *1:* 33–34
    aquifers, *1:* 39
    automobiles, *1:* 41
    bats, *1:* 76–77

Index

bioregionalism, *1:* 71, 73
Bureau of Land Management, *2:* 427–429
California food system, *2:* 283
clean up programs, *2:* 378–379
climate change, *1:* 120–122
coal, *1:* 125, 126–127; *2:* 292
Comprehensive Environmental Response, Compensation, and Liability Act, *1:* 140–142
Conservation Reserve Program, *1:* 56–57
consumption, *1:* 151–152, 153
desertification, *1:* 166–167
drought, *1:* 171–174
ecotourism, *1:* 216
electronic waste, *3:* 533
endangered species, *1:* 224
energy conservation, *1:* 232, 233–235
environmental justice, *1:* 236–240
environmental law, *1:* 243–244, 245
family planning and contraception, *3:* 504–505
food deserts, *2:* 273
food system, *2:* 281
food transport, *2:* 391–392
fossil fuels, *2:* 292, 295, 296
fuel cell vehicles, *1:* 45
geothermal power, *2:* 309
government employment, *1:* 110
green jobs, *2:* 369
greenhouse gas emissions, *1:* 114–115; *2:* 324
hydraulic fracturing, *2:* 341–345
industrial farming, *2:* 458
intergenerational responsibility, *2:* 355–357
invasive species, *2:* 362, 363–364
irrigation, *2:* 265
Kyoto Protocol, *1:* 246
mass transit, *2:* 397–398, 400–401
mining, *2:* 410–411, 412–413
mountaintop removal mining, *2:* 410
municipal solid waste, *3:* 625
natural gas, *2:* 420–421
North American Free Trade Agreement, *2:* 299–300
nuclear power, *2:* 448–449, 450
oil, *3:* 463–464
oil spills, *3:* 466–467
pesticides, *3:* 478

pollution regulations, *3:* 497–498
population, *3:* 501
precautionary principle, *3:* 509–510
preservation, *3:* 511–512
recycling, *3:* 533
shale rock oil, *3:* 465
soil pollution, *3:* 558–559
solar power, *3:* 562–563, 567
surface mining, *2:* 408–409
sustainable farming, *2:* 268
Transition Towns movement, *3:* 592
transportation, *3:* 593
urban sprawl, *3:* 610–611
war, *3:* 618–619
waste disposal and recycling, *3:* 529
waste management, *3:* 622 (ill.), 623
wasted energy, *2:* 383
water conflicts, *3:* 630
wildlife management, *3:* 644–646
zero waste, *3:* 656
Universal Declaration of Human Rights, *2:* 333–334
Universal wastes, *2:* 328
Upcycling, *3:* 603–605
Upgraded Family Well, *3:* 631
Uppsala Conflict Data Program, *3:* 617
Ural mountains, *3:* 499
Uranium, *2:* 447; *3:* 619
Urban areas
    automobiles, *1:* 45
    bicycles, *1:* 232
    biomimicry, *1:* 68
    building design, *1:* 90
    ecological footprint, *1:* 181
    food systems, *2:* 282
    food web, *2:* 289–290
    heat islands, *3:* 582–583
    land use, *2:* 380
    locavores and the local food movement, *2:* 394
    mass transit, *2:* 397–400
    noise laws, *2:* 439
    planning, *3:* 612
    public health, *3:* 520–521
    transportation, *3:* 596, 597
    urban farming, *3:* 605–607
    urban sprawl, *2:* 379 (ill.), 398; *3:* 610–611
    urbanization, *3:* 608–613

Index

Urban farming, *3:* **605–608**
Urbanization, *3:* 574–575, **608–613**
U.S. Agency for International Development, *3:* 632

V

Vaccines, *3:* 502
Valley of the Drums, *2:* 332
Van En, Robyn, *1:* 136
Vectors, invasive species, *2:* 360
Vegan and vegetarian diets, *2:* 457
Velocity of money, *2:* 388
Vietnam War, *3:* 616–617
Vinyl chloride, *3:* 537–538
Vitamins, *2:* 456
Volcanoes, *3:* 554
Volunteers and volunteering
    citizen science, *1:* 104–106
    citizenship, *1:* 108
    green jobs, *2:* 370
Voting, *1:* 107–108

W

Wackernagel, Mathis, *1:* 179
Wages. *See* Income and wages
Walden (Thoreau), *1:* 143
War, *2:* 378; *3:* **615–620**, 617 (ill.), 630–631
Warren County, NC, *1:* 237–238
Wasps and gypsy moths, *3:* 484
Waste management, *3:* **620–627**, 622 (ill.). *See also* Hazardous waste
    batteries, *1:* 49–50
    bioplastics, *3:* 488
    building design, *1:* 90, 93
    composting, *1:* 137–139
    consumption, *1:* 151–152
    food waste, *2:* 284–286, 304
    Great Pacific Garbage Patch, *3:* 642, 643 (ill.)
    hazardous waste, *2:* 330–331
    industrial ecology, *2:* 351–354
    nuclear power, *2:* 450–451, 452–453
    plastics, *3:* 486–487
    pollution, *3:* 494
    recycling, *3:* 529–534, 531 (ill.)
    solar power, *3:* 566
    upcycling, *3:* 603–604
    zero waste, *3:* 653–656
Wasted energy, *2:* 383
Wastewater, *3:* 629 (ill.)
    building design, *1:* 92–93
    ecovillages, *1:* 218–219
    hydraulic fracturing, *2:* 341–342, 344
Wasting, *2:* 456
Water
    aquifers, *1:* 38–39
    building design, *1:* 92–93
    climate change effects, *1:* 117
    conservation, *1:* 147
    desertification, reversing, *1:* 168
    drought, *1:* 174–175
    energy production, *1:* 228
    food systems, *2:* 283
    geothermal power, *2:* 309
    industrial farming, *2:* 265, 277
    irrigation, *2:* 265
    livestock, *2:* 459
    soil, functions of, *3:* 555
    sustainable farming, *2:* 269
    thermal pollution, *3:* 581
Water access and sanitation, *3:* **627–633**, 629 (ill.)
    building design, *1:* 92–93
    food security, *2:* 274
    public health, *3:* 520
    sewage and sewage treatment, *1:* 218; *3:* 624, 643
    water pollution, *3:* 640–641
    waterborne diseases, *3:* 638–639
Water cycle, *1:* 38; *3:* **633–637**, 635 (ill.)
Water desalination. *See* Desalination
Water hyacinth, *2:* 362
Water pollution, *3:* **637–644**, 643 (ill.)
    acid rain, *1:* 5, 21
    aquaculture, *1:* 35
    bioaccumulation and biomagnification, *2:* 329
    coal, *2:* 293
    environmental law, *1:* 245
    ethanol production, *1:* 62

Everglades restoration, *1:* 210
hydraulic fracturing, *2:* 341, 342, 343–345
hydropower, *2:* 349
industrial farming, *2:* 264–265
mining, *2:* 410–411
monoculture, *2:* 270
nitrogen, *2:* 436
nuclear power, *2:* 450
oil spills, *2:* 294
plastics, *3:* 486–487
soil pollution, *3:* 559
Water power. *See* Hydropower
Water Resources Development Act, *1:* 186
Water vapor, *2:* 319–320
WaterAid, *3:* 632
Watersheds, *1:* 71
Wave power, *1:* 31
Weather
acid rain, *1:* 4, 6
atmospheric brown cloud, *1:* 20
climate change, *1:* 121
climate *vs.* weather, *1:* 111
ecosystems, *1:* 204–205
food production, *2:* 272
food systems, *2:* 283
greenhouse gas emissions, *2:* 323
polar melting, *3:* 491, 492
thermal pollution, *3:* 583
urbanization, *3:* 611
water cycle, *3:* 636
West Nile virus, *2:* 362
Wetlands, *1:* 210; *3:* 579, 641
Wheat, *2:* 274–275; *3:* 546
White nose syndrome, *1:* 76–77
Wild and Free-Roaming Horses and Burros Act, *2:* 428
Wild fish, *1:* 34
Wilderness Act, *3:* 513–514
Wilderness areas, *3:* 511–516
Wilderness Society, *1:* 145; *3:* 514
Wildfires, *1:* 174
Wildlife
conservation, *1:* 143–149, 145–147
monoculture, *2:* 416–417
wind power, *3:* 650
Wildlife management, *3:* **644–648**

Wilson, Edward O., *1:* 52, 223
Wind power, *1:* 30, 92; *3:* **648–651,** 649 (ill.)
Windbreaks, *2:* 269
Wingspread Conference, *3:* 509
Wolves, *1:* 187, 226
Women
Convention on Biological Diversity, *1:* 58
microloans, *3:* 551
Millennium Development Goals, *2:* 403–404, 405
Workplace issues. *See* Labor issues
World Bank, *1:* 25; *2:* 335
World Commission on Environment and Development. *See* Brundtland Report
World Day of Social Justice, *3:* 550
World Economic and Social Survey, United Nations, *3:* 573
World Fair Trade Organization, *2:* 255–256
World Health Organization, *1:* 19; *2:* 437; *3:* 517–518
World Nuclear Association, *2:* 451
World Social Forum, *1:* 26 (ill.), 27
World Solar Challenge, *3:* 564–565
World Summit for Social Development, *1:* 201; *3:* 550
World Trade Organization, *1:* 26–27; *2:* 298, 300–301
World War II, *3:* 482, 485
World Water Day, *1:* 147
World Wildlife Fund, *1:* 224
Wrangell-St. Elias Wilderness Area, *3:* 513 (ill.)

Y

Yard, Robert Sterling, *3:* 514
Yasuni National Park, *1:* 55, 55 (ill.)
Yellowstone National Park, *1:* 187, 226
The Yosemite (Muir), *1:* 147–149
Yosemite National Park, *1:* 146, 146 (ill.), 147–148; *3:* 511
Young, Alison, *3:* 558
Yousafzai, Malala, *2:* 405 (ill.)
Yucca Mountain nuclear waste site, *2:* 452–453
Yunus, Muhammad, *3:* 551

Index

Z

Zahniser, Howard, *3:* 514
Zebra mussels, *1:* 74; *2:* 362
Zero-emissions vehicles, *1:* 45
Zero waste, *3:* 625–626, **653–657**
Zimbabwe, *1:* 69; *3:* 631
Zion National Park, UT, *1:* 144 (ill.)

Matawan Aberdeen Public Library
165 Main Street
Matawan, NJ 07747
(732) 583-9100